Music and Monumentality

ALEXANDER
REHDING

Music and
Monumentality

Commemoration and Wonderment

in Nineteenth-Century Germany

2009

OXFORD
UNIVERSITY PRESS

Oxford University Press, Inc., publishes works that further
Oxford University's objective of excellence
in research, scholarship, and education.

Oxford   New York
Auckland   Cape Town   Dar es Salaam   Hong Kong   Karachi
Kuala Lumpur   Madrid   Melbourne   Mexico City   Nairobi
New Delhi   Shanghai   Taipei   Toronto

With offices in
Argentina   Austria   Brazil   Chile   Czech Republic   France   Greece
Guatemala   Hungary   Italy   Japan   Poland   Portugal   Singapore
South Korea   Switzerland   Thailand   Turkey   Ukraine   Vietnam

Copyright © 2009 by Oxford University Press, Inc.

Published by Oxford University Press, Inc.
198 Madison Avenue, New York, New York 10016

www.oup.com

Oxford is a registered trademark of Oxford University Press.

Library of Congress Cataloging-in-Publication Data
Rehding, Alexander.
Music and monumentality : commemoration and wonderment in nineteenth-century
Germany / Alexander Rehding.
    p.   cm.
Includes bibliographical references and index.
ISBN 978-0-19-538538-0
1. Sublime, The, in music.   2. Music—Germany—19th century—History
and criticism.   I. Title.
ML3877.R45 2009
780.943'09034—dc22   2008043837

9   8   7   6   5   4   3   2   1

Printed in the United States of America
on acid-free paper

ACKNOWLEDGMENTS

IT IS IN THE SPIRIT OF MONUMENTALITY THAT NUMEROUS INVIS-
ible hands have labored behind the scenes toward the final product. Over
the years, and in the many places that I have researched at toward this book,
the number of people to whom I owe a debt of gratitude has continually
grown into a list that is far longer than I can enumerate here. In organizing
my thanks chronologically and geographically, I have happy recollections of
passing through the stages and places to which this project took me.

It all began during a conversation with Dean Kolbas in the coffee shop at
Waterstone's in Cambridge, at a time when it was still new and exciting to
have a coffee shop in a bookstore. I thank John Harvey for suggesting a title
for the book, long before I knew it was a book project, and Serena Olsaretti
for critiquing it. I am grateful to Cary Howie for reminding me that the step
from the sublime to the ridiculous can be small, and to Ron Gray for his vast
knowledge of Schiller and Beethoven. I thank Roger Parker for drawing my
attention to Music-with-a-*k*, John Deathridge for showing me the way out of
an impasse just when I needed it, Peter Franklin for always being present,
even when he was in the background, and Daniel Chua for his usual striking
originality. I am grateful to Gerardo Fragoso for being patient with me. I
thank Paul Yates for reading early drafts. I thank the staff of the Cambridge
University Library and the Pendlebury Music Library. I am grateful to Savino's
for good coffee, and lots of it.

At UPenn, I am grateful to Lucy Shanno for her careful reading, fiery discussions and very long jogs. I thank Liliane Weisberg for her interest in the
project before I knew it was a project. I thank Jennifer Conway for her strong
coffee and her strong liberal views. I am thankful to Chris Hasty and Jeff

Kallberg for listening. I am grateful to the staff of the Van Pelt Library, and to *Pizza Rustica* for their impeccable *crema* on their espresso.

At Princeton, I am grateful to Alexander Nehamas from whom I learned more *zwischen Tür und Angel* than he probably realizes. I am grateful to Branden Joseph and Tom Levin for taking me away from this subject, and to Scott Burnham for bringing me back to it. I thank Constanze Güthenke for eerie long-life milk and philology. Giulio Boccaletti deserves thanks for introducing me to the wonderful world of the ocarina and for his unflinching love of high modernism. I thank Tracy Strong for his continued interest, Philip Bohlman for, as always, having been there long before me, and Brian Hyer for knowing German idealism better than anyone else. I thank David Kasunic for opening his home to me. I am grateful to Mary Harper for making the Society of Fellows a home away from home. I thank the staff of the Firestone and Scheide Music Libraries, and Small World Coffee for providing Princeton, and the universe, with a center.

At Harvard, I thank Carolyn Abbate for petit(e)s croissants and for reading the entire manuscript. I thank David Trippett for help with the musical examples, and Jonathan Kregor for his bibliographical help. I thank Matthias Röder for the bourgeoisie. Eric Nelson must be thanked for encouraging me to see the larger picture. I am grateful to Ingrid Monson and Kay Shelemay for giving the project a big push, Karen Painter for her sheer enthusiasm, Tom Kelly for being a critical and attentive listener, Suzie Clark and Sindhu Revuluri for always being there, Sean Gallagher for long talks, and Mauro Calcagno for providing an Italian perspective. I thank Reinhold and Dorothea Brinkmann for wonderful dinners with attitude. I thank Richard Taruskin for his patience with German music, and James Hepokoski for his characteristically incisive comments on the manuscript. I am grateful to the helpful staff of Harvard's Eda Kuhn Loeb Music Library, Fine Arts Library, Houghton Library, Lamont Library, and Widener Library. And I thank Burdick for their hot chocolate.

In Berlin, I thank Albrecht Riethmüller for Wagnerian Water metaphors, Walhalla and unWavering support. I thank Frank Hentschel for great party music and discussions on Brendel (though not at the same time), and for reading the entire manuscript. I am grateful to Christian Thorau for leitmotives and cake on a lake in Charlottenburg. I thank Ryan Minor and Michael Puri for their critical readings of the manuscript. Christa Brüstle must be thanked for her expert knowledge on Bruckner. I thank Sepp Gumbrecht for his continuous presence. Alexander "Chip" Steinbeis—thank you for the music. I thank the Department of Music at Basel, who gave me a helpful grilling. I am especially grateful to Bevil Conway for sharing dessert. I thank the staff of the library of the Staatliches Institut für Musikwissenschaft, the Staatsbibliothek Berlin I and II, the Goethe and Schiller Archive and Anna Amalia Library at Weimar, the Bavarian State Library, Munich, and Café Einstein for mélange and Apfelstrudel.

And finally, Suzanne Ryan and Norman Hirschy must be thanked for their professionalism and good cheer, and for confidently steering this project through its various stages. I am grateful to Stephanie Attia and Karla Pace for their careful attention during the copy-editing process.

Earlier versions of two chapters, chapter 2 and the epilogue, have appeared elsewhere: "Liszt's Musical Monuments," *Nineteenth Century Music* 26/1 (2002), 52–72, with permission of the Regents of the University of California Press, and "'Ode to Freedom': Bernstein's Ninth at the Berlin Wall," *Beethoven Forum* 11/1 (2005), 33–46, with permission of the University of Indiana Press. Sections from an essay first published in German, "Souvenirs aus Weimar," *Im Herzen Europas: Nationale Identitäten und Erinnerungskulturen,* eds. Lothar Ehrlich, Detlev Altenburg, Jürgen John (Weimar: Böhlau, 2008), 355–366, made their way into chapter 3.

I gratefully acknowledge financial support received through a Research Fellowship at Emmanuel College Cambridge, an Andrew W. Mellon Fellowship at the Humanities Forum at the University of Pennsylvania, a Cotsen Fellowship at the Princeton Society of Fellows, the Stiftung Weimarer Klassik, and the Alexander von Humboldt Foundation.

CONTENTS

Music and Monumentality

Introduction

Perspectives on Musical Monumentality

DESPITE ITS GRAND ASPIRATIONS, MUSICAL MONUMENTALITY IS deceptively simple. In fact, every concert goer has a very good intuitive understanding of what monumental music entails. We are likely to expect certain grand effects and outsize forms in the vein of, say, Wagner's and Berlioz's orchestral music. When asked to imagine monumental passages or works of music, we may well recall before our mind's ear such musical effects as over-powering brass chorales, sparkling string tremolos, triumphant fanfares, glo-rious thematic returns, and the like. From this angle, we think of musical monumentality as a stylistic property, which we might describe informally as an uplifting, awe-inspiring, overwhelming, or sublime quality—or, negatively, as effects whose immediacy seems slightly distasteful, which can seem bom-bastic, gothic, pompous, or over the top. We all know these musical effects, and we can probably list incisive examples in the works of Beethoven, Liszt, Wag-ner, Brahms, Bruckner, Mahler, and others—or, to step outside the Austro-German repertoire, in Tchaikovsky, Berlioz, Saint-Saëns, Verdi, *e tutti quanti.* Because of the self-evident nature of monumental music, a stylistic taxonomy of such musical effects, one imagines, could be drawn up without any great problems.

Given this apparent self-evidence, it is perhaps surprising that a compre-hensive taxonomy of musical monumentality does not exist in the musico-logical literature. (The sole explicit attempt in musicology to capture monu-mentality as a musical style, by Arnold Schering, will be revisited in chapter 1.) Despite the significant role that monumentality indisputably plays in nineteenth-century music, it is not a well-defined musicological concept. To be sure, it is on occasion found in music-historical literature, yet it seems the authors assume that their readers know exactly what is meant, so no explanation is required. Alfred Einstein, for one, introduces monumentality as a reaction against classicism; for him it features primarily as a symphonic gesture.[1] Theodor W. Adorno mentions the term "monumentality" in passing in his Mahler monograph; for him, monumentality is primarily associated with the *neudeutsch* aesthetic and becomes a touchstone of difference between Mahler and Bruckner.[2] It was the prolific Carl Dahlhaus who was more interested in monumentality than most other musicologists. He took the notion a little further by surreptitiously introducing a number of monumentalities, derived from either grand opera or the symphonic tradition, and implied that a monumental style comes with certain formal demands (which, in his assessment, are fulfilled by Bruckner, but not by Tchaikovsky).[3] Dahlhaus remained conspicuously vague, however, as to what characterizes these formal demands, or how to describe the stylistic principles on which his conception of monumentality rests.[4]

It seems, paradoxically, that the very self-evidence of musical monumentality constitutes a hurdle to academic reflection. It does so in at least three ways. First and foremost, it poses a challenge to the self-understanding of musicology as an intellectual discipline: monumentality is so glaringly obvious that there seems to be little left to be said. As the academy is above all in the business of complicating things, as Hans Ulrich Gumbrecht brilliantly pointed out,[5] it would seem that monumentality is too simple to be worked into sophisticated musicological pursuits. More often than not, as we shall see, the most monumental effects are bafflingly simple, so much so that detailed music analysis often seems redundant. It seems difficult—and Dahlhaus's abortive efforts may count as a case in point here—to get beyond stating the obvious, bare observation that monumentality is somehow about big gestures and grand effects.

Second, musical monumentality poses an aesthetic problem. The negative lens through which monumental music is often viewed is at least partly an expression of the perception that alongside its sweeping grandeur goes a certain perceived superficiality. The positive and negative attributes, which we initially bestowed on musical monumentality, are, needless to say, an expression of such deep-seated aesthetic ambivalence. As Dahlhaus puts it, monumentality is primarily "decorative façade."[6] Moreover, its immediacy holds great and unabashed popular appeal—monumental music is often music for mass audiences. Again, I would venture that this is related to its simplicity: monumental music appears to speak for itself—it is immediately intelligible to anyone and does not seem to require any theoretical reflection. More often than not, the musical effects we commonly associate with monumentality are achieved less by rhetorical finesse or compositional intricacy than by a combination of straightforward musical content and sheer overwhelming sonic force.

I am, of course, speaking in generalities here, and many readers will have the understandable desire to save a favorite composer from being tarred with the same monumental brush as others. It is noticeable, however, that individual composers associated with monumentality are usually exempted on account of some redeeming feature: think of Adorno's subversive physiognomy of Mahler's music, or the recent interest in Tchaikovsky's biography and sexuality in relation to his music. Put starkly, in "rescuing" individual composers from the "reproach" of monumentality, we simultaneously confirm that the idea of monumentality as a whole should remain unredeemed.

And third, monumentality is weighed down by its ideological baggage. The step from the popular to the populist can be small, and monumental music has proved to be an extremely useful tool in the hands of the totalitarian regimes of the first half of the twentieth century. No one has summed this up more incisively than Thomas Mann, who noted a propos of Wagner that the bourgeois nineteenth century handled monumentality, by which he meant outsize forms, "as though size in itself were the natural attribute of morality."[7] The triumphant fanfares, the celestial harp arpeggios, and the rousing sonorous string tapestries, of which nineteenth-century monumental music often availed itself, appeared to exude moral authority. We should, however, ask: the moral authority of *what?* This critical question, which often gets swamped under the uplifting sounds, is much less easy to answer. In any case, the ideological use for which monumental music has been co-opted under totalitarian regimes—notably under the National Socialists, but also in Fascist Italy and Soviet Russia[8]—has shown once and for all that the imaginary link between morality and monumentality is entirely spurious. Yet we remain in thrall to it—on one level, it simply remains enticing to believe in it.

To plunge right to the heart of the matter, take the fanfares from Liszt's symphonic poem *Les Préludes,* shown in example I.1, a passage that has the doubtful distinction of being firmly associated with the National Socialist *Deutsche Wochenschau,* the weekly news program. (In that context the fanfares were often referred to as *Rußlandfanfaren* or *Siegesfanfaren,* though this epithet was obviously not related to Liszt's programmatic conception of the symphonic poem, but rather to the current political situation of the 1940s.[9]) In a pioneering study of the uses of music during the National Socialist regime, Hanns-Werner Heister and Jochem Wolff have pointed out the numerous differences between Liszt's original and the version that was used to announce the war-time news. They note that in the cinematic jingle the fanfare is torn out of its context, bypassing the long motivic build-up that climaxes in Liszt's

EXAMPLE I.1 The passage from Liszt's *Les Préludes* (1856), which became known in the 1940s as *Rußland-fanfaren* or *Siegesfanfaren*, served as a theme tune for the weekly news program in Nazi Germany. This example shows the beginning of the fanfares in the original version.

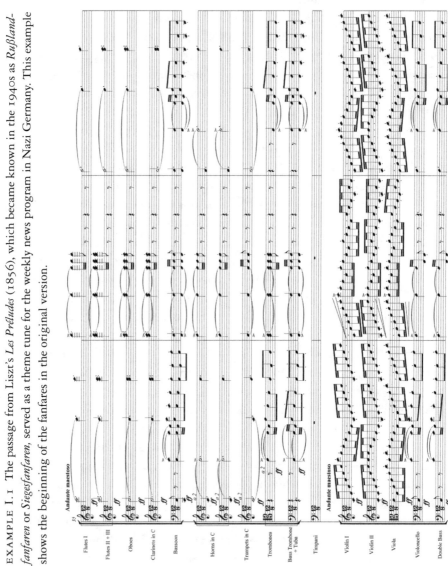

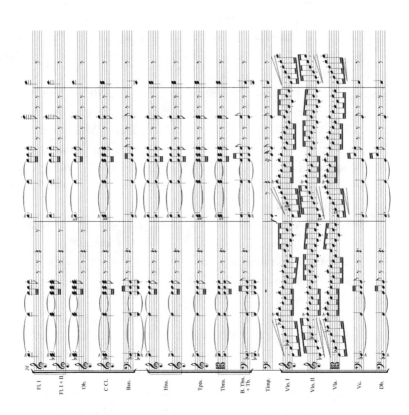

original fanfares. Moreover, the version in which the passage gained notoriety as a news jingle did not observe the original score, but presented the music in an arranged, simplified version, which they describe as follows: "The texture appears pared down, the string passages as well as the polyphonic voices are practically inaudible. The percussion, by contrast, is all the more evident: the solo passages of the timpani, which replace the strings, sound almost like grenade explosions."[10] Heister and Wolff present a finely differentiated analysis of the factors that make the music suitable for such an adaptation. The implication is, meanwhile, that Liszt should not be held responsible for this usage, since his original score did not lend itself so readily to this ideological appropriation and first had to be adapted and simplified. Complexity, it seems, would function as a safeguard against ideological appropriation of monumentality.

While Heister and Wolff are not primarily concerned with issues of monumentality, this short example reveals a number of aspects that will be relevant for the concept as I develop it over the next few chapters. Above all, musical monumentality has an uncanny ability to attach itself to various elements: not only is it capable of having an uplifting psychological effect on a rapt listenership, and of glorifying the action thus heralded, but it also somehow reflects back on its composer (here turned negative, as the underlying efforts to extricate Liszt from the tainted monumentality of his music reveal). We will encounter this phenomenon, which I refer to as the "Midas touch" of monumentality, at various points in the following chapters. As we shall see, it is closely related to Mann's observation that monumental music seems to exude moral authority without specifying the carrier of this authority, or indeed the nature of such morality.

Heister and Wolff's example may be an extreme case of the ideological use of music—indeed, one in which the political use completely overshadows the cultural or the musical aspects of monumentality and which, to be sure, is equaled by few other examples—but it is representative insofar as the experience of the National Socialist years have left their indelible mark on the notion of monumentality. The punch line of Woody Allen's famous quip, "I can't listen to that much Wagner. I start getting the urge to conquer Poland," pivots on this entrenched association, summing up the problem of how far monumental music from the German repertoire has become associated with its uses and abuses under the National Socialist regime. At the same time, Allen's observation is strongly suggestive of the precariously irresistible power of monumental music. Stated with a good dose of preposterous exaggeration, he hints at its power to make us commit immoral acts, even against our will.

To return to our initial situation, our outline of the principal hurdles that have prevented critical investigations into the idea of musical monumentality shows that it appears intellectually impoverished, aesthetically questionable, and morally suspect. In other words, the character and the principles of musical monumentality are so simple as to be obvious—indeed, its very nature demands that they be obvious. Not only does monumental music not necessitate, but in fact it actively discourages any kind of critical engagement. This explanation might suggest itself as a reason that monumentality has not received much critical attention in musicology in its own right, but such a conclusion is obviously a red herring. For all we achieve in casting aside the concept of monumentality is merely to reaffirm its seductive power and its ideological dangers while ridding ourselves of any opportunity to understand its workings. We can only arrive at a better understanding of this power, and its underlying mechanisms, if we start a critical examination of its persuasiveness with the paradox that monumentality itself discourages any critical engagement.

It might be useful at this point briefly to take stock of the ground we have covered so far. This will also help us revise the three points raised initially; for the concept of monumentality has begun to metamorphose into something more complex. First and foremost, musical monumentality is no longer merely about musical structures. The stylistic taxonomy proposed initially would fail to capture what seems critical about monumentality in music: it is not just about big musical effects per se but also about what they stand for and how they are used. Rather than any kind of "bigness" in its own right, monumentality is better understood, for now, as the imaginary link between musical bigness and greatness, and this link, in order to appear natural and self-evident, needs to be forever forged anew.

Second, in describing what music critic Adolf Weißmann startlingly called music's efforts "to break our will,"[11] I have come close to personalizing monumental music, to attributing agency to it. This is doubtless a dangerous move—especially given its ideological susceptibility—for such music does not issue forth by itself. Yet, as we shall see, an essential ingredient of the trappings of monumental music is a pronounced theatricality, which endows it with the appearance of agency.[12] We will have the opportunity to examine this theatricality more closely in the following chapters.

And third, while the concept of monumentality characteristically avails itself of the appearance of ahistorical transcendence, it is not the monolithic concept that it appears, but is rather subject to historical change. That is to say, if our reservations against monumentality are representative of an attitude toward a particular cultural-political situation—which Thomas Mann memorably labeled the "bad nineteenth century"[13]—then we would be well advised not to limit the idea of monumentality to particular musical effects and to analyze them in a vacuum but also to explore the cultural situations that call for these effects. On one level, this point may be a truism of hermeneutics, but considering monumentality's marked tendency to theatricality, a critical hermeneutic position is a highly effective means to counter the appeal to immediacy and transcendence that is so easily seen as the defining feature of monumentality.

From this angle, then, the apparently self-explanatory nature of monumentality itself demands an explanation. These three points complicate our inquiry into musical monumentality, in the sense that nineteenth-century monumentality is not simply a phenomenon that can be hermetically contained in the nineteenth century, but instead requires us, as author and reader, to write ourselves into the story. In other words, we do not hear with the same ears as did listeners in the nineteenth century—our musical experience is indelibly marked by the experience of the twentieth century, and as we have already seen and will further see, this is of critical consequence to the phenomenon of monumentality.

The Germanist Andreas Huyssen has observed that our own age is characterized by a schizophrenic twofold approach to monumentality: "monumentalism of built space or monumental tendencies in any other medium continue to be much maligned, but the notion of the monument as memorial or commemorative public event has witnessed a triumphant return."[14] It is worth underlining here that Huyssen adds a new dimension to the concept of monumentality, that of commemoration. This has so far played no part in our considerations, but will become important shortly—it might be useful to bear in mind that the word "monument" itself is derived from the Latin *monere,* to exhort or remind.[15]

Huyssen shows in an elegant argument that nineteenth-century monumentality, and its rejection under the banner of modernism, has led to a late-twentieth-century phenomenon he calls anti-monumentality, a self-conscious effort to counter the overwhelming nineteenth-century heritage with a more recalcitrant memoryscape that does not give up on the commemorative aspects of the monument and that may even allow for a coy re-enjoyment of its seductive power while resisting simplistic interpretation and appropriation. Such postmodern forms of anti-monumentality assume a similar cultural function to old-style, nineteenth-century monumentality, with the important difference that they are, by their very nature, less easy to pin down and hence, presumably, less susceptible to ideological appropriation. The concept of anti-monumentality Huyssen proposes, as "fundamentally informed by the modernist spirit of a fleeting and transitory epiphany but . . . no less memorable or monumental for that,"[16] is ultimately a plea to find new ways to recapture

FIGURE I.1 Christo and Jeanne-Claude: *Wrapped Reichstag, Berlin, 1971–1995.*
© Christo 1995. Photo: Wolfgang Volz (laif/Redux).

the pleasure—which is not necessarily the same as light-hearted enjoyment—
of the monumental.

Post-unification Berlin is the chief site of this anti-monumentality, and
especially the temporary artwork, *Wrapped Reichstag, Berlin, 1971–1995* by
Christo and Jeanne-Claude, shown in figure I.1, could be described as the
paragon of "anti-monumentality" in Huyssen's sense.[17] The artists shrouded
the Reichstag in a silver fabric that from a distance looks like a light veil, as
a counterpoint to its familiar, history-laden, somewhat stodgy Wilhelmine
architecture. As was noted widely, by making the building invisible for the
duration of a few weeks, Christo and Jeanne-Claude ironically succeeded in
highlighting the presence of the architectural structure. The project enjoyed
enormous popular success at the time, attracting five million visitors. Many
of them made the most out of this joyous respite from the imposing architectural and historical portentousness of the site and thereby turned it into the
most popular picnicking spot of the season.

Huyssen's diagnosis of the split of monumentality in contemporary culture into near-obsessive commemorations and the simultaneous rejection of
the heaviness and permanence of the physical monument helps to explain the
veritable boom of memory studies that various humanistic disciplines have

witnessed in recent years, spearheaded by the French historian Pierre Nora. Nora introduced the important concept of *lieu de mémoire,* usually translated as "memory site," which he defines as "any significant entity, whether material or non-material in nature, which by dint of human will or the work of time has become a symbolic element of the memorial heritage of any community."[18] Since some of Nora's concepts play a significant part in the idea of musical monumentality as it will be developed in the following chapters of this book, even where he is not explicitly invoked, it is worth briefly introducing some of his key ideas here.

Nora's concept, with its emphasis on communal remembrance, rests significantly on a shift in the conception of memory that goes back to the Bergsonian-turned-Durkheimian sociologist Maurice Halbwachs.[19] Halbwachs's idea of a "collective memory" wrested the concept away from the psychological-philosophical purview of such thinkers as Freud, Bergson, and Proust—for whom memory was firmly associated with the individual, not shared among a group of people—and carved out a space for memory as communal practice.[20]

Nora's interest does not centrally focus on monumentality per se, so his own explanation for the resurgent fascination with memory follows a slightly different route than Huyssen. His somewhat nostalgic concept of *lieu de mémoire* is born out of a sense of crisis in the present: "Memory is constantly on our lips," he begins elegiacally, "because it no longer exists."[21] Nora views this crisis of memory, the acute loss of its last vestiges, as a crisis of identity in the contemporary world.

Like Huyssen, Nora builds these ideas on a tripartite historical model. In Nora's model, pre-modern agrarian society was once characterized by a continuous, unself-conscious sense of the inseparable bond between past and present that was perpetuated in rituals, traditions, and forms of memory—which Nora pointedly calls "real memory."[22] This *milieu de mémoire* with its authentic, all-encompassing practices of memory, he argues, gave way with the emergent industrialization to a new form of administering time: by introducing history, which for Nora means the chronologically divided perception of time into discrete levels of past, present, and future. In this modern, rationalized world governed by history, he continues, memory could only survive in pockets—reservations, as it were—as *lieux de mémoire,* in which time is perceived as continuous and perpetual. (Emphasizing the constructedness of the *lieu de mémoire* perhaps more than Nora would himself have done, the cultural historian Wulf Kansteiner has pointed out that these *lieux de mémoire* no longer constitute real memory, but rather "first-order simulations of natural memory."[23]) It is on these *lieux de mémoire,* which provide the community with a vital connection to its shared mythical past, that the idea of the nation could be built and sustained in the nineteenth century. In the postmodern stage of Nora's model, our own age, the last vestiges of a sense of belonging and the communal past are now at stake, where a distinct threat is perceived to emanate from modern mass media. It is from this acutely felt threat—which is disputed by some of his critics—that Nora's project receives its sense of urgency and nostalgia.[24]

The proximity of certain ideas espoused by Nora to other theories of cultural identity has been noted—among others, Benedict Anderson's *Imagined Communities,* Eric Hobsbawm and Terence Ranger's *Invention of Tradition,* and Alois Riegl's *The Modern Cult of Monuments* have been singled out.[25] Insofar as Nora's *lieux de mémoire,* along with the whole burgeoning field of memory studies, constitutes simultaneously "diagnosis and symptom"[26] of a particular situation, the concept does not so much constitute a clear-cut methodology as an aspiration, or, given the strong popular resonance it enjoys, perhaps something of a cultural project.[27] Nonetheless, it forms an important impulse and inspiration for this study. Nora's ideas will be complemented or counterpointed at various stages by other voices, such as Jan and Aleida Assmann, Susan Stewart, Thomas Carlyle, Thomas Nipperdey, and notably Friedrich Nietzsche.[28] Nor is Nora's groundbreaking study of the cultural symbols that define the nation and tie it together particularly concerned with music at any stage, save for the *Marseillaise.* Its subsequent German counterpart, *Deutsche Erinnerungsorte,* however, notably includes articles on Bach, Wagner, *Schlager* (that particular German tradition of easy-listening pop music), the *Gesangverein* (choral society), *Hausmusik* (domestic music-making), the National Anthem, as well as on that most monumental of musical works, Beethoven's Ninth Symphony—a broad collection that no doubt reflects the great importance that music, in its various forms and practices, holds in the German collective memory.[29]

Nora's concept of *lieu de mémoire* has a complex, twisted relationship with history.[30] He takes noticeable pride in the spontaneous, subjective, messy, and quasi-religious nature of memory that eschews clear-cut, rational historical inquiry.[31] To be sure, the opposition Nora posits between history and memory might be taken to legitimize opening the floodgates to complete methodological arbitrariness and has understandably sent up some red warning flags. (Critics have noted with reassurance, however, that most of the contributions employ a fairly traditional historical methodology.) Some of the characteristics Nora attributes to memory, meanwhile, could also be applied to the idea of musical monumentality, as it will be developed here over the next few chapters—or, to be more precise, these traits are categories within which monumentality operates, and by means of which it generates a sense of immediacy and of presence. The "Midas touch" of monumentality and its pronounced penchant for theatricality can be seen as indicative of these qualities, which make it a distinctly unwieldy topic for a straightforward music-historical inquiry.

One thinker who has recently come into focus as an early, irreverently insightful commentator on cultural memory is Friedrich Nietzsche. While Nietzsche was also supremely knowledgeable in musical matters, it is less his explicitly musical writings that matter in this context than his second *Untimely Meditation,* "On the Uses and Disadvantages of History for Life" (1874). This essay is often regarded as Nietzsche's first mature work, foreshadowing the powerful cultural critiques of his later writings, notably the *The Gay Science* (1882), *Thus Spoke Zarathustra* (1883), and *The Genealogy of Morals* (1887).[32] As we shall see at various junctures, the ideas proposed in this essay, supplemented by other key texts of Nietzsche, are of particular relevance to this project as in it Nietzsche addresses the particular role of monumentality and its relation to different modes of historiography in nineteenth-century Germany.

With this brief foray into the territory of cultural memory, we have already moved a long way from the initial idea of musical monumentality. It gradually accumulated conceptual baggage as it changed from a pointedly simple musical stylistic concept, via an aesthetic mass phenomenon, to an object of seduction and ideological distrust, and finally an object of commemoration that is capable of linking the present with a perpetual past. Let us now take one final step here and further transform the idea by actually jettisoning an element from our initial conception: we should drop the notion, dictated by common sense, that all monumental music necessarily needs to be big or loud at all times.

This is in fact a direct consequence of the path we have taken: once we place the commemorative function of musical monumentality in the limelight this inevitably alters the musical characteristics of what constitutes monumentality. To take a famous example, think of the musical greeting Brahms penned on a postcard to Clara Schumann in 1868, reproduced here in figure I.2, which was to feature prominently a few years later as the horn solo in the final movement of his First Symphony. Taken in its narrow sense (as "big" music), the sounding monumentality of this small musical sketch itself is nil, while its commemorative value as a memento is enormous and continues to fascinate Brahms researchers and biographers.[33] It is doubtful, had Brahms not enshrined this greeting in his symphony, that the postcard—as a mere souvenir—would have received the same attention. At the same time, but for the postcard, the horn solo of the symphony would be merely sound without definite meaning. Both components establish a network of monumentality in which they are

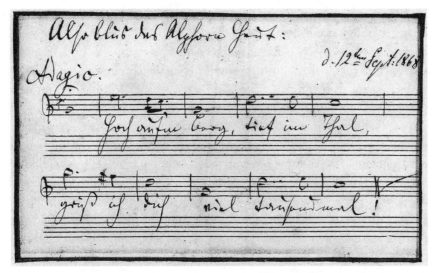

FIGURE I.2 Postcard from Johannes Brahms to Clara Schumann (1868). Reproduced by permission of Staatsbibliothek Berlin, Preussischer Kulturbesitz, Musikabteilung mit Mendelsohnarchiv.

enveloped and mutually reinforce each other's significance. Even without going into any details here, once we reestablish the link between the very private commemorative import of the postcard and the romantic sound world of the rather more public First Symphony, with its evocative horn call resonating over the shimmering string surface, we can get an idea of how even an object that is ostensibly silent, like a modest postcard, can resound monumentally. It is in this link between the private and the public, between the small and the outsized, between the commemorative and the sublime that monumentality resides.

It is for this reason that the idea of a transformation is quite central to the approach to monumentality pursued here. Each of the case studies that make up the main chapters examines a transformation of musical material—typically an "arrangement," taken in a broad sense. In our exploration of monumentality, we will encounter a range of musical objects that would be described as ephemeral in standard music histories and that rarely find themselves in the limelight of musicological attention: a commemorative festival cantata, operatic piano arrangements, a concert overture, a philological edition, a soundtrack from the early days of cinema, and finally a full-blown modern media spectacle. These apparently ephemeral objects are placed in dialogue with canonical works, as such forgotten musical objects were often instrumental in positioning the central canonical works in the cultural space that they occupy now.

What is common to these arrangements is that they all are material—often tangible—manifestations of a musical work. The material component of these musical objects is foregrounded here so as to focus our attention on the function that such monuments fulfill in musical culture and to reveal the embeddedness of monumental music in a network of cultural and musical connections most clearly. The focus on arrangements here is neither to say, of course, that a monument can *only* be an arrangement nor that *any* arrangement is automatically monumental. It is to say, rather, that the machinations of monumentalization can more often be laid bare in arrangements and offer instructive insights on the workings of monumentality—more so, in many cases, than compositions that have inherent pretensions to monumentality and that have garnered a lasting place in the canonical Hall of Fame. We will therefore forego extended discussion of certain prized monumental musical compositions, say by Mahler or Strauss, in favor of a focus on broader cultural and historical, indeed archaeological, questions, by examining the events and conditions that made such musical monuments possible.

The case studies themselves are not so much selected to demarcate all the stations along the German canon of monumental music. Rather, they were chosen with the view to exploring the variety of monumentalities that music has to offer. The chapters tend to be arranged in double vignettes that juxtapose pairs of conceptual opposites—large/small, progressive/classical, performative/philological, elite/popular—so as to bring them in dialogue with each other under a multifaceted notion of monumentality that continually changes as we (and it) progress through the nineteenth and twentieth centuries. Over the last few pages, the attempt to reassemble the various parts of the monument and bring together the object of commemoration with the much-maligned soundscape of the nineteenth century, following Huyssen's diagnosis, has already transformed the idea of musical monumentality, and it will further have a bearing on the way in which its "monumental history," to use Nietzsche's influential term, is written.

Ultimately, this study itself is inextricably bound up with the symptoms of the schizophrenic situation Huyssen describes: it is a twenty-first-century hermeneutics of nineteenth-century music, marked by the events of the twentieth century. It would be churlish to want to conceal a certain ambivalence toward the phenomenon it seeks to explore. On the one hand, it tries—I try—to create and develop a discursive space in which musical monumentality is enabled to resonate while, on the other hand, presenting a critical examination of this monumental siren song, which for that very reason needs to be held at bay. The aim, meanwhile, is not to lend further support to this ambivalence, but to situate it and to turn it into a more productive starting point for this investigation. I hope to arrive at a richer understanding of musical monumentality and our ongoing fascination with it by engaging with monumental music and musical monuments from both the inside and the outside, and by attempting to come to terms with its seductiveness, its popular appeal, its capacity to commemorate, as well as with its ideological susceptibility. The following chapters may offer elements of a critique of musical monumentality, but they are also, and cannot help being, a celebration of it.

CHAPTER ONE

The Time of Musical Monuments

Making Music Last

At the dawn of the nineteenth century, in March 1800, the *Allgemeine musikalische Zeitung* decided the time was ripe for musical monumentality. Johann Friedrich Christmann, Lutheran pastor, composer, and regular contributor to the journal, waxed lyrical in a paean to the century just passed.[1] Germany had produced a great many gifted composers that laid the foundation for the present glory of German music throughout Europe: "You gave us a Handel and a Gluck, a Graun and a Hasse, and through them you established respect of the genius of the Germans at the banks of the Thames, the Tiber, and the Seine."[2] The idea of honoring the great composers of the eighteenth century, of preserving their memory, was all the more important as their work was by its very nature ephemeral and especially endangered. No other artistic work, the *Allgemeine musikalische Zeitung*'s founding editor Friedrich Rochlitz emphasized, "contains so much that is perishable within the imperishable, so much that is mortal within the immortal" as that of the musician.[3]

Calls for "musical monuments" in the sense of collections of historical works had, in fact, appeared repeatedly in the previous years.[4] Johann Nikolaus Forkel (who was to erect a national monument to Johann Sebastian Bach with his patriotic biography of the composer in 1802)[5] had also made an urgent plea in 1792 to make rare, historically significant musical works more widely available. Likewise, the Viennese musician Joseph von Sonnleithner announced his plan to produce a "history of music in monuments" in the *Allgemeine musikalische Zeitung* in 1799.[6] Unfortunately, this ambitious project was nipped in the bud: apparently the printing plates of the first volume, just finished, fell victim to the Austro-French war in 1805 and were forged into bullets.[7] It seems that music was perishable in more ways than Christmann may have imagined.

The monuments that the *Allgemeine musikalische Zeitung* had in mind for the change of the century were more lasting, and it peeked beyond the borders of the German lands for comparison. Abroad everything was much easier, sighed the *Allgemeine musikalische Zeitung:* England had London, and London had its Westminster Abbey; similarly, France had Paris, and Paris had its Pantheon—both nation-states had successfully institutionalized the honoring of their worthies, including musicians. And what did Germany have to offer? Germany had no central "capital (only capitals) and cannot have one, because of her statistical conditions"—by which he meant that Germany had no genuine political unity—"and therefore she cannot have a Pantheon or a Westminster Abbey."[8] In this dire political situation, international recognition of German music was all the more important. The fact that Handel had even made it into Westminster Abbey was a case in point for Christmann: "Albion's mausoleum had to accept the urn with the ashes of a Handel."[9] This ceremonial burial abroad was not only a testament to the outstanding quality of Germany's music that was recognized abroad but also underlined the urgency of Germany to follow suit and create its own Hall of Fame. This would not happen for another forty years, when the Walhalla was opened near Regensburg at the behest of the Bavarian King Ludwig I, as shown in figure 1.1. But even then, as the *Allgemeine musikalische Zeitung* presciently recognized, the results would be somewhat parochial.[10]

The root of Germany's problem, the journal asserted always with an envious sideways glance toward France and England, was its lack of a cultural center that would promote a unified taste and artistic manner.[11] For now, all that could be done in Germany, Rochlitz concluded, was to mark important sites—birthplaces, death places, or places of work of the great masters—by dedicating plaques or columns to their memory, as had already been done with Haydn at Rohrau, C. P. E. Bach in both Weimar and Hamburg, and Mozart at Schloss Tiefurt near Weimar (figure 1.2a). Just to show what was possible elsewhere in comparison with these rather humble memorials, he added an illustration of the spectacular sculpture of Handel in Westminster Abbey, which effortlessly blends an apparently realistic likeness of Handel at work on *Messiah* with an allegory and glorification of his musical genius (figure 1.2b).[12]

It would take several decades before any artist's countenance was represented in Germany in an even remotely comparable manner to the London Handel memorials in Westminster Abbey and Vauxhall Gardens. But underneath Rochlitz's musings on the sorry state of monuments emerged another

FIGURE 1.1 Leo von Klenze, "Die Walhalla bei Regensburg" (1841) © Bildarchiv Preussischer Kulturbesitz/Art Resource, New York.

thought. Germany may not have been able to provide an infrastructure that would support the honoring of its great composers, so it would be a true test of the strength of German music to effect a role reversal: German music would become its own monument.

The *Allgemeine musikalische Zeitung* could fall back on other important reflections on the nature of monuments. In his groundbreaking *Allgemeine Theorie der schönen Künste* (1771), Johann Georg Sulzer had defined the monument, in a pronounced curatorial vein, as a "work of art located in public sites that is meant to perpetually sustain, and disseminate to posterity, the memory of noteworthy persons or objects."[13] The most basic monument was writing, Sulzer mused: a simple inscription would fulfill the minimum purpose. However, insofar as Sulzer considered the purpose of art to reside in the emotions and evoke virtuous sentiments, the essence of the artistic monument for him ultimately coincided with that of art itself.[14] From this perspective, music's monumental task was its natural destiny.

More than Sulzer and intellectuals at the time, however, the *Allgemeine musikalische Zeitung* was more concerned with how such a feat would actually be possible to achieve. Whereas the cultural-political bases in the scattered, decentralized German states were insufficient, the institutional structures necessary for musical production and reproduction were plentiful, as Christmann

FIGURE 1.2a German monuments to Haydn, Mozart and C. P. E. Bach. From *Allgemeine musikalische Zeitung,* March 12, 1800, Beilage. Reproduced by permission of the Eda Kuhn Loeb Music Library of the Harvard College Library.

detailed in his paean to the eighteenth century. Besides the wealth of great German composers, Christmann's personified eighteenth century had also bestowed another important gift upon humankind: modern musical print, particularly the "beautiful invention of the Saxon musical typeset under Father Breitkopf."[15] This invention was providential, he proceeded to argue, as it allowed composers' fame to spread far beyond their immediate sphere of influence.

FIGURE 1.2b Handel's monument in Westminster Abbey. From *Allgemeine musikalische Zeitung,* March 12 1800, Beilage. Reproduced by permission of the Eda Kuhn Loeb Music Library of the Harvard College Library.

Christmann addressed himself directly to the eighteenth century, in assessing the value of Haydn, one of the principal heroes of his reflections:

> Perhaps you sensed the value of this rare man [Haydn] even before he could compete for the laurel wreath which now decks his brow. For like a tender mother, who takes care of the abiding happiness of her children with great foresight, you, too, were concerned to protect the spiritual fruits of the muses by this great foster-child of the art and of nature, and alongside him those of other excellent composers, to protect them from falling into oblivion in future epochs and to deliver them to posterity.[16]

Christmann went on to outline the institutional achievements of the eighteenth century, such as they are: besides his gratitude for the great composers and for musical typeset, he also lavished praise on the instrumental pedagogical treatises of his time, the publishing industry, a recognition of musical talent, the evolution of German opera, and finally even music criticism, theory, and the musical chroniclers of the century, Burney and Forkel. Music had performed commemorative and celebratory functions before—think of Josquin's lament of Ockeghem or Couperin's Apotheosis of Corelli and Lully—but only now was such music in a position to reach out beyond a specialist circle into the public sphere and become a driving force of culture.

With all these institutions in place, it seems, music could overcome its perishable state. No longer did it need to be likened to the fragrant scent of perfume—as Kant, for one, had argued: a fleeting, incidental phenomenon, which engaged the senses but not the intellect, at best pleasant, at worst annoying, as it invariably envelops the general public without allowing dissenters a way out of its sphere.[17] With these achievements handed down by the eighteenth century, music now received its own rigorous pedagogy, wide circulation of compositions, enjoyment by an educated public, a national repertory that would soon become canonical, critical attention by the guardians of taste, and, last but not least, its own history. It became a force that was there to last. Bolstered by this institutional support, the curtain could rise for German music singing its own praises.

This new task for music required one further move. The heterogeneous musical practices and traditions scattered across the German lands had to be unified and subsumed under music's higher mission. "What the new century will have to offer, we do not yet know," the *Allgemeine musikalische Zeitung* concluded in another comprehensive survey of the eighteenth century by Johann Karl Friedrich Triest, theologian and regular contributor, but "on the level of the particular, where art depends on genius, study and taste, it is the work of humans, who can be commended or reprimanded for their progress or regress. As a *whole,* however, we may only imagine music as the workings of a higher force which can never, *ever* take any real steps backwards—or else, the highest in the world is nothing but a soap bubble."[18] The whole is greater than the sum of its parts—with this thought began the unparalleled rise of German music to pre-eminence in the national consciousness as well as in subsequent music history books. At the cusp between the eighteenth and nineteenth centuries, the scene was set for musical monumentality.

When compared, in hindsight, with our knowledge of the later nineteenth-century musical repertoire, one thing is particularly noticeable in the centennial reflections of the journal: its authors kept silent about the nature of the music that was to become monumental. One might think that this was because they felt that the music of the eighteenth-century composers they singled out as exemplary spoke for itself. In fact, however, when we read the *Allgemeine musikalische Zeitung* carefully, we find that they were acutely aware of a lack of certain components in their conception of musical monumentality. Thus, it was in a footnote that Triest added to his reflections on the eighteenth century that music was still missing two things: a "proper aesthetic theory" for this new music, one that would ideally "treat music metaphysically," as well as "truly musical German poems," which should be sonorous, singable, and at the same time of a high literary standard.[19]

The *Allgemeine musikalische Zeitung* was by no means a radical, or at that time even a particularly progressive forum: it championed primarily vocal music and had little interest in the new developments in instrumental music that were going on elsewhere around the same time. (A review in the *Allgemeine musikalische Zeitung* of a work by Beethoven, his sonatas for violin and piano opus 12, reacted predominantly with distaste to the dramatic gestures and harmonic maneuvers of the music.[20]) But it was exactly around this body of wordless, instrumental works that another, well-known assemblage of musical thinkers—E. T. A. Hoffmann, Jean Paul Richter, Johann Gottfried Herder, Wilhelm Heinrich Wackenroder, and Ludwig Tieck, to name but the most important ones—built precisely the metaphysical music aesthetics that Triest imagined, which made music absolute and let it be fully monumental as a musical work.[21] As Bernd Sponheuer puts it, the national cultural myth began with "the formation of an imaginary 'spiritual realm' of German music in which absolute music retroactively furnishes a meaningful identity."[22] The *Allgemeine musikalische Zeitung* had outlined the institutional base, as it were, to the Romantics' philosophical superstructure of absolute music. With the new found confidence in music, Horace's *exegi monumentum aere perennius* (I have erected a monument more lasting than bronze) could also be applied to music itself.

The idea of absolute music has been thoroughly contextualized, historicized, critiqued, deconstructed, and rehabilitated in recent years.[23] What matters for our purposes here is that monumental music is subtly but distinctly different from absolute music. Put briefly, with its important task of invoking memories, the monument is meant to *mean*. As an artifact that carries a message, coded or explicit, abstract or concrete, monumental music is by definition neither self-contained nor devoid of social function. In other words, monumental music cannot be absolute—in the narrow sense of wordless, non-referential, and non-functional musical entities. And as we shall see in the six case studies that make up the following chapters, musical monuments tend to be conceived less as self-contained, abstract works than as objects, concrete manifestations of music, which in some cases can, and are supposed to, be literally possessed and cherished. It is for this reason that the monuments examined in the following chapters are all musical arrangements of sorts, as these arrangements show most clearly the multifarious ways in which the monument plays with, instantiates, or manipulates the "higher" concept of music, which Triest and others called for. The concept of *Werktreue,* or fidelity to the work, came to mean something very different in the context of musical monumentality.

Strictly speaking, as an entity that is neither necessarily self-contained nor functionless, monumental music should rather be understood as *non*-purposive *with* a purpose; it therefore doubly falls short of the Kantian categories for beautiful art, which also eventually came to set the standards for the musical work.[24] Yet musical monuments are unthinkable without the rise of the idea of absolute music: as absolute music came to mean so much more over the course of the nineteenth century, as the musical work conquered the whole metaphysical realm of the absolute in the romantic imagination, monumental music partook of (or, depending on one's viewpoint, became parasitic on) the new prestige of music, along with its rituals, practices, and authorities. It came to inhabit part of the same rarefied aesthetic sphere as absolute music. Both suggested that the here and now can be transcended.

Thinking Big

The monument performs work. The *Allgemeine musikalische Zeitung* with its emphasis on the institutional basis, rather than the musical sound world, seems to have had an implicit understanding of this—including the double meaning of the concept, where "work" stood for both *labor* and *opus.* The monument needs to perform labor, at times in secret, in order to create the sense of being a self-sufficient musical object that radiates greatness as though out of itself; and it piggybacks on the newly minted work-concept that had bestowed new prestige on the art of music and that only made this monolithic, self-reliant impression possible.

The work that the nineteenth-century musical monument was to perform effectively consists in bringing together two distinct types of magnitude: one component, historical greatness, can be summarized under the modern keywords of collective memory and identity formation, while its other component, physical size, shows a marked tendency toward dramatic proportions (or even lack of any proportionality) that would elicit astonishment from its audiences. This tendency, which is often associated with the sublime and which manifests itself in the grandiose (or bombastic) qualities already touched upon, is perhaps better understood as an aesthetics of wonderment.[25] Since these two components will be critical to the concept of nineteenth-century monumentality in music, which resides precisely between them, it is worth reviewing each in turn in somewhat greater detail here.

The historical component of the monument was perhaps best captured by the Austrian art historian Alois Riegl. Writing in the early twentieth century, in an age where modern museum culture took off, the question of monuments was for him in the first place determined by curatorial issues of preservation and explanation. As we will have the opportunity to examine some of Riegl's work more closely in chapter 5, it suffices to say for now that for him, the "cult of the historical monument," as he called it, was inextricably bound up with a tangible conception of historicity. He explained at the outset of his reflections: "Everything that has been and is no longer we call *historical,* in accordance with the modern notion that what has been can never be again, and that everything that has been constitutes an irreplaceable and irremovable link in a chain of development."[26] In such an evolutionary frame of mind, every object becomes worthy of collecting and commemorating, as each object contains the developmental history of the whole. In principle, then, even the least remarkable scrap or pebble could achieve the status of a monument, a commemorative object, if only it somehow succeeded in triggering the imagination in this historical dimension. Monumentality in this conception is therefore based on the idea of an evolutionary history, that "each successive step implies its predecessor and could not have happened as it did without that earlier step,"[27] a concept that accords privileged importance to heritage and traditions. Historical monumentality approaches the fundamental question of who we are by telling us where we come from. It instructs us simply to look backwards for an answer.

The physical, or aesthetic, form of monumentality is principally associated with architecture. In its purest form, it excludes the historical dimension and concentrates instead on the immediate and present effect. The purpose of this kind of monumentality is to inspire, by means of splendor and representation of power, what historian Lewis Mumford has called "awesome terror"[28] (in obvious parallel to Edmund Burke's rather more restrained "delightfull horrour," which characterized for him the sublime).[29] In a German context, this form of aesthetic monumentality was articulated in Goethe's early essay "Von deutscher Baukunst" (1772) in which he used the Gothic Strasbourg Minster to bring together the aesthetics of the sublime and the revolutionary, original genius who created the building.[30] These ideas were swiftly transferred to the music of Handel and Bach—who, as we saw, were considered key players in the idea of musical monumentality.[31] Aesthetic monumentality answers the question of identity by reassuring us of our greatness and our lasting ability to overcome the challenges of others, by suggesting that we will go far. It tells us to look around ourselves and to have confidence in the everlasting future.

Historical and aesthetic monumentality both demonstrate persistence and suggest longevity—one by surviving over generations in traditions and commemorations, the other by grandiloquence and the sheer force of art. Both sides exhibit a tendency to self-stylization, which can be affective, emotional or representational, but which results in different forms. Historical monumentality suggests that what has prevailed has withstood the trials and tribulations of time; physical magnitude demonstrates that strength will be victorious. One side appeals to memory, while the other particularly avails itself of awe. Both of them demonstrate, on the one hand, immortality and, on the other hand, a superhuman quality, which implicitly miniaturizes the individual and the everyday.

With this somewhat schematic separation of historical and aesthetic aspects of the monument in mind, we should now turn to the ways in which monumentality was taken up by musical thinkers. It was in fact well over a century after the appeal of the *Allgemeine musikalische Zeitung* before anyone attempted to capture monumentality in exclusively musical terms. In 1935 the musicologist Arnold Schering proposed a succinct definition, according to which the monumental is a "grand, significant" object that is worthy of "being permanently preserved in the remembrance of posterity."[32] (The date is no coincidence here: during the twelve-year reign of the National Socialist regime questions of monumentality were discussed with particular vigor.) We see in this definition that both aspects that we just took apart temporarily, historical and aesthetic, appear in neat unity. As if in keeping with the eighteenth-century roots of musical monumentality, Schering's idea was epitomized by Handel's and Bach's music.

Meanwhile, such clear-cut definitions are few and far between. The majority of nineteenth-century commentators remained on the metaphoric level. In the absence of concrete examples, a ubiquitous image to capture monumentality in music was that of the mountain range. A stock-in-trade figure of the sublime, the use of this metaphor may still seem surprising in this function, as the image of the mountain range cannot convey either associations of musical sound or commemorative values. Regardless of their historiographic and political leanings, music historians of the nineteenth century tend to be in agreement on the usage of such mountainous metaphors. Thus, the Leipzig editor of the progressive *Neue Zeitschrift für Musik* and founder of the New German School, Franz Brendel, who will feature prominently in chapter 3, wrote in 1859 in his brochure *Franz Liszt als Symphoniker:* "To a later era, the whole epoch [from Mozart to Liszt and Wagner] will appear as *one* great mountain range with various summits. I repeat: the principle is the same for all of these greatest artists; only within it can particular modifications be differentiated."[33]

To take a figure from the other end of the spectrum, let us consider the Berlin philologist and Bach researcher, Philipp Spitta, who will be discussed at greater length in chapter 5. He elaborated further on the mountain metaphor a propos of the inauguration of his series *Denkmäler deutscher Tonkunst* in 1892:

> When talking of the great German composers of the past, we still think first of Haydn, Mozart, and Beethoven. We have gradually grown accustomed to the fact that Handel and Bach should also be included. But in the public imagination they rise up like peaks in the wilderness. . . . If there are figures in the history of art that are unanimously accorded towering greatness, it does not follow that less great artists are negligible for posterity. With the same justification we could argue that the alpine landscape should be done away with for the sake of a few of the highest peaks.[34]

The correct mode of appreciating Bach and Handel, Spitta concluded, is in relation to their context, to use them to survey the whole great alpine landscape of the musical past: "Bach's and Handel's creations are like two great mountains, from which vantage point the eye can perceive how rich and flourishing the world used to be around them."[35]

It is immediately apparent that Brendel and Spitta twist the mountain metaphor in two different directions, corresponding to their respective interests and proclivities. Brendel was eager to counteract a dusty classicist music

aesthetic, guided by Mozart's example, which he aimed to broaden dialectically so as to include Liszt and Wagner as well.[36] Spitta, by contrast, used the
triumvirate of the Viennese classicists as a starting point to push it back in
time to the era of German baroque, beyond the "old classics," Bach and Handel, all the way back to Heinrich Schütz and his contemporaries. The mountain metaphor transfers temporal distances to the spatial realm, suggesting
a contemporaneity of timeless genius, and thus allows Spitta and Brendel to
look both forward and backward in time. They can do so by referring to the
higher purpose of music in terms of abstract, overriding categories, as Triest
and others had proposed around 1800. While individual peaks might be dissimilar, their particular differences are all subsumed under the vast mountain
range. Despite the vast ideological gulf that separates the two thinkers, this
idea is at work both in Brendel's "one principle" and in Spitta's "alpine landscape." As the Janus-faced logic of monumental history suggests, to look forward is to look backward.

The mountain metaphor has obvious shortcomings, notably in its lack of
reference to sound or collective memory, but these do not seem to be an im-
pediment to its efficacy. For modern-day critics it might be tempting to overcome these limitations by positing a finer distinction between two paradigms
of monumentality, to which Spitta and Brendel would subscribe respectively—
along the lines of a historicist Bach paradigm paralleled by an aesthetic Beethoven paradigm—but in practice, again, such a neat separation between these
two poles very rarely held in the context of nineteenth-century monumentality.[37] Rather, the mountain metaphor seems to initiate a particular mode of
thought that complements the concept of monumentality: it seems that the
mountain range functions so well because it allows a series of ambiguities,
which only show up at closer inspection and therefore allow the leap between
our two kinds of magnitude with such ease—the overwhelming physical size
of the mountains is metaphorically transferred into colossal artistic or historical greatness. Moreover, it suggests that these supreme peaks of human
achievement are as durable as the mountains themselves. The mountains
represent apparently irrefutable norms of eternal validity. The fact that both
historians, Brendel and Spitta, use these implications of immutability to expand their mountain ranges by their respective favorites is less an irony of circumstance than precisely the reason for the proliferation and popularity of
the mountain metaphor. For while the mountain metaphor implies a clear
historical model, the image itself connotes an essential timelessness. Even
for a philologist like Spitta, the mountain metaphor is ultimately not about
well-founded historiography so much as about the establishment of cultural
norms.

No one has put this as concisely as Friedrich Nietzsche, for whom this conception characterizes the essence of "monumental history":

That the great moments in the struggle of the human individual constitute a chain, that this chain unites mankind across the millennia like a range of human mountain peaks, that the summit of such long-ago moments shall be forever still living, bright and great—that is the fundamental idea of the faith of humanity, which finds expression in the demand for a monumental history.[38]

Nietzsche was quite skeptical of monumental history, and we do well to take this apparent celebration of monumentality with a large grain of salt here—he would point out the pitfalls in the very concept of monumental history only a few paragraphs later.[39] Such skepticism, however, was rare in the nineteenth century, and his description, ironic though it is to a certain extent, perfectly describes the spirit in which the mountain metaphor was typically employed at the time.

The ambitions and stakes of Brendel's and Spitta's project suggest that the mountains conjured up here are less Parnassus than Olympus. The task of monumentality covers great cultural acts; its protagonists are not effete "sons of the muses" but rather superhuman heroes, who commit great deeds in the musical and cultural realm. The impact of Nietzsche's monumental history will be a central theme in chapter 2. As we shall see there, in some cases, a heroic composer issues forth directly out of the mountainous nature—as in Schumann's ironic suggestion to have Beethoven's likeness hewn into a great mountain.[40] This musical Mount Rushmore clinches all the riches that the metaphor has to offer.

Most often the monumental mountain range is encountered in a form that has already transferred the nature image into the cultural realm: as a frieze, a series of busts or inscriptions of the names and countenances of great masters, whose communion forms a circle of perennial validity in which they guard the grand concert halls of the nineteenth century. (We shall encounter such classicizing busts again in chapter 4.) Alfred Einstein, for one, begins his reflection, *Greatness in Music,* from his American exile in 1941—here the date is no coincidence either—with precisely this image: "In Munich, where I was born, there is still in use today a concert hall of classical style—the Great Odeon Hall—with a wide apse for the orchestra, in the semi-circle of which are a number of round niches, filled with busts of musicians. They are of plaster; materially and artistically their value is nil."[41] The ideal value of these plaster figures, however, was all the greater. Einstein remembers how this collection of timeless greatness was continuously adapted to the changing times: for the inauguration in 1811 Michael Haydn stood next to his brother, and closely followed by Cimarosa, while at the beginning of the twentieth century, Liszt and Wagner found themselves beside the firmly established busts of Beethoven, Schubert, Schumann, and Weber. Einstein is unsure whether Mendelssohn managed to keep his place throughout the twentieth century.[42] Nothing is quite as provisional as the immutability of eternal values.

But is it really the composers who constitute the heroes of monumental history? We noticed that Spitta and Brendel tend to speak about great works, while Nietzsche talks of great moments; it is only in the plaster busts that the composers themselves are represented. In fact, it is precisely the flexibility at the core of the concept of monumentality that allows these imaginary connections between composers, their work, or even the effects of their work to be linked in creative ways. This is the "Midas touch" that the machinations of monumentality exercise and that is capable of extending its qualities to everything within its reach—gilding and solidifying it by association.

Ultimately, this is the strength of the mountain metaphor: it refuses to pin down anything; it does not explain anything but it presents everything in suggestive and awesome ambiguity. The image of the mountain conjures up monumentality itself, stages it as a theatrical event, and turns it into a veritable "experience." It is no coincidence that cragged, shapeless mountains are part of the standard repertory of the sublime at least from Burke onwards: just as the sublime itself, which exceeds human imagination, enters into the realm beyond representation, so the concept of monumentality, with its cognates of the "colossal" and the "monstrous," transcends conventional conceptions of proportion and beauty.[43]

In fact, the invocation of mountain ranges is as frequent as thorough explanations of the nature of monumentality are rare. As Riegl noted in 1903, the monument had been the token of the conviction throughout the nineteenth century that there was an immutable canon of art and an artistic ideal of indisputable, absolute validity.[44] The awkward fact that no one had succeeded in delineating this ideal with general rules did not deter historians of the time from continuing to have faith in and endorse this transcendent but elusive canon. In this respect, too, the Alpine image may have been helpful: the authority emanating from the majesty of the mountain commands silence from any disbeliever.

Transcendence and Beyond

On the metaphoric level, the mountain range might successfully integrate the historical and aesthetic aspects of the monument and pretend that there is a smooth, seamless connection. But the most refined rhetoric can only get us so far. We should now explore how some of the ideas we have covered so far can be conceptualized so as to get closer to a working model. How can we integrate the commemorative aspects of the monument with its sounding surface?

The doyenne of modern German cultural memory studies, Aleida Assmann, conceives the monument, though not necessarily the musical monument, as that "which is determined to outlast the present and to speak in this distant horizon of cultural communication."[45] In comparison with the rather more self-absorbed, iconic mountain metaphor, her focus is on communicative potential: in her conception, the monument is a conscious sign for posterity, a message addressed to an implied future interlocutor, which in this way aims to bridge two levels of time.

We can juxtapose her, too, with a figure from the other end of the spectrum, Arnold Schering, who also tried to capture the musical monument in its capacity for communication—although, admittedly, in a rather different sense. For him the significance of monumentality resided in its ability to inspire posterity by means of its greatness, as he saw exemplified in Bach's and Handel's works. We should, however, take this with some caution, as we will further see in chapter 6. Schering was clearly aware of the monumental sound world of the nineteenth century. He explained: "While every age has its great composer, and especially the nineteenth century has characteristically striven for monumental effects, there are only few composers"—by which he was referring to Bach and Handel—"with whom we can associate this concept so completely and unreservedly."[46]

A musical monument can only be "something grand, significant," Schering explained, "of which one can assume that the force of its contents will still be able in the most distant times to appear alive and capable of creating moments of elation, of pride, of self-confidence."[47] He made a dual demand on the musical monument, which for him primarily builds on the aesthetic aspect of monumentality: the monument is not only concerned with the representation of greatness, celebrating it in sound, but at the same time it is supposed to be awe-inspiring itself, to enact this greatness. The other aspect of monumentality, its historical magnitude, is subsumed by this conception: for Schering, the temporal distance between a monumental artwork and the observer is a sign of the success of the monument. In other words, once a musical work has prevailed for centuries in cultural memory, as is the case in Bach and Handel, it has succeeded historically, which for Schering is tantamount to eternal validity. The central concern of Schering's investigation, then, is the question of which musical means produce the kinds of effects that he considers to be in force in a truly monumental musical work.

The mountainous monuments aspired to an apparently autonomous effect in timeless space, which is to say that the agents who secretly removed the obsolete sculptures or enriched the canon with their musicological arguments were only allowed to act out of sight behind the scene. Schering's argument, by contrast, inscribes a forward-looking temporality into the monument, as it is obliged to project its identity-shaping authority into the future. This difference between Assmann's and Schering's conception of the monument is crucial: Assmann concentrates on the means of communication, that is the "how," the mediating elements in monumentality, while Schering is centrally concerned to identify the "what," a specific musical essence of the monument. Thus, while Schering is convinced by the mysterious "force of contents,"[48] which he holds to be responsible for the monumentality inherent in a work of music, neither forces nor contents seem to matter much in Assmann's model. This focus in Schering's essentialist model therefore leads us inevitably to the origin of the monument—the only point in time that is fixed and identifiable, from which the "forces of contents," which characterize Schering's model, emanate.

The central question of how such a monument should be constituted in order to make optimum use of its special capacities was tackled in the nineteenth and early twentieth centuries with rather less compunction than nowadays. For Schering's musical physiognomy may ostensibly build on Bach and Handel, but it ultimately aims to capture something more general, something similar to what Nietzsche expressed when he claimed that Wagner's prelude to *Lohengrin* was music capable of hypnosis[49]—both possessed "forces of content" that exerted a immediate and lasting impact on their environment and on posterity. To be sure, Schering's efforts represent the only sustained attempt to compile a physiognomy of musical monumentality, but there is no shortage in the psychological-empirical aesthetics of the later nineteenth century of efforts to concretize the notion of the sublime in music, which were largely congruous with Schering's ideas.[50] Thus, Adolph Zeising, for one, attached central importance to various structural elements such as fugatos; for Arthur Seidl, such events as rallentandos or pedal points were signs of the sublime in music; while Hugo Riemann considered large orchestral tutti to exceed the capacity of subjective imagination—which was determined for him by the human voice—in both range and force. Hermann Stephani, meanwhile, regarded intensification and contrast more generally as characteristics of sublime music.[51]

Even without going into any detail here, it is obvious that such typologies can easily be applied, and have been, to many of the chief works of the long nineteenth century. This is, after all, the age of Wagner's *Ring,* Brahms's *Ger-*

man Requiem, Mahler's *Symphony of a Thousand,* Strauss's *Alpine Symphony,* and Schoenberg's *Gurrelieder.* Or, since the idea of musical monuments was obviously not limited to German culture alone, we can expand our view beyond the Germanic cultural borders: it is also the age of Tchaikovsky's *1812* overture, Berlioz's *Les Troyens,* Verdi's *Requiem*—that is, of works that might well confirm Schering's hopes of radiating the force of their musical contents into the most distant future.

The list, however, does not end here. Is this also the age of Joachim Raff's oratorio *Weltende—Gericht—Neue Welt* (1880)? Of Siegmund von Hausegger's *Natursymphonie* (1912)? Or of Franz Schmidt's *Buch mit sieben Siegeln* (1937)? These works are second to none as concerns scope, ambition, and overwhelming size, but their place in the collective memory is highly doubtful. Worse still, works that fall into the category of what Alois Riegl would call "intentional monuments,"[52] explicitly commemorative works—take, for example, Beethoven's *Wellington's Victory,* Brahms's *Triumphlied,* or Bruckner's *Helgoland* —have largely fallen out of favor, notwithstanding the stature of their composers and the high esteem in which they themselves may have held these works.[53] Issues of canonicity, monumentality, and the sublime may indeed have close associative ties, but the compositional factors Schering foregrounds— force, nature, and means of musical expression—are not in themselves sufficient to guarantee monumentality in the historically significant sense that Schering grapples with. Nor does it seem possible, conversely, to identify the canonical value of a composition analytically: attempts to determine the boundaries between greatness and bombast or *Kitsch* by means of detailed analysis, as had been popular up until the 1960s, are now considered untenable.[54] In other words, Schering has talked himself into a corner: historical significance is not a consequence of musical effect.

One common reaction is to defuse this precarious situation by reverting to a differentiation between "monumentality" as a mere stylistic notion of the over-proportionate and bombastic, and the "monument" as such, which fulfills a representative commemorative function.[55] As we recall, this is very much the case in late twentieth-century German culture: embarrassed by the supremacist excesses of fascist culture in the middle of the century, monumentality as a style is all but defunct; meanwhile the monument, as an object of remembrance, is more widespread than ever. In any case, with such a categorical distinction between the (commemorative) monument and the (overwhelming) style of monumentality, any attempt to approach the issue of musical monumentality from the stylistic angle, as Schering did, would necessarily be doomed. Nonetheless, it would mean to throw out the baby with the bathwater to cut the connection between monumentality in the sounding

EXAMPLE 1.1 Arnold Schering illustrates the sound of monumentality with a short snippet of music from Handel's *Utrecht Jubilate Deo*. Very similar moments are found in Handel's *Messiah* and the anthem *O be Joyful in the Lord*—each time to the word "Glory."

structure and the monumental, commemorative contents that are communicated in them.

Schering had highly specific ideas about the sound of monumentality: as example 1.1 suggests—the only music example he presents in his essay, taken from Handel's *Utrecht Jubilate Deo*—he was particularly interested in expansive blocks of static sound overlaid with sparkling textures. We need not go as far as Schering did to see that, nonetheless, in the nineteenth century there is undeniably something of a monumental style, parts of which are captured quite well by the phenomenology of the musical sublime.[56] The crux is, rather, that the existence of such a style alone does not lead to any historical guarantees.

A more fruitful approach would be to scale back the ambitions of monumentality. The appeal to transcendence on which monumentality operates must be historicized. This is to say, the mysterious "force of contents" that Schering conjures up must be examined more closely, and the "most distant future" into which monumentality allegedly projects its values needs to be more firmly identified than Schering was willing to do. To understand how musical monumentality works, the invisible hands that removed the Cimarosas and Michael Haydns from the Munich Odeon Hall, the imagined stonemasons carving Beethoven's countenance into the mountain, and the authorities behind the musicological verdicts must be brought out into the sunlight.

Acknowledging that there are invisible hands at work is not the same as to argue that these works, composers, or histories should not be there. Nor is it to say that they are arbitrary and easily replaceable by others. On the contrary, it serves to underline that they are there for a reason, and that they are fulfilling a very specific purpose, which often could not be fulfilled by another composer or piece of music. *Contra* Sulzer's earlier argument that every work of art is a monument, we should further specify that while every work of art *could* be a monument, not all of them *are* monuments at all times. This simple distinction—we could also call think of it as monument *in potentia* and *in actu*—is fundamental to understanding the workings of the monument: it might be useful at this point to recall that musical monumentality is far from being the self-evident, self-sufficient musical effect as which it habitually presents itself, but rather the product of surprisingly complex cultural mechanisms. Both the specificity of the sounding structure and the particular context in which it is sounded remain crucial to its monumental work, and both need to be carefully scrutinized.

Wagner's Romantic harmony always looms large in all matters monumental and can serve as an example here. According to the music historian August Reissmann, Wagner availed himself of the stylistic means of Meyerbeer's grand opera but concentrated them by focusing on its harmonic expression, as Reissmann explained in a number of examples. He commented on these examples: "Catchy harmonies, such as [example 1.2], may not lose their effect on the layman, but for the professional musician who knows the mechanics of these procedures they will soon lead to tedium, even when he ignores all other demands and fully submits to the effect of the music."[57] The catchiness of

EXAMPLE 1.2 August Reissmann demonstrates in a few chords that Wagner's bag of tricks may enchant amateurs but has no substance to offer to experts.

these harmonies mainly consists in third-related progressions and chromatic variants. Reissmann particularly complained about Wagner's undifferentiated application of these stylistic means, which he, as the examples demonstrate, employed in very different dramatic situations. It is by no means a paradox that the passages that Reissmann dismissed as banal and overused are the same kind as those to which Nietzsche assigned hypnotic power.

Without being aware of what he was doing, Reissmann's observation also brings into play a factor that is crucial to the concept of musical monumentality: Reissmann conceded that the audience reacts differently to such musical effects. The mass of amateurs, whose artistic instincts Reissmann did not trust, is highly susceptible to those effects that are also claimed by monumentality. To accept this discrepancy as significant, and to accept the layperson's reaction as fully legitimate, however, would lead to painful consequences. It is no less than an admission that monumental effect and normative artistic values might diverge. An approach, however, that aims to pinpoint monumentality in the structure of the composition, such as Schering's, cannot accommodate a differentiated listening experience because a piece's artistic values are supposed to be conveyed by means of the sounding structure. A legitimate mode of reception, under Schering's regime, would necessarily have to be unified.

It would be wrong to argue that the listeners' response is irrelevant to Schering's model—he spoke, after all, of "moments of elation, of pride, of self-confidence"[58]—but for the most part he nonchalantly committed those moments to the most distant future and no longer considered them in his examination. However, as soon as we lend more weight to the reaction of the masses, the communicative character of the monument shifts away from the origin, from the sender of the message, toward its recipient. Riegl's concept of the historical monument, too, draws attention to the fact that as soon as the concept of "eternal values" conveyed by the monument is given up, we are necessarily referred back to the values of the present.[59] For it is only with the view to the values of the present—which in this case is the "present" of the group of recipients whenever they lived—that we can explain how and why an artistic object may be assigned the status of a monument.

It is precisely at this point that the crucial difference to Assmann's cultural-anthropological approach comes to the fore: Schering has salvaged the element of transcendence in his model so that it conveys, in his words, "the impact of the initial impression across all ages."[60] Not unlike a Voyager missile on its indefinite trajectory into outer space, Schering's monument carries its man-made message to whomever it may concern, confident that it will speak for itself. Assmann, meanwhile, speaks of two distinct temporal dimensions, two epochs that come into contact by means of the monument. For her, the monument is an "established sign, codifying a message" that is "directly related to an addressee."[61] Assmann's monument, in other words, is staged so as to become legible for posterity and to facilitate a dialogue between two ages. With this, the context of the recipients also contributes decisively to a notion of monumentality and instructs us to consider its mass effects as part of the concept. At the same time we can get beyond the idea of universal canons or transcendent values and instead concentrate on an examination of how these coded values are received in specific situations.

Masses for the Masses

By combining the hermeneutic aspects from Assmann's cultural-anthropological model with a modified version of the specific musical aspects that are Schering's main concern, both the commemorative and the sounding aspects of musical monumentality can be captured and brought together in one concept. When viewed from this angle, the idea of musical monumentality turns out no longer to be identical with the musical sublime itself. It should rather be understood as the attempt to convey the sublime to the masses.

In this much less self-confident formulation, the troubling aspect of transcendence only remains as an aspiration. The ambition of the monument to convey high culture and eternal values to the audience, which had turned out to be largely untenable, is no longer pre-supposed as the automatic effect of the monument, but rather the key to the work it performs. It cannot quite be laid to rest, for no monument can liberate itself completely from the nimbus of transcendence without putting at risk its very claim to monumentality.[62] The effect of transcendence should rather be understood as the result of a successful monumentality. At the same time this means that the attempt to convey the sublime to the masses may well fail, in a way that can be no less spectacular than its success.

It is also for this reason that many, though not all, of the following chapters cast a spotlight on musical objects that are no longer present in the collective memory, that no longer possess the monumental power they were once endowed with. Rummaging through the proverbial "dustbin of history"—a term that by its very definition seems irreconcilable with the transcendental aspirations of monumentality and that, needless to say, should be used with gingerly circumspection—may in fact remind us of our own cultural forgetfulness and can help us to clarify the demarcations and limits of our collective memory. The differences that separate us from the figures of the past often allow a clearer view of the mechanisms and authorities that once made possible and sustained the illusion of transcendence.

Of course, we should not stop here: if a renewed acquaintance with some of the forgotten music discussed over the next chapters served to rekindle our interest in these musical objects, if we agreed to pick them out of the "dust-bin of history" and, indeed, if we rethought the very notion of a dustbin of history in conjunction with the vicissitudes of monumentality, then we will have come a long way in dialectically recuperating a monumentality for the twenty-first century. And perhaps we will find, at least in some cases, that the differences are not so great after all. In other words, a deepened engagement with those forgotten musical objects may make us question in turn precisely how those differences that appear to set us apart from the figures of the past have come about in the first place and may cause us to examine more closely the mechanisms and authorities that prop up visions of transcendence in our own musical culture. This would be the first step toward de-solidifying monumentality, toward demystifying its claims to transcendence, and toward understanding the golden shimmer that it once received thanks to its "Midas touch."

It is impossible to give an adequate description of the mechanisms and authorities that sustain monumentality in the abstract. But it may nonetheless be useful to sketch out some of the basic interactions of the critical institutions on which this form of monumentality relies, as we will encounter these or similar ones again and again in ever-changing constellations over the following chapters.

The scaled-back ambition of a monumentality that is no longer transcendent does not make its work any easier. On the contrary, its job comes close to squaring the circle. The monument is charged with the task of both celebrating the loftiest achievements of a culture and presenting them in an immediately appreciable form, their intellectually demanding and often also elitist nature notwithstanding. From this angle, again, monumentality emerges as the attempt to bring together two distinct quantities, which result from their temporal and aesthetic aspects, respectively. Here the quantities in question are immediacy, as a consequence of the overwhelming effect of physical monumentality, and permanence, as the correlate of the longevity of historical monumentality. These two aspects are juxtaposed in such opposites as fashion vs. classicity, entertainment vs. education, popular culture vs. canonical high culture, or newness vs. age.[63] The monument promises to bring both aspects to the fore—mass appeal and elite—as if there were no tension between the two. In a word, the monument must do no less than to heal the rifts of modernity, or at least, it is supposed to bandage them.

Theodor W. Adorno famously held Mozart's *Magic Flute* to be the last example in music in which popular culture and high art could cohabit.[64] It was a farewell to an idealized eighteenth century of a harmonious equilibrium between pleasure and enlightenment, an age before the indomitable spirit of modernity and progress unleashed the combined forces of class, history, and nation onto nineteenth-century culture. In combination, this triumvirate, the three pillars of nineteenth-century European culture, formed an exceptionally close interactive system that both gave rise to the monument (in its nineteenth-century guise) and was in turn held together by it.

Let us briefly sketch these pillars and their interactions here. The rising bourgeoisie, to begin with, with its self-definition based on *Besitz und Bildung* —property and education—increasingly gained the role of the principal carrier of culture.[65] Second, historicism, understood in its broadest terms as the valorization of the past as a key source of knowledge over the present, formed the background against which the identity-shaping forces of the monument came to the fore (as Nietzsche above pointed out).[66] And third, cultural nationalism provided the illusion that class differences can be leveled out with the view to a higher spiritual community, commensurate with national or cultural borders, building on the traditions, rituals, and spiritual links to the past that historicism provided.[67] Music, with its "community-shaping powers," as Paul Bekker memorably put it, became an important instrument within this triumvirate.[68] As monumental music, indeed, it seemed to increase this power exponentially.

With this in mind, we can now turn to the interactions between the three pillars. Given that the aristocracy typically formed the foil for bourgeois ambitions in the nineteenth century, it is no surprise that the modes of representation the bourgeoisie settled on for monumentality were primarily oriented by the monarchic monuments of the eighteenth century. (Nor should it surprise us that Handel is such an important figure in the establishment of musical monumentality, despite his complicated position within German music.) In the field of sculpture, the monuments of the eighteenth century had mainly celebrated military and political rulers; in the nineteenth century this space came to be increasingly occupied, sometimes literally, by monuments to the cultivated nation (or *Bildungs- und Kulturnation*), as historian Thomas Nipperdey calls it, with its heroic writers, philosophers, and artists.[69] Not only did the bourgeoisie exert a growing economic and social influence, but the cult of the genius, celebrated in these monuments, also became a central institution in the writing of history. To speak with Hegel, the world spirit manifested itself through the genius and history actualized itself through his works.[70] The Germanophile Scottish historian Thomas Carlyle expressed this in his unmistakably titled lectures *On Heroes, Hero-Worship and the Heroic in History* (1840): "The History of the World . . . was the Biography of Great Men."[71] Carlyle's heroic historicism had given up Hegel's idealistic outlook and embraced a reverential empiricism bordering on religious worship of the heroic deeds of great men.

As sociologists have been arguing for some time now, however, the relation between bourgeoisie and genius is reciprocal. In other words, the genius only exists *qua* genius—that is, not as a creator merely of works, but of *great works*—in symbiosis with its community of admirers who recognize it as such and praise its achievements. In other words, the community of admirers is united around a set of shared interests, which are attached to the genius, but which also, first and foremost, reflect the values of the group itself.[72] The community creates a canon of values for itself and installs the genius as its representative and authority figure.[73] *Pace* Carlyle, the genius *is made* to make history.

What matters, then, is the relationship between the groups of recipients and the monument, no matter whether this is the sculpture of a musical genius or the experience of his or her (though usually his) music. It is with this in mind that the revised definition of the musical monument, as the attempt to convey the sublime to the masses, should be understood. This new definition brings with it one further complication: the masses are not further specified, as identification only occurs around and under the influence of the monument. The nameless masses are not a priori identical with the nation. There is no compelling reason why the musical monument, or genius worship, would have to take place in a national framework. (As Ernest Gellner cautioned, a desire to belong to groups may be natural, but there is nothing natural about the specific desire to belong to a nation.[74]) In the nineteenth century, however, where nationalism became a driving force, monument and nation came to be almost inseparably commingled. There are some good arguments for this: if we approach the nation as an "imagined community," in Benedict Anderson's influential term, it draws, like the monument itself, on a strong concept of education that is determined by selective historical reception as well as by a firm belief in the perpetual presence of the past.[75] That is to say, the musical monument becomes the petrified, sonic impulse that brings together this imagined community and enables it to identify as a group.[76]

Again, it was Nietzsche who pinpointed, caustically but concisely, the stakes of the monumental task of German music. With reference to the increased importance of nationalism in the wake of the revolutions of 1848/49, he wrote:

Today German music is more than any other, the music of Europe, if only because it alone has given expression to the transformation of Europe through the Revolution. Only German composers know how to lend expression to an excited mass of people, creating an immense artificial noise that does not even have to be very loud—while Italian opera, for instance, features only choruses of servants or soldiers, but no "people" [*Volk*].[77]

Nothing would be more misguided than to consider Nietzsche's appraisal of a European quality in German music as an admission that he would buy into the frequent claims of its cosmopolitan nature. On the contrary, the privileged position German music assumes among the chorus of national styles is only in tune with a European spirit insofar as it reflects the spirit of the times: German music has learned to perfect its tasks and powers in representing, shaping, and homogenizing the *Volk*. Where the revolutions may have failed on the political forum, music continues its cause from the aesthetic realm. We need not go into great detail here—though it is tempting to think of Wagner's *Meistersinger* here as a paragon of that "immense artificial noise" that can at times be quiet—to see that the monument joins forces with communal identity by representing a fixed point, often suggesting a stable, immutable origin.

With this thought, we return to the point at which we started this section —the rise of monumentality among the vicissitudes of modernity. Thinkers from Novalis to Georg Lukács and beyond have identified the modern condition as a kind of transcendental homelessness.[78] When monumentality came to the fore in the nineteenth century, it acted as a probate remedy against this transcendental homelessness by providing a compelling vision of stability within the unstoppable surge of progress.

Turning Back

The call for monuments made by the *Allgemeine musikalische Zeitung* in 1800, at the moment that time folded in on itself to begin another centennial cycle, was born out of an impulse to take stock at the turn of the century. Matthew Head has shown, in a fascinating examination of issues of canonicity, historicity, and monumentality surrounding Haydn's *Creation,* how important the precise starting point of the new century—1800 or 1801?—was to the contributors of the *Allgemeine musikalische Zeitung.*[79] They finally offered an ingenious musical solution to this conundrum, presented with an ironic wink,

FIGURE 1.3 A short four-part fugue on the theme "When does the nineteenth century start?" From *Allgemeine musikalische Zeitung,* September 18, 1799. Reproduced by permission of the Eda Kuhn Loeb Music Library of the Harvard College Library.

to be sure: as figure 1.3 shows, a centennial four-part fugue worked the theme "When does the nineteenth century start?" into an imitative whole, in which the beginning and end of the subject were impossible to pinpoint with absolute certainty. As we will have occasion to observe in greater detail later on in the book, anniversaries of any kind offer a heightened psychological incentive to look forward and backward in time, to contemplate where we stand and who we are—precisely the questions that the monument promises to be able to answer. And yet, with the view to the monumental music of the later nineteenth century, it was much more than just a timely reflection. It was also a sign that the times demanded this kind of historical awareness, and that from now on this reflexivity was going to stay with music. The centennial reflections of 1800 also showed that it was time to consider the new tasks for art and to prepare its role as a self-conscious cultural agent.

As we have seen, monumentality was not just a matter for composition itself, but for everybody and everything associated with music. Triest knew that this included the crucial relationship to its audiences, and that a bond needed to be formed between them that would allow music to unfold its capacity for wonderment and awe. In this sense, Triest exhorted his readers to "lavish all conceivable attention on those who have demonstrated their inner calling, through genius and diligence, for the creation and elevation of an art whose ambitions exceed the value of a fleeting means of sensual delight, nay which, like the creative spirit that molds it, is capable of perfection into the infinite."[80]

Without calling it such, Triest's call for a new music in the nineteenth century brought together all the germane aspects of monumentality—including the call to the public to revere composers and creation as one, which, as we saw above, made the sprawling "Midas touch" of monumentality possible. With the united forces of all the institutions of music—chief among them composers and performers, pedagogues and educators, critics and historians, editors and publishers, and last but certainly not least listenership and public—it would be possible to fix music historically and gain "perfection into the infinite." In other words, by the time the nineteenth century came around, the time had come for German music to take on its monumental task.

It goes without saying, by now, that the very notion of the nineteenth century was not excluded from the twists and turns of monumental history. It is only fitting, then, that the reflexive, multi-referential view of music established *circa* 1800—which was to clear the path for the timeless "mountain range" view of monumental history—embraces much more than the chronological nineteenth century. Just as the nature of the monument is characterized by excess at all levels, so it becomes impossible to keep the nineteenth-century monument neatly confined to its period: its commemorative aspect allows it to extend backwards toward an apparently stable point of origin, while the aesthetic aspects projects a utopian point promising an everlasting future. Thus, within the confines of monumental history and its capacity to forge associative connections, it is no problem at all that figures such as Heinrich Schütz or historical events such as the German reunification of 1989 can feature prominently under the banner of nineteenth-century musical monuments. As we shall explore in the following chapters, both are firmly anchored, irrespective of their position in chronological time, in complex constellations that link it back or forth with the compositions, institutions, traditions, or with the ideology of the nineteenth-century monument.

Triest and the other thinkers of musical monumentality circa 1800 may not have envisioned the extent to which the concept would turn into the vast, sprawling phenomenon that it was to become over the course of the century, and beyond. To be sure, none of the facets that Triest and his colleagues consider to be constitutive of the foundations of monumentality can be said to be monolithic and immutable: the eighteenth-century sublime was hardly the same as its nineteenth-century equivalent; fundamental notions of canonicity, listening experience, musical media, and musical education were subject to wide-ranging changes; and last but not least, as the political systems changed between monarchic, democratic, militaristic, and totalitarian forms in the course of German history, so did the appearances and usages of musical monuments. In this sense, the image of Beethoven that forms the basis of the monument we will encounter initially on our journey through the next six chapters, at the Bonn Beethoven festival of 1845, can hardly be said to be the same as the one we finally revisit in the Epilogue in 1989, indelibly marked and irreversibly altered as it is by the intervening experiences of German history in the later nineteenth and twentieth centuries.

Nonetheless, across these transformations, the monument works to establish a sense of continuity that counteracts all the vicissitudes of modernity. It continually seduces us into believing that these traditions, and what they stand for, must abide—that the two Beethovens of 1845 and 1989 really could be one and the same, that the circle of monumental history can be squared. More than that, the musical monument encourages us to *experience* that this is so.

| Musical Apotheoses

Liszt's Apotheoses

> Let me express to you, best of men, my astonishment at your *enormous*
> *productiveness!* You have a Dante symphony in your head, have you? And
> it is to be finished in the autumn? Do not be annoyed by my astonish-
> ment at this miracle! When I look back upon your activity in these last
> years, you appear superhuman to me; that must truly have its special
> significance.[1]

With this accolade, Wagner began what was to become a rather famous letter
to Liszt in Weimar, dated June 7, 1855. He could hardly have chosen a better
attribute than "superhuman" for Liszt. For, as the reverent biographer Lina
Ramann put it in 1887, Liszt's Weimar activities included "groundbreaking
reforms" as a conductor and "groundbreaking reforms" in keyboard pedagogy, which produced a number of star pianists.[2] In addition, his theoretical
writings are a "triumph of genius"—which is tantamount to saying that he
introduced groundbreaking reforms—and his symphonic works "introduce
[a new] period of music history," which was no less than the fulfillment of
Beethoven's heritage.[3] In fact, by the time Wagner wrote his letter, Liszt had
virtually completed a consciously Beethovenian set of nine full-length symphonic works, most of which he had shown to Wagner.[4] Wagner's epithet
refers in particular to these symphonic works.

What is more, "superhuman" may also refer to the musical style of Liszt's
compositions of those years. As the continuation of Wagner's letter shows,
he regarded the connection of life and music as the essence of artistic existence:

"However, it is very natural that we only find pleasure in our creation, that it alone makes life bearable to us. We are what we are only what we are in our creation, all the other functions of life have no meaning for us, and are at bottom concessions to the vulgarity of ordinary human existence, which can give us no satisfaction."[5]

Needless to say, the notion that the creations and the biography of an artist are inextricably linked is one of the cornerstones of nineteenth-century criticism and was perhaps brought to perfection in the case of Wagner himself. This line of criticism culminated in the intriguing reversal suggested by Paul Bekker in 1924, that Wagner did not write *Tristan und Isolde* as a creative outlet for his amorous feelings for Mathilde Wesendonck, wife of his Swiss patron, but rather that he started an affair with her *because* he was working on *Tristan* at the time.[6] If Wagner's letter to Liszt insinuates a similarly close relationship between life and works, notably in the statement "we are only what we are in our creation," Liszt's "superhuman" nature would also suggest itself to Wagner through the music that he describes in his letter.

The strategy of mapping a composer's life onto his works, or vice versa, smacks of unbridled Romanticism and may seem suspect. At the same time, however, there is some comfort in the conceit that within Liszt's theatrical and often carefully choreographed life a stable point of reference should be found in his music. After all, Liszt told Ramann that he wished to be remembered according to the Goethean motto: "Er lebte dichtend, und er dichtete lebend." given the strong imaginary flavor of the German word *Dichtung*— which for Goethe was opposed to *Wahrheit* [truth]—this may be translated roughly as: "His life was poetic fiction, and his fictional poetry was life."[7] Under this motto, critics have recently begun to re-examine Liszt's compositional and performing career as an integral part of his biography.[8] And in this sense, it is quite easy to discern how Liszt's symphonic music may have sounded "superhuman" to Wagner.

To illustrate this point, we might consider Liszt's second symphonic poem, *Tasso, Lamento e Trionfo* (begun 1848), with which Wagner was familiar at the time that he wrote the letter. Example 2.1a shows the main theme, played by the bass clarinet and accompanied softly by hushed horns, pizzicato lower strings, and harp. As Liszt informs us in his programme notes, this theme represents a Venetian gondoliers' song and refers to the opening lines of Tasso's poem *Gerusalemme liberata:* "Canto l'Armi pietose e'l Capitano / Che'l gran Sepolcro liberò di Cristo" (in Edward Fairfax's translation: "The sacred armies, and the godly knight, that the great sepulchre of Christ did free, I sing"). Liszt explains what he imagines to hear in his musical setting:

The motive itself is plaintive, slow and mournfully monotonous; but the gondoliers give it a quite special character by dragging certain notes, holding back their voices, which, heard from a distance, produce an effect similar to that of rays of light reflected from the wave. This song had already so powerfully impressed me, that when the subject of Tasso was suggested to me, I could not but take for the text of my thoughts this enduring homage rendered by his nation to a genius of whom the court of Ferrara had proved itself unworthy.[9]

Example 2.1b shows the same theme, which has now shed its plaintive guise and returns in the major, in full splendor and triumph, marked "Moderato pomposo," to conclude the symphonic poem: Tasso's genius finally shines through —or rather, later generations recognize the "monument" that was Tasso. And here Liszt pulls all the stops: the full orchestra, including the sizeable brass and percussion apparatus, comes together in fortissimo for the glorification of this theme (and thus, symbolically, the glorification of Tasso), before the final stretti.

Most of Liszt's symphonic works employ a similar strategy, ending in a similar manner, with the principal theme returning triumphant. These moments usually go by the name of "apotheosis" and are comparable to the one just discussed.[10] Everything in these works points to the superhuman—even the title and subject matter of most the works refer to heroic mythical figures, such as Prometheus and Orpheus, or fictional and historical ones such as Mazeppa or Tasso.[11]

To today's ears, this kind of musical apotheosis has become the paragon of late nineteenth-century bombast, which has come to stand for Thomas Mann's "bad" nineteenth century.[12] The particular technique in which it was achieved is particularly associated with Liszt, at least since an influential study of his symphonic works in 1911, on the occasion of the Liszt centenary, examined the transformational processes of his thematic and motivic material in his symphonic music.[13] The notion of "thematic transformation," as it is generally understood,[14] is precisely the mechanism just described: the main theme, which may by and large be considered as characterizing the hero, is presented in its constituent elements blown up beyond all proportions and, because it is typically slowed down tremendously, is split up into smaller segments. In other words, if the theme characterizes the hero, the technique used for the apotheosis presents it no longer as a contiguous melody but as the gigantic, larger-than-life—in short: superhuman—object of admiration and glorification.[15]

EXAMPLE 2.1 (a) Franz Liszt, *Tasso, Lamento e Trionfo,* Gondoliers' Song (beginning). The theme that characterizes Tasso is presented by a lone bass clarinet.

EXAMPLE 2.1 (b) Franz Liszt, *Tasso, Lamento e Trionfo,* Tasso reemerges triumphant in this final apotheosis (beginning).

In Leonard B. Meyer's words, the effect of the apotheosis in nineteenth-century music is that of a powerful climax, of a statement of majestic affirmation:

> Such climaxes constitute a new source of unity. For by literally over-whelming the listener, their force and magnitude make prior unrealized implications, diversity of materials, contrasts of expression, and even gaucheries of technique irrelevant. Unity is established, so to speak, by the transcendence of the sublime—a kind of statistical, rather than syntactic, subsumption.[16]

The apotheosis is not a subtle rhetorical device; it persuades the listener by sheer force. Any technical deficiencies are overruled by irresistible strength; technique and musical logic become irrelevant beside the unequivocal closure which it provides. As Meyer concludes, the apotheosis was successful in the nineteenth century because it appealed particularly to less educated bourgeois audiences. Put bluntly, it taught them to clap in the right place. Meyer views such musical apotheoses as products of romantic (and largely elite) egalitarianism.[17] While he clearly recognizes the ideological potential of such musical gestures, the power of such music to overwhelm could also harbor the seeds of certain totalitarian features: the apotheosis is a climax that does not permit objections.

No big surprise, then, that since the Second World War Liszt's symphonic music has not fared well.[18] Most critics view it with suspicion; they tend to regard the very superhuman quality of the music as vacuous bombast. A recent Liszt critic, disagreeing with this sentiment, notes nonetheless that one "reason sophisticated modern audiences have often rejected Liszt's symphonic poems has to do with the notion that optimistic and jubilant musical climaxes must be in bad taste."[19]

The suspicion with which the symphonic poems are mostly regarded can be described quite well by a term Wagner coined in his major theoretical treatise, *Oper und Drama* of 1851: *der Effekt.* Wagner deliberately uses the foreign word, as opposed to its German equivalent *Wirkung,* to underline his derogatory tone. The theatrical *Effekt* in this charged sense is an "effect which is without cause" (*eine Wirkung, die ohne Ursache ist*),[20] a senseless bombastic display, a vacuous showy monumentality. As music critic Charles Rosen observes shrewdly: "[Liszt's music] is the zero degree of musical invention if we insist that invention must consist of melody, rhythm, harmony and counterpoint."[21] The palpable transformation of the musical theme into an apotheosis of itself—and the means by which it is achieved—would be a striking demonstration of Rosen's point.

Der Effekt *as Style and History*

It is intriguing that Friedrich Nietzsche used the same notion of the *Effekt*— as a *Wirkung ohne Ursache* (albeit in their more learned Latin forms)—in his essay "On the Uses and Disadvantages of History for Life," where he introduces his concept of monumental history. This parallel is no coincidence: at the time, Nietzsche was in close contact with Wagner; it is quite likely that Nietzsche borrowed this concept directly from Wagner's *Oper und Drama*.

Nietzsche explains that monumental history focuses on the great struggles of humankind and presents them in such a way as to suggest that past greatness is repeatable and should therefore be taken as an example for future aspirations. He envisages it as a succession of transcendent moments of greatness that link mankind across the millennia, as the maintenance of the perpetual presence of greatness in a kind of everlasting Hall of Fame.[22] Following Schopenhauer, he describes monumental history as "the belief in the solidarity and continuity of the greatness of all ages and a protest against the passing away of generations and the transitoriness of things," amplifying this notion with the image of a mountain range to capture the sublimity and transcendence of greatness on which "monumental history" dwells.[23]

To be precise, Nietzsche uses "monumental history" in two senses throughout his essay. This transcendent type of monumental history just described is the first sense, and it is perhaps better understood as a particular mode of narration, singling out the great and heroic moments in the history of mankind. At the same time, the idea of monumental history has a different, though related sense, when Nietzsche maintains that the use of such monumental examples (that is to say, the *application* of monumental history) results in a cyclical narrative, where individuals or nations, particularly in times of distress, are encouraged to repeat the great deeds of former times, and the heroic past is held aloft as a corrective to the misery of the current circumstances.[24] In other words, Nietzsche's "monumental history" in its two aspects implies both the history *of* monuments and history itself *as* monumental.

The notion of the *Effekt* and its associated pretences come into this precisely in the disparity between the two concepts of "history"—between the transcendent mountain range on the one hand, and the cyclical phenomenon on the other:

> [Monumental history] will always have to deal in approximations and generalities, in making what is dissimilar look similar; it will always have to diminish the differences of motives and instigations so as to exhibit the *effectus* monumentally, that is to say as something exemplary

and worthy of imitation, at the expense of the *causae:* so that, since it as far as possible ignores causes, one might with only slight exaggeration call it a collection of 'effects in themselves,' of events which will produce an effect on all future ages.[25]

The only way to sustain the illusion of this transcendence and timelessness is by ignoring the historical causes that led to the great achievements in the first place. The second aspect of monumental history, its cyclical conception, which holds that present or future generations can partake of the achievements of the past, is predicated on the very idea of this transcendent greatness. In other words, only if the achievements of the past are seen as results in themselves and are divorced from the historical context in which they occurred can the present be regarded as repeating or even surpassing these achievements. Nietzsche's criticism of monumental history on the basis of the *Effekt* is really a critique of the transcendent validity of greatness.

Nietzsche was primarily thinking about the history of political events and of great men, but it is not difficult to see how his concept of monumental history could be applied to nineteenth-century music history—which has also been written, on one level, as a history of great men. So, with the bridge of the *Effekt* between Wagner (where it is part of a stylistic critique) and Nietzsche (where it is a historical one) it becomes possible to consider the notion of the stylistic monumentality of Liszt's symphonic music together with the historical consciousness of monumentality in mid-nineteenth-century Germany. There is, in other words, a two-fold task ahead. First, we need to develop further the concept of the musical monument as both an aesthetic and a historical object and examine its application in nineteenth-century music history. And second, we need to investigate how the musical monument supports the imagined connection between Liszt's life and work, so as to result in something that Wagner would admire as "superhuman."

"What Does a Monument Want?"

It is a truism that for the nineteenth century there was no composer quite so transcendent as Beethoven. Accordingly, we shall begin our investigation with the first Beethoven monument in Bonn of 1845 (figure 2.1) before we return to Liszt's involvement with the monument and the monumental history written around the two.[26] As we shall see, Liszt's involvement in the inauguration festivities was an important stepping-stone towards his "superhuman" status.

L. v. BEETHOVEN.

FIGURE 2.1 The Beethoven Monument in Bonn by Ernst Julius Hähnel, 1845. From Heinrich Karl Breidenstein, *Festgabe zur Inauguration des Beethoven-Monumentes zu Bonn* (Bonn, 1846). Reproduced by permission of the Syndics of the University Library, Cambridge.

Beethoven was the first composer in Germany to be honored with a statue in a public place, and it fell to his native town Bonn—not Vienna—to celebrate him.[27] The monumentalization had begun almost immediately after his death in 1827. Although the first public call for a Beethoven monument in Bonn was made in 1832, the plans did not get under way until three years later, when a Beethoven society was founded.[28] Its principal task was the realization of a Beethoven statue, and to this end it issued an appeal for money on what would have been Beethoven's 65th birthday, December 17, 1835.[29] Despite the efforts of individuals (notably Robert Schumann, the English Beethoven supporter Sir George Smart, and later Franz Liszt) to get the enterprise off the ground financially, progress was exceedingly slow.[30]

While donations were given reluctantly, the fund-raising campaign could not complain about lack of contributions on the critical front. One of the most astonishing critiques came from the poet Jean Paul, who pointed to the paradox that lies at the heart of every monument dedicated to artists, a paradox that in some ways resonates with the aporia expressed in Nietzsche's comment on the *Effekt*. Jean Paul phrases his critique as a cryptic Romantic fragment: "What does a monument want? Impossible to lend immortality—because each [monument] already presupposes [immortality]. It is not the canopy [*Thronhimmel*] that carries Atlas but the giant who carries the sky [*Himmel*]."[31]

Jean Paul's paradox, then, is as follows: it is not the monument that bestows immortality on the great artist, but conversely, it is the great creation of the artist remembered that only gives rise to the erection of the monument in the first place. If Beethoven's creation itself glorifies the artist, then why does Beethoven need a physical monument? Or, put differently, had Beethoven not written his immortal symphonies, no one would dream of giving him a monument. Either way: the planned Beethoven statue seems to be a redundancy; Beethoven is immortal already.

But Jean Paul offers a way out: he considers the monument to be a work of art *on* a work of art. In his words, the monument attempts to express "two ideals" at once: it represents a "spiritual" ideal through a "physical" one.[32] The point of a monument is for posterity to express its admiration for the great work of the deceased. And this, Jean Paul explains, can only be achieved by a work of art in its own right. He personally favored sculpture because it particularly appealed to the masses.

Jean Paul may have concluded by speaking up for the Beethoven statue— and it should not surprise us that in 1841 he himself was honored with a statue in his native Bayreuth—but other critics were less easily swayed. For instance, Robert Schumann voiced his concern along very similar lines to Jean Paul (this despite the fact that he had offered his financial support for the Beethoven project).[33] Expressing his views in an editorial in his influential journal *Neue Zeitschrift für Musik* in 1836, Schumann (speaking as Florestan) began with an onslaught against the very idea of a monument for Beethoven: "A Greek sculptor, who had been approached for a proposal for a monument for Alexander the Great, suggested carving his statue out of Mount Athos. In his hand, the statue would hold aloft a city. The man was declared insane. Truly, he is less insane than these German attempts at raising pennies."[34]

Schumann here implicitly disagrees with Jean Paul's proposed way out by drawing on the sublime in Beethoven's music by insisting that it is humanly impossible to give Beethoven an adequate representation. He shows only scorn for the mediocrities that Schumann imagines the committee would finally come up with—which bear striking resemblance to the composers' monuments that the *Allgemeine musikalische Zeitung* had complained about in 1800 (see figure 1.2a): "a moderately tall slab of stone, a lyre, on it the year of his birth and death, above it the sky, and a few trees around it."[35] In this situation, he concludes, it is best not to attempt to represent the unrepresentable. All that the craze for monuments reveals is that we do not comprehend Beethoven's greatness. Schumann-Florestan remarks with regretful irony that Beethoven was evidently *not* great enough to be given *no* monument.[36]

One of the reasons that Schumann felt uncomfortable with a representation of Beethoven's greatness becomes clear later, where he turns to the historical implications. We have already seen that the monument can be a sign set in defiance of transitoriness and in celebration of the transcendence of great works, inspiring posterity to carry them into the future. This means nothing less than that monuments affect the way the future shapes up. Each monument casts a trajectory into the future, setting out guidelines for the mode in which the hero is to be remembered.[37] It carries with it moral obligations; it keeps us on one particular track and invites loyalty to the tradition that his example established.[38] The cause of Schumann's concern is not related to Beethoven's tradition per se, but rather the danger that this tradition might be misrepresented by the philistines—a thought that constantly haunted Schumann. In other words, if the monument channels the response of posterity, if it reifies Beethoven's legacy, then it automatically exposes itself to abuse. In this situation, *no* representation remains the safest option.

Schumann, now speaking as Jonathan, bolsters his criticism by casting doubt on the legitimacy of Bonn to honor Beethoven, who, after all, spent most of his creative years elsewhere. What would happen, he wonders, if other cities also staked their claim, say Vienna or Leipzig, and decided to build monuments of their own? Which memorial would be the authoritative one? How ought we to remember him?[39]

In singling out this point Schumann showed good judgment of the underlying dangers, for the appropriation of Beethoven by Bonn as an emblem for the town became one of the principal features of the four-day celebrations surrounding the inauguration of the monument in 1845. It is perhaps best summed up in the Festival Ode, which the Director of Music of Bonn University, Heinrich Karl Breidenstein, composed for the occasion:

> It is thou, Master, treasure of tones,
> Whose lofty image
> Was revealed before our eyes,
> At this place,
> Where once your cradle stood,
> For here with us, at the German Rhine,
> No matter that every country would call thee theirs,
> Oh mighty one, here is thy fatherland.[40]

Schumann's hopes that multiple Beethoven statues would cause so much confusion that the mutually exclusive claims would cancel each other out were not fulfilled until the 1880s, when the Beethoven monument in Vienna was inaugurated. Nevertheless, his concerns did play themselves out on numerous levels in the events surrounding the 1845 Bonn monument. In such a context one thought suggests itself above all: if a place could use the monument to promote itself, why should a person not be able to do the same?

Rivalries

It should come as no surprise that the whole inauguration festival (August 10–13, 1845) was competitive and hostile, especially since a number of individuals and factions involved were only too aware of the unique historical opportunities that this event offered.[41] The Englishman Henry Chorley reports his recollections:

> It appeared as if some of the guests had come thither with no other purpose than to see the matter fail, and to sneer at the universal discomfiture. A. would not sing. B. (which was almost more annoying) *would* play. C. wrote anonymous letters to apprise every one that D. was

of character too infamous to be allowed part or share in so sacred a rite. Every one seemed to have set his or her heart on accompanying "Adelaida!" Then what business had Liszt to permit his own *Cantata* to be performed, when E. had his psalm ready, and F. his Hymn of Praise, and G. his choral *symphony* as good as Beethoven's, and twice as difficult? Then H. and F. and I. were spirited away by Meyerbeer, who was accused of fixing the rehearsals for the King of Prussia's concerts at Brühl and Stolzenfels, at the precise time best calculated to thwart the operations of the Bonn Committee.—Then the wranglings for place and precedence at the dinner-tables at "The Star" every day!— and the sneers and the slanders, and the confidences in by-corners, and the stoppages on the stairs to relate some new hope of an utter break down—some new story of ill-usage and neglect. It was the plague of Envy, called into open and active life by mismanagement, in its fullest perfection.[42]

Every move was political. For the musicians among the well over two thousand international visitors, the Beethoven festival was a unique opportunity to make, or break, a career.

There were a number of rivals among the celebrities, all of whom had a vested interest in seizing the opportunity to establish or consolidate their entitlement to Beethoven's legacy—chief among them, Schumann, Louis Spohr, Anton Schindler (Beethoven's shady amanuensis), Breidenstein (who represented the interests of the organizing committee), and, last but not least, Franz Liszt. All were in direct competition with each other to garner a performance before a vast and influential audience (including international press coverage), though all of these rivals had different claims and motivations.

First, it is imaginable that Schumann should have been at the forefront of the events, but he only drew attention to himself by his absence, as the press did not fail to notice.[43] One might imagine that this celebration would have been too philistine for him. In fact, however, he had indeed planned to attend the festivities, confirming this with Liszt as late as August 1845, but had to return home after he became unwell.[44]

Second, Breidenstein was in a highly strategic position, since he was also the chairman of the organizing committee. As it happened, however, this position turned against him, since the organization was blamed for any glitch during the festivities—and there were many. Perhaps his worst error of judgment had been his neglecting to hand out free tickets for the attending newspaper journalists.[45] Probably in recompense, the reviews of his "Ode" were overwhelmingly negative:

Even though Herr Breidenstein may have had the understandable wish, as the president of the committee, as the local director of music, to occupy himself during the festival, he should never force his compositions on us, where Spohr, Lindpaintner, and many others present at the festival, would have been much more entitled to such an honor due to their famous names. Indeed, as surely every modest man would have done if the committee had invited him to compose a festive chorus, Herr Breidenstein would have done well to refuse the honor, which ought only to be made available to the most senior of the foremost living German composers.[46]

Although ulterior motives may of course have been at play, the critic himself mentions an important, perhaps decisive criterion: it does not merely fall to anyone to celebrate Beethoven's monument and memory. Rather, the position of the celebrant, his relation to the celebrated hero, is of crucial importance. To alter a *bon mot* by Goethe slightly: he who commends, condescends.[47] Breidenstein, a mere local hero, could not offer a genealogy worthy of this office. In other words, there is an implicit understanding that the act of honoring Beethoven in return bestows honor on the celebrant. And conversely, in order to be worthy of performing this honorable act of honoring, a certain prior reputation or validation is required.

Our third candidate, Louis Spohr, would have the necessary credentials, since he was the most famous living composer at the festival. But Spohr had no interest in the Beethovenian legacy. As he confessed in his autobiography several years later, he did not understand the late Beethoven and thought that the Ninth Symphony and the *Missa solemnis*—the very two works at the center of the Beethoven festivities in Bonn—were artistic failures due solely to Beethoven's tragic deafness.[48]

The only other musician who was active during the festival was Liszt. As indicated earlier, at that time Liszt enjoyed European fame as a piano virtuoso, although, unlike Spohr, he had next to no reputation as a composer or conductor. Nonetheless, he was commissioned not only to play the solo part of Beethoven's Fifth Piano Concerto but also to conduct part of the festival's concerts. Further, he was commissioned to write a festive cantata, which was the only such commission apart from Breidenstein's doomed Ode. Liszt had joined the festival committee in 1839 and had made a donation of 10,000 fr towards the monument, which covered almost a quarter of the overall cost.[49] Needless to say, many observers immediately suspected a connection between Liszt's generosity and his prominence during the festival.

Beethoven's self-appointed secretary and confidant, Anton Schindler obviously had both the background and sufficient interest in presenting himself as the authentic mouthpiece of Beethoven's legacy, a privilege that he guarded jealously. He was not a creative musician, however, and his influence was purely destructive. He particularly objected to Liszt's participation:

> Far be it from me, neither to the pleasure of some nor the displeasure of others, . . . to put a *sordino,* that is, a damper on to the excessive racket about Mr. Liszt. The truth must in any case be weightier than ten thousand francs. . . . However, some gentlemen in Bonn bow their knee before [this sum of money], because its sound is just the kind that affixes itself best to their aural nerves. . . . I was going to recommend the Munich Court *Kapellmeister* to the committee as a festival conductor, . . . since he is the only one among them who over many years encountered Beethoven's music in Vienna in the Master's understanding, [and who] has been musical director for eighteen years and is therefore no 'walk-on' [Improvisirter]. Lachner is surely also of the conviction that anyone who wants to conduct . . . the Ninth Symphony and the *Missa solemnis* must rehearse it himself with chorus and orchestra so as to work himself into the music, no matter how much experience he may have. It is not good enough to come, on the trust in one's famous name, like a high-ranking general taking over the musical corps for the parade. . . . However, what good is a man like Lachner? What good is Spohr, if Liszt is present? Did Lachner buy the right to musical direction with a large sum? It is likely that his contribution = 0. But 0:10000 is a terrible disproportion; consequently we cannot invite Lachner.[50]

As always, Schindler was trying to capitalize on his personal relationship with Beethoven, fiercely defending this privilege against other potential claimants. An anonymous respondent immediately leapt to Liszt's defense by pointing out that he had previously conducted Beethoven's Fifth and Seventh Symphonies to great acclaim.[51]

One earlier incident from Liszt's biography evidently also nagged Schindler: in 1823, the eleven-year-old Liszt had been introduced to Beethoven by none other than Schindler himself and played the piano before the composer. The composer was apparently so enraptured by the performance that he stormed onto the stage and kissed the young Liszt on the forehead.[52] Liszt subsequently attached great significance to this event, which was soon stylized into a symbolic act. Schindler felt threatened and tried to undermine

Liszt's position. He even sank so low as to forge Beethoven's conversation books to evoke the impression that Beethoven had disliked Liszt.[53]

To cut a long story short, Schindler disqualified himself from the struggle for Beethoven's mantle precisely because of such foul play. Eventually the tide turned against him; he was effectively silenced in the run-up to the festivities by the disclosure of a letter by Beethoven unknown to Schindler, in which the composer wrote: "Write back as soon as you receive this letter; I will send you a few lines for Schindler, this despicable object, since I do not like to be in immediate contact with this wretch."[54] Beethoven did not mince his words, and the letter is authentic. It is not difficult to imagine the glee that the publication of this passage must have caused among Schindler's numerous adversaries.

The final candidate in the wrangling about Beethoven's monument is, perhaps surprisingly, King Friedrich Wilhelm IV himself, the only non-musician among the rivals. Like Schindler, he could not hope to make claims to Beethoven's musical legacy, but Beethoven's stature posed a considerable threat to his own political position, since the committee placed some significance on the location in which the statue was to be deployed. Placed squarely on the Münsterplatz opposite the cathedral, it was to occupy a space previously reserved for kings and statesmen.[55] In fact, the insistence of the committee on this location had been largely responsible for the considerable delay between the initial petition, submitted in 1836, and the eventual inauguration, in 1845. Not only had King Friedrich Wilhelm III vehemently opposed statues to bourgeois heroes, he had also refused to grant a royal permit to the committee. It was not until his death and the ascendance of his son, Friedrich Wilhelm IV, that the project could finally go ahead in 1840. Beethoven, the bourgeois hero, could symbolically knock royal figures off their pedestals.

Working at Cross-Purposes?

Given the anti-royalist implications of the Bonn Beethoven monument, it seems strange that at the same time the committee placed the utmost importance on the presence of the king at the festivities. The committee went so far as to move the actual date of the unveiling so that King Friedrich Wilhelm IV and his wife Queen Elisabeth could attend—and, better still, bring their guests of honor, Queen Victoria of England and Prince Consort Albert, who were fortuitously visiting Germany at that time.[56]

This curiously twisted relationship between the committee and the royal house was typical of the *Vormärz* period, the years leading up to the revolutions

THE INAUGURATION OF THE STATUE OF BEETHOVEN, AT BONN.

FIGURE 2.2 The Unveiling of the Bonn Beethoven Monument, August 12, 1845. From *Illustrated London News* August 23, 1845. Reproduced by permission of the Syndics of the University Library, Cambridge.

of March 1848. The committee had designed the whole Beethoven project as a demonstration of democratic power and national consciousness. A contemporary newspaper illustration, reproduced in figure 2.2, even suggests the possibility that liberal black-red-gold flags were in evidence during the ceremony. Nevertheless, a royal presence at the festival was indispensable to the success of the enterprise and functioned as a kind of seal of approval. The choreography of the Beethoven celebrations demanded this royalty. Ideally, the liberal nationalists would have liked to be seen in charge over the royal house, while in fact both sides compromised heavily. The royal house, on the other hand, played along because they had no other choice: they were keenly aware of the ever-growing power of the bourgeoisie.[57]

From the committee's perspective, the deployment of the monument was intended as a demonstration of national sovereignty. As historian Thomas Nipperdey has pointed out, during the *Vormärz* period the invocation of the nation usually implied a sense of democratic provocation against monarchic powers.[58] There were, however, other forces that brought a more aggressive style of nationalism into the debate, hoping to turn the event into a demonstration of national superiority.[59] While the initial appeal for funds had been announced internationally, certain voices made themselves heard, condemning the international involvement in a project concerning the glorification of Beethoven as a national hero. For instance, a review of a charity concert given in 1836 in aid of the monument stated:

> There is just one aspect that I would have wished to be different, namely the acceptance of contributions from abroad. The German nation should erect a monument to such a genuinely German composer as Beethoven purely out of itself, and without accepting any support (no matter how well-intentioned) from foreigners, who are, after all, not capable at this time of recognizing and feeling the true and full value of the great deceased.[60]

In such an aggressive climate, one might ask whether there were hostile voices objecting to Liszt's participation on nationalistic grounds, since he would seem to be an obvious target. In fact, this question has been raised repeatedly since the later nineteenth century, first of all by Ramann herself.[61] The notion, however, that Liszt was Hungarian—and therefore foreign—must not be taken too seriously, since this viewpoint is indebted to the narrowly focused and more aggressive form of Wilhelmine nationalism of the 1880s. At the time, by contrast, the concept of national identity was defined along more flexible lines. Thus none of the journalists present at the inauguration commented on Liszt's foreignness at all. On the contrary, in the opinion of Hector Berlioz, who was reporting from the Bonn festival for the French *Gazette musicale,* the musical direction was firmly in German hands: "Nothing could have been more appropriate than that Spohr and Liszt, both of them Germans, should have been entrusted with the direction of the three concerts of this German celebration."[62] In the Romantic nationalism of the *Vormärz* period, marked by the absence of a unified state, an Austro-Hungarian cosmopolitan such as Liszt could very well be counted as German.

What is more, Liszt's international fame was of crucial importance to the nationalistic spin that certain groups were trying to give to the monument project, since his reputation as a virtuoso added international glamour to a festival otherwise widely criticized for its parochialism.[63] Unlike other ambitious demonstrations of national significance at the time—such as the planned completion of Cologne Cathedral (conceived as the tallest structure in the world), or Walhalla, the German Hall of Fame erected on the Danube near Regensburg, which left a lasting, widely visible mark in the landscape—this one critically depended on international recognition to bolster the symbolic significance of the project.[64]

Thus the situation presented a fortunate constellation between the interests of the committee and those of Liszt. The nationalists needed Liszt, and Liszt was prepared to take advantage of this situation. From the committee's perspective, Liszt posed no threat to the nationalist reading that the committee proposed for the Beethoven monument; on the contrary, his cosmopolitan appeal emanating from a firmly German background could only help its international success. Moreover, Liszt evidently had no interest in tampering with the nationalist message of the inaugural festivities. This becomes clear in Liszt's compositional contribution to the festival: a cantata on a celebratory text by the Jena professor and poet O. L. Bernhard Wolff.[65] Besides Breidenstein's own occasional chorus, this would be the only original composition played at the festival. The text on which his Festival Cantata is based is in itself a thinly veiled anti-royalist program for monumental history:

> If the Prince represents his people
> In subsequent annals,
> Who represents their pain,
> Who announces how they suffered?
> Who rises up for them in the book of World History?
> Makes their name radiate across the course of times?
> Poor Mankind, cruel fate!
> Who is sent out by you at the end of the day?
> The Genius!
> Eternally great in his works![66]

For all this, it seems, the committee was willing to let Liszt be the main actor at the festival. From Liszt's perspective, the Beethoven commemoration offered a unique opportunity to round off his reputation:[67] he would capitalize on his international fame as a brilliant virtuoso—a position which, for all its glamour, had always smacked of charlatanry and immorality—to become a serious (that is, great) composer. Most people around him were just as aware of this opening as Liszt must have been himself. Thus Wagner wrote to him just weeks before the festival, in wonderfully mixed metaphors: "You are just on the point of crowning your important participation in the erection of the Beethoven monument; you are for that purpose surrounded by the most important musicians of our time."[68] One wonders who is actually being crowned. Characteristically, Wagner was writing to use this moment in Liszt's career for his own interests, but his analysis of the situation was correct. For three days Liszt would take a position center stage, watched by the international musical elite.

Liszt could be sure of an international audience of leading musicians, and he knew full well that the Beethoven festival was his opportunity to consolidate his reputation as the chosen heir.[69] Liszt participated in the festival in no fewer than five separate functions: as the chief donor, committee member, soloist, and not least as a conductor and composer. All in all, Liszt would be the minister to a congregation of Beethoven worshippers. He had every interest in instrumentalizing Beethoven to further his own immortality. And he had every reason to be confident that his calculation would succeed: a local newspaper hit the nail on the head when it reviewed the festival under the headline "Beethoven Festival in honor of Franz Liszt."[70]

Liszt's Beethoven Cantata

The climax of Liszt's involvement in the celebration was the concluding concert of the Beethoven festival, at which Liszt's cantata was to be premiered.[71] There is a certain irony in the circumstance that, once again, the presence of the King was indispensable to the success of the composition, though not in a way that anyone would have imagined. For King Friedrich Wilhelm and his entourage were not actually present when the concert began. Apparently, the King had given specific orders not to wait for him, but Liszt nevertheless tried to postpone the start.[72] After about a half hour's delay, the audience became so restless that Liszt could put things off no longer, and he began conducting his cantata. To cut a long story short, the performance was a disaster—neither the orchestra nor the singers performed up to their expected standard. During the final bars, however, Friedrich Wilhelm appeared as a veritable *deus ex machina*. Liszt did not hesitate to seize the opportunity that this unexpected arrival offered and simply repeated the whole half-hour cantata from the top. It was a risky decision, but he was probably hoping that the audience would believe that he had acted at the special request of the King. In true fairy-tale fashion, the second performance was a great artistic success.

Here is the newspaper critic who had ridiculed Breidenstein, this time reviewing Liszt's cantata:

> Even though the composition on the whole lacks some unified form, as well as some unified idea, it is still possible to discern something extraordinary in the totality of the composition. . . . I consider this

composition not only as one of the most interesting works among Liszt's compositions, but in the field of contemporary composition on the whole. With this work, Liszt has raised great expectations for the future.[73]

What had happened? How was Liszt's composition deemed worthy where Breidenstein's had been dismissed as blasphemous? Liszt had in fact employed a clever compositional device: for the moment immediately succeeding the verse that first mentions that "genius," he brought in a quotation from Beethoven's Archduke Trio. Liszt's version first introduces it as a chorale, a kind of "secular Sanctus,"[74] in praise of Beethoven, and Liszt even follows some of the variations that Beethoven had himself composed. Eventually, however, he monumentalizes the theme, using the same technique of "thematic transformation" discussed initially: where the original is an intimate piece of chamber music, Liszt's final version (shown in example 2.2), significantly marked "Andante religioso," inflates the theme into gigantic proportions, played *fff* by the grand symphony orchestra and chorus, to the words "Heil, heil, Beethoven!"[75]

With this artistic ploy, Liszt steered clear of the awkward position of seeming to condescend to praise Beethoven. On the contrary, audience and critics registered it as a graceful bow toward the master. Liszt let Beethoven speak for himself—and let him praise himself. Or so it would seem, because, as in Breidenstein's failed attempt earlier, such praise is always reciprocal. It is once again Ramann who seems to have best captured this ambiguity: "With this device, he [Liszt] had characterized the essence of the genius of Beethoven and glorified it as though through himself."[76] Through Beethoven's genius or Liszt's?—The grammatical ambiguity would seem precisely the salient point. While Liszt *appeared* to let Beethoven speak for himself, he in fact used Beethoven as a ventriloquist's dummy, and let him speak for Liszt.

Liszt's autobiographical writing is sparse, but he evidently attributed great significance to this event: in 1881 he was shown the proofs of an encyclopedia entry on his life and works. The first substantial addition he made was: "He has notably contributed to the monument for Beethoven erected at Bonn in 1845."[77] If it were possible to pinpoint a moment in Liszt's life that was the starting point of his career as a self-consciously great composer, as superhuman, it would be this day, August 13, 1845.

Although Jean Paul and Schumann would probably not have approved, Liszt had answered their earlier points regarding the problem of capturing Beethoven's greatness in a monument: Liszt's musical monument was a work of art on another work of art, an artistic commentary on artistic greatness. By borrowing his material directly from Beethoven, and by using it for a musical

EXAMPLE 2.2 Franz Liszt, Cantata for the Inauguration of the Bonn Beethoven Monument (1845). The apotheosis of Beethoven uses a quotation from the *Archduke Trio* opus 97, third movement, which is scored here for large orchestra and chorus, to the words "Hail, hail, Beethoven!"

commentary, he avoided the representational problems that Schumann had envisaged. In his powerful and overwhelming orchestration, he had even answered to Jean Paul about the necessity of mass appeal in a monument.

This was not the first time that Liszt had used this technique of thematic transformation for a final apotheosis. In fact, it had occurred twice before in his operatic paraphrases, the *Réminiscences de Norma* and *Réminiscences de Lucia di Lammermoor.*[78] Still, the question of genre is crucial: the cantata was Liszt's first composition for orchestra and voices, the first public work for large forces. Here Liszt stepped self-consciously into the sublime symphonic tradition.[79] (It is hardly a coincidence that the orchestral and vocal forces of the Cantata are virtually identical with Beethoven's Ninth—English reviewers in particular noted similarities to Mendelssohn's *Lobgesang.*)

We could even go further and conclude that the nature of the arrangement itself supports the new claim to apotheosis that Liszt makes in his music: where the operatic paraphrases reduce orchestra and voices to a piano texture, here the piano trio is expanded to the vast scale and monumental forces of orchestra and voices.[80] The symphonic apotheosis was, thus, Liszt's virtuosic apotheosis turned inside out: underneath the vast orchestral and choral mass lay a musical miniature. Just as Liszt's career on the whole had been transformed from flashy virtuoso to serious composer, apparently anointed by Beethoven himself, so the device of apotheosis itself had changed from a vehicle of piano virtuosity to that of the musical sublime with the performance of the Beethoven Cantata in 1845.

Liszt's Apotheosis

We should return to the problem of cause and effect in monumentality itself—and to Nietzsche's and Wagner's double critique of the *Effekt.* We have seen how the Beethoven monument served interrelated endeavors of self-monumentalization—monumentalizing history, monumentalizing Liszt, monumentalizing the nation, even monumentalizing monumentality—and how, given the right predisposition, the monumentality that emanated from Beethoven's statu(r)e could be applied to almost any object. To invoke Nietzsche again, this is due to the vacuity of the *Effekt.*

How does this effect of monumentality take hold?—It is worth bearing in mind that Nietzsche took a deliberately extreme stance in his critique, which he later modified and mollified. For the sake of the argument, let us continue in Nietzsche's uncompromising vein for now: could the nineteenth century not see through the vacuity lurking at the bottom of such monumentality? Is it imaginable that they would not hear that the technique of thematic transformation, with which Liszt achieved his greatest monumental effects, were figuratively and literally stretching out the musical material so far that these moments, put provocatively, may have contained almost no substance? Nietzsche's critique continues:

> That which is celebrated at popular festivals, at religious or military anniversaries, is really such an 'effect in itself': it is this which will not let the ambitious sleep, which the brave wear over their hearts like an amulet, but it is not the truly historical *connexus* of cause and effect—which, fully understood, would only demonstrate that the dice-game of chance and the future could never again produce anything exactly similar to what it produced in the past.[81]

If we follow Nietzsche, we have to concede that nineteenth-century culture itself calls for the *Effekt* and its monumentality. Wolff, the poet of Liszt's Beethoven cantata, makes the same insinuation with the first few lines of his libretto:

> What assembles this multitude here?
> What business summoned you here?
> Judging by the crowds,
> It must be a day of celebration today.[82]

As Nietzsche suggests and Wolff describes poetically, the principal occasion here is the celebration as an end in itself—what matters is the drawing together of the crowds *through* the celebration. (The occasion of the festivity, by contrast, seems of much lesser significance; it is not mentioned until the end of the poem, almost as an afterthought.)

From this perspective, the Beethoven festival is itself an affirmation of the belief in monumental history. In other words, the vacuous *Effekt* is instilled with meaning in the context of nineteenth-century festival culture, which gives monumentality the semblance of a historical causality that it would not otherwise possess. Because of this, monumentality can be seized and appropriated by anyone, provided their interpretation is powerful or convincing enough to sway the masses—which closely reflects Schumann's objections to the Beethoven monument. Liszt's position in 1845 as a celebrated and a charismatic virtuoso, noted for his limitless talent and relentless energy, was the ideal vantage point: it provided the persuasiveness required to fill the Nietzschean void at the core of the monument.

This kind of monumental history is the history of the strong man; it is the self-fulfilling prophecy that history is made, and that it is *possible* to make history. It encourages the strong to write themselves into history. As Nietzsche remarks elsewhere, now less outré, this self-monumentalization must be re-enacted over and over again:

> For an event to possess greatness two things must come together: greatness of spirit in those who accomplish it and greatness of spirit in those who experience it. No event possesses greatness in itself. . . . It can also happen that a man of force accomplishes a deed which strikes a reef and sinks from sight having produced no impression; a brief sharp echo, and all is over. History has virtually nothing to report about such as it were truncated and neutralized events. And so whenever we see an event approaching we are overcome with the fear that those who will experience it will be unworthy of it. Whenever one acts, in small things as in great, one always has in view this correspondence between deed and receptivity; and he who gives must see to it that he finds recipients adequate to the meaning of his gift.[83]

Given the precarious nature of greatness, the great man—the strong man, intent on writing himself into history—must continually convince his audience of the greatness of his actions. If this is so, there is a sense in which one should consider all of Liszt's subsequent symphonic poems, with their almost inevitable final apotheoses, as a reminder of Liszt's own apotheosis during the 1845 Beethoven celebration.

When Wagner referred to Liszt as "superhuman" in his letter of 1855, at a time when Wagner's own position in music history was far from self-evident, he may have had not only Liszt's compositions in mind but also the historical claims founded on them. Perhaps, in thus alluding to Liszt, he might have heard in the apotheoses an echo of Liszt's successful effort to write himself into music history, and ultimately a continual re-enactment of the moment when greatness was first bestowed—when he was first admitted to the canonical Hall of Fame.

CHAPTER THREE

Sounding Souvenirs

Souvenirs Public and Private

Let us stay with Liszt a little longer. In 1849, while the revolution swept through Europe, the small provincial town of Weimar prepared for a big celebration. That year, on August 28, saw the one hundredth return of Goethe's birthday, an anniversary that was celebrated in great style in Weimar, where he had spent the most important years of his artistic life. The extraordinary court *Kapellmeister* of Weimar, Franz Liszt, was busy organizing the celebrations for the big day.[1] For the central festivities, he wrote a number of new compositions: besides the overture *Tasso,* intriguingly not based on Goethe's drama but rather on Byron's poem of the same title, these were all occasional works.[2] No expense was spared; the festivities drew on anything that promised to be of high artistic quality or, failing that, was at least available at considerable cost. Nonetheless, with the exception of *Tasso,* which was then performed in its original form, the compositions are now almost completely forgotten.

The musical program began with an orchestral Goethe Festive March, followed by a four-part male chorus accompanied by lower brass on a setting of Goethe's last words, "Mehr Licht," an anthem titled "Weimars Toten" (To the dead of Weimar) on a text of Franz Schober for low male voice and orchestra, a solo vocal quartet on "Wanderers Nachtgesang," one of Goethe's most celebrated poems, and a setting of the angelic chorus from *Faust Part II,* for female and mixed choirs with piano solo or, predictably perhaps, alternative harp accompaniment. The scoring for these five pieces is conspicuously wide-ranging, employing a luxurious variety of instruments: while the whole orchestra was available and indeed used for the March, Liszt tended only to use particular groups of instruments—the low brass for Goethe's sublime last words, or the harp for the angelic choir. In part, these decisions have rather mundane reasons, and can be explained with reference to the particularities of the performance for which they were written. The *Leipziger Illustrirte Zeitung,* which covered the festivities in some detail, reports that "Mehr Licht" was performed in the hall of the Grand-ducal library (which had been under Goethe's directorship during his lifetime)—a much larger ensemble would hardly have found enough space in that room. The *Illustrirte Zeitung* continues its report: "After the conclusion of the celebration, an elegant and luxurious gift 'in memory of the celebration of August 28, 1859 at the grand-ducal library at Weimar' containing interesting facsimiles was distributed among all those present."[3] In other words, the commemorative event was in turn commemorated by means of a souvenir. A similar souvenir album was also produced of Liszt's music, which was handed out under the title *Fest-Album zur Säkularfeier von Goethes Geburtstag am 28. August 1849.*

Weimar's culture of commemoration was a well-oiled machine.[4] Just in time for the jubilee, three days before the celebrations, the *Illustrirte Zeitung* published a notated version of the chorus "Mehr Licht" in a richly illustrated print, spanning three full pages of the newspaper. The title illustration, reproduced here in figure 3.1, aims to capture artistically the sublimity of Goethe's immortal dying words. The scene it depicts shows how the transfigured *Dichterfürst,* or prince of poetry, is drawn heavenwards by an angelic genie. Goethe moves away from the dark, infernal scene in the lower corner of the image, in which grimacing faces can just about be made out: a female figure, dancing frenetically in the foreground, brandishes a scourge. Sparks can be seen flying out of her agitated pointy headgear. A lecherous figure in a priest's robe with a large hat and white clerical bands, the face close to the dancing female, stares at her agape—the eyeballs of both figures glow white out of the darkness of the eerie scene. The concupiscent priest seems to clasp a male figure by the neck, who seems to be running rapidly out of breath as he is being choked by the priest. In the background, a horned figure raising his arm up is barely visible in the dark. Further faces disappear into the background. In the bottom far left, a small bat lends this hellish scenario the final eerie touch.

Further up, the left margin of the image indicates a grassy hill from which three entangled stems grow up. Their outsize proportion and their tendrils continue the eeriness of the infernal scene below, but soon turn into gigantic floral ornaments that frame the upper half of the scene. The partition is further marked by an eagle with wide spread wings who, like Goethe himself,

FIGURE 3.1 Liszt's setting of "Licht, Mehr Licht." From *Illustrierte Zeitung,* August 25, 1849. Reproduced by permission of the Herzogin Anna Amalia Library, Klassik Stiftung Weimar.

lifts up majestically from the abyss and forms the sublime counterpart to the derisory little bat. The body and the wing of the genie, which form a right angle, provide the remaining sides of this inner frame. Just as the eagle's wing seems to support Goethe from below, so the angelic wing is held protectively over Goethe's head, and is reminiscent of a canopy, or perhaps a halo.

The genie's astral body, merely wrapped into a light cloth and glowing in white brightness against the already white background, is set off from the dark infernal scene with exaggerated clarity. With great tenderness, he holds

Goethe by the hand, which the poet barely extends. Goethe, too, is wrapped in a cloth, covering his whole body, which looks half like a classic toga, half like a shroud. The upper end of the cloth flutters backwards and underlines in this way the upwards motion of Goethe's body. The face of the genie is turned backwards but his earnest gaze looks beyond Goethe towards the margin of the picture into infinite space. Goethe, by contrast, seems to look straight into the genie's face. Behind the genie's head the axis continues to the torch of wisdom that the genie holds aloft and whose flame, pointing left, indicates the direction from which both fly. Incidentally, it is the genie, not Goethe, who wears the laurel wreath, which seems to underline further the spiritual link between the two. The diagonal axis finally leads to the title of the whole, "Licht, mehr Licht," and illuminates the letters of the title. At the same time, the text is written into the sky and supports in its slight curvature the rays of the, one assumes, rising sun, which lightens up a stark but Arcadian landscape behind hills and sea.

This long description mainly serves to show one thing: the whole scene depicts something of an overkill of sublime motives, in which any number of symbols of light and dark known to nineteenth-century culture are employed and offered up for immediate consumption. In short, it can easily be recognized as *Kitsch*—that slippery and deceptively complex aesthetic phenomenon of nineteenth-century mass culture.[5]

Liszt's musical setting seems to replicate the grand sweeping gesture of this image. He deploys all that nineteenth-century progressive harmony has to offer: mysteriously interrupted six-fours, surprising third-related sequential patterns, and ominous chromatic relations. On the whole, one could easily think of this setting as a study in chromatic third-relations, as the six verses of the ode are all based on the same material but develop it in different directions. The only feature common to all verses are the brash effects in which distant harmonies are juxtaposed. In fact, it would not be out of line to assume that the chorus is actually little more than a compositional sketch, an act of musical doodling, that made it into print: as Rena Mueller has shown in her study of Liszt's sketches, his working method usually consisted in working out material by circling around one musical idea, developing it in various directions and continually returning to it.[6] In this case, the deliberately rough and sketchy quality of this chorus would actually be its central musical feature; it allows a glimpse, but not more than that, into unheard-of musical regions. It is, like the overripe image surrounding its reprint in the *Illustrirte Zeitung,* the overly clear gesture of sublimity, whose content remains tantalizingly unclear. And it must remain so: its very unhewn quality is the compositional device for our incomprehension.[7]

Perhaps the best indication of this strategy of mystification that the piece plays out is in the plain opening motive A-G-C, which is played in sequence C-B-E. Played as it is in emphatic octaves, it exudes the mystique of a cryptic code. It could well be heard as a remote Beethovenian echo (*"Muß es sein?"*), or as a reference to his own *Les Préludes* (1848).[8] Nor would it be far-fetched to assume that the pitch names A-G-C could be an encrypted reference to Carl Alexander, the Grand-duke of Weimar and Liszt's benefactor. But again, it matters much less that we understand and decipher the code than that we acknowledge the existence of a code, as well as admitting our inability to know for sure what it stands for. This acknowledgment, and the circumstance that the riddle is unsolved, heighten the mysteriousness of the music, and hence the veneer of its importance.

In pursuing this strategy, a fine line needed to be trodden: in what is only apparently a paradox, the mysteriousness of the music could only be effective if everybody was made aware of it. This might explain the unusual format in which the chorus "Mehr Licht" was published. It stretches the imagination to suggest that the readers of the *Illustrirte Zeitung* would form small male choruses to re-create the piece in their homes, let alone that the majority of the readership was musically literate. To be sure, the *Illustrirte Zeitung* did circulate musical works in this form from time to time, but it was usually solo songs or patriotic hymns, and never compositions of such difficulty. At the same time, no other score in the *Illustrirte Zeitung* was decorated as lavishly as this commemoration of Goethe. It seems that the wide distribution of the score, with the illustration that suggested an interpretation from the visual domain, mattered more than the performance of the music.

The curious illustrated score in the *Illustrirte Zeitung* presents yet another form of the souvenir, this time of a much less personal nature than the keepsake album handed out after the Weimar festivities, more complex and more modern perhaps, but no less distinctive in its function.[9] Like a snow globe harboring a small plastic model of the Eiffel tower, this musical souvenir does not fulfill any practical function—it is not meant to be used, that is to say performed; rather it is an object of contemplation. If it has a purpose, it is one of commemoration. However, the commemorative function of the musical souvenir is a very peculiar one: for most readers of the *Illustrirte Zeitung,* the events in Weimar of August 28, 1849 could not evoke any particular memories, not least since the actual celebrations were an exclusive affair. And yet, the souvenir invites the wider world to partake of this commemoration (this is probably also the reason for its publication three days *prior* to the actual event).[10] Like our cheap, mass-produced Parisian snow globe, which more often than not is presented as a gift to friends and family left at home, this musical souvenir, with its extremely wide dissemination, is not so much reminiscent of any particular memory of the performance, but rather it *substitutes* for the actual experience. It is the souvenir's invocation of a familiar iconic image—of the Eiffel tower just as much as Goethe—that allows this shared act of commemoration far beyond any particular place and time. What is more, thanks to the souvenir, the public commemoration can take place in private, in the comfort of one's own home and at one's own leisure.

Such a souvenir is not characterized by its subtlety. Rather, its success lies in its immediacy. The souvenir thrives on the incisiveness and density of its referentiality: as in the example of "Mehr Licht" with its overabundant symbols of sublimity, the souvenir often crosses the imaginary line between art and *Kitsch*—and it is no coincidence that these categories were beginning to separate at roughly the same time.[11] It is in this way that the souvenir miniaturizes and domesticates the monument, and mass-produces it in unlimited quantities; in short, the souvenir commodifies commemoration.

Old and New

Liszt's second big project for the year 1849, besides the Goethe anniversary—or rather, the other half of what was essentially the same project—was the staging of Wagner's latest opera, *Tannhäuser und der Sängerkrieg auf Wartburg.* Again, the occasion was an anniversary: February 16 was the birthday of Carl Alexander's mother, the Grand-Duchess of Weimar Maria Pavlovna, which was celebrated every year with the performance of a new opera.[12]

Wagner's *Tannhäuser* was not strictly speaking new, as it had already been performed in Dresden in 1845, but its subject matter was of great symbolic relevance to the Weimar dynasty: reconstruction work on the Wartburg in Eisenach, shown in figure 3.2, had begun in 1838 under the management of the grand-ducal family. Already in the mid-nineteenth century the Wartburg was what would nowadays be called a *lieu de mémoire,* holding a special place in the German national imagination.[13] Not only had Luther translated the Bible into German while hiding there from prosecution, laying in the same stroke the foundation stone for a standardized German language, but it also had become a cultural-political symbol for German unity more recently, with such important events as the 1817 national students' meeting, celebrating simultaneously the three-hundredth anniversary of the Reformation and the fourth anniversary of the victory over Napoleon. For Carl Alexander, the rebuilding of the Wartburg was not only a task of supreme cultural, though avowedly not political, importance but also, on a more personal level, a way of firmly

FIGURE 3.2 The Wartburg near Eisenach, picture postcard from the nineteenth century. Reproduced by permission of the Fine Arts Library of the Harvard College Library.

associating his family name with the medieval dynasty of the Margraves of Thuringia. The craze for medieval lore—fanned by Romantic writers such as Schlegel and Wackenroder—was at its peak at that time, not least because it provided a model of national significance: the Holy Roman Empire of the German Nation, whose unholy, much belated, end had been brought about by Napoleon in 1806.

The story of Tannhäuser—and more so, the other half of the title of Wagner's opera: the singers' war at the Wartburg, which apparently took place in 1206/07—was therefore an ideal vehicle for dynastic representation and would virtually guarantee that Carl Alexander's project was placed in the limelight. Liszt went out of his way to forge a link between the two projects. In his essay outlining the project of a Goethe Foundation, he provided his overview of the highlights of German literature:

> Germany thus saw song and poetry flourish in the thirteenth and eighteenth centuries. The most famous names and most weighty memories of these two epochs were evenly distributed among the beautiful areas of Romantic Thuringia. To begin with, it was its Margraves who immortalized their names by means of the protection that they afforded to the most famous poets of their time: Wolfgang von Eschenbach, author of *Parsifal,* Walther von der Vogelweide, Heinrich von Ofterdingen, native of Eisenach, Bitterolf, etc. dwelled at the court or frequented it. At the picturesque Wartburg, for many centuries the residence of the Margraves, the Singers' War took place, which will forever remain engraved in the people's memory.[14]

It takes a good while in this synoptic account of the culture of Thuringia—and hence, following Liszt's claim, the whole of Germany—before Liszt finally moves on to the later cultural peak in the eighteenth century and to Goethe, who is after all the main topic of the essay.

Nineteenth-century Weimar, in its so-called "Silver Age," was the center of cultural commemoration in Germany.[15] The name was a token of its biggest problem, as the runner-up implications of the name "Silver Age" suggest. Since Goethe's death, Weimar had become the *Musenwitwensitz,* in Heinrich Heine's snide but not unfounded expression, the "seat of the widowed muses," whose principal occupation had become the nostalgic remembrance of its glorious past. Against the background of this conundrum, it becomes understandable why a work such as *Tannhäuser* would hold such promise for Weimar. Here was a modern work by what was by all accounts a progressive and controversial composer. What is more, the invocation of Thuringia's glorious past in this opera would simultaneously provide continuity into the future. *Tannhäuser* might succeed in alchemically turning the melancholy "Silver Age" into a renewed "Golden Age."

Wagner's aesthetic problem, and the problem of nineteenth-century progressive music, was diametrically opposed to Weimar's situation. Franz Brendel, the editor of the *Neue Zeitschrift für Musik* and tireless promoter of Wagnerian music, explained the specific problem of progressive music, referring here to music in Germany since roughly the age of Mozart, in stark terms:

> Our music is too widely distributed to be a self-contained art, to count among its admirers only participants who have followed their calling, but also too narrowly: it is too unpopular in its innermost being to appear as the genuine art of the people, to be truly and fundamentally theirs. We therefore find in the present the preponderance of a bad dilettantism, which always imperils art. . . . On the level that our music has assumed particularly since the second half of the [eighteenth] century, it cannot stand up to such profusion. It is destroyed in its innermost substance without being able to have a lasting fertilizing effect on the masses.[16]

For Brendel, the state of contemporary music was caught in a force field between progress and popularity. As a card-carrying Left-Hegelian, Brendel was a fervent believer in progress in music, but he admitted that these progressive artistic values were actually impeded by the wide availability of music.[17]

In Brendel's analysis of the situation, progressive German music—"our music"—found itself in an unhappy medium: on the one hand, it was not exclusive enough to withdraw into splendid isolation completely, while on the other, it would never attain mass popularity. Brendel conceded that in principle there was such a thing as "good" popularity, but this was an almost utopian hope, which he could not bank on. It was better to think of its lack of popularity as an immanent feature of progressive music—or rather what the nineteenth century instinctively understood by progress: an ever-increasing complexity and difficulty, which in music translated into expansive phrasing, unconventional syntax, and the increasingly liberal treatment of dissonance. Its innovations invariably made greater demands on the listener; progressive music therefore had an inherent bent towards unpopularity and was accepted by its audiences, if at all, only slowly and grudgingly. Brendel complained particularly that the drive toward progress stigmatized the kind of music he promoted as somehow artificial—or rather, as not being the "genuine art of the people."

At the same time, Brendel was far from proposing an embrace of mass audiences as a remedy to the problem of modern music. Rather, he seemed to be afraid of mass popularity: as soon as music is consumed by the masses, it would seem, it invariably loses something of its essence—which Brendel saw as a kind of aesthetic germinating power—that would prevent it from "fertilizing" the audiences for the appreciation of further advancements. For the time being, therefore, the prevailing compromise was so inartistic as even to put art itself in danger. This compromise was the specter of dilettantism.

We find in Brendel's assessment a complex, if by no means uncommon, conflation of artistic values with its social situation that is worth unraveling: the state of art was positioned on a bipolarity, which combines a number of dimensions: high-brow, complex, exclusive pretensions of progressive music were contrasted with low-brow, simple, readily available, popular art—which at this low end is in danger of losing its very status as art. Brendel did not in fact position the music he promoted at one extreme of this axis; on the contrary, he argued that one part of the conundrum of contemporary art was that it was not exclusive *enough*. For Brendel the multiple dimensions of this axis were firmly associated with one another. A change in social factors, if music aimed to appeal to mass audiences, would usher in grave aesthetic consequences. Such a sell-out would compromise or forfeit its artistic character.

Brendel may not seem to be able, or indeed willing, to suggest a way out of the dilemma of modern music here, but the Weimar performance of *Tannhäuser* that Liszt was planning might offer just that, by overlaying Brendel's bipolar axis with yet another layer, which cut across all the other dimensions: that of monumentality, and in particular the kind of monumental history that had worked so well for him at Bonn a few years previously. Liszt gave expression to this synthesis of new and old, elite and mass, difficult and simple, high-brow and low-brow, under the mantle of monumental history with an aphorism *a propos* of Wagner: "The present, determined by the past, gives birth to the future."[18]

Big and Small

In monumental history, past and future connect. This is no more so the case than in anniversaries, as Liszt in Weimar was keenly aware.[19] Thus, a few years later he would begin an essay on Wagner's *Rheingold,* "On January 1, 1855." The opening tag was not only a marker in time but also the subject of his reflection on his Janus-faced conception of monumental history.[20] Nor was the date a coincidence, as it allowed Liszt to begin with a reflection on the psychology of anniversaries. In his rhetorical gambit, he used the date of New Year to liken the organic cyclicity of the seasons to the periods of the arts. Just as the recurring event of New Year both encourages summarizing reflections of the results of the past year and inspires curiosity for the coming one, so this period of time, palpably on the cusp between two artistic eras, gives rise to inquisitiveness about the works of art that are to characterize this new period. In other words, an anniversary is nothing but a monument in time.[21]

Liszt made the connection between this cyclical history and monumentality explicit a little later when he waxed lyrical over Wagner's latest oeuvre:

> Do you see this shimmering dot at the distant horizon? It is the gigantic outline of a majestic grand edifice, the likes of which we have never seen on our path. Perhaps you will be bewildered, perhaps you will find the style too sublime, the plan too enormous, the abundance of ornaments too rich—but you will have to concede that it is the grandest among the existing monuments.[22]

Surprisingly, this form of praise did not go down well with Wagner. He immediately responded to this article in a letter to Liszt where he expressed his dismay. Publication had not been agreed with him beforehand, and it seems that for the time being he had planned to keep the newly finished score of *Rheingold* under the shroud of secrecy.[23]

What is more, Wagner took particular issue in Liszt's article with the invocation of monumentality for his work. Where Liszt's reflections on monumentality were particularly concerned with its historical implications, Wagner was mainly concerned with matters of size:

> And yet, when you hold out my work as something tremendous [*Ungeheures*], I feel you must be confusing the basic standard: what strikes me as utterly insignificant and pitiful are present-day audiences and the spirit of our means of presentations, etc., whereas my works are simply of decent human proportion and appear gigantic only when we attempt to force them into so unworthy a framework. Thus, whenever we claim

that our intentions are chimerical and eccentric, we are really only flat-tering the current unworthiness of present-day audiences, and ultimately giving them the seal of respectability. We should not suggest this to the public.[24]

In other words, for Wagner, size is relative. Like Gulliver, strapped down by the Lilliputians, his work is of normal—human—size but shackled by an age of musical small-mindedness. More striking than this assessment, though, is Wagner's obvious horror of monumentality. Where Liszt used attributes such as "sublime," "enormous," and "rich" to describe Wagner's work, Wagner only focused on the potential for excess in Liszt's description and replaced these terms with much more negative ones, which took Liszt's acclamation in a very different direction: *das Ungeheure* invokes much more terrifying associations of the "monstrous" than does its usual English cognate, "the tremendous,"— associations that Wagner confirmed with the later attributes "chimerical," and "eccentric." He concluded with another admonition to secrecy: the pub-lic was better off not being made aware of any of this.

It would seem surprising that Wagner was so concerned not to be associ-ated with monumentality, considering especially that he was just writing the *Ring des Nibelungen*—a work that could justifiably be described as the single most monumental work in music history—but he was concerned at the time to appear to write music "of the folk." In fact, Liszt may have been somewhat mischievous in emphasizing the monumentality of Wagner's oeuvre, since Wagner had recently rejected any notion of monumentality at the outset of his "Mitteilung an meine Freunde" ("A Communication to my Friends") of 1852, which heralded the inception of the *Ring des Nibelungen* but which also had a very different understanding of monumental history.

In that essay, Wagner had explained that the monument for him signified that which transcended its own time and which had, by the same token, noth-ing to do with any period of history at all. That was not what Wagner—then still very much under the influence of the Young Hegelians and the 1849 rev-olutions—had in mind for his art. The crucial propensity of the work of art, as Wagner imagined it, was precisely "that it proclaims itself in sharpest defi-nition by Time, by Place, by Circumstance; therefore that it can never come to living and effective show, unless it appears at a given time, in a given place, and amid given circumstances; in a word, that it strips off every vestige of the *monumental*."[25] While this conception of the work of art would be an almost word-perfect definition for what Liszt had propagated at the Bonn Beethoven festival, it seems Wagner understood something very different by the term "monumentality": his work of art related to a monument, he argued, as does a living human to a marble statue. For him, the quality of monumentality implied such characteristics as "the absolute," and "the un-present"—in short, Wagner associated monumentality with the very classicizing aesthetic from which he was at pains to set himself off.[26]

In its resistance to contemporary relevance, Wagner argued, monumentality was the precise opposite of fashion, which was only concerned with the present. (Wagner's German term, *Mode*, is rhetorically more powerful than its English equivalent, since not only does it form a suitably Wagnerian assonance with its opposite *Monumentalität*, but it is also etymologically related to modernity.[27]) In its frivolity and endless chase for the *dernier cri*, faddish fashion was for Wagner a concept just as devoid of humanity as monumentality itself. Any artistic turn toward monumentality in art is therefore born of disaffection with the present—as Wagner saw in contemporary art. The inevitable consequence of this move, to make monumentality itself fashionable, was no viable solution to the problem but rather a false synthesis; it was Hegelian "bad infinity"—the spurious kind of dialectic that does not lead on to a higher level but instead lingers in unending one-sidedness. By making the "un-present" an issue of contemporary relevance, the living spark that Wagner looked for in his artworks would be doubly banned from art. Instead, in Wagner's conception, both monumentality and fashion had to be annihilated, to yield to the forever-present work of art.[28]

Wagner was, of course, prone to such apocalyptic tones. This was part of his radical stance with regard to his own music in relation to the music history that preceded it.[29] The difference in his position toward monumentality from that of Liszt can easily be explained as a consequence of his theatrically radical rejection of the musical past, which forced him to dismiss works of the past as irrelevant marble statues. Against this background, Wagner's vision of the "true" dialectic of fashion and monumentality resulting in the ever-present work of art was not in fact all that different from Liszt's (or indeed Brendel's) thoughts on the matter. The only difference was that Liszt believed, *pace* Wagner, that such works already existed and would continue to be created, and, *pace* Brendel, that it was possible to cut across the seemingly irreconcilable (but askew) opposites of progress and popularity.

Virtuosity and Dilettantism

But let us not get ahead of ourselves. Back in the 1840s, Wagner was not yet the artistic giant—or outsized monster—nor the political fugitive that he was soon to become. He was little more than a provincial *Kapellmeister* of moderate if controversial reputation, desperate for his artistic breakthrough. In fact, he had even tried to petition the King of Prussia to accept a dedication for his opera *Tannhäuser*. With this he hoped to garner wider recognition for the work outside of Dresden, where it had been premiered in 1845.[30] In response, Wagner was told that the King only accepted works already known to him and was advised to send some arrangements of individual numbers for military band to acquaint his majesty with the music.[31]

Wagner did not follow this well-intentioned if patronizing piece of advice. Nonetheless, the idea of arranging individual pieces from the opera to make it better known was in fact a good one. Thus, on February 26, 1849, Liszt informed Wagner of his intention to arrange two numbers from *Tannhäuser* for piano: the overture, which would "meet with few executants capable of mastering its technical difficulties," and Wolfram's *Abendstern* cavatina, conceived to be "within easy reach of second-class pianists."[32] Wagner did not raise any objections, far from it:

> Before I knew anything about your intention, several years ago, when I was writing the overture, I wondered whether I should ever hear it played by you. I should never have mentioned it to you, for such matters one must not be too forward, but now that I hear you are employed in making this piece your own, after your own fashion, I must tell you that I feel as if a wonderful dream were realised. Is it possible? Why not? *All* is possible to you. About the "Abendstern," dear friend, do exactly as you like.[33]

Wagner kept his silence over the fact that he had already arranged both pieces for piano himself in 1845, and the overture additionally for piano duet.[34] Conspicuously, Wagner's response took up a figure of speech Liszt used in his earlier letter, of "appropriating" the composition "in [his] own fashion": an arrangement from Liszt, the foremost pianist of his age, was in a completely different league, as far as recognition and sales were concerned. A performance by him, as Wagner knew well, was even better.

Liszt's sharply distinguished categories between the two arrangements demonstrate that he knew what he was talking about: he conceived the overture as a virtuoso piece of extreme difficulty, and the *Abendstern* scene as a popular and rather more playable salon piece. Central to Liszt's assessment, which he communicated to Wagner in uncharacteristically sober terms, were not aesthetic issues, such as musical beauty, compositional skill, or suitability for the piano, but rather the technical difficulty of the arrangement—and hence, by implication, its marketability and likely dissemination. These arrangements would open the music to a market to which Wagner, as a *Kapellmeister*

EXAMPLE 3.1 (a) A violin descant accompanies the pilgrims'
theme in Wagner's *Tannhäuser* Overture (1845).

EXAMPLE 3.1 (b) Liszt's challenging pianistic version of the Overture to *Tannhäuser* (1849) makes the descant more complex and supplies it with intricate fingering.

and opera composer, would himself have had little access.[35] When elsewhere Liszt referred to the two arrangements as "humble propaganda on the plain piano for Wagner's lofty genius" he hit the nail on the head.[36]

Both arrangements are quite faithful to their sources. They adhere to the form of the original and keep textural changes to a minimum.[37] Interestingly, Liszt is as likely to add to Wagner's orchestral textures as he is to pare them down; questions of complexity or performability are often independent from the musical material of the source. Thus, the overture, in itself already a patently unpianistic piece of music, is actually made *more* complex in Liszt's transcription. The descant violin line that accompanies the pilgrims' theme in its *ff* version at measure 38, reproduced in example 3.1a from Wagner's score, is a single descending line. In Liszt's arrangement, shown in example 3.1b, the same descending violin line becomes a more complex figure that looks rather unwieldy on paper and indeed demands consummate pianistic technique, with each figure beginning in octaves and the second sixteenth-note only sounding the lower octave. The fingering seems to be of utmost importance to Liszt, and is, as usual, critical for the desired effect, marking traces of pianistic performance.[38]

It seems that in the complex texture of these measures Liszt was experimenting with a kind of "four-hand effect," as if to trump the famous "three-hand effect" with which his rival, the virtuoso pianist Thalberg, dazzled his audiences.[39] In Liszt's version the chorale is set in full chords in the middle register—in deviation from the orchestral scores, which only has the trombones play the choral melody—the bass line is kept apart from the repeated accompanying chords, while the descending octaves mark the top register. The aural effect of these distinct registers suggests that four hands are constantly at play; no wonder that Wagner opted for an actual set of four hands in his own rather more perfunctory arrangement for piano duet.

This passage evidently captivated Liszt's pianistic imagination. When in 1857 he set out to make a separate arrangement of the Pilgrims' Chorus of Act III, he did not simply lift identical passages from his arrangement of the overture, as Wagner had by and large done in his orchestral score, but transcribed them again. And yet again, he added a layer of complexity. Example 3.2 shows the descending octave figures, which were now no longer just reinforced by their octaves but rather set as intervals filling out the underlying harmony. In Liszt's hands, clearly, Wagner's music became a vehicle for a display of technical brilliance and virtuosity.[40]

The other arrangement Liszt described in his letter to Wagner, Wolfram's Hymn to the Evening Star, a much more accessible piece of music, became a showpiece in its own right, though of a very different kind. In the recitative it retains the arpeggiations that both underline Wolfram's bardic status as a medieval *Minnesinger* and that, on a more abstract plane, were a signifier of virtuosity in the overture. But in fact, here they serve to simplify the texture: in the original this passage has a chordal basis played by the lower brass. The subtleties of the spacing, the skilful transference of effects from the orchestra to the keyboard precisely by treating them liberally, are also at work here, but in the service of a different aim. As the two parts of example 3.3 show, in Wagner's score sustained trombone chords accompany the recitative, while the harp only adds a sprinkle of texture every now and then, whereas in Liszt's version arpeggiations become the only form of accompaniment, though in smaller note-values than Wagner has his harpist play. The ominous trombone chords are left out completely. (Liszt's editor Peter Raabe suggests that the melody be played in its entirety just with the thumb of the right hand—which does not add much to a subtly shaded phrasing, but at least ensures that every note rings out over and above the harp figures.) What remains, then, is the gesture of virtuosity, though not its technical difficulty, in what is an attractive salon piece. The whole number is transposed up a semitone, which may be less handy to read but in fact puts it in much easier reach for

EXAMPLE 3.2 Liszt tries his hand again on the violin descant, this time in a separate piano arrangement of the Pilgrims' Chorus (1861), and produces a very different version of the same passage.

EXAMPLE 3.3 (a) Wolfram's Hymn to the Evening Star (beginning) from Act III of *Tannhäuser* in Wagner's score, with sonorous trombone parts.

(b) In Liszt's pianistic version of Wolfram's aria (1849) the trombone parts are nowhere to be found in the arrangement, instead the harp part has become more virtuosic.

the fingers. Graciously enough, this number bears a dedication to Grand-Duke Carl Alexander.

The two arrangements could hardly be more different. Of course, their respective sources are markedly different: Wolfram's aria is one of the most intimate moments, while Wagner's overture is, in Liszt's words, a "grand symphonic composition."[41] But Liszt could have easily chosen other parts from the score, for instance, the very popular Entry of the Guests, the Act II chorus, "Freudig begrüßen wir die edle Halle," which Wagner himself had already singled out for an arrangement for solo piano.[42] It seems that Liszt's primary concern with these two arrangements was to target the two distinct levels of piano music of his time: the virtuoso showpiece, on the one hand, and the more dilettante salon piece, on the other.[43]

The difference between the two genres is not merely one of technical demand, but also of social space: the virtuoso piece is in the public domain, while the salon piece is the product of the bourgeois private sphere. That Liszt's arrangement of Wolfram's aria seeks, on one level, to imitate the showmanship of the virtuoso overture, gesturing toward its filigree passage work without really replicating its complexity, is no coincidence but rather the consequence of the genre of salon music, which seeks to bring the veneer of virtuosity into a domestic setting.

In musical circles, salon music was something of a guilty pleasure. Enormously successful, and in many ways the precursor of the popular sound media that were not invented until later in the nineteenth century, it drew the ire of many music critics, who feared that exposure to a facile and flashy salon music might impede access to truly great works of music. Joachim Raff, composer and conflicted Wagner critic, saw a direct line between the popularity of opera, virtuosity, and salon music. His parodistic social analysis of nineteenth-century virtuosity fits Liszt's two types of arrangements of Wagner's *Tannhäuser* so acutely that it deserves to be quoted at length:

> Opera became the main public musical spectacle for everybody, and simultaneously influenced the direction of what kind of music was made in the salons of the new society. The chamber virtuoso had the choice between disappearing in a large orchestra and isolating himself. If he opted for the latter, he had to capitalize on his dexterity. The symphonic style of concertos did not allow him to do this. Instead, for the demonstration of his virtuosity, he would use a backdrop that, being familiar to everybody, would not challenge anyone's attention, but would rather embrace it and invite the listener to concentrate on the dexterous skilfulness of the artist; these were the '*motifs de l'opéra.*' In this way, a virtuosic style emerged in which music is a pretext for the presentation of unusual finger, lip, or throat formations.—In the entourage of opera the virtuosic style could also sneak into the salons of the nobleman and the rich bourgeois, as well as into the reception rooms of the middle bourgeois music lover.[44]

On its way from the operatic stages and away from the symphony halls to the upper- and middle-class salons, Raff presents virtuosity as a kind of physical deformity. Judging from his description virtuosity appears as a phenomenon that one should rather expect to encounter at fairground attractions. Perhaps his perplexing notion, however, is less far-fetched than it might first appear: consider, for instance, Schumann's strange athletic exercises that led to his ring finger stiffening and eventually forced him to give up his career as a pianist.[45]

Raff went on to explore the triumphal entry of virtuosity into the salons. In his view, the virtuosic style—which he personifies and assigns agency in his account—ran into problems, as it first had to get rid of the two predominant musical genres there:

> But here it first had to overcome two obstacles: one was the lyrical po-etry of songs, which had developed independently alongside the *Lied*—a privilege that no 'daughter of the house' would willingly give up. The other was social dance, influenced by fashion and determined by national elements—a cult that formed a popular appendage to any social evening. In this situation, it [the virtuosic style] stumbled upon the piano, which had become indispensable for song and dance, as well as upon a youth who would know how to handle this most general of instruments in a manner befitting the salon. This youth would only have to remove the words from the song, and the legs from the dance, and hey presto—the salon style was born.[46]

Bodily images return in this part of Raff's account: where the special skills of concert virtuosos above were depicted as over-developed and mutated body parts, in the salon, by contrast, Raff's protagonistic virtuosic style first amputates parts of the music before it offers it up for consumption.

The importance Raff places on the "youth" (*Jüngling*) performing in the salon (a male youth at that) suggests that the visual aspect of the performer, young age and youthful looks especially, was of heightened significance, and may have stood in for the presumably compromised technical skill that could be expected at social evenings. The young male pianist that is in Raff's concept at the center of the truncated virtuosic display in the bourgeois salons is contrasted with the "daughter of the house" who had previously sung lyrical *Lieder* in the same space. However intriguing, Raff's gendering of salon music is not confirmed by most other contemporary sources, in which salon pianists are generally held to be female.[47] Playing the piano, besides conversational French, were in fact the most important skills of the standard education for bourgeois females in nineteenth-century Germany.[48]

There can be no doubt about Raff's value judgment inherent in these images: as deformities of performers, or indeed of music itself, virtuosity with its associated manifestations on the concert platform and at home, constituted for Raff not only a form of musical aberration but rather a form of degeneration. As is common in the nineteenth-century discourse of degeneracy, this pathological diagnosis is just the physical manifestation of an underlying ethical problem—and this helps explain Raff's curious rhetorical strategy of assigning a form of agency to performer and musical style alike: they are not fully distinguishable.[49] Ultimately, Raff puts the blame for all this squarely on Wagner. At bottom, Raff argues, Wagner's operatic style already displays an affinity with the piano virtuosos:

> Wagner only does what piano virtuosos do, who have been trying hard for the last twenty years, to work vocal melody into their instruments (in truth his way of figuring violins above the melodic line in the tenor is quite similar to the manner of modern piano composers). But this sin against style does not exculpate him from his own. Lewdness in artistic creation is always avenged by a sickness of the art, which in turn has a dangerous effect on the artist.[50]

For Raff, whose apodictic lines on Wagner caused considerable embarrassment among his progressive colleagues, Wagner's music was part and parcel of the problem of contemporary music, of which piano arrangements were just another manifestation.[51] For Raff, music was an art form in fragile health, which needed to be protected for it to maintain its high values. It was easily corrupted by the likes of Wagner and, though he is not mentioned by name, Liszt.[52]

Raff's critique of virtuosity on the stage and in the salon, and its degenerative effect on music as a whole, was no doubt extreme. Yet it reflects certain critical attitudes that were widespread in the mid-nineteenth century. Critical voices abound complaining about the bad quality of arrangements: not only are they often shoddily made but also only give a very partial representation of the orchestral or vocal original.[53] This latter point was more widely seen as a flaw of the genre: as Thomas Christensen has pointed out, a comparison was habitually made between copper engraving and piano arrangements, as opposed to oil portrait and orchestral original, which both appear in full colors.[54] Against this criticism, supporters immediately leapt to the defense of the genre: just as copper engravings can help familiarize us with art that would otherwise not be available in its original, so piano arrangements can expose musicians to a whole new world of music and enhance an understanding of difficult compositions, such as Beethoven symphonies.[55]

Needless to say, one of such difficult and rarely heard compositions was Liszt's cantata for the Beethoven monument. Early in 1847 the *Allgemeine musikalische Zeitung* advertised for its arrangement for piano duet in typically grandiloquent prose:

> The numerous friends and admirers, as well as the opponents, of the famous composer, whose efforts for the Beethoven monument are indisputably highly meritorious, will appreciate the opportunity finally to attain [*erlangen*] his frequently reviewed and highly praised cantata, at least in a lavishly ornate piano score . . . , and to obtain closer knowledge of the work—as far as that is possible in such a guise—which at any rate belongs to the best and most interesting ones by this composer.[56]

This advertisement touches on a point that Brendel had also raised: new works require increased and intensive study fully to appreciate their intricacies. The piano arrangement here functions as an object of study; its lack of orchestral colors, the advertisement seems to suggest, is compensated by the material luxury of the edition. At the same time, the piano duet arrangement conversely serves to keep the work in the limelight—given the extraordinarily close connections between the work and the place and occasion for which it was written, despite its success, it was unlikely to be performed again. The special significance that the single performance had for the work seems to be captured in the rhetoric that slipped into the advertising prose, notably in the strange verb *erlangen,* which is somewhere between "acquire" and "achieve," and the oddly modest adverb "at least": both seem to indicate that short of the real thing—personal attendance of the performance in Bonn in honor of Beethoven—the piano arrangement offers the next best substitute. "Attaining" the cantata meant in the first place to possess the piano arrangement.

The idea that an arrangement can serve as a spiritual link to a particular past performance is not far-fetched. Even the incomplete piano sound, another critic argues, can trigger the memory of the orchestral whole:

> We should bear in mind the function of an arrangement, that is to remember the impression that the work originally made on us, by means of recalling the musical material, and in this way to enjoy the work once again. Given this function, we find not only for instrumental works but also with vocal ones requiring larger forces, a certain necessity and, so to speak, apology for an arrangement.[57]

Here the function of the arrangement as an *aide-mémoire* is clearly foregrounded. It represents little more than a stripped-down, easily reproduced version of a performance that took place in the concert hall. Put more confidently: the piano arrangement is a souvenir.

With these widely differing views of the pros and cons of piano arrangements, we can return to Brendel's earlier problem. Here too, the enmeshment of values of high art and issues of popularity and dissemination were on display: while new and difficult art works cannot gain access to the hearts and minds of the audiences unless they are played as often as possible, piano arrangements could provide a solution.[58] This is only possible, though, in the guise of partial representations, which are in danger of compromising the full artistic value of the original work. It is imaginable that this problem could be addressed simply by further differentiating between "good"—faithful and instructive—and "bad"—showy and shallow—arrangements. The maverick music critic Johann Christian Lobe, for one, argued that like every genre, piano arrangements come in all shapes, forms, and varieties. This notwithstanding, the immense popularity of piano arrangements showed that they were in tune with the *Zeitgeist:* "Instead of rejecting and condemning salon music unconditionally and outright, one should perhaps rather say that in modern times the good spirit of musical art has fled into this music—of course not speaking of bad specimens here."[59] But in practice such a qualitative distinction was rarely made. Lobe himself was conspicuously quiet as to the basis on which such a distinction between good and bad arrangements should be made. Indeed, how should it? If the function of arrangements was educational, how could the uneducated know which type of arrangement was before him—or more likely, her?

Liszt's two arrangements of *Tannhäuser* are a case in point. The overture stretches the limits of what is possible in piano performance and is thereby protected from the overuse and purported profanation in the salons that Brendel and others feared. But does that also mean that it is better music than the much simpler *Abendstern?* That claim would be very hard to sustain. Rather, what is at play here is the conflation of the difficulty of virtuoso showpieces and the maintenance of high artistic values—they both display a form of elitism and are apparently only accessible by a minority. In this way, the genre of the piano arrangement, which cuts across all these dimensions, breaks open the bipolar distinctions that dominate the discourse about progressive music and wreaks havoc with them.

Past and Future

Liszt's multiple efforts for Wagner's *Tannhäuser* bore fruit three times over: first of all, the performance at Weimar was a considerable success, much more so than its Dresden premiere four years earlier.[60] Partly this may have been due to the revisions Wagner had carried out since the premiere, which smoothed out some parts in the score that had not had the desired effect. Partly this was also due to a more even cast of singers at Weimar, who had both the vocal and dramatic qualities required for the lead roles.[61] Wagner himself could not officially attend the Weimar performance: in the meanwhile, he had been outlawed and had to flee from Dresden. On the way to his Zurich exile, however, he briefly stopped in Weimar and secretly attended a rehearsal of his opera.[62]

Second, to promote Wagner's cause where he could not speak up for himself, Liszt wrote two essays in the wake of the Weimar performance of *Tannhäuser*. (As was his wont, he wrote in French and gave his essay the misspelled title "Tannhaüser," which, he argued, made pronunciation easier in French.) With this essay he aimed to prepare the wider readership for the opera and set the paths that would channel its future reception—notably in Paris, where *Tannhäuser* would gain notoriety as a *succès de scandale* in 1861.[63] The importance of this essay is considerable, prompting music historian August Wilhelm Ambros to note in 1860 that Liszt's "brilliant book and his performance in Weimar has paved the way for Wagner's works as if with a wave of the magic wand."[64]

And third and most importantly, Liszt's piano transcriptions had begun to set the standards for a whole range of arrangements that were to follow in the wake of *Tannhäuser's* triumphal march through the German opera houses. By 1852, it was performed in Schwerin, Riga, Breslau, Frankfurt, Freiburg, Leipzig, Wiesbaden, Posen (Poznan), Darmstadt, Hamburg, Königsberg, and Cologne—plus another fifteen stages in the next few years. At the same time, a welter of piano arrangements of excerpts and *"motifs de l'opéra" Tannhäuser* were published.

The numbers Liszt selected in his groundbreaking transcriptions proved a good choice: in the arrangements of the 1850s most use the Pilgrims' Chorus, which opens the overture, in a prominent place.[65] (Only few of the early arrangements, among them Charles Voss's *Tannhäuser de Wagner, Grande Fantaisie pour Piano* of ca. 1855 and Joachim Raff's *Sextett aus Richard Wagners Tannhäuser,* refrain from using this theme.[66]) The *Abendstern* cavatina, likewise, features widely in the arrangements. The settings of these and other numbers, however, showed a staggering variety. By far the simplest arrangement is Heinrich Alberti's piano duet (ca. 1860), which is part of an aptly named series "fantaisies amusantes et instructives sur des Thèmes d'Opéras favoris."[67] Instructive it certainly is: transposed to C major, the primo player plays little more than the chorale melody. Where in the middle section of the Pilgrims' chorale, starting with the upbeat to measure 17 in example 3.4, the melody leaps up an octave in characteristic dotted rhythms, and both players would awkwardly have to cross hands, the arranger came up with a bold idea

EXAMPLE 3.4 Heinrich Alberti's four-hand arrangement, *Petite fantaisie sur des motifs de l'opéra Tannhäuser de Wagner* op. 25 no. 7 (ca. 1860) proposes a bold solution to the middle-range melody. The motivic octave-leap, in the passage starting with the upbeat to measure 17, is divided between both players.

EXAMPLE 3.5 (a) Despite his voluble protests, Joachim Raff cannot help himself in his *Fantasie über Motive aus Richard Wagners Tannhäuser* op. 61 no. 3 (1853), but to add a descant over the tenor melody, which gains motivic significance and ties parts of the fantasy together. This excerpt shows the very beginning of Raff's arrangement.

that is musically perhaps less than ideal: the first melodic note of the dotted rhythm is played by the *secondo* player (while the *primo* player adds the upper seventh), and *primo* then completes the melodic phrase. A charitable interpretation might hold that this distribution forces the players to fine-tune their musical relationship and truly perform it as if played by one, whereas a bleaker (but more likely) view would suspect lacking care in the making of the arrangement, which was a common complaint against the genre of arrangements. By comparison, most other piano duet arrangements, including that by Wagner, take care to keep this passage in the hands of one player only.

Perhaps the most skilful link between the overture and the *Abendstern* is achieved by none other than Joachim Raff, in his *Fantasie über Motive aus Richard Wagners Tannhäuser* op. 61 no. 3 of 1853. The fantasy begins, as shown in ex-

EXAMPLE 3.5 (b) Further into the *Fantasie über Motive aus Richard Wagners Tannhäuser,* when Raff fantasizes over Wolfram's aria, he recalls the descant figure from the beginning.

ample 3.5a, with a minor version of the pilgrims' theme, which is interspersed with filigree thirty-two-note figures outlining added sixth chords. The same figuration returns later in the piece, as accompanying figures to the *Abendstern* cavatina, in example 3.5b, and make one wonder whether these are in fact the kinds of figurations above the tenor melody that he would decry only a few years later.

On the whole, the fantasies concentrate on a small number of pieces—favorites among them being the Entry of the Guests, the Act I finale sextet, and Tannhäuser's song. In like spirit, the conservative music critic Otto Jahn, who had given *Tannhäuser* on the whole the thumbs down, exempted from his verdict only the sextet and the hall scene.[68] In other words, mainly the conventional and musically conservative numbers were considered for arrangements; surprisingly, perhaps, Elisabeth's arias are completely omitted from those early arrangements. Only one of the arrangements of this period, by G. W. Marks (ca. 1854)—a pseudonym for a whole host of arrangers, one of whom was the young Johannes Brahms—alludes to the luxurious chromaticism of the Venusberg scene.[69]

Alfred Jaëll even dedicated his paraphrase, "Aus Richard Wagner's *Lohengrin* und *Tannhäuser,*" opus 35 (ca. 1854) to Franz Liszt.[70] Yet his arrangement of the Pilgrims' Chorus could not be more different from Liszt's example: as seen in example 3.6, Jaëll replaces the violin descants with a flickering arpeggiation across the keyboard, marked "grandioso," (beginning in measure 3 of

EXAMPLE 3.6 Did Alfred Jaëll's hand gain its unsightly deformation from playing passages like this? From Jaëll, *Aus Richard Wagners Lohengrin und Tannhäuser* op. 35 (ca. 1854).

the example) that has no basis in the original. There is a certain irony in this arrangement, and in the dedication to Liszt, since both of them were pitted against each other as pianists. The Munich satirical journal *Punsch* published a "psycho-physiological riddle," shown in figure 3.3, in which Liszt's spindly hands were juxtaposed with Jaëll's rather stubby fingers. "Yet," the paper concludes laconically, "both are equally good pianists." The caricature seems to recall Raff's degenerative effects of virtuosity. Each hand clearly reflects the music it brings forth in playing as well as in writing. However—and this is the very important wider point that the *Punsch* caricature is making—the difference in difficulty does not translate into a simple difference in quality judgment.

The new arrangements of *Tannhäuser* that flooded the market were stiff competition for two other highly popular operas in those years, Friedrich von Flotow's *Martha* and Meyerbeer's *Le Prophète*.[71] Like their rivals, these arrangements of *Tannhäuser* were on the whole less concerned with the virtuosic end of the market than with the domestic sphere, where dissemination (and hence sales) could be assumed to be most widespread. The wide proliferation of the music of *Tannhäuser* in this form also had another effect with weighty aesthetic

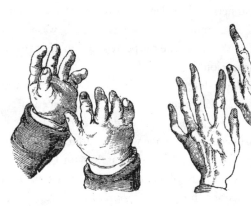

Pfychophyfiologifches Räthfel.

Jaell's Hände   Liszt's Hände
und Beide find fie gleich gute Clavierfpieler!

FIGURE 3.3 "Psycho-physiological Riddle." From
Ernst Kreowski and Eduard Fuchs, *Richard Wagner in der
Karikatur* (Berlin: B. Behr, 1907). Reproduced by permission of the Eda Kuhn Loeb Music Library of the Harvard
College Library.

consequences. For this, let us turn back to Wagner for a minute in his Swiss exile.

In Switzerland Wagner had stopped composing; instead, he had begun to channel his creative energies into the grand theoretical edifices of the early 1850s, the so-called Zurich writings that were *Kunst und Religion, Oper und Drama,* and, crucially, *Das Kunstwerk der Zukunft.* The notion of the "Artwork of the Future" immediately left its mark on the public discourse of music, and within few years—arguably even months—the parodistic form of "Music of the Future," *Zukunftsmusik,* was born.[72] Brendel later tried to argue that the very notion was a contradiction in terms: its exclusive focus on music was irreconcilable with Wagner's concept of the *Gesamtkunstwerk.*[73] Yet his efforts were in vain: *Zukunftsmusik* was the term that stuck.

Due to the fast promulgation of the notion of *Zukunftsmusik*—by word of mouth, rather than by individual study—and the simultaneous, slightly delayed reception of *Tannhäuser,* many listeners assumed that the Zurich writings were an a posteriori reflection on the earlier operas, *Tannhäuser* and *Lohengrin.* (And who could blame them? It would be difficult to deny that *Oper und Drama* was based at least in parts on Wagner's Dresden experience.[74]) And like so many of Wagner's concepts, his term—let alone its bowdlerized, popular version—had little to offer in the way of a specific technical description but was rather an idea within a broader agenda of cultural politics. This did not stop many listeners and readers from trying to understand what exactly this notion entailed, or more generally, what exactly was new about Wagner. They subjected *Tannhäuser,* as the purported exemplar of the music of the future, to rigorous inspection.

This was yet another side-effect of the rise of piano arrangements: by making music easily available, they exposed it to unprecedented analytical scrutiny.[75] Or, as Liszt put it, "once this beautiful work is better known, one will begin to dissect its skeleton, and one will not fail to count all its joints."[76] One of these analytically minded listeners was Johann Christian Lobe, who made the *Tannhäuser* overture the object of a painstaking analysis, examining in turn its melody, harmony, form, and program and urging his readers at least to follow his analysis in a piano score. To be fair, Lobe was well aware that *Tannhäuser* belonged to an earlier period within Wagner's oeuvre, but since his supporters made such bold claims as if it were an exemplar of the artwork of the future, Lobe decided to put it to the test.[77] Often, it seems as if Lobe just engaged the old strategy of arguing that the parts that were new were not good, and those that were good were not new. But while this might sound like a dismissive verdict, Lobe's judgment was actually a lot more measured than other critics of his time. Yet the selectivity of Lobe's observation is interesting: he printed the entire melody of the Pilgrims' Chorus and proceeded to criticize its opening part for its periodic and symmetrical phrase structure and its end for its similarity with a passage from Meyerbeer's *Robert le diable*. (The reception of *Tannhäuser* had come a long way since 1846, when Hanslick had cautioned that "audiences do not like music from which one cannot take home a few hummed eight-measure march tunes from the first performance that are then immediately applied to the fortepiano."[78])

Lobe was oddly silent on the middle section of the Pilgrims' Chorus, shown in example 3.7a. This passage is harmonically most adventurous—its sliding chromaticism and minor-thirds relations are difficult to pin down by conventional harmonic analysis. In fact, this passage is just as adventurous as the Venusberg passages following it, here reproduced in example 3.7b from Liszt's essay. By contrast, these passages were subjected to the minutest critical scrutiny by Lobe.[79] The similarity between the two passages mattered little to Lobe's analysis. Another commentator on the overture, Wagner's friend Theodor Uhlig, spelled out the tacit difference between the two passages: it is only the circumstance that this slippery chromatic passage is in essence vocal music that saves it; had it been found in an instrumental work, he contended, one would have to worry about Wagner's dangerous chromatic proclivities.[80] Unlike the Venusberg music, the Pilgrims' Chorus on the whole exudes an air of reassurance that would put it beyond the suspicion of *Zukunftsmusik*. It was in this guise that the daring Wagnerian sounds were allowed to enter into the living rooms and parlors of his more reluctant audiences.

Lobe's analysis and purported demonstration may be based on a dubious premise, and Wagner's subsequent texts, "A Communication to my Friends," as well as the letter known as "Zukunftsmusik" were attempts on Wagner's part to clarify this misunderstanding. However, it is also possible to view this confusion as a productive engagement: the notion that *Tannhäuser* contained something radically new did not seem so outlandish that it could be dismissed out of hand. Liszt, for one, praised *Tannhäuser* for precisely those features that were to come to the fore in Wagner's subsequent works: "In *Tannhäuser* he introduced a conspicuous innovation for opera, in which the melody not only expresses, but represents, certain emotions, by returning at the moment where they reappear, by being replayed in the orchestra, independently of what is sung in the scene, often with modulations that characterize the modifications of the passions to which it corresponds."[81]

Nor did Lobe deny that there are new things to be discovered in *Tannhäuser*, starting with the overture. With the comforting benefit of hindsight, the most forward-looking element turned out to be the Rome narration of Act III, a piece that played a comparatively minor role in this context.[82] At any event,

EXAMPLE 3.7 (a) Sections from the pilgrims' music are closer to the slippery chromatic *Venusberg* music than Johann Christian Lobe lets on. This piano reduction originally featured as an example in Liszt's essay on "Tannhaüser."

(b) The *Venusberg* music, in a piano reduction from Liszt's essay on "Tannhaüser." The boxes, added here, indicate the chromatic minor-third sequences that this passage has in common with the middle section of the pilgrims' music.

this (mis)apprehension put *Tannhäuser* in a strange position at the intersection between the progressive forces of the mid-nineteenth century and domestic dilettante musical practice—unlikely bedfellows, to say the least. And this constellation was unique: compared with *Tannhäuser,* piano arrangements of *Lohengrin* are far fewer in number, and they decrease further in Wagner's later oeuvre.[83] At the same time, of course, there were fewer numbers available in the later stage works to single out for arrangement. Raff summed up the development of Wagner's style as follows:

> In *The Flying Dutchman* we still find incidental scenes, such as the lyric sailor, the spinning room, the scene between the two ships in the last act: in *Tannhäuser* there's a landscape scene . . . and an "Evening Star." In *Lohengrin*, there's nothing of the sort: everything has emerged immediately and necessarily from and in relation to the subject-matter.[84]

This gradual development is similar to that which Wagner draws up in his "Communication to my Friends." But there seems to be more about the intermediary position of *Tannhäuser* than either Wagner or Raff would seem to realize. Franz Brendel—the Wagnerian editor of the *Neue Zeitschrift der Musik* who staked his career on promoting musical progress—put his finger on it when he precisely located the position of *Tannhäuser* within the discourse of musical progress: "*Tannhäuser* is the work of transition. It is an opera, on the one hand, liberated from the nonsense of recent times; Gluck's opera reborn on a higher sphere and with richer means. On the other hand, however, it already contains many elements of progress.[85]" This transitional status of *Tannhäuser* is also clearly reflected in the number of arrangements made. It is not for nothing that Wagner extends a trajectory in his "Communication to my Friends" that links the works from *Tannhäuser* (more so than *The Flying Dutchman*) to *Tristan* in a single uninterrupted line.

As Brendel knew only too well, familiarity was the biggest stumbling block on the path toward the acceptance of progressive music—and, given the nature of progress, there was no easy way around this problem. As far as Brendel was concerned, this lack of familiarity had also been the principal problem of *Tannhäuser*'s lukewarm reception at its premiere in Dresden.[86] Against this background, the manifold arrangements of *Tannhäuser* would be the approbate remedy. The complex sounds of progressive music with its advanced aural and intellectual demands on operatic audiences, and the soothing dilettante piano sounds emanating from the bourgeois salon would blend euphoniously. Modernity and *Kitsch* would unite in the souvenir.

Anniversaries, Souvenirs, and Monuments

Like the many anniversaries that marked Weimar's "Silver Age," so, too, are souvenirs monuments that transcend spatial limitations. This is nowhere more evident in the musical realm than with operatic piano arrangements. For while the performance of opera is confined to few places, and exclusively so, the music becomes widely disseminated by means of transcriptions, in the guise of which it can enter into middle-class homes. In this spirit, Theodor Uhlig appraised Wolfram's Cavatina in the *Neue Zeitschrift für Musik:* "How few will there be who would not exclaim in their hearts: 'how beautiful this is!' and how many did not feel tears well up when they reminded themselves of this scene sitting at the piano."[87] For the purpose of promoting progressive music, playing Wagner's music at the piano is of crucial significance: it can serve to overcome the obstacle of progressive music Brendel identified, that of lack of familiarity.

What is more, the piano arrangement allows for a broad part of the population to familiarize themselves with this music—far more so than would be able to frequent opera houses, whether for reasons of space or indeed of economic constraints. It was exactly for this reason that Liszt's piano arrangement of Wolfram's Cavatina was praised in 1850: "[as an arrangement] it will, one hopes, gain that level of propagation that its excellence merits, but which it can hardly achieve without a transcription, since *Tannhäuser* has been performed on so few stages to date."[88]

But unlike the anniversary, the piano arrangement as souvenir is not bound to a particular date, it is not fixed in time. It follows its own time, which is, in Susan Stewart's expression, one of interiority: not only is the arrangement readily available in the privacy of one's own home whenever desired but it also offers a foreshortened experience of the musical work it invokes. Concentrated on a few highlights—nowhere more so than in the blossoming genres of fantasias on *"motifs de l'opéra"*—the miniaturized operatic experience existed on its own level of time, providing what was presented as the quintessence of the score. And indeed, perhaps it is this most maligned genre that actually corresponds most closely to the way memory works, flitting as it often does from one highlight to the next without any apparent logical coherence.

Like the modern souvenir, then, which can substitute for the first-hand experience of a tourist destination, the piano arrangement can stand in for the experience of listening to a new operatic work. And it is irrelevant here whether the memory triggered by the piano arrangement is of a past performance, as our critic from *Allgemeine musikalische Zeitung* argued above, whether it replaces an actual performance that could not be attended by many, as in the case of the piano duet arrangement of Liszt's Beethoven Cantata, or indeed whether it serves to prepare for an actual performance in the future.

In the case of *Tannhäuser* and the debate surrounding *Zukunftsmusik* especially, the piano arrangements helped achieve a particular twist that was neither accurate nor intended, but nonetheless highly efficacious. The arrangements allowed the apparently threatening "music of the future" into the homes and salons in this miniaturized and easily consumable form. In more than one sense, they commemorate the future. Due to the widespread reception of the Zurich writings, based on an insufficient reading, or indeed on second-hand knowledge of the sources, progressive musical forces, for once, went hand in hand with the sentimental sounds of the bourgeois salons.

FIGURE 3.4 Advertising poster for Römhildt pianos, Weimar. Reproduced by permission of Museum für Kunst und Gewerbe, Hamburg.

In a way, the arrangements of Wagner's *Tannhäuser* are a response to his conception of the work of art lodged between the modern Scylla and Charybdis of fashion and monumentality. The dialectic here is one that Wagner might have rejected but that in fact was a potent mixture. In this miniaturized guise, even Wagner's self-proclaimed megalophobia is addressed: the arrangements are in fact Brobdingnagians in Lilliputians' clothing.

This curious marriage of convenience between progress and popularity was only possible under the banner of the commercialization of art. And perhaps this is not surprising, given the gradual rise of the bourgeois classes and the increasing importance of leisure and consumerism—as well as of musical literacy. In this sense, it seems entirely appropriate that a Weimar piano dealer would aim to capitalize in turn on the association of famous composers with his town. In his commercial print, in figure 3.4, Liszt, Wagner, and von Bülow are united around an upright piano of the Römhildt brand. An audience in formal evening wear, which can only be described as classy, is visible in the background, and the palm tree adds a touch of luxury probably restricted to wealthier bourgeois salons. Issues of popularity, progress, quality, magnitude, and class come together in this beautiful utopian location. And before anyone can start wondering whether a mere upright piano is not an incongruous object in this scene, we are made aware of Beethoven's reassuring presence in form of a plaque on the wall, which provides the final artistic seal of approval. One can only hope that what von Bülow, sitting at the piano, is playing, is Liszt's arrangement of Wagner's *Abendstern*.

| Classical Values

Strange Encounters

Franz Brendel was not alone in observing a natural affinity between Wagner
and Gluck, the two great operatic reformers of the eighteenth and nineteenth
centuries. In fact, however, the two did not hit it off at first. Rather, Wagner's
first encounter with Gluck was a big disappointment. While in Vienna as
a nineteen-year-old, Wagner attended a performance of *Iphigenie auf Tauris,*
Gluck's best-known opera at the time, with a cast full of first-rate singers.
"Yet," he reminisced,

> I must honestly confess that the work bored me as a whole, which was
> all the more painful as I did not dare admit it. My conception of Gluck
> had inevitably attained gigantic dimensions from my reading of Hoff-
> mann's well-known tale: I assumed I would find in him, whose works
> I had not yet studied, an overpowering dramatic fire, and applied to
> my first hearing of his most famous work the standard set for me on
> that unforgettable evening when Schröder-Devrient had sung in *Fide-
> lio.* With some effort I succeeded in bringing myself during the great
> scene of Orestes with the Furies into a halfway comparable state of
> ecstasy. I spent the rest of the opera waiting in solemn intensity for an
> effect that never came.[1]

Wagner's listening expectations are easily recognized as staples of the romantic imagination: he was waiting for an ecstatic musical experience; in actual-
ity, only one of the numbers from Gluck's score could evoke this effect. It
should hardly surprise us that the number Wagner singles out is the frenetic

Chorus and Dance of the Eumenides in Act II. (Wagner, who prided himself on his Classical education, knew his Greek mythology better than Gluck's librettists Guillard and Du Roullet: while being furious, the Eumenides are strictly speaking Furies; it is only later that Athena turns them into happy creatures.) With the view to Wagner's own progressive artistic outlook, it fits the romantic bill that the frenzied and chromatic choruses of Act II would prove particularly memorable.

At the same time, Beethoven is also factored into the equation, albeit in a slightly roundabout fashion. The yardstick Wagner applied to Gluck's composition was to measure it against Beethoven's *Fidelio*, and what is more, against a particular performance of it: he referred to Wilhelmine Schröder-Devrient, who was as famous for her outstanding dramatic talent as for her complete lack of any vocal beauty. Her interpretation of Leonore left a lasting impression on the young Wagner and served as an ideal throughout his theoretical writings. It is not by coincidence that when, just a few pages before the disappointing *Iphigenie,* he described her singing in *Mein Leben*—"demonic fire," "ecstatic experience,"[2]—he used almost the same attributes to describe her performance as he did for his expectations toward Gluck. All these impressions, which are partly located in the score, partly in the performance of the work, seem to contribute to the expectation of "gigantic dimensions" with which he approached Gluck.

Even though we only have his own recollection of this experience to rely on, dating from thirty years later, Wagner's intense disappointment points toward a profound disconnect between historical and musical greatness: Gluck's stature in music history is undoubted, and even though Wagner did not explicitly mention it in this instance, it is safe to assume that in 1832 he was well aware of Gluck's significance in operatic history. For this reason, Wagner seemed to feel obliged to appreciate this historical greatness, but he could not find it reflected in Gluck's music, which appeared to lack, for the most part, the progressive spirit that one might well associate with revolutionary ideas. And yet, strangely, despite this unfortunate meeting of minds, Wagner continued to return to Gluck throughout his life. In many ways, Gluck came to occupy a unique position in Wagner's thinking: there is no other composer from an earlier century—not even Bach, whom he revered—who keeps Wagner's interest sustained over so many years and about whom he writes with such remarkable consistency across the profound changes in his thinking.

The Wagner we encounter in this chapter is a very different one from the figure we examined through the miniaturized and domesticated *Zukunfts-musik* in the previous chapter: here Wagner is turning his gaze backwards, and actively engaging, indeed intervening, in the music of the past. He strove to restore Gluck to a musical greatness that he felt the older composer deserved and that was not forthcoming in his own age. As we shall explore, he tried to rescue Gluck from a false sense of monumentality, to correct his position in history, and he did so in ways that came most naturally to him—as a composer, as a conductor, and as a pamphleteer.

What is perhaps most curious about Wagner's earliest encounter with Gluck is the fact that these expectations were shaped by a piece of prose fiction, the novella "Ritter Gluck" by the romantic polymath E. T. A. Hoffmann—all the more so, since the nature of the title character of the novella itself would hardly invite any grand claims of authenticity. Quite the contrary, the story circles around the question of the identity of the main character of the story: the novella recalls a number of encounters between the narrator and a mysterious elderly gentleman, who is evidently highly musical. Invariably, their discussions turn to Gluck's operatic works. During their final encounter, the mysterious musician plays the whole score of *Armide* on the piano and invites the narrator to turn the pages for him—"but at the right moments," he admonishes the young man. To his astonishment, the narrator finds that the pages show nothing but empty staves; over the ghostly performance, which teeters between faithful recreation and a virtuosic improvisation, the mysterious character proclaims: "I am Ritter Gluck."[3] As this purportedly true event took place in 1809, which is to say almost a quarter-century after Gluck's death, this final exclamation raises more questions about the character's identity than it is able to solve.

The idea of a nameless romantic hero doubtless had considerable appeal to Wagner, as such characters were to feature again and again in his own operatic works. In fact, the question "Who is Ritter Gluck?" has been asked many times.[4] In countless interpretations, Hoffmann's mysterious figure has variously been described as a madman, an ingenious impostor, an epigone, a ghost, a figment of the narrator's imagination, the undying "Wandering Jew," or the manifest essence of Gluck's genius.[5] Yet Wagner stands alone in proposing that Hoffmann's shady character could offer any insights about the real Gluck and his music—as he did in the run-up of the performance of the Viennese performance of *Iphigenie*. We can interpret Wagner's reaction in two ways: either he takes Hoffmann's allegedly true account at face value and conceives of Hoffmann's Gluck as a kind of "Elvis" figure of classical music, whose death is disbelieved but who makes irregular appearances in likely or unlikely places; or he takes this fictional account as a covert piece of Hoffmann's music criticism.

This latter possibility was not uncommon in the nineteenth century: Wagner himself was to write a number of novellas himself, chief among them

Eine Pilgerfahrt zu Beethoven and *Ein glücklicher Abend* ("A Pilgrimage to Beethoven" and "A Happy Evening") with which he would simultaneously propound his music-aesthetic views. Apparently Heinrich Heine praised these prose works by pronouncing, much to Wagner's delight, "Hoffmann himself could not have written such a thing."[6] If we assume that Wagner took Hoffmann's prose as a piece of music criticism, however, his reaction to hearing Gluck's music is difficult to explain: he seems to have more faith in Hoffmann than in Gluck. For the duration of the whole performance in Vienna, Wagner never ceased to wait for the expected ecstasy. When confronted with Hoffmann's account of Gluck's music and his own rather different experience of it, he showed reluctance to revise the standards that Hoffmann set. Rather, if Gluck turned out not to live up to the "gigantic dimensions" in which Hoffmann had described him, then it is Gluck who should be changed.

This retroactive readjustment turned out to be more difficult than expected. As Wagner realized at various junctures in his engagement with the older composer, the place assigned to Gluck in history was quite firm: Gluck had become precisely the monumental marble statue—a "classic"—that Wagner so abhorred.[7] Wagner believed that what backed Gluck up and affirmed his place in music history was a strong performance tradition, against which Wagner battled continuously. He realized he had to change this tradition if he wanted to change Gluck at all. Only by reuniting the historical figure with appropriate sounds in performance could new life be breathed back into the marble statue that Gluck had been turned into. Wagner was to act predominantly on the theoretical and essayistic platform; his strategy would consist overwhelmingly in picking holes in the imagined connection between music history and the prevalent performance tradition, and mending them in a new way that would bring the two aspects into line the way he envisioned it. Once he had formulated his theoretical views, he would then put his ideas into action and endeavored, from the arranger's desk and from the conducting podium, to promote his sounding music history in performance.

Gluck between Mozart and Beethoven

It is perhaps no coincidence that Wagner would start first thinking about Gluck again during his first sojourn in Paris in the 1840s. It was in Paris that Gluck really had attained "gigantic dimensions": his bust, shown here in figure 4.1, flanked the entrance of the *Opéra* besides those of Rameau and Lully, and bore the inscription *Musas Praeposuit Sirenis* ("He preferred the muses to the sirens"), clearly in reference to Gluck's opera reforms in the previous cen-

FIGURE 4.1
A copy of J. A. Houdon's bust of
Gluck (1775). Reproduced by
permission of the Royal College
of Music, London.

tury.[8] Yet it was less Gluck's dramatic skills that interested Wagner at that
stage in his life than one specific work, the overture to Gluck's *Iphigenie in Aulis*.

This focus on an overture, an instrumental form, may seem a curious approach, but it is an important part in Wagner's reconsideration of Gluck's
stature. As Thomas Grey has indicated in a thoroughgoing study of Wagner's
aesthetics of the overture, Wagner's historical narrative can offer enlightening insights precisely because in discussions of instrumental forms he tends
to be less anxious to foreground his own music-dramatic achievement. This
is not to say, of course, that we should read Wagner's history of the overture
with the view to gaining well-supported, unassailable music-historical insights.
But in marked contrast to his theories of the music drama, Grey notes a rather
more "conservative tone" in his discussions of non-operatic music.[9] As we
shall see, this will have a critical bearing on Wagner's views of Gluck and his
overture to *Iphigenie in Aulis*.

In his essay, "De l'Ouverture" (or "Über die Ouvertüre"), which first appeared in French in the *Gazette et revue musicale* in 1841, Wagner placed Gluck,
like his *Opéra* bust, beside two other great musical composers in Wagner's
pantheon: Mozart and Beethoven. For Wagner, the overture, as a form in its
own right, did not exist before Mozart, at least not in the sense that he was
interested in and that he was going to develop in his essay. Any previous overtures or opening sinfonias—Wagner singled out Handel's *Messiah* in this

context—were nothing but a blunt sign, serving no other purpose "than to tell the audience that singing was the order of the day."[10] Beyond that, the overture had no dramatic function, Wagner continued, as at that time "purely instrumental music was not sufficiently matured as yet to give due character to such a task."[11] This lack of expressivity had a direct effect on its form: instead of a dramatic development, Wagner explained, the early overture could only avail itself of technical means, that is fugal sections, to expand its dimensions.[12]

While gradually a tripartite model of fast-slow-fast became the standard form for overtures, Wagner's historical narrative continues, it was only with Mozart and Gluck that a closer connection with the ensuing drama was established in the overture. Gluck's masterwork in this respect was the overture to *Iphigenie in Aulis,* and equivalently, Mozart's that to *Die Entführung aus dem Serail.* Of Mozart's overtures, Wagner writes:

> Without toiling to express what music neither can nor should express, the details and entanglements of the plot itself—which the earlier Prologue had endeavored to set forth—with the eye of a veritable poet he grasped the drama's leading thought, stripped it of all material episodes and accidentiae, and reproduced it in the transfiguring light of music as a passion personified in tones, a counterpart both warranting that thought itself and explaining the whole dramatic action to the hearer's feeling.[13]

In the course of Wagner's discussion, the parallels between Mozart's and Gluck's examples become quite apparent: both manage to capture something of the character of the drama as a whole, but both avoid going into any specifics, which would in any case be, in Wagner's view, beyond the power of music at that time. Furthermore, both have clear thematic connections with the first scene—in the case of Gluck's *Iphigenie in Aulis* the overture does not even close musically but segues into the first scene. Mozart, by contrast, tended to keep his overtures musically self-contained—with the important exception of that to *Don Giovanni,* which Wagner considered to be Mozart's most significant achievement in this field, and which transitions into the opening scene without any kind of musical caesura. (We should not worry too much about the similar superlative that Wagner had bestowed on Mozart's *Entführung* just a few paragraphs previously—this was simply part of Wagner's exuberant prose style.)

When Beethoven comes into the picture, in Wagner's model, he already oversteps this perfect balance between drama and music that the overture represented with *Iphigenie in Aulis.* With Beethoven, music has learned to speak for itself. Wagner writes about Beethoven's third *Leonore* overture: "Far from giving us a mere musical introduction to the drama, it sets that drama more complete and movingly before us than ever happens in the broken action which ensues. This work is no longer an overture, but the mightiest drama in itself."[14] With the overture *Leonore III,* the ensuing drama has become redundant.

This thought stayed with Wagner throughout his life. Three decades later, he expressed the same idea much more drastically, when he asked: "What is the dramatic action of the librettist's opera 'Leonora' anything but an almost repulsive watering of the drama we have lived through in its overture?"[15] But even in this early article, the problem of *Leonore III* was clear: its genius, as well as its problem, lay in its double closure—it is both musically and dramatically complete.

Mozart's *Don Giovanni* functioned as the counterexample. It reached up to the same dizzying heights as did *Leonore III,* Wagner argued, but it differed from the latter in two fundamental respects—it lacked a musical ending, and it made little thematic reference to the ensuing drama:

> Had Mozart but added the fearful termination of the story, the tone-work would have lacked nothing to be regarded as a finished whole, a drama in itself; but the master lets us merely guess the combat's outcome: in that wonderful transition to the first scene he makes both hostile elements bow beneath a higher will, and nothing but a wailing sigh breather over the place of battle. Clearly and plainly as is the opera's tragic principle depicted in this overture, you shall not find in all the musical tissue one single spot that could in any way be brought into direct relation with the action's course; unless it were its introduction, borrowed from the ghost-scene—though in that case we should have expected to meet the allusion at the piece's end, and not at its beginning.[16]

For Wagner, Mozart's *Don Giovanni* was so compelling because, in contrast to Beethoven's equally compelling counterexample, it is both musically and dramatically incomplete. Unlike *Leonore III,* Mozart's example necessitates the ensuing operatic drama. But here Wagner was a little too much concerned with sharply contrasting types from one another—his argument actually implies a second, somewhat different point, a point that reaches over to the musical novella that he was writing at the same time, *Ein glücklicher Abend* ("A Happy Evening"), and that can only be fully understood in the context of this other writing. *Ein glücklicher Abend* also proposed a sharp differentiation between Beethoven and Mozart: unlike Beethoven's overpowering dramatic force, Mozart was compelling by predominantly musical means.[17] It is this differentiation that also stands at the background of Wagner's argument here, but it only comes out in the detail of his language: while Beethoven's overture already encompasses *the* entire drama of *Leonore,* Mozart's overture would be "*a* drama in itself." Thus, Mozart's overture is not anticipating the ensuing drama of *Don Giovanni*—but for its lacking an ending, it would stand as a "complete whole" in music.

Both *Don Giovanni* and *Leonore III* are special cases, which transcend that which Wagner considered typical of the overture. In his view, the ideal overture should be musically complete in itself, while being dramatically contingent on the opera: "In this conception of the Overture, then, the highest task would be to reproduce the characteristic idea of the drama by the intrinsic means of independent music," Wagner argued, "and to bring it to a conclusion in anticipatory agreement with the solution of the problem in the scenic play."[18] This is the special, dual task of the overture: it must stand up as a piece of music in its own right, following the autonomous laws of "pure" instrumental music, as Wagner called it in this context, but at the same time still carry a certain dramatic message.

This is where Gluck and his overture to *Iphigenie in Aulis* come into the debate: Wagner outlined in detail what he considered so special about this particular example and summarized the dramatic content of the overture. Like *Don Giovanni, Iphigenie* begins with a clash of two hostile elements, though in this case it is the conflict of classical tragedy: the army of Greek heroes versus the life of Iphigenie, the collective mass versus the individual. Both were represented, in Wagner's view, in the two main themes—on the one hand, the forceful, intransigent unison theme of "the mass unified in one single interest" and the following theme, on the other, of the "suffering tender individual," respectively, eliciting alternately feelings of terror and pity.[19] Wagner was thinking here of a kind of motivic technique, which he applied as a tool for the formal understanding of Gluck's music.

Given that Wagner began his argument with a dismissal of Baroque overtures and their fugal forms, it is curious that he refrained from saying any more about the form of the overture than this—a conflict of two themes is often seen as a staple of overtures, and of nineteenth-century approaches to sonata form in general.[20] Wagner's approach to form was not like those of his more analytically inclined contemporaries Adolf Bernhard Marx or Johann Christian Lobe; he was more interested in the poetic object that is expressed in music.[21] At any rate, it is not difficult to recognize the idealist heritage of Hegelian theories of tragedy behind Wagner's notion of the overture, hinging dialectically on the conflict between the universal and the particular.[22] Wagner concludes that Gluck's overture leaves the listener with a "sublime-excited feeling," in preparation for the drama that will unfold before the audience, and it is this musical effect that at the same time reveals the "ultimate meaning" of the tragedy before the curtain rises, without giving away any of the plot:

> May this glorious example serve as a rule in future for the framing of all overtures, and demonstrate withal how much a grand simplicity in the choice of musical motives enables the musician to evoke the swiftest and plainest understanding of his aims, no matter how unusual they might be.[23]

Gluck's overture is so successful, Wagner explained, because it remains a work of "pure" instrumental music, and as such subject to its own rules, while at the same time capturing something profound about the dramatic essence of the play. It neither anticipated the full drama in great detail, as Beethoven's *Leonore III* did, nor did it capture the "drama's leading thought in a purely musical but not in dramatic shape," as did Mozart's *Don Giovanni*.[24]

In other words, Wagner presented here a typology of overtures, with Mozart as the example of a consummately musical conception of the overture, Beethoven with an equally consummate dramatic conception of the overture, and Gluck in the happy medium, with a classical balance between music and dramatic elements. The epithet "grand simplicity," which Wagner used for Gluck above, would seem to echo Winckelmann's classic definition of classicism as *edle Einfalt, stille Größe* ("noble simplicity, quiet grandeur").[25] Initially in his argument Wagner followed a chronological order, where Gluck and Mozart (or, to be precise, the Mozart of *Die Entführung aus dem Serail*) form the first generation of overture composers, followed by a second generation comprising Beethoven and Cherubini; by the end of his argument, meanwhile, this generational difference between the three first composers has all but disappeared: Cherubini has been dropped, and each of the remaining three has been turned into an ideal type, which forms one necessary part of the triumvirate. For Wagner, all three were equally important, and music history would only emanate from the union of them, as he stressed in the concluding sentence: "In the triad, *Gluck, Mozart and Beethoven,* we have the lodestar whose pure light will always lead us rightly even on the most bewildering path of art; but anyone who should single out *one* of them for his exclusive star, of a surety would fall into the maze from which but one has ever issued victor, namely that One, the Inimitable One."[26]

The warning signal—and the glorification of Weber, whose name does not even need to be spelled out in this context—with which Wagner ended his exploration of the overture hints at the implicit conception of music history that he envisaged as shaping up around them. In Wagner's view, Weber was the only composer who had been successful in taking the drama-oriented

Beethovenian path further by developing the overture into what he calls a "dramatic fantasia."[27] As it relinquishes part of its musical self-sufficiency in the service of its dramatic representation, the danger on this path is one of musical fragmentation. Others who tried their luck in this direction—Wagner mentioned Spontini, Rossini, and Hérold—were less felicitous and ended up with the potpourri overture, which Wagner regarded as a degenerate musical form.[28]

A similar danger would consist in making music too loquacious, as it were, and an example from Johann Christian Lobe would be a case in point.[29] Lobe proposed a model overture on *Wallenstein,* where each of the three themes represents one chief character from Schiller's plays. Wallenstein, Thekla, and Max Piccolomini are all different manifestations of an underlying thematic complex, whose dramatic interactions are depicted by means of harmonic layout, contrapuntal interaction, and orchestral presentation. This plot-driven working-out of the material, Lobe imagined, would hold the listener captive and "force him to be engaged by the performance in tense excitement."[30] Composers, he exhorted, would likewise do well to keep their intentions and musical expression clear and intelligible. Even contemporary program music lacked the sufficient clarity he envisioned for his form of overture. Although Lobe offered his thematic material for *Wallenstein* to any young, unknown composer eager to make his career, this call remained without musical response.[31]

But Mozart's example on its own also harbors certain dangers. Wagner did not say any more about the Mozartian line with what might be called its "symphonic" tendencies—and given Wagner's understanding of his own position in music history, it is not difficult to see why. But we can interpolate for him that the exceedingly musical conception of the overture is a dangerous path: an overture that is musically consummate would be in danger of stopping to "speak" and of failing to relate to the opera it is supposed to introduce. Where Beethoven's example was so dramatic that it made the drama redundant, in its extreme form Mozart's musical example would refrain from introducing the drama, or would at best be arbitrarily attached to it. It is tempting, and not quite unwarranted, to read out of this pairing of the Mozart-versus-Beethoven ideal types elements of the later Hanslickian split in music aesthetics that Wagner anticipated here.

For Gluck's stature, Wagner's triumvirate meant no less than a considerable upgrading in music history, which despite his status as a reformer of opera, had long been regarded with some ambiguous feelings. To take Brendel's influential *Geschichte der Musik* as an example, there Gluck was presented as Mozart's precursor: theoretically on firmer ground than Mozart, but musically clearly lagging behind him in imagination and musical power. "Gluck is like a closed bud, while Mozart is the flower unfolded in richest fullness," Brendel rhapsodized, only to revise this judgment immediately: "Our opera culminates in two summits, Gluck and Mozart; both have in some sense achieved the highest goal, depending on one's viewpoint."[32] Gluck, it seems, was the guilty conscience of a music historiography caught between the immediate appeal of the musical highlights it singled out and the stern need for a continuous narrative of progress.

When Brendel found that Gluck was lacking in musical liveliness, and likened his "ancient grandeur" with marble statues—"multi-dimensional [*plastisch*], like those marble images, but also cold and unmovable"[33]—his verdict finds a distant echo in Wagner's images of Greek tragedy that he conjured up in his reassessment of Gluck's *Iphigenie.* Both seem to concur that Gluck embodied truly classical values (in the sense of Wagner's "bad" monumentality that he so abhorred in the case of Liszt's extolments of his *Ring*).[34]

This notion is finally set in stone in the position accorded to Gluck within the triumvirate, in the *juste milieu* between the two extremes of Beethoven and Mozart. Its specific function seems to be to hold the two other divergent types together. His overture epitomizes, according to Wagner, the perfect balance between music and drama—or, to extend the idealist framework with which Wagner operated in explaining his views on tragedy—between form and content. But what is the "future" of this "glorious example" that he invoked earlier in his hymnic address? It seems, rather, that the consummate balance of Gluck's type would have its own problematic historical dimension: in a word, perfection itself is a problem. On the one hand, it does not harbor any particular dangers of verging too far into the musical or dramatic domain; nor does it, on the other hand, invite any further developments. Or, if we tried to fold these two sides into one, the specific issue with Gluck's example would seem to be that it engenders no progress, only eternal repetition. It is hard to envisage how Gluck's example should be carried forth into the future. Given that Wagner's historical trajectory operated on a timeline of instrumental music's growing capacity for distinct expression, it would seem that the Gluckian paradigm can only continue to rest in itself.

Gluck's Antiquity and Actuality

As already seen in Brendel's comparison between *Tannhäuser* and Gluck's operas in the previous chapter, a number of subsequent Wagnerian exegetes tried to forge strong links between Wagner and Gluck, as the two chief reformers of opera. Thus, one early commentator of 1861, the year of *Tannhäuser* in Paris, begins with a biographical parallel: "Like Wagner, Gluck chose from his operas for his debut of his Paris career that which in its diction fully represented the new principle."[35] Another saw their commonality in their reaction against outmoded forms of expression: "Gluck and Wagner: they both pursued the same principle, they destroyed the old form of opera, they also helped to reinstate the poetic arts in sung drama and thus led to a close relation of tone and word, of a kind that our old classics Lessing, Herder and Klopstock had been dreaming."[36] And the fervent Wagnerian Ludwig Nohl saw in Wagner the executor of Gluck's promise. In *Gluck und Wagner*, which not coincidentally was published at the height of German Francophobia in 1870, he asked: "How is it that a whole century had to pass, despite all the signs of an ardent desire for the goal to which Gluck had most successfully paved the way, before the goal itself was reached—indeed, how is it that Gluck could only see his efforts fulfilled abroad and, what is more, in the most unmusical of foreign nations, among the French?"[37]

Satisfying as such a direct trajectory from Gluck to Wagner might be, where Gluck became a kind of "John the Baptist" to Wagner's "Messiah,"[38] as was commonly claimed, this is not in fact what Wagner himself envisioned. What is striking, rather, is Gluck's relative absence in Wagner's Zurich reform writings, particularly *Oper und Drama.* He is mentioned, to be sure, and in more positive terms than several other composers from the past, but none of this goes much beyond what would be considered courteous, even against the background of the *creatio ex nihilo* of music drama that Wagner constructed in these treatises.[39] The closest Wagner came to enlisting Gluck in a music-historical trajectory was when he argued that "Spontini is the last member in a series of composers whose first exponent is found in Gluck."[40] In other words, Wagner sets himself and his music drama off from the long development initiated by Gluck, whose reform efforts rather leads into a dead end.

For Wagner, Gluck seemed to belong fully to another era of music history. This is part of his classicism, which in this case, as we have already seen, carries with it clear overtones of antiquity. In 1847, back in Dresden, Wagner had the opportunity to deepen his engagement with *Iphigenie in Aulis,* when he adapted the opera for nineteenth-century audiences. His particular interest was to understand the ancient conception of tragedy:

> People were amazed at that time to hear me talk with particular vivacity about Greek literature and history, but never about music. In the course of my reading, which I zealously pursued, and which drew me away from my professional activities into increasing solitude, I was soon

impelled to turn my attention to a new and systematic study of this all-important source of culture, in the hope of filling the perceptible gap between my boyhood knowledge of these eternal elements of humanist education and my current desolation on the terrain caused by the distractions of the life I had been leading. . . . I began anew with Greek antiquity and was soon filled with such overwhelming enthusiasm for it that whenever I could be brought to talk, I would only show signs of animation if I could force the conversation around to that sphere. Once in a while I found someone who was willing to listen to me; but in the main people only wanted to discuss the theater with me, because, especially after my production of Gluck's *Iphigenia,* they believed me to be an authority on the subject.[41]

It is a commonplace of music history that—unlike the visual and poetic arts—music has no *exempla classica* in antiquity, since modern music is fundamentally different from its ancient Greek counterpart.[42] Instead, the music and aesthetics of the late eighteenth century stand in for these ancient exemplars. Yet, Wagner's conception of classicism here is markedly more oriented toward antiquity than one might expect.[43] Wagner was no fan of Euripides, the author of *Iphigenie in Aulis,* who had been held in disdain since Friedrich and August Wilhelm Schlegel had all but banned him from the classical canon.[44] Where Aeschylus represented for Wagner "birth out of music," Euripides was its *"décadence."*[45] What interested him here was a more general sense of antiquity, which he coupled with Gluck's musical classicism.

Some commentators have noted with curiosity that Wagner refrained from appropriating Gluck for the German cause. Gluck was something of a special case, in that his career was almost entirely founded on successes abroad, particularly in Italy and France. Numerous later writers, notably those who see a direct link between Gluck and Wagner, simultaneously aim to stress his ties to German culture. In this spirit, Nohl cited Wagner from his 1840 essay "De la musique allemande," where Wagner rehearsed the nationalist topic—prevalent in German musical writing at least since J. J. Quantz—of the quintessential heterogeneity of Germanic culture:

The German genius would almost seem predestined to seek out among his neighbours what is not native to its motherland, to lift this from its narrow confines, and thus to make something Universal for the world. Naturally, however, this can only be achieved by anyone who is not satisfied to ape a foreign nationality, but keeps the German birthright pure and undefiled; and that birthright is Purity of feeling and Chasteness of invention. Where this dowry is retained, the German may do the grandest work in any tongue and every nation, beneath all quarters of the sky.[46]

When Nohl maintains that both Gluck and Mozart are implied in this pan-egyric, he has to stretch Wagner's thought a little: while Mozart was almost definitely meant, as Wagner says explicitly in the following paragraph, Gluck's name is most noticeable in its absence from the entire article.[47] Given that this essay was written around the same time as "Über die Ouvertüre," which we encountered above, it is hard to imagine that Gluck's name might have been omitted purely by an oversight. Where the *Opéra* busts of Gluck, Lully, and Rameau are a grouped together as a small pantheon, unmistakably a tri-umvirate of French opera, the nationalist associations of Wagner's triumvirate Gluck–Mozart–Beethoven are surprisingly understated.[48]

In a way, it seems more likely that Gluck was not part of Wagner's na-tional pantheon because his music fulfilled a very different role in Wagner's conception. In *Oper und Drama,* written ten years after "De la musique alle-mande," Wagner brought up the question of Gluck's nationhood explicitly. In this explanation, Gluck came dangerously close to being likened to Meyer-beer, Wagner's Jewish nemesis:

Meyerbeer passed through all the phases of this Melody's development; not from an abstract distance, but in a very concrete nearness, always on the spot. As a Jew, he owned no mother-tongue, no speech inextri-cably entwined among the sinews of his inmost being: he spoke with precisely the same interest in any modern tongue you chose, and set it to music with no further sympathy for its idiosyncrasies than just the question as to how far it showed a readiness to become a pliant servi-tor to Absolute Music. This attribute of Meyerbeer's has given occasion to a comparison of him with Gluck; for the latter, too, although a Ger-man, wrote operas to French and Italian texts. As a fact, Gluck did not create his music out of an instinct for language (which in this case can only ever be one's mother tongue); what he, as a Musician, was con-cerned with in his attitude toward language, was *speech,* that utterance of the lingual organism which merely floats upon the surface of this myriad of organs. It was not from the generative force of these organs that his productivity ascended through speech to musical expression, but rather he returned to speech from detached musical expression, merely so as to give that baseless Expression some ground of vindica-tion. Thus every tongue might well come equally to Gluck, since he was only busied with speech: if Music, in this transcendental line, had been able to pierce through speech into the very organism of language, it must then have surely had to entirely transform itself.[49]

We can see through how many intellectual hoops Wagner had to jump in order to rescue Gluck from being labeled a homeless Jew, like Meyerbeer, who would avail himself of any language and any fad he could lay hands on. In this conception, Gluck turns in effect into a composer of instrumental music to which words happen to be attached. (In fact, this explanation is fully consistent with Wagner's earlier focus on Gluck's particular achievements in the genre of the overture.) Not the meaning of language, which in its foreign guises must remain obscure, but the sound of speech guided Gluck's composition. And since Wagner elsewhere also declared instrumental music to be a particularly German genre, Gluck could be readmitted into the circle of German composers.

What is most noticeable, however, is that Wagner did not seem to care particularly about Gluck's national status: his argument, despite its transcendent appeal, remains fairly weak. By contrast, Mozart, who as a composer of Italian operas was in a broadly comparable situation, was unquestionably considered as a German, without any mental gymnastics.[50] (In the same spirit, Wagner gave short shrift to Gluck's operatic reforms: they were simply a success in the perennial power struggle between composer and performer.) When viewed purely in terms of music history—which was often for Wagner also a history of the pre-eminence of German culture—it seems that Gluck, *malgré tout,* simply did not matter to Wagner.

Correct Score and Correct Performance

The ties to Gluck that Wagner forged were not historical, but of a musical, and hence supposedly much more immediate, nature. He returned to the overture of *Iphigenie in Aulis* one more time, in 1854, while in exile in Zurich, in order to produce a version of the overture that would be suitable for the concert hall. There was already a concert ending in existence, ostensibly written by Mozart, but Wagner found it wanting. In reality, this concert ending was composed by a much less sensational composer, Johann Philipp Schmidt, but Wagner never doubted the authenticity of Mozart's authorship. In fact, what makes this episode so enlightening—given that the central question is one of authority—is that Wagner had no qualms stepping over Mozart's authority and instead supplying his own ending, which he considered superior.

The problem with the "Mozart" ending, Wagner believed, was that it was based on a faulty understanding of the tempo and had been duped into this

FIGURE 4.2 First page of Gluck's *Iphigenie in Aulis*, piano arrangement by F. Brißler (Berlin: Challier, ca. 1839). The Allegro section begins after the first nineteen measures, as it did in the non-extant Spontini version. Reproduced by permission of the Eda Kuhn Loeb Music Library of the Harvard College Library.

misconception by a corrupted score of the overture. In composing his concert ending, Wagner studied the score closely and found that he—and everybody else—had profoundly misunderstood the internal logic of the overture. For the score of *Iphigenie* that was in common usage on German stages in Wagner's time was a version arranged by Spontini, now lost. Wagner initially based his concert version on this score but soon became mistrustful of the tempo indications in Spontini's score. As is common in eighteenth-century overtures, the slow introduction, which spans the first nineteen measures and is shown in figure 4.2, is followed by an Allegro section. It was only when Wagner compared this version with the old Parisian score, as reproduced in figure 4.3, which he had sent to him especially for this purpose, that he found that there was no tempo change: the "impudent tempo indication"[51] Allegro was missing.[52]

Wagner had already been struck in 1840 by the fact that the overture segued into the first scene, but now this observation turned into an important argument: the first scene begins with a restatement of the opening material from the overture, and for this reason the tempo had to be continuous throughout.[53] The "Allegro" part, Wagner concluded, was therefore already inscribed in the notes themselves: the fast figuration is fast because of its short note values, not because of a tempo change. When this material reappears, in Act I, scene 2, beginning in measure 3 of example 4.1, introducing Kalchas's recitative, it returns in halved note values (sixteenth notes of the overture turn into eighth notes here), and this time the tempo marking is Allegro.[54] (Wagner saw the motivic relation as given, whereas the similarities are in fact only approximate.) As the music should presumably be played at the same tempo both times, Wagner concluded, the overture could not have been marked Allegro. This misunderstood tempo was the key to the problem Wagner had always experienced with Gluck's music. The fault lay with the misdirected performance tradition.[55]

The traditional way of performing the overture, as marked in the "Spontini version" with both the Allegro marking and the sixteenth notes, Wagner argued, is therefore twice as fast as Gluck intended. For Wagner, this is nothing short of a "deformed" version of the music, a "trivial noise," as "anyone with taste and reason will be able to judge."[56] It is only with the restoration of "Gluck's original intention," residing in its correct performance, Wagner argued, that its inherent greatness comes to the fore: "By grasping the tempo in the only correct way I at once arrived at a sense of the great, the powerful and inimitable beauty of this tone-piece, whereas it had always left me cold before—as already mentioned—though I naturally had never dared to say as much."[57] It was only with Wagner's restoration of the score, which coincided

FIGURE 4.3 Two pages from Wagner's score of Gluck's *Iphigenie* (ca. 1790), with pencil markings in Wagner's hand. Reproduced by permission of the National Archives of the Richard Wagner Foundation, Bayreuth (Burrell Lot 107).

for him with a restoration of Gluck's true intentions, that he felt that its real greatness could be appreciated anew. At the same time, Wagner's reading acted as a defense against the apparently false ideas of Gluck's music that were prevalent in nineteenth-century concert halls. There is a distinct echo to his first encounter with Gluck, all those years ago in Vienna, when Wagner had not dared to speak up, intimidated by the aura of music-historical reverence

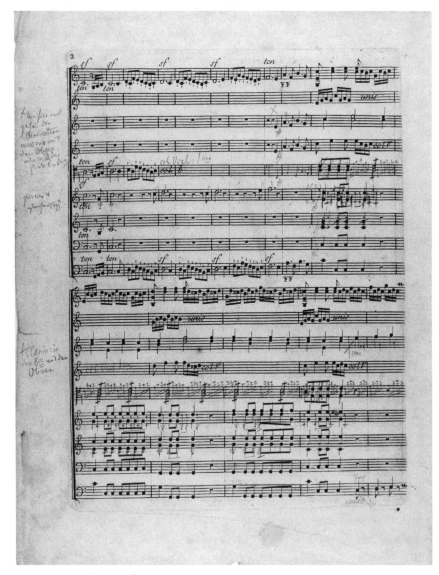

FIGURE 4.3 (*continued*)

that surrounded the older composer—even though this reverence was apparently based on a profound misunderstanding of his music.

With the removal of the misapprehension of Gluck's *Iphigenie,* Wagner moved on to a new reappraisal of its form: this time the form of the overture is not only determined by the struggle between the individual and the collective, but by four dramatic motives, which he described as follows and which are reproduced in example 4.2: a "motif of the call from painful, gnawing sorrow of the heart;" the "motif of force, of awe-inspiring, over-powering demand"

EXAMPLE 4.1 The beginning of Kalchas's recitative from Gluck's *Iphigenie in Aulis,* Act I, scene 2. Wagner was very interested in the rapid figuration, starting at measure 3. While any motivic resemblance is vague, Wagner argues that this figuration is a return of material from the overture in doubled note values (the sixteenth-notes of the overture are eighth-notes here). This is proof for Wagner that the "Allegro" marking of the overture is false and that it inevitably trivializes the overture in performance.

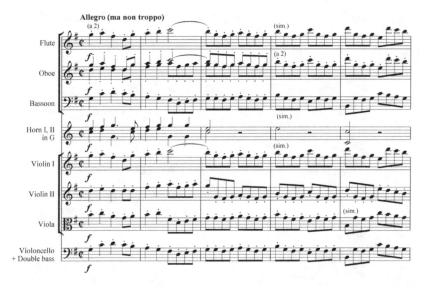

replaces the "unified general interest of the overwhelming mass" of the Greek army; the "motif of gracefulness, of virginal tenderness," which is identical with the earlier "particular interest of salvaging a single human life;" followed by a "motif of painful, tormented compassion." The entirety of the main part of the overture constitutes itself of the last three motifs, of a "continuous, diverse alternation" between them, which induces a feeling of "compassion of a sublimely tragic conflict," and leads directly into Agamemnon's opening scene.[58]

Wagner took this "continuous, diverse alternation" of motives as a starting point and aimed to be as little invasive as possible, that is to use as little new material as possible. This was in pointed opposition to the end supposedly composed by Mozart, which would fall into the category of "exultation overture" [*Jubelouvertüre*] that Wagner explicitly rejected, reproduced in example 4.3. The Mozart concert ending made use of earlier material but palpably cranked up the level of excitement, very much in the manner of final stretti: the ending begins with a startling harmonic swerve to E major and reshapes a number of motives in new contexts. Thus, twenty measures into the Mozart ending, the unison "motif of force, of awe-inspiring, over-powering

EXAMPLE 4.2 Wagner identifies the emotional content of Gluck's motives.

1. Motif of the call from painful, gnawing sorrow of the heart

2. Motif of force, of awe-inspiring, over-powering demand

3. Motif of gracefulness, of virginal tenderness

4. Motif of painful, tormented compassion

demand" is being developed and adapted so as to begin on different scale degrees; similarly, the opening motive of the big unison theme, which sounds suspiciously like the opening of Mozart's Jupiter symphony, comes into its own as a closing gesture. This kind of conclusion was not one that Wagner envisioned, mainly, one assumes, because of the dramatic tasks that the overture fulfilled in Wagner's thought: such a jubilant conclusion would signal the ending of the drama—and a false one at that.

Wagner's own version, shown in example 4.4, practiced restraint: it availed itself of the material with which the first scene opens and which harkens back to the opening of the overture. Conveniently for Wagner, the first sung entry is on the dominant, corresponding exactly to measures 12–19 of the overture. All that Wagner now had to do was to find a return to the tonic, for which he could use the opening measures. The only additions Wagner made to Gluck's music are a chromatic ascent in the top parts and the closing eleven measures, which reuse what he calls the motive of "painful, tormented compassion." As a token of how much he subjugated his own artistic will to Gluck's material, he even reverted to Gluck's original orchestration, which means that the instruments Wagner added in his arrangement—two clarinets, two additional horns, two trombones—fall silent toward the end. It seems that the authenticity of orchestration fell outside of what Wagner considered essential to musical fidelity, as long as the parts he reused in pursuit of his revision of the score were retained in their original form.

EXAMPLE 4.3 The "Mozart" ending to Gluck's overture to *Iphigenie in Aulis* was in fact composed by Johann Philipp Samuel Schmidt (shown here in piano reduction).

This ending has interesting implications for the form of the overture and its purported role in music history. The slow introduction is now a framing device, to which the overture returns at the end. It has no continuous dramatic development but is rounded in its form. This might not seem remarkable in its own right, but in the larger context of aesthetic debates at the time, this compositional decision has perhaps greater weight than first meets the ear. For 1854, the year Wagner completed the concert ending, was also the year in which Eduard Hanslick's treatise *Vom Musikalisch-Schönen* appeared,

EXAMPLE 4.3 *(continued)*

and the schism between autonomous instrumental music, on the one hand, and programmatic-dramatic music, on the other, which had been simmering throughout the nineteenth century, was finally complete.

At the same time, Wagner had sharpened his views on instrumental forms since 1840, the year of "Über die Ouvertüre." The notion of an "alternation" [*Wechsel*] of motives, which he first employed for Gluck's *Iphigenie* overture, was an important formal concept to Wagner at that time. He distinguished it from that of another fundamental principle, "development" [*Entwickelung*]. The over-ture with its slow-fast-slow form had originally been all about "alternation"

EXAMPLE 4.4 Wagner's concert ending. Wagner practices considerable restraint and mostly reuses Gluck's material. As the first measure of the example shows, the instruments Wagner added in his version—horns, clarinets, trumpets—drop out in Wagner's concert ending as soon as he departs from Gluck's musical text.

because, Wagner argued, its origins lay in dance. As such, this form is fundamentally not suitable for the representation of a dramatic idea, which would necessitate a "development."[59]

Gluck's *Iphigenie* is so successful as an overture, he argued, precisely because it eschews the developmental model:

> As you may remember, I once set up Gluck's Overture to *Iphigenia in Aulis* as a model, because the master, with surest feeling of the nature of the problem now before us, had here so admirably understood to open his drama with a play of moods and their opposites, in keeping with the Overture-form, and not with a development impossible in that form.[60]

This development-less form might have been the ideal form of the overture and its underlying principle of alternation. This was also the problem of the "Mozart" ending: in its final apotheosis and more supple motivic development, it suggested a clear goal-directed structure climaxing in the conclusion, which would have been difficult to reconcile with Wagner's ideal image of Gluck.

Wagner conceded that this formal ideal was never to be repeated: Beethoven's overtures already followed the dramatic path in his *Leonore III*—and Wagner's views on this work are unchanged from his earlier reflections on the overture. This time, however, his criticism is much more direct, as a clear attack on sonata form:

> But he who has eyes may see precisely by this overture how detrimental to the master the maintenance of the traditional form was bound to be. For who, at all capable of understanding such a work, will not agree with me when I assert that the repetition of the first part, after the middle section, is a weakness, due to which the idea of the work is deformed almost beyond recognition, all the more so since in all the other parts, especially at the end, the dramatic development is recognizable as the master's only determining principle?[61]

Now it was no longer the misguided tradition of the potpourri overture that deformed the idea of the overture, but the very tradition of sonata form itself, which with its need for recapitulation undermined the concept of "development." The only solution Wagner saw out of this dilemma was a more radical one—and his response to Hanslick's formalism: in pursuit of the progressively developmental tendencies of instrumental music, sonata form would have to be jettisoned altogether. The overture has either to retain its "alternation form" or lose its recapitulation altogether.

In the context of the debate, Wagner's polemical argument invariably leads to a glorification of Liszt: it is in his symphonic poems, which no longer rely on outmoded sonata forms, that Liszt has followed this developmental path to the utmost consequence, and his symphonic works must therefore be seen at the forefront of music history.[62] But the other winner from this polemic is Gluck: it is here that Gluck's *juste milieu* triumphs, its "alternation" form is forever original—even if this comes at the price of never being modern.

Reproducing/Producing Gluck

When Wagner said it was the false tempo that led to the misapprehension of Gluck's *Iphigenie,* and the misunderstanding of his genius, we might be led to assume that he was making a strong philological claim, trying to recuperate Gluck's true intentions on the basis of notation, as it can be recaptured from the written score in its earliest source as close to the original as possible.

But this form of appreciation is pointedly not historical; Mozart, who in Wagner's conception was from the same generation as Gluck, would presumably have had a keener historical appreciation of Gluck's style. In fact, Wagner cozied up with Gluck against Mozart: Wagner's argument implicitly deprecates Mozart's stature, for it claims no less than that Mozart—or Schmidt, for that matter—had not been able to see through the musical error he built on, and compounded, in composing the concert ending. (The fact that the arranger was not Mozart but Schmidt, who may or may not have been a lesser composer, is not a relevant counterargument: as mentioned above, Wagner never questioned the authenticity of the Mozart ending.) Despite Wagner's reassurances to the contrary, his account would give rise to concerns about Mozart's limited musical understanding.[63]

As José Bowen points out in an important study of Wagner's conducting aesthetics, Wagner was the first conductor who "sought to recreate the original external sound of an earlier work."[64] While one could call this arrangement "authentic" in tendency, in so far as Wagner believed he subjugated his own artistic opinion to that of the earlier composer, we should be careful to distinguish Wagner's particular branch of authenticity from the historicist performance traditions that later gained ground in the twentieth century and to which Wagner's conception owed very little. Rather, Wagner's claims reach much more unabashedly into the metaphysical realm. The significance that Wagner accorded to the tempo in his effort to restore the "great, powerful and inimitable beauty" of the overture implies two points: first, the correct appreciation of Gluck's music could only be warranted in performance, relying on music's temporality, it did not simply reside in the work as an abstract entity; and second, the correct performance of the work had to be based on the internal logic as communicated by the score, which provided an implicit, "intended" performance practice.[65]

So, when Wagner talked above about "the only correct way" to understand the *Iphigenie* overture, he was quite serious—for him, the tempo was not a mere matter of taste or personal preference, but one of inner necessity.[66] And it is also Liszt who was crucial in Wagner's non-historical appreciation of past masterworks because it was only through Liszt's performance of them that Wagner learned the transcendent value of great art. Wagner seems to have had this epiphany repeatedly with a number of different works—it was through Liszt's performance of Beethoven's *Hammerklavier* sonata,[67] Bach's C sharp minor fugue,[68] or Beethoven's final sonatas, that Wagner realized that Liszt's rendition went a long way beyond a mere reproduction of past masterworks:

> Whoever had frequent occasion to hear Liszt play Beethoven, for instance —particularly in a friendly circle—must surely have always been struck with the fact that there was no question here of re-production, but of genuine production. To accurately lay down the line that parts both functions, is much harder than one commonly assumes; thus much, however, has grown clear to me, that to be able to reproduce Beethoven one must oneself be able to produce.[69]

Liszt's performance caused Wagner—who was not a performer himself—to blur the line between performance and composition, or between reproduction and production, as Wagner calls it here. Performance, in Wagner's emphatic sense, comes to be an appropriation of another composer's work and a reshaping of the work in the correct, composer-intended way. In Wagner's concept, this idea does not grant license for arbitrary or personal performance preference, to stamp one's own personality on someone else's work. On the contrary, it is the strictest form of what he called the "correct performance," which borders on a mystical union between composer and performer.

Wagner's argument was blatant in its effort to transfer Liszt's undoubted fame as a performer to his much shakier reputation as a composer of symphonic poems: "What others achieve with pen and paper, he accomplishes himself at the piano," added Wagner, just to hammer home his point.[70] But it would be wrong to dismiss Wagner's argument, on this basis, as merely tendentious or borne of the heat of the polemic against Hanslick, in which the argument was used. Rather, he also considered his own conducting as a form of "productive reproduction," a performance on the orchestra, as it were, and developed this thought much further as an element in his own poetics.

The standard of "correctness" does remain a problem in Wagner's conception, founded as it necessarily is on an unquestionable and unchanging notion of musicality. He expressed this most clearly in an important letter to his friend Theodor Uhlig, a propos of Beethoven, the undisputed pinnacle of musical greatness:

> The poetic object of a composition by Beethoven can only be surmised by a composer because—as I remarked before—Beethoven communicated himself, involuntarily, only to the composer who feels exactly as he does, who shares the same training, and who has almost the same creative powers; this man alone is capable of giving the layman an understanding of these works.[71]

Wagner here drew a hermeneutic circle of musicality: the greatness of a Beethoven can only be understood by anyone who is his artistic equal (or nearly so).[72] Wagner's conception of the reproductive act is based on complete empathy with Beethoven's productive act, but for Wagner reproduction must go beyond production, as it further carries a communicative function: it explains Beethoven's greatness to the wider masses, who, Wagner contended, would not comprehend without the conductor's mediation.

Wagner does not explicitly refer to Gluck in this context, but we will see shortly how Wagner's performance practice of Beethoven is crucial to his "correct" understanding of Gluck in performance. As the letter to Uhlig underlines, Wagner's concept of musical greatness in performance seems to be predicated on two conditions, one apparently manifest and the other metaphysical: the correct reading of the score based on the internal logic of the work, and a spiritual, transcendent bond between composer and conductor (who must also be a composer). The conductor becomes the medium of past musical greatness.

Given Wagner's self-assurance that he satisfied both conditions with regard to Gluck's overture to *Iphigenie,* it should be astounding that Wagner's correct performance of the work in Dresden (as part of the whole opera, not with the new ending) was anything less than a resounding success, finally bringing Gluck's music back to the glory that it had unjustly been denied. Yet, the critics were not satisfied; in particular, the prominent Dresden critic Carl Banck was horrified by the rendition of the overture.[73] Wagner dismissed his objections by arguing that Banck was simply not used to his interpretation—which is to say that the problem lay merely with the communication between Wagner and his lay audience, not in the mystic dialogue between composer and composer-conductor. But Wagner went on to concede that there were certain points in his interpretation that played into the hands of the critics:

> At certain places, where the contrast between the main motives rises to the violence of passion, and particularly towards the end, in the eight bars before the last return of the great *unisono,* to me an acceleration of the time seemed indispensable; so that with the last re-entry of the main theme I had, just as necessarily for the character of this theme, to slacken down the tempo to its earlier breadth of flow.[74]

The critic saw this as a sign that the earlier tempo modulation was inconsistent and did not have any internal stringency. Wagner concluded in turn that the critic had not listened properly but was resigned to the thought that, as a critic, Banck would always have the final word.

It seems hard to disagree with the critic's argument that the internal logic of the tempo was not demonstrated in the performance. Wagner even seems to admit as much. But Wagner's theory of conducting practice—of which the critic evidently did not approve overall—makes it clear that there was no inherent contradiction for Wagner.

Wagner differentiated sharply between two conducting styles and, again, Mozart and Beethoven serve as the paradigms: Mozart, he argued, can be conducted straight through, without any tempo modulations, whereas Beethoven's music requires constant tempo modulations, even where they are not written out in the score.[75] In other words, Wagner's theory of conducting would require a distinction between two types of tempo modulations, which we could call structural and agogic (that is, dramatically or emotionally motivated). In the case of Gluck's overture, Wagner had demonstrated, at least to his own satisfaction, that the music required no structural tempo modulations, in contradiction of the standard performance tradition. It seems, however, that Wagner's interpretation of Gluck did call for agogic tempo modulations, and the case he made above was clearly motivated by the expressive content of the music.

The consequences of this performance decision, however, are weighty: it implies no less than that Wagner's performance of Gluck followed a Beethovenian model of conducting practice, not a Mozartian one. This impression is further strengthened when Wagner goes into the details of his performance of *Iphigenie.* The "motif of gracefulness, of virginal tenderness," reproduced

EXAMPLE 4.5 The "motif of gracefulness," Wagner argues, should be performed with a crescendo ending in a sudden piano—a technique he discovered in Beethoven's Ninth Symphony.

here in example 4.5, should be performed in Wagner's understanding with a particular effect: a crescendo ending in a sudden piano. This dynamic articulation is even applied twice in the course of the short two-measure motif.

It was precisely this motif that had always caused Wagner the greatest problems in its earlier, overly fast tempo: he had found it "risible."[76] But with its new dramatic dynamic shading Wagner had ennobled this motive, for this particular effect Wagner had learnt from none other than Beethoven, as he explained in his essay on the performance of the Ninth Symphony:

> The characteristically Beethovenian *crescendo,* ending, not in a *forte,* but in a sudden *piano:* this single nuance, so frequently recurring, is still so foreign to most of our orchestral players, that cautious conductors have made their bandsmen reverse the latter part of the *crescendo* into a sly *diminuendo,* to secure at least a timely entry of the *piano.*[77]

This Beethovenian performance practice is in stark contrast to the different formal model that Beethoven, as the representative of the failure of the "developmental" overture, represents vis-à-vis the "alternating" form of Gluck. Yet in the more rarefied realm of reproduction, where composer and conductor enter into a musical dialogue in a purely musical dimension, these formal differences paled into insignificance. In his performance practice, therefore, Wagner clearly aligned Gluck with Beethoven. In all likelihood this was an unconscious act, for Beethoven's name is never mentioned as a model in the context of the performance of Gluck's *Iphigenie.* And with good reason: for Wagner's very concept of the "correct" performance is based on its autonomous coherence of his reading of the musical text and a required immediacy in the spiritual bond between producer and reproducer.

Through the correct tempo, Wagner felt he quite literally breathed life into the marble statue that Gluck had become in the ears of his nineteenth-century audiences. In this spirit, he reminisced about his Dresden performances of the work, that as soon as the orchestra had got over its old habits and its initial trepidation, the "warm and lively-colored interpretation" met with the "most popular"—that is, for Wagner, the "least affected"—success.[78]

In this way, finally, Gluck's "gigantic dimensions" could be brought out through his music. This eventual "meeting of minds" between Wagner and Gluck, so different from their initial encounter a quarter-century earlier, took place in the apparently unmediated mystical space of musicality between producer and reproducer. It is ironic, and at the same time part and parcel of Wagner's artistic conception, that this immediate transcendent dialogue was only enabled by the mediation that Beethoven's model provided.

Gluck's Ghostly Return

Over the twenty-five years in which Wagner concerned himself with Gluck, his image of the classical composer had sharpened significantly from the initial expectations with which he approached his first performance of *Iphigenie in Tauris* as a nineteen-year-old. But in many ways, he did not go beyond the romantic image of the composer that E. T. A. Hoffmann had created in his novella and that had determined his impression before he came to Gluck's music—the first impression abided. Wagner's Gluck remained that mysterious character who never had a fixed place in his music-historical conception: as a truly classical composer, he existed outside his own time, ageless and undying, forever present but never modern.

For Wagner, Gluck's greatness only existed in performance. And just like the ghostly performance of *Armide* at the hands of "Ritter Gluck" with which Hoffmann's story climaxed, which was both an act of production and reproduction at the same time, Wagner's "correct" understanding of Gluck, his restoration of the apparently "original intention" of the score, was a creative act in the spirit of recreation. The problems arising from the tension between Wagner's at times liberal handling of the musical material, on the one hand, and his claim to textual fidelity, on the other, were reconciled under his transcendent notion of musicality, which erased the difference between production and reproduction and returned Gluck to his rightful place in the musical pantheon. Narrative and sounding music history were finally reunited—or so Wagner hoped.

It seems that, for Wagner, Gluck's perceived lack of modernity could be turned into a virtue: this made Gluck in many ways as great as Beethoven, but completely different from him. Wagner no longer expected to hear from Gluck the sounds with which Wilhelmine Schröder-Devrient had brought Leonore to life. Rather, he had managed to give Gluck his own "gigantic dimensions" through Beethoven, but independent from him. Not dissimilar from his idealization of ancient Greece, Gluck's music presented for Wagner a prelapsarian moment of immediacy before the onset of modernity, with its unstoppable process of progressive fragmentation, had begun. Such a moment was no longer possible, or indeed desirable, in composition, but it could be (re-)created in performance, though only if the performance was artistically impeccable.

Wagner was not normally given to backward-looking tendencies, and he was fully aware of the unusual position that Gluck fulfilled in his thinking. He ended his reflections on Gluck with a joke directed at his hostile critics, above all François-Joseph Fétis, hoping to get a rise out of them if they read the passage outside of the context. For this reason he even had it printed in widely spaced *Sperrschrift* to make the paragraph leap off the page:

> I hold it the most rational course for us, to perform nothing whatever of Gluck and confrères any more; for this reason, among others, that their creations are mostly performed so unintelligently that their impression, coupled with the respect instilled into us from our youth up, can only make us utterly confused and rob us of our last grain of productivity.[79]

Wagner was not renowned for the subtlety of his humor.[80] And this joke with its pretended iconoclasm was certainly no laughing matter: there is a sense in which Wagner was dead serious with every word he wrote in this paragraph. He explained the punch line: the proposed ban on Gluck was meant as a jibe against all those who had contributed to the misapprehension of Gluck's musical greatness, and who had replaced it with a merely textbookish awe in music history. They did not understand, in Wagner's eyes, that the only correct interpretation of Gluck's music could come from a musician with a disposition that equaled the composer's talent (or "very nearly," as he had written to Uhlig, which in this rather pessimistic context seems a crucial addition). That Mozart would, by implication, also have to be included in this list was a price it seems Wagner was prepared to pay.

CHAPTER FIVE | Collective Historia

Giants on the Shoulders of Dwarves

"Have you got the first *Monuments* volume?" wrote a noticeably delighted Brahms to his friend Eusebius Mandyczewski in 1892. Brahms, who was not easily roused to such enthusiasm, could hardly contain his excitement and continued impatiently, in a letter full of ellipses and fragmentary sentences:

> Beautiful organ works. And are you wallowing in contemplation and admiration for him, and—regarding Bach? What a great and deep nature he had, and of what great interest—considering Bach—everything is that concerns counterpoint, fugue, chorale and variation! What a rich summer this is! A new volume of Schütz has arrived, one of Bach is due out soon.[1]

Brahms may be forgiven in his euphoria for forgetting to mention in his letter what these organ works that caused such elation actually were: Samuel Scheidt's *Tabulatura nova* of 1624. This edition by Max Seiffert had appeared as the inaugural volume of one of the grandest editorial projects of the age, the *Denkmäler deutscher Tonkunst* series, or monuments of German musical art. Given that his enthusiasm was not so much directed at these works per se as rather at their significance in relation to Bach, it almost seems as if Scheidt's name was of secondary importance to Brahms.[2]

Or perhaps Brahms expected Mandyczewski to be au courant with this groundbreaking publication: the *Denkmäler deutscher Tonkunst* series was the philological pinnacle of an age steeped in historicism, it was conceived as the crowning glory of philological-critical work in nineteenth-century musicology.[3]

As its editor-in-chief, Philipp Spitta, explained, the *Denkmäler deutscher Tonkunst* series comprised "works whose historical and artistic significance have a right to continue to dwell among the German people"—as long as they dated from the sixteenth to eighteenth century and were written by a German composer.[4]

The political dimensions of the *Denkmäler* project recast music history along strict national boundaries. This was made more complicated by the relatively recent political reality of the unification of Germany of 1871 under Bismarck, where Austria had been excluded from this union, which ensured unrivaled predominance of the Prussian state.[5] Even a philologist deeply involved in the *Denkmäler* project, the Handel expert and avid gardener Friedrich Chrysander, recognized the problems with such political demarcations for music history, writing as early as 1874: "The *musical* German Empire is larger than the political one, as Austria is part of it. This bare fact alone should suffice to liberate us from this patriotic bombast."[6] The attempt to separate the musical traditions of Austria from Germany, however, after the political separation had been achieved, was one of the inevitable consequences of this project. In a dramatic reversal of fortunes, the composers most affected by this and the first victims of this political division of the cultural sphere were the eighteenth-century cosmopolitan Europeans—chief among them none other than Gluck, who had the misfortune of being born on Bavarian soil into a Bohemian family and working in Vienna for a large part of his life. A life of such cosmopolitan complexity was not easily classified along the exigencies of the modern political boundaries. After some quibbles, once it became clear that a complete edition was not forthcoming in 1914, a compromise was reached: selected works by Gluck were eventually divided between Austria and Germany.

In his excitement at the publication of Scheidt's *Tabulatura nova,* Brahms, who was famously a fervent supporter of Bismarck even when he lived in Vienna, showed no awareness of this political dimension. In fact, both he and Mandyczewski were well informed about the potential implications, being members of the editorial board of the Austrian rival series *Denkmäler der Tonkunst in Österreich,*[7] a counter-project that arose more out of political than musical necessity: in the preparations for the launch of the series in the 1880s, the *Denkmäler* series had briefly been conceived as a joint German-Austrian enterprise, but the venture had eventually bowed to the political and financial realities. Both sides went their separate ways—with subsidies, editorial work, and publication confined to strictly national contexts.[8] The German *Denkmäler* were sponsored by the Prussian state, edited from Berlin by Philipp Spitta and published by Breitkopf und Härtel in Leipzig, while the *Denkmäler* in Austria, under Viennese sponsorship, were edited by Guido Adler and initially published by Artaria in Vienna.[9] Meanwhile, the slight change in the Austrian title, *Denkmäler der Tonkunst in Österreich*—stressing the geographical rather than cultural-linguistic boundaries—reveals the particular problems in the conception of Austrian nationhood, as compared with the *Kulturnation,* which Germany had considered itself ever since Herder.[10]

Brahms's blithe wallowing in Scheidt's pre-Bachian chorale variations did not betray that on the political platform the publication of the *Tabulatura nova* caused considerable embarrassment: the Austrian ministry for culture, which sponsored the Austrian series, had evidently been unaware of the existence of a German rival project and curtly demanded an explanation from Guido Adler, the editor in chief of the *Denkmäler der Tonkunst in Österreich.* That this impression might have prevailed is hardly surprising: like Spitta in Prussian Germany, Adler had kindled the state officials' interest in the project with a specimen volume that highlighted the protection of the musical arts under the royal rulers of the previous century—Spitta had invoked the court of the enlightened Prussian monarch and passionate flutist Frederic the Great, while Adler had put together three volumes of compositions associated with the Habsburg Empire.[11] Both had tapped into the representational potential that such a project might offer to the state—they both invoked Freiherr vom Stein's *Monumenta Germaniae Historica* (founded 1819), a philological-critical edition of nationally important medieval documents. And both met with the financial support they had hoped for, though Spitta first had to convince Prussian state officials of the benefits of subsidizing even music beyond the Prussian boundaries.[12] Eventually, the cataloguing of the music of the two nations could begin.

The fractured and politically volatile nature of the *Denkmäler* projects, therefore, was hardly coincidental in these times of imperial rivalry. Nor was it a big surprise that this state-supported and politically motivated enterprise should become the central prestige project of the young discipline of musicology.[13] Even some German regions managed to claim musical independence within the *Denkmäler* project, where political independence was not a viable option: in 1899 the state of Bavaria also broke away from the Prussian-based project and initiated its own regional subseries, though, like the political entity it represented, it remained under the German umbrella.[14]

It is not easy to define what exactly constitutes a musical *Denkmal* in the philological-critical sense that the likes of Otto Jahn, Philipp Spitta, Friedrich Chrysander, and Guido Adler employed, beyond the proposition that they are works by composers deigned to be remembered by the nation: the *Denkmäler* that appeared in the respective national series are predominantly dedicated to selected works by little-known composers like Samuel Scheidt—

in other words, to composers that German music historians would habitually refer to as *Kleinmeister,* or "minor masters"; yet any such qualified terms are noticeably avoided in the explanatory commentaries of these musicologists.[15] And it is easy to see why they would shy away from such value judgments: the key to the philological method of the young discipline of historical musicology, as they saw it, lay in the abstention from aesthetic judgment, in favor of a "respect for that which has come to pass" (*Respekt vor dem Gewordenen*), in the famous expression by Philipp Spitta, which turns Rankean historicism into a moral obligation.[16] Any question of greatness had to be deferred, though it was far from defunct: the philological resurrection of these forgotten composers from the distant national past was justified with reference to historical figures whose central position in the musical canon was uncontested.

Thus, Spitta contended that the "oldest and perhaps most consequential 'monument of German musical art'"[17] was the complete Bach edition, launched in 1850 by the Leipzig *Bach Gesellschaft* in celebration of the composer's centennial. It was soon followed by the complete Handel edition, in 1859, likewise to mark the Handel centennial. The project was co-edited by Friedrich Chrysander, who supported his printing press from the sale of cucumbers and peaches grown in his garden, and the maverick literature scholar Georg Gottfried Gervinus. The concept of the later *Denkmäler* series is inextricable from these complete editions that centered on the two *Altklassiker,* Bach and Handel.[18]

The *Denkmäler* project is a collection on the grand scale—a collection of collections. While the complete works associated with the overall *Denkmäler* project constitute closed collections with pre-determined outlines, the *Denkmäler* series proper is an open-ended collection. As its stated goal is to represent the whole nation, it necessarily eschews completion. Its overall domain is so vast that it can only replace the goal of completion with that of providing a representative sample. As cultural historian Susan Stewart cautions, we always have to take it on trust that collected specimens in museums, libraries, and other collections really are representative of the whole.[19]

The hierarchy between the great composers Bach and Handel, on the one hand, and those largely unknown entities that needed to be resurrected through the *Denkmäler* series, on the other, was primarily expressed in the size of the editorial projects: the *Denkmäler* volumes were each dedicated to a different composer or a group of composers, whose works were published in selections, while the towering figures of music history were celebrated with a complete edition. These latter figures have to be imagined, to invert the familiar expression, as giants on the shoulders of dwarves: the principal interest of the *Denkmäler* series ultimately lay outside the works and minor composers thus resurrected, but rather in the additional light that these rediscovered works might shed on our historical understanding of their great successors. The crucial aspect of the *Denkmäler,* therefore, lay not in the individual works but in their relation and contribution to the later achievements of German music. In other words, as the dwarves carry their giants on their shoulders, they themselves grow stronger.

Brahms's somewhat oblique enthusiasm vis-à-vis Scheidt's *Tabulatura nova* was precisely in line with the basic idea of the *Denkmäler* project: the particular significance of the *Tabulatura nova* only unfolds its full web of meaning in the context of its musical progenitors and successors, which Brahms clearly recognized in his eagerness to relate Scheidt's works to those of Bach. In fact, in its very appearance, the *Tabulatura nova,* the first piece of German keyboard music to be printed in open score, could be seen as a brilliant demonstration of the effect of the *Denkmäler* idea, as the trajectory from obscure beginnings to the towering achievements of later generations. The newness announced in the title of the *Tabulatura nova* promised an innovative form of notation, different from the six-line staves common in Dutch and English music and from the letter tablature common in Germany.[20] In this layout, the *Tabulatura nova* has been thought of as a starting point of a pedagogical contrapuntal tradition leading up to Bach's *Art of Fugue;* foregrounding variation forms and the characteristic treatment of chorales, this imagined trajectory appears to highlight the pre-eminence of chorale fugues in German Baroque. It is hard to imagine a work that would more convincingly and emphatically mark a beginning from humble origins. In actual fact, however, the reason for choosing Scheidt's *Tabulatura nova* was much less high-flying: as a recent dissertation produced under Spitta's supervision, Seiffert's edition happened to be available when it was needed.[21]

As the web of relations is cast from earlier minor masters to the later great canonical figures—and back again—the editors appeared at times to get entangled in their conflicting aims: on the one hand, the interest in those figures was always predicated on an unquestioned admiration of Bach and Handel, while, on the other hand, they were at pains to stress the intrinsic qualities of these forgotten composers. This is where Spitta's alpine mountain range, discussed in chapter 1, becomes critical: just as Spitta treasures the whole landscape over a few individual towering summits, so lesser composers are needed for an enhanced appreciation of the eminent and great composers.[22] Spitta's colorful image of the alpine world shows that the *Denkmäler* project was not trying to shake up the musical canon: the hierarchies were clear and immutable. Dwarves would not turn into giants themselves. But rather, by locating the highest peaks in context, the horizon would broaden—Bach and Handel would emerge not as isolated phenomena, but as *primi inter pares* within a historical landscape.

No figure made this conflict between relatedness and intrinsic interest clearer than the case of Heinrich Schütz, Bach's and Handel's senior by exactly a century, who found himself at an intermediate stage. Contemporary thought would not place him in the same league as Bach and Handel, but it was conceivable that with some additional—that is, philological—support, he could stand on his own. In 1885 Schütz was granted a complete edition in his own right, again under the editorship of Philipp Spitta, and again to mark an anniversary. Spitta acknowledged the greater difficulty in legitimizing this project, as Schütz did not benefit from the same place in historical consciousness: "To the majority of our musicians, turning back by yet another century to Heinrich Schütz seemed like an antiquarian folly, to which they could not relate. Even those who judged this project more cautiously regarded it with dubious amazement."[23] However, in Spitta's view, increased exposure also leads to heightened appreciation. While it remained doubtful, even for Spitta, that all of Schütz's music would be loved, his complete edition at least generated further interest in the music of earlier times.[24] In other words, while Schütz was originally resurrected to enhance our understanding of Bach and Handel, the reassessment of his significance in music history—given material expression in the fact that he was granted a complete edition—in turn requires further contextualization of Schütz. Once the artistic links from the past are better understood, what may have seemed like antiquarian folly would shine out in full historical splendor:

> In order to recuperate [the connection to the unwonted forms common in Schütz's music], nothing is more beneficial than to show how a whole century thought musically in these and similar forms, how Schütz was the greatest among his contemporaries, but still pulled his weight alongside them. Then, that which is typical will separate itself from the individual, the former will be understood most easily in that way. On this foundation, it will gradually become easily intelligible and finally familiar. Thus Schütz presupposes our familiarity with Andreas Hammerschmidt, with Johann Hermann Schein, and Samuel Scheidt. At least, the latter two were the pride of their age and may well, in a few generations' time, become our pride again.[25]

This gigantic network of greatness across the ages would not have been possible to motivate but for the strong historicist leaning of his age: Bach and Handel, who are clearly at the center of the enterprise, cannot be properly understood without the "powerful forces that were active before and alongside them, which helped them to attain such greatness."[26]

As the *Denkmäler* delve further into the past, it is difficult to determine where to stop: when Spitta comes to the Scheins, Scheidts, and Hammerschmidts, the classic hermeneutic problem, which already beset the canonization of Schütz, unmistakably comes to the fore: the interest in these figures is predicated on our interest in Schütz, at the same time Spitta is at pains to present them as intrinsically worthy of our interest. There is no good reason to stop there: if Schein, Scheidt, and Hammerschmidt should be restored to the status that they possessed in their time, they would also deserve a more thorough contextualization—leading, potentially, to infinite regress. It is difficult to keep a lid on an open-ended collection. The only boundary to be found resides in the national exclusivity of the project. Thus, important Italian composers such as Monteverdi or Schütz's teacher Giovanni Gabrieli, whose influence on Schütz's music was decisive and demonstrable, do not get a mention in this context and remain outside the collection.

Schütz's example also demonstrates the sheer power of philology in the later nineteenth century, its active participation in the formation of musical trajectories and in the processes of music history. It is not for nothing that the second half of the nineteenth century has been described as the "heroic age" of musical scholarship.[27] Hugo Riemann even went so far as to end his *Geschichte der Musik 1800–1900* with a chapter on recent developments in musicology. To be sure, not everybody would have agreed with the notion that musicological work had become the driving force in musical culture, self-evident as it may have seemed to the music chroniclers of the late nineteenth century. An alternative view would be to regard it as an expression of the new self-confidence of the recently institutionalized discipline of musicology—the belated realization that those who write history are also empowered to make history. This undeniable tendency toward self-aggrandizement, however, is only a partial aspect in the overall endeavor. For many, the philological muscle of musicology became necessary to compensate for the shortcomings of contemporary composers. Regeneration, it was felt, could only come from a reflection on music's own past. It was to history, musicologists urged, reading the signs of the times, that composers should turn.

Spitta explicitly forbade musicologists in his methodological musings from judging ongoing processes.[28] But this proscription did not stop him from pronouncing doom on the state of contemporary music:

> There was a time when German composers felt rich enough to live on what they came up with by themselves. This self-confidence is beginning

to crumble. But they need not despair: they are backed up by a precious heritage that they can rely upon. At this stage, they can hardly sense just how sizeable it is. The *Denkmäler deutscher Tonkunst* will help reveal its size and its greatness.[29]

Salvation will come from the glorious past of the nation. The nationalistic tone of Spitta's peroration may seem typical of the time, but this should not distract us from the radical historicist departure from the discourse of monumentality that the *Denkmäler* project attempts. Most noticeable is the discrepancy between Spitta's diagnosis of the problem and the suggested remedy: while composers from the past were creative without the need for reflection, the modern age has lost this immediacy, and with that loss its creative power has stalled.

The solution Spitta has in mind is not to restore this "unexhausted youthful power,"[30] as he calls the achievements of past composers elsewhere, or to encourage creative independence in other ways, but rather to channel the inevitable need for reflection by providing the right material for such reflection. This must come, needless to say, from the national past. A new Golden Age cannot hope to regain the immediacy and richness—recalling the naïve/sentimental distinction in Schiller's sense—of the previous one, but must rather found its renewed self-confidence in reflection on the past. And for this task, only musicologists can lead the way.

Aesthetics and Ascetics

While the editorial and text-critical work of Spitta, Chrysander, and others undeniably enlarged the repertory of early music considerably, the consequences for the assumed integrity of these works that arose from their philological approach were not universally welcomed. Thus, in 1869 a propos of a performance of Gluck's *Armide*, none other than Eduard Hanslick complained about the "party of artistic zealots" who rejected any form of modernization of old works: the artist who adapts the works with conscientious cuts or a well-conceived reorchestration "seems more righteous in the interest of the work of art than those purists, who would rather sacrifice the living effect for the sake of philological faithfulness to the letter. They would rather see a work of music that seems to us insufficiently orchestrated fail in its original form than to resurrect it to renewed, living effect using modest help."[31]

Although Hanslick had mentioned no names in his review, Chrysander immediately picked up the gauntlet. The circumstance that a year later, in

1870, Hanslick was appointed the only full professor of musicology at the University of Vienna, and therefore appeared to speak with the full authoritative force of the academy, did not go unnoticed by the philologists, who in turn prided themselves on the scientific objectivity of their historical work and their rigorous academic training, often in the Classics.[32] (Chrysander, whose academic route had been more circuitous, was exceptional in this generation.[33]) Indeed, the bitter argument that unfolded during those years can best be understood in the light of competing paradigms, between the assumed immediacy of great musical works, and the postulated fidelity to the conditions of their creation—or, in the common shorthand of the time, between aesthetics and history.

At the core of the debate were arrangements of vocal works of Bach and Handel by the composer Robert Franz, which enjoyed considerable popularity and which were notably endorsed by Hanslick.[34] Franz used the published volumes of the new critical Bach and Handel editions for his own arrangements of these works, but he arranged them in a manner that frequently deviated from the established text and was considered irresponsible in the eyes of the philologists.

Franz's arrangements took the problem of figured bass realization as a starting point. Rejecting the keyboard instrument—harpsichord, organ, or indeed the modern piano—that was habitually used for the basso continuo of Bach's time, he opted instead for an orchestrated version of the continuo part.[35] In this he favored the use of clarinets and bassoons, as in his opinion, these instruments blended well and created a sonic world oriented by the organ sound he particularly associated with Bach's music. This orchestral effect, he asserted, "made one almost forget that it no longer lay in the hand of one person, the former accompanist."[36] For the harmonization of the figured bass, Franz preferred a highly contrapuntal realization, which often introduced free motivic imitation, using the "rich figuration, which surely could not be without a purpose" of these scores as a point of reference. At last, the organ sound was added here and there as reinforcement of tutti passages, to lend a festive touch to the whole and to add "any splendor still lacking."[37]

Franz admitted to taking a "liberal position vis-à-vis the original." He typically considered Bach's texts, even in their philologically edited versions, to be in "sketch-like form"[38]—in a state, in other words, that still awaited completion by the arranger. Occasionally, he would modify the vocal line, where he deemed this necessary, or he would deviate from the score where he felt the archaisms of the musical text could no longer be justified.[39] These adaptations were carried out, Franz explained, with the view to carefully familiarizing the larger public with Bach's works and musical expression, taking into account

EXAMPLE 5.1 (a) The opening of the tenor aria "Geduld" from Bach's *St. Matthew Passion,* scored for obbligato viola da gamba. Philipp Spitta found it difficult to recognize the *Bach Gesellschaft* edition underneath Robert Franz's lavish contrapuntal realization of Bach's figured bass for large orchestra.

the predilections "of the modern taste." This "modern taste" meant for Franz the emblematic employment of selected sonic features of Bach's music: Bach's prolific counterpoint becomes a synecdoche of his style, while the organ, now divested of its structural function, returns as a sounding signifier of Baroque splendor.

The results of Franz's arrangements look as shown in example 5.1a and 5.1b, taken from Bach's *St. Matthew Passion.*[40] Where the original text of the tenor aria "Geduld," reproduced in example 5.1a, is only accompanied by a bass line, scored for obbligato viola da gamba, Franz's version in example 5.1b adds a sonorous orchestral body of flutes, clarinets, bassoons, and full string orchestra.[41] Franz was evidently proud of his version of this aria, its intricate individual shadings in dynamics and articulation, and highlights it in the

EXAMPLE 5.1 (b) Robert Franz's version of the same aria Bach's *St. Matthew Passion* (1867). In his arrangement Franz was careful to mark the parts that were not originally by Bach with an "F" in front of each added staff.

preface of his edition. The solo part in this contrapuntal framework is thoroughly diffused right from the beginning. While each of the newly composed parts shows some polyphonic independence, giving the appearance of a colossal nine-part counterpoint, much of the part-writing is derivative or partly doubles other parts. (Take the eighth notes of the first violin part in measure 2: but for the phrasing, it could be taken as a motive derived from the opening cello line; this impression is fully dispelled when first clarinet and first bassoon join this line on each successive eighth note.) The comprehensive dynamic, expressive, and performance marks make up for what Franz perceived as a lack on Bach's part in that domain.[42] Franz's idea of Bach's music was completed in the "richness of euphony" (*Fülle des Wohllauts*), as an anonymous reviewer noted approvingly.[43]

Franz may have felt he was doing little more than "filling in the gaps" in what seemed to him like defective and incomplete passages in Bach's text, which prepared the music for an adequate contemporary performance.[44] For Franz, the crucial part to understanding Bach's music was the accompaniment, since the "actual center of gravity of [Baroque] music resided in it."[45] Difficult though it might seem to grasp the resemblance across the two scores of "Geduld," Franz's complex polyphonic textures, which give rise to the towering orchestral sound effects, can be traced back to the figured bass of Bach's text.

Needless to say, the philologists' camp soundly rejected Franz's arrangements of Bach's music. His mistake arose, allegedly, from the very fact that he took the accompaniment for the central ingredient. Heinrich Bellermann, Spitta's colleague in Berlin and author of an influential counterpoint treatise, took the most extreme adverse position in his claim that the ideal of Bach's time was informed by the *a capella* sound, even where instruments were included in the score. Voices were so central, Bellermann contended, that the organ was only required in a supporting role where the vocal forces were not of sufficient quality to carry the musical fabric by itself. The music of Bach and his contemporaries was therefore essentially vocal, "as they were surely still conscious that the origin of all music is in song."[46]

Bellermann's conjecture had clearly left solid philological ground. To be sure, his allies Spitta and Chrysander had somewhat more nuanced views on the matter. What was clear to all, however, was that the crux lay in the meaning of Bach's figured bass in his time and in theirs. Spitta explained:

One cannot help, in light of the facts, but feel that a performance of Bach's instrumental solos with figured bass which would have been to his satisfaction has become impossible for us. However, if the master had considered his way of accompanying as crucial to the overall effect, he would have written out an obbligato piano part.[47]

Spitta and Franz could agree that the tradition of improvising figured bass, which had become all but extinct in the nineteenth century, and particularly Bach's fabled art, had been irrecoverably lost. The consequences arising from this circumstance, however, led the two in very different directions.

It would be difficult to find fault with the compelling simplicity of Spitta's argument. Accordingly, in his editions he typically opted for a simple chordal realization of Bach's figured bass.[48] Brahms, who edited several volumes for both the Bach and Handel critical editions, would even go further than Spitta and argue that ideally no pre-given realization should be included in the editions, in line with the historical conventions.[49] Franz's most voluble supporter, the Breslau music director Julius Schaeffer, was aghast at Brahms's apparent laissez-faire attitude in this matter; he wrote to Franz: "[Brahms] said he had left the [harmonies over the] bass empty so that one could play 'anything one pleases' on the basis of it; he himself would play something completely different from what he had written; this latter [written version] might be assailable, and he might do something totally different again eight days later."[50]

For Schaeffer and Franz the possibility that the accompaniment might not be fixed carried a considerable risk, as it would leave open the possibility that the performed accompaniment could be inappropriate or unworthy of Bach.[51] The very complexity of the contrapuntal textures with which he filled the "gaps" in Bach's scores, were to vouchsafe the highest standards.

The simple chordal accompaniments favored by Spitta grew ultimately out of a similar insecurity.[52] The inability to know what Bach would have done, however, led him to the opposite conclusion: the less elaborate the proposed accompaniment, the smaller the risk is that anything wildly inappropriate might be performed—in this way, the intrusion into the established text is minimized. In other words, a chordal accompaniment is at least not wrong and could at best function as a form of damage control. Brahms seems to have argued in a similar vein. As Kallbeck reports, when asked, "'Do you think that Bach sitting at his organ accompanying arias would have been satisfied by the simple harmonic realization of the figured bass?' he replied: '*Quod licet Bacho not licet Francisco.*'"[53] Ironically perhaps, Brahms's adaptation of the Latin proverb, "what is permitted to Jupiter [Bach] is not permitted to an ox [Franz]," was quite right: the realization of figured bass was first and foremost a question of authority.

The diametric opposition in approach to the same situation speaks to their self-consciousness and their perceived function in the Bach revival. Franz emphatically approaches the task from the perspective of the artist: the more artful the realized accompaniment, the closer his version might be to Bach's fabled skills. He showed, supposedly, fidelity to Bach's artistic greatness, to his spirit, though not the letter of his music. To justify his artistic solution, Franz relied on a moment of inspirational epiphany, in which the correct realization came to him as a solution of the contrapuntal demands of the music: "And behold: to my pleasant surprise suddenly everything came to life, the voices only seemed to have waited to be written down and were obviously premeditated."[54] As the old masters, Franz continued, habitually played their accompaniments themselves, the mere figures were sufficient *aides-mémoire* to re-create the full sonic image. All that he, Franz, had done, was to re-create their polyphonic intentions in writing.[55]

Spitta's philological fidelity, by contrast, required that all intrusions must be kept to a minimum. Franz's contrapuntal excesses were particularly perilous as they might obscure the bass line—the only part of the accompaniment that was unquestionably authentic and fixed in writing.[56] This led to a paradoxical situation, where Chrysander and Bellermann tried to dismiss Franz for his subjectivity, his reliance on his own taste, and the fashion of his own time, while Franz and Schaeffer, tried insistently to discredit Chrysander's harmonizations on account of their technical weaknesses. Pedantically, though perhaps not fully without justification, Franz and Schaeffer list pages after pages of illegitimate consecutive fifths and octaves in Chrysander's editions, so as to underline that he lacked the artistic qualifications necessary for such a task.[57] As Elaine Kelly has noted in a recent reassessment of the debate, most of the passages singled out were actually harmonized by Brahms, who took this criticism very badly.[58]

For Franz, flawless counterpoint stands in for the lost art of Bach's extemporization—an art that philology cannot hope to recover, whereas for Chrysander and Spitta, the imposition of a second artistic personality necessarily results in a chimerical product. In other words, what they criticized in each other was that Chrysander was not an artist, while Franz was not an historian.

The two camps, which ended their acrimonious battle in forever new stand-offs, opposed each other in mutual misunderstanding. For the "aesthetes," Franz and his two spokespeople Hanslick and Schaeffer, the ascetic fearful philologists ended up with paper tigers, with bloodless corpses that make no effect on modern listeners.[59] For the philologists around Chrysander and Spitta, on the other hand, the full effect resided in the authentic treatment of the sources and could only be regained under full fidelity to the historical import of the work. Chrysander complained in a review about a performance of

Handel's *L'Allegro ed il Penseroso* (the *il Moderato* part was omitted), while unwittingly revealing himself as bearing precisely the characteristics of the "artistic zealot" of Hanslick's description:

> One hopes, after this yet again successful attempt, that the academy will achieve a complete performance of the *Allegro*. In this we follow the above reviewer in his wish that the original orchestral accompaniment (excluding any bothersome modern "arrangements") should be used, since it is only through those that the full effect is guaranteed. What would it be other than an act of barbaric tastelessness if one were to paint over old paintings? Is it not the same in music?[60]

In this creed, Chrysander left no doubt about his views on arrangers of Franz's ilk. Franz could certainly be reproached for taking the predilections and anxieties of his own age too seriously, at the expense of any historical fidelity. Yet his example sheds light on a question that the philologists had to face: can they afford to disregard the taste of their age? Does the effect of early music really shine forth simply by virtue of fidelity to the sources, as Chrysander seems to say?—Where Franz suffers from what could be called a Nietzschean *effectus* without *causa,* the opposite seems to be true in the case of Chrysander and his colleagues: their work is all about the *causae,* but their stated confidence that the *effectus* will automatically follow suit is rather more questionable.

Chrysander's comparison, however, of musical arrangements with "painting over old paintings"—or, put more neutrally, the restoration of historic art works—points to the wider implications of this debate. And, to be sure, the answer is less obvious than Chrysander might imagine here in his polemics. For the restoration and preservation movement of the late nineteenth century was concerned with precisely those issues. The positions embodied by Spitta–Chrysander–Brahms and Franz–Schaeffer–Hanslick can therefore usefully be reframed in the terms of Alois Riegl's conception of the historical monument, which we briefly encountered in chapter 1.

Let us take a step back to review the terms of the debate in context. To be sure, the Austrian art historian Riegl, a major figure in the historical preservation movement, explicitly eliminated musical monuments from his discussion, as he held "aural creations"[61] to be identical with their written scores; yet his ideas have a direct bearing on these musical debates. In the late nineteenth-century, Riegl noted a marked change in attitude toward monuments and the preservation movement, which particularly impinged on the way in which commemorative objects from past ages were tied to present-day concerns. The most common practice for the most part of the century, Riegl explained, had been to present old artifacts in modern guise, to present their exterior in as pristine and complete a fashion as possible, thus emphasizing what Riegl called the "newness-value" of old artifacts. Riegl explained that this practice aims "to remove every trace of natural decay, to restore every fragment to achieve the appearance of an integral whole,"[62] so as to present the artifact in forever fresh beauty.

The change that Riegl noted turned away from the "newness-value" and toward an attitude that cherished the "age-value" of the artifact instead, finding intrinsic value in its visible traces of age and decay. "Age-value" and "newness-value" were, needless to say, mutually conflicting, but they coincided insofar as they both derived their appeal from immediately visible features on the surface of the artifact—either its fresh appearance, or the traces of its age—and both, Riegl pointed out, held immediate appeal to the masses. The question for him was how newness or age were used in the construction of "historical value"—by which Riegl meant the more elusive quality that could only be determined by specialists, and that formed the basis of the evolutionary narratives on which commemorative institutions such as museums and collections commonly rest.

In other words, the preservationist movement had to pursue a different strategy if it wanted to preserve some of this "age-value" and respond to this interest in age as a quality in its own right. Obviously, the most radical appreciation of "age-value" would be to allow the artifacts to decay further. But barring the Romantic fascination with ruins, such an approach could not be in the preservationists' interest. To use Riegl's terms, the combination of "historical value" with "age-value" was carried out with the aim of maintaining "as genuine as possible a document for future art-historical research."[63] This combination, however, is much harder to sell to the public: "based as it is on scholarly research," he mused, it "is as little capable of winning the masses as are the doctrines of philosophy."[64]

Using his categories, we can construct Franz's position in light of the conventional nineteenth-century practice of preservation, where the historical value of a monument is predicated on the sensory appeal of its newness-value (which, in an extreme scenario, is nothing but the metaphorical "painting over of old masters" to freshen up their faded colors). The new approach, focused on the preservation of age-value, obviously corresponds to Spitta–Chrysander's position. Their philological editions offered a solid basis, which would be beneficial for posterity, but they certainly gave little immediate gratification. Small wonder: the performance of the works was not a primary concern, but came clearly after the establishment of a text that could be considered to be historically and philologically sound. The artistic purpose of the philological editions was far from self-evident, but the stakes were set high: the circle of beneficiaries was not immediate, but was supposed to lay the groundwork for all future times. The ideal that Spitta and Chrysander pursued within the logic of their museum-like historical collection was not the individual performance, but rather the promise of completion.

Historians Making History

After the fierce debates with Franz, Schaeffer, and Hanslick of the 1870s, it is no surprise that Spitta was keen to introduce a strict separation between the concerns of creative artists and those of philological musicologists: "The paths of work of artistic science," by which Spitta meant particularly musicology, "and of art must never run into each other."[65] The differences for Spitta lay in the "being" of the individual artwork for the composer, and the "becoming" as the central category of the musicologist's endeavor. The musicologist complemented the artist's sense of beauty with a deep-running commitment to truth; the composer's subjective, individual, and absolute work contrasted with the musicologist's objective, synoptic, and comparative approach, which necessarily led the musicologist beyond an engagement with the individual artwork to the composer's personality and the relative significance of the work to the whole age.[66]

Yet this separation brought along some difficult consequences. If artists and musicologists were to co-exist in peaceful if somewhat tense relations without ever trespassing onto each other's turf, why were musicologists necessary at all? The suggestion that a regeneration of musical composition could only come from a correct engagement with the past was obviously part of a philological program that had a glaring tautology at heart: musicologists had diagnosed a problem with contemporary music, which they claimed could only be remedied with history, and it fell to musicologists to provide that history. The framework of historicism provided both the diagnosis of the crisis and its cure. But it is not at all clear that either the diagnosis or the cure were similarly compelling outside this self-sustaining academic circle.

Faced with this difficult question, Spitta remained convinced that in certain circumstances, particularly in preparing the revival of musical works from the past, practicing musicians required the help of their academic colleagues. Spitta's conception of the strictly separated roles of musicians and musicologists seems somewhat limited, certainly in comparison with those earlier heady days of academic self-confidence: now the musicologist had nothing at all to do with either creative inspiration or with the performance of works. For both these artistic tasks, Spitta argued, full immersion in the work is required, whereas the scientific objectivity that a musicologist must retain at all times by the same token precluded such involved activities. The musicologist "cannot demand to unite in him what is by nature mutually exclusive."[67] It fell into the artists' domain both to create works, whether in composition or performance, and to mediate them to their audiences.

It was owing to the vicissitudes of modern life, Spitta argued, that such mediation between artist and audience was necessary—in effect, an artist's statement had to explain the work and set the correct mode of reception. Even where this meant that artists would have to leave their preferred non-verbal mode of expression, such literary mediation was indispensable: "Once the necessity of literary mediation is acknowledged, it has to be the artist himself who provides it. The discomfort that this may cause him will be bearable if he is convinced that this is a vital issue."[68] Reflection on artistic activity to convey its significance to the broad public, Spitta contended, was as important as the activity itself. Only in cases where artists were not in a position to issue such statements by themselves, which is to say when they were dead, would philologists have to take over this part. The sole task that remained for musicologists, in other words, was to be the mouthpiece of artists from the past who could no longer speak for themselves, or rather, whose living musical traditions had made such mediation unnecessary in their own times. Spitta explained:

> No work of art produces an effect without pre-conditions. It is always related to its background, which with its customs, views, and mentality forms the age in which it was created. In the course of the centuries, however, this background shifts or may collapse completely. The works of art appear in skewed relations, or even stand isolated and alien in desolate space. To give them back their necessary tools, the philologist first needs to apply his craft.[69]

Here Spitta's historicist creed comes to the fore: only the sober objectivity of the musicologist can re-create the original conditions that alone, in Spitta's view, explain the achievements of past composers. The musicologist is needed for turning the desolate musical space of the past into a richly flourishing landscape in which individual great works can shine forth from their natural, their historical habitat.

Spitta's historicist stance is pitted against the timeless dogmatic aesthetics so central to the thinking of Hanslick and his generation, as perhaps best expressed in Thibaut's venerated *Reinheit der Tonkunst:* "Genius is not bound to any age, and the Classical is imperishable."[70] Against this form of classicism, Spitta argued that even those great works from the past, which apparently stand up on their own, were not excluded from this gradual decline of their original historical conditions. Even Handel's *Messiah,* or other works whose performance history and popularity were virtually continuous, could not count as proof of a self-sustaining, transcendent kind of beauty:

> There are a few old works of art, which have a forever convincing and powerful effect up until the present day, no matter how far they are separated in time. One tends to rely on these works when one claims that the truly beautiful is the same at all times. It would probably be more appropriate to say: in these works the full richness of artistic content of both the artistic personality and its entire age issues forth with such strong energy that the viewer or listener is irresistibly drawn back into the past, but in such a way that what is strange seems immediately familiar, and what is an arbitrary custom of the age seems artistically necessary.[71]

From his historicist vantage point, Spitta suggested instead that the seeming familiarity and artistic necessity must be seen as special cases of the strangeness and difference that characterizes the past, and still require the view through the historian's lens. What aestheticians might consider as timeless greatness (a word Spitta tried to avoid at all costs here, describing it instead as "a forever convincing and powerful effect") was for Spitta based on both the individual creative personality and the age on the whole. While these factors were necessary, however, they were not sufficient for the effect of transcendent beauty. In Spitta's view, a particular circumstance or rather a kind of historical acoustical illusion was further required: what is in fact a strange musical experience *sounds* familiar, and what *seems* like artistic necessity is in fact nothing but the stylistic convention of a bygone age. For Spitta, it is the surplus element, the semblance of immediacy and the apparent absence of strangeness, that lends these works their special status. Here, too, the historian is therefore required to mediate an understanding of their beauty.

While Spitta was anxious to make the case against transcendent beauty, his explanation, drawing on mysterious energies, came close to equipping other instances, such as artistic personality and the genius of the age, with equivalent traits instead. What he seemed to suggest here is that certain artists had succeeded in channeling the full artistic achievement of their age into a single work of art, and that this level of achievement was immediately appreciable by audiences from later ages. This "second immediacy" is nothing but transcendence in sheep's clothing—except in one important respect: Spitta's explanation does not lend the work of art eternal presence, but rather absolutizes its pastness.

By and large, Chrysander agreed with Spitta's views (so much so, in fact, that Julius Schaeffer referred to them as a fused entity with the double-barreled name Spitta-Chrysander.[72]) The supreme works of the past—those which have attained the status of "classics" in the emphatic sense common in the late nineteenth century, also invoked by Thibaut above[73]—offered us a path to a thoroughgoing encounter with the past:

> Nothing higher exists in art than the individual perfect work, and no greater phenomenon does art history have to offer than the artist who has been able to achieve such a work. The reverence paid to the few so-called classics among the composers is therefore justified; their works show us art in its entirety, to be sure, not in its complete breadth and length but in a cross-section and at the highest level. The possession of the classics in print and performance will therefore always be the quickest and most general way to achieve the total enjoyment of art.[74]

Unlike Spitta, however, Chrysander was less anxious to deny the transcendent significance of these classic works of music. For him, it was not unthinkable that works of art could possess significance that transcended their own age and set an absolute standard, but this property of certain outstanding works could only emerge over time:

> In its own time [a supreme work of art] only possessed relative significance, as the best among many similar attempts of contemporaries. But soon it turned out, at first showing in the fading production among competitors, that its significance was *absolute* and that, in the final analysis, the work was neither created as a lucky accident, nor merely rose to fame as the consequence of a beneficial constellation of external circumstances, but that new spiritual forces were active at its inception, ideas of a characteristic kind, which caused it to come into being as a completely new creation.[75]

Like Spitta, Chrysander mystified the actual creative process in those supreme great works and sought its foundation in the outstanding artistic personality of the creator as the bottom line. These slight difference between Chrysander's and Spitta's notions of greatness, however, would lead to considerable consequences.

Spitta's insistence that the great works of the past do not possess eternal presence, but rather enable us to be drawn into the past, makes it hard, if not indeed impossible, to make good on his earlier promise that the engagement of the great works of the past will have a regenerative and inspiring effect on composers of the present—to give German composers back their former "self-confidence" by leading them back to their "precious heritage." Instead, it was Chrysander who rejected any creative import of the works of the past on present composers—even though the "absolute" status that his classics could achieve would presumably make them ideal models for posterity. Chrysander refused the notion that the works of the past can be models for the present:

> It flies in the face of nature that these forces, these ideas, would come into effect a second time under similar or equivalent conditions. All design is individual. Just as the same original thought cannot be conceived by two people at the same time and considering the same object, so the repetition and renovation of artistic creation in subsequent ages is utterly impossible.[76]

Chrysander placed even greater importance than Spitta on the artistic individuality of the creative personality—even though this would not necessarily follow from Chrysander's position vis-à-vis the "classics" and the absolute values that they represent. And while Chrysander's position may be read as an implicit criticism of Spitta, it also sounded rather like Nietzsche's caricature of monumental history gone awry—the historians who, disappointed by the present, hold aloft the past for its own sake and contend that "the monumental is never to be repeated, and to make sure it is not, they invoke the authority which the monumental derives from the past."[77] Historicism, in Nietzsche's view, reveals itself as a struggle for the authority over history, and therefore over the present.

The figure of Nietzsche and his trenchant criticism of the uses of history in his own time may not be out of place here, as Chrysander and Spitta's project clearly exhibited leanings that can be described as simultaneously "monumental" and "antiquarian" in Nietzsche's sense—two mutually opposing tendencies of the historicist age.[78] In their ambitions, the philologists have indeed become entangled in a number of glaring contradictions: first, they reject, on the one hand, the normative aesthetics of Hanslick while praising empiricist history, but, on the other hand, they admit *exempla classica* through the backdoor, which achieve (in Spitta's case in all but name) absolute normative status. Second, Spitta's ambition, on the one hand, to teach present musicians through exposure to the past is denied, on the other, by Chrysander's insistence on the irreducibility of historical facts. And third, the emphasis on abstract, synoptic relations, and "becoming," which Spitta considers as the salient features of musicological work, seems directly contradicted by Chrysander's and Spitta's unflinching interest in the biography of one particular composer: Handel and Bach, respectively.

These apparent discrepancies are solved in a maneuver that is as elegant as it is methodologically questionable. By arguing that the *exempla classica*—Bach and Handel—offer synoptic insight into their whole age, Chrysander and Spitta managed to cut the Gordian knot.[79] These dialectics would probably have left Hegel breathless: the universal *is* the particular, the "breadth of perspective" that characterized philological work can be gained from the special focus on one outstanding composer. History and aesthetics are united here in unholy matrimony, which, however, holds up in mutual support: the empiricist collection of material becomes the basis of aesthetic values, while the normative standards of the aesthetic derive their legitimacy from history.

But let us not be rash in criticizing these scholars. Before we dismiss this mixture of history and aesthetics as an ill-conceived chimera, we should remember that some of the most basic products of philological work are based on this mixture of assumptions.[80] Even a concept as common as that of editions of complete works, surely no controversial idea, rests significantly on it.[81] Outside a philological framework, in which completion is a token of scholarliness and functions as the principal justification of "complete works," it is not easy to explain why *every* work by a composer should be taken up in an edition of a composer's works, regardless of its individual artistic value.

In fact, the *Thomaskantor* Moritz Hauptmann reacted to Chrysander's complete Handel edition in typically cantankerous fashion: "Instead of a complete edition of Handel all we need are a few arias—the whole contains an awful lot of trash [*Schlendrian*] and trifles."[82] It takes Chrysander's central creed to explain this cornerstone of philological thinking:

> Breadth of perspective [*Fülle der Anschauung*] remains the foremost foundation of true and complete knowledge about art. Only with this at its basis can one particular danger be averted that often besets aesthetic examinations, that is the danger to raise individual observations to the level of general laws.[83]

The same directive also underlay Spitta's thought when he explained the necessity of complete critical editions: "Using Bach, Handel, and Schütz," he argued, "it could be shown for the first time to the world that for the historical understanding of an artistic personality from the past the precise and complete knowledge of all their works is indispensable. That sounds so self-evident that it might seem unnecessary to spell it out."[84]

In Spitta's view, a "general history of music cannot be written as long as one does not know the deeds of those men who made history."[85] One might well object that not every single work by Bach "made history," but Spitta would counter that only with the full "breadth of perspective" can we decode Bach's artistic personality. For Spitta, musical works—and that includes every single one, regardless of its individual historical impact—were the key to the artistic personality, which in turn opened up a full understanding of the age:[86] "The representation of the individual personality spreads into its environment, its age, and its pre-history: the light, lit brightly in one point, casts its shimmer over the surrounding darkness."[87] It is ultimately with reference to this "breadth of perspective" that a number of editorial policies and decisions can be explained. The search for ever new material with which to explain the position of the composers of the past only makes sense under this philological regime. Even Spitta and Chrysander were happy to admit that most this newly discovered music stood little chance of being loved, but this was simply not a relevant category in their philological framework.

This position may be historically responsible, but particularly the emphasis on the "breadth of perspective," Spitta's directive that history of music cannot be written until the evidence is complete, casts the *Denkmäler deutscher Tonkunst* project in a gloomy light. After all, its very nature as an open-ended collection precludes completion. It may be possible to collect the entire works of one composer, but as soon as we cast the net beyond individual composers, the whole search will necessarily remain fragmentary. The scholarly ideal of completion can only remain a vague promise.

This situation offers two equally bleak perspectives, which were analyzed sharply by Nietzsche, who was not coincidentally trained as a classical philologist himself. Either, he argued, the writing of history could get caught up in infinite regress, in endless antiquarian gathering of data at the expense of evaluation: "the habit of scholarliness continues without it and rotates in egoistic self-satisfaction around its own axis."[88] Nietzsche's prediction for the historian is dire: "Often he sinks so low that in the end he is content to gobble down any food whatever, even the dust of biographical minutiae."[89] In this scenario, the collection of newly discovered *Denkmäler* could become an end in itself and lose a sense of the higher value behind the enterprise. It turns into mere antiquarianism, where oldness and rarity become ends in themselves.

Or alternatively, Nietzsche argued, philological history becomes embedded in the paranoid search for self-identity, which gets bogged down in the referential interpretation of every triviality. In this case, the evaluative aspect of historical work is at the expense of the data collected:

The possession of ancestral goods changes its meaning in such a soul: *they* rather possess *it*. The trivial, circumscribed, decaying and obsolete acquire their own dignity and inviolability through the fact that the preserving and revering soul of the antiquarian man has emigrated into them and there made its home.[90]

Here every scrap of information, the most mundane compositional sketch, becomes charged with the politics of identity. This is Riegl's historical monument gone wild.

There can be no question that Spitta's and Chrysander's work was of supreme importance to later generations of musicologists, but the question of how their efforts relate to the regeneration of musical life as a whole is a little more difficult to answer. In light of Nietzsche's criticisms, we should review Spitta's claim that "it is only necessary to fill the imagination of mankind once again with the ideas [*Anschauungen*], which used to form the prerequisites of the works of art to educate them to connect these in vivid fashion, and then the artworks themselves . . . will start breathing again."[91] Spitta's service to living composers is not so much his suggestion that they all compose like Bach—he would probably have to agree with Chrysander that this is no longer possible—but rather to convey a sense that they are all part of an artistic movement that is larger than themselves, and that finds its completion and culmination in the nation.

Completing the Nation

The strict separation of labor between artists and musicologists that Spitta proposed also furthered the split between philological scholarship and musical practice: it was not necessary for musicologists to cater to either musicians' or audiences' tastes. More generally, the performance, the experience, of their edited works was not a central interest of the *Denkmäler* project. The principal concern was reserved for the establishment of the correct text. Whatever else followed would at least be carried out on solid philological ground. Thus, even Max Seiffert, the editor of Scheidt's *Tabulatura nova,* agreed that only parts of the collection had stood the test of time:

> Not everything that Scheidt proffers us in his 'Tabulatura nova' has retained its refreshing power up to today, but the few twigs that are still green are worthy of attentive contemplation to the fullest degree. One need merely plant them in soil that suits them, and in the hands of a valiant organist they will flourish again to become those viable creatures that used to edify the hearts of pious church-goers in former times.[92]

Again, the ideal of completeness guides and motivates the edition of this collection, while concerns about musicians' responses clearly take a back seat.[93] Unkindly but not without justification, a critic described the editions as a "mummified corpse dressed up in splendid robes."[94]

No one summed up the revolutionary potential in the philologists' concept of monumentality better than Spitta himself, when he declared in introducing the *Denkmäler* series: "I consider it to be one of the most important steps of progress of recent times that . . . works of art are regarded as documents, and that one is striving by all means to read and interpret them correctly, regardless of any aesthetic enjoyment."[95] Where Robert Franz and other composers stressed above all the sonic impact of music, created in performance or in their own compositions, Spitta countered this commitment to beauty with a categorical commitment to truth, a truth that would answer only to philological methods and textual criticism.[96] The philological ideal of *Fülle der Anschauung* had replaced Franz's earlier sonic ideal of *Fülle des Wohlklangs*.

Needless to say, the cornerstone of this commitment to truth was a historicist approach to musical greatness. Spitta took away from the idea of self-generated and self-generating genius and the belief in *creatio ex nihilo*, common in the nineteenth century, in favor of a contextual and empirical approach:

> Only few people have knowledge of that which exists around [Handel and Bach] although even the most basic historical experience would suggest that these composers could not have risen to their enormous heights without powerful forces that were active before and alongside them, which helped them to attain such greatness.[97]

In Spitta's conception, musical monumentality could no longer reside solely in isolated peaks, the highlights of the musical canon, but in the full alpine landscape—in Spitta's philological sublime, it was the sheer magnitude of the material covered that expressed the greatness of the musical tradition.

That such a monumental collection of musical *Denkmäler* need not be motivated by nationalist ideology shows Chrysander's similar effort in the 1860s and 1870s: he launched an editorial series titled *Denkmäler der Tonkunst* —without any national attribution. Instead, he described its task as presenting "such works from the past which possess abiding artistic value or were epochal in the evolution of musical art but might, due to their rarity, be known only to few."[98] Included in his series were a wide range of works by composers from the period "from Palestrina to Gluck and Haydn," but none of them were German: motets by Giovanni Pierluigi Palestrina (edited by Heinrich Bellermann, 1869), oratorios by Giacomo Carissimi (edited by Chrysander himself, 1870), string works by Arcangelo Corelli (edited by Joseph Joachim, 1871), harpsichord works by François Couperin (edited by Johannes Brahms, 1871)—followed, a little later, by volumes with works by Francesco Urio and Agostino Steffani.[99] As Chrysander had not placed much emphasis on commentary in this project, it is difficult to fully reconstruct the underlying rationale for each selected composer. It is safe to say, at least for the first four volumes, that he considered each of these composers to be exemplary in their respective genre or to be the origin of a compositional tradition in this genre.[100] The second batch, with works by Urio and Steffani, were edited explicitly with the view to Handel's compositions: both volumes contained works from which Handel had borrowed.[101]

It may well have been the radically open-ended nature of the collection, or the lack of a clear direction, that ultimately caused the series to fold after only a few years. The belated focus on Handel suggests that some guiding criteria were necessary to order and limit the flood of possible contenders. Building on Chrysander's first attempt, the new *Denkmäler* project in the 1890s was recast along national lines, which set clear constraints and made, in the spirit of the times, for a more successful enterprise. As Susan Stewart explains: "The collection is not constructed by its elements; rather, it comes to exist by means of its principle of organization."[102] It is in the nature of the collection to be significantly concerned with the formal aspect of classification: in the collection, history is synchronized—selected elements exist beside each other, in a hermetic biosphere. (The emphasis Chrysander placed earlier on "possessing the classics" comes literally true here.[103]) The contextualization that Spitta considered so central to his *Denkmäler* project is therefore also a form of decontextualization—as seen, for instance, in the refusal to acknowledge Gabrieli and Monteverdi as significant forebears of Schütz, since neither fulfilled the formal requirements of acceptance as German composers.

If the collection indeed precedes the inclusion of any of its elements by focusing on pre-existing criteria as its principle of organization, then Spitta's hope that the *Denkmäler* series will function as a fount from which contemporary composers would regain their lost self-confidence can only mean that they would, in the future, be deigned to become further specimens in this open-ended collection that represents the musical tradition of the German nation. In other words, the key to our initial question as to how exactly composers could benefit from the *Denkmäler* series would be the possibility that one day they themselves might form part of this gallery of immortal German composers, and that they might carry the torch to continue the tradition of German music.

It would not be up to Spitta—or to any musicologist, for that matter— to decide who qualified for inclusion, as part of his understanding of the task of the historian explicitly precluded him from commenting on ongoing artistic processes. Thus, after a glowing review in *Leipziger allgemeine musikalische Zeitung* of Brahms's *Triumphlied* of 1872—his most affirmatively nationalist musical work, memorably described by Wagner as "Handel, Mendelssohn and Schumann bound in leather"[104]—Joseph Müller, the editor, who was close to the circle around Chrysander and Spitta, added a postscript. He felt moved to dissent from the effusive praise lavished on Brahms—that 1870 was not merely a victory of German arms but also "a new epoch of art, at least of music"— asserting instead that historical judgments are not justifiable in this context.[105]

Some twenty years later, it seems, the time had come to make this categorical historical judgment on Brahms. Spitta wrote: "The way he stands now, he belongs to the powerful protectors and contributors of the age-old realm of German musical art. Posterity will not find anything to correct in this judgment."[106] A single contemporary composer that Spitta would admit in the *Denkmäler deutscher Tonkunst* might not seem like much, though perhaps quantity is not the issue in this case: as an exemplary specimen, Brahms would be able to go on, in Spitta's conception and given the proper philological support, to represent the entire age to future generations.

| Faustian Descents

Descending to the Mütter

Consider the most enigmatic scene in Goethe's *Faust II,* the "descent to the Mothers." In order to extend his powers beyond the Christian world, Faust needs to travel to the mysterious realm of the *Mütter*—a realm that no one has entered before. The *Mütter* are, as Mephistopheles explains mysteriously, "the unexplorable, never to be explored, the unimplorable, never to be implored."[1] So inexplicable are the *Mütter* that no one can quite tell who they are or how to get to their realm: they dwell outside of time and space, in a wholly different dimension.[2] It is not even clear whether one should descend or ascend to them.[3] Faust is simply instructed to stamp his foot on the ground and to disappear into the earth.[4]

The journey to the *Mütter* has long been recognized as a return into the womb and has been read as a primal scene, as it were, of Freudian ideas.[5] The *Mütter* are not anyone's mother, but "mothers" in the plural and in the abstract: they are a formidable maternal force, the quintessence of the Eternal-Feminine.[6] This awe-inspiring prospect, even hearing their name, terrifies Faust. He shudders—a perfectly appropriate response, which is at once a reassertion of his human nature in the presence of the sublime and a physical response to the overwhelming super-personal emotional force that the *Mütter* embody.[7] And he shudders with good reason: as Faust disappears into the earth, Mephistopheles wonders nonchalantly whether we shall ever see him again.[8]

As mothers, "goddesses"[9] even, the *Mütter* are the mystical source of life, an unmediated *Ur*-existence; they are a force of pure instinctual creativity, an unreflected lived experience. They lead a primeval existence in an originary

chaos—"some will be seated, some will stand or walk, there is no rule"[10]—
preceding any order, any laws, or indeed any words. This is why there is so
little to be said about the *Mütter:* they remain forever outside of representation. Words simply fail them in every sense. Even when Faust successfully returns from his sojourn at the *Mütter*'s realm, all he can relate of his experiences
are, by conventional standards, paradoxes: the "limitless" *Mütter* are both lonely
and gregarious; they are surrounded by the images of life that are simultaneously "lively" and "without life."[11] He can only stammer nonsense in his
attempt to describe a realm where logic, words, and concepts, do not prevail.
Nor can the *Mütter* see Faust. They can only see schematically, they "perceive
wraiths."[12] Nothing relating to them can be understood rationally, everything can only be intuited: yet what they have to offer is a deeper reality than
our rational world—the *Mütter* have access to the Platonic idea itself.

The figure of Faust, of course, had long been seen as the quintessential
"German character"—as early as 1918, Oswald Spengler announced the end
of the Faustian Age along with the whole decline of the West.[13] Perhaps more
than other ideologies, however, musical literature and musical thought under
the National Socialist regime was particularly beholden to this scene—the
musical realm of the mothers came particularly to the fore in the 1930s and
1940s.[14] When in 1944 Friedrich Blume declared in his attempt to define
a German quality in music that the "realm of the *Mütter* is not to be decoded
by a Faustian urge for knowledge,"[15] he only summarized what had been a
commonplace of interpretation over the previous ten or so years: the transcendent German quintessence—which had become a tireless quest of a National Socialist-inspired musicology[16]—or what, at any rate, passed for it, was
not to be found by rational or scholarly means, in other words by conventional
intellectualism. Instead, the academic traditions of their intellectual forefathers
—the generation of Spitta, Adler, Jahn, and others—had to be overcome by
reaching beyond their philological approach and delving into a realm of in-
tuitions and deeper spiritual truths.[17]

Modern commentators sometimes rashly dismiss such irrational talk as
wishy-washy and mystifying rhetoric, as it does not allow a handle on the subject at hand and seems to wallow in an indistinct instinctual "feeling," which
valorizes the subjectivity of the *Erlebnis* (or lived, unmediated experience)
over reflection. But the very significance of irrationalism as an argumentative
structure needs to be taken very seriously to understand this facet of German
musical thought.[18] Hans-Joachim Moser struck a similar tone at the end of
his *Kleine deutsche Musikgeschichte* of 1938, whose peroration is a paean of the
irrational in German music:

What we want in art is not the physical but the metaphysical, not the conveniently near but the distant idea, not clever awakeness but the childlike dream, not the dazzling dexterity of the nihilist show-off but the bitter seriousness of the ultimate meaning, even in the semblance of artistic play. . . . What we want (not just in Romanticism) is music as the expression of the humanly essential, as the representation of things in the center of feeling, as the festive presentation of a secret not expressible by other means; it may well be a lighthearted, smiling, happy secret, but a piece of spiritualism must be conveyed in it. And the urge to say that which is unsayable by words continuously guides the Germans toward instrumental music, as a language of communication with the spirit, and the spirits beyond that which is plainly communicable, as a sealing of symbols.[19]

Moser's dichotomous argumentative structure, typical of the time, does not shy away from polemical opposites that verge on the bizarre (would anyone opt for "the dazzling dexterity of the nihilist show-off"?). It is essentially an affirmation of the romantic metaphysics of absolute music with all its well-known, and by that time somewhat clichéd, attributes of articulating a truth that lies beyond words. In this sense, it might seem as if politically sanctioned musical thought of the 1930s did not progress much beyond the established traditions of nineteenth-century musical metaphysics.

Moser, it is true, builds on these traditional foundations, but it is easy to miss among Moser's well-worn stereotypes a surprisingly concrete conception of how to convey that which instrumental music has to say. Moser speaks of the "festive presentation" (*feiertägliche Bindung*)—or more literally, the "connections tied during or by means of holidays"—through which music's secret could be communicated.[20] In the broadest terms, the idea of such a "festive presentation" goes along with the unspoken ideology of absolute music, in the sense that it serves to lift its audiences beyond the everyday. The explicit functionalization of absolute music for celebratory purposes, however, would compromise its purposeless status.[21] There is an irreconcilable conflict between the alleged deeper reality of the realm of the *Mütter*, representing the higher wordless truths of instrumental music, and the appropriation for *Fest-* and *Feiertage* with their social message. In other words, the very notion of the unspeakability of music was to be articulated in the service of the festive celebrations under the National Socialists.

This functionalization of absolute music in the service of awe makes it into "higher utility music" (or *höhere Gebrauchsmusik*), to alter Heinrich Besseler's influential concept.[22] In many ways, Hitler was right on the mark when he explained that there is nothing quite like the eternal language of great art to silence the narrow-minded complainer.[23] We should be mindful of the fine difference between the awe-struck quiet contemplation that monumentality encourages and the shutting-up of complainers, as practiced by the National Socialist regime. Yet we must ask to what extent musical monumentality was complicit in this. Or could, contrariwise, a critical exploration of musical monumentality help us uncover the unspeakable secret of musical festivals under the National Socialist regime?

A New Space for Music

The most far-reaching programmatic suggestions as to such a "festive" functional appropriation of music came from the corner of early music scholars. In these attempts, the concept of "musical space," that is a space that music itself created in performance, not the performance space itself, was of paramount concern. Thus, in 1935, as we saw in chapter 1, Arnold Schering pondered the nature of musical monumentality, which he sought to exemplify in Bach and Handel.[24] "Magnitude" was the decisive criterion here—by which Schering meant not so much the duration of a piece during performance, but rather an imagined musical space that was articulated through its tonal structure:

> A monumental piece of music can never be imagined in a restricted musical space. Its expanse is achieved by sounding a broad tonal basis, the predominance of simple and full harmonies and a certain splendor and fullness of sound. The imagination does not conceive of these effects as a mere reinforcement of the normal—far from it—instead, the sensual impression is completed toward a representation [*Vorstellung*] by unconsciously reproducing the acoustical space corresponding to these extraordinary sonic events.[25]

Monumental music, in other words, would articulate and fill in vast imaginary tonal spaces. Ideally, these spaces would convey a sense of infinity and transcendence.[26] The key to this effect lay in the simplicity and clarity of the musical compositions—Schering suggested cantus firmus and ostinato techniques as well as fugal forms as exemplars of such clarity and simplicity. Fugal forms may seem like an odd choice, given their usual association with learnedness. All these techniques were linked, however, in that they were all supposed to convey a sense of a "single law" at work, an image which carried—at least since Kant—clear overtones of the sublime.[27]

FIGURE 6.1 Albert Speer's "Cathedral of Light" (1937). Photo by Heinrich Hoffmann © Bildarchiv Preussischer Kulturbesitz/Art Resource, NY.

It is difficult not to think of Albert Speer, Hitler's chief architect, and his idea of "light cathedrals" here. Using powerful floodlights against the night sky, which shone up their beams as vast colonnades of bright light, Speer created the illusion of overwhelmingly vast spaces that reached for the skies, as shown in figure 6.1. A favorite device for outdoors political rallies and cultural events, the "light cathedrals" enveloped and domed the sites of such important spectacles, and forged the participants into one community within this virtual space. Surrounded by such spectacular light effect, the individual crumbles against the overwhelming virtual space and turns, together with the other participants, into a mass ornament, an integral component blending into this utopian space.[28]

Music was never far off from such effects. Propaganda events habitually included fanfares to surround the audience with sound from all sides, as a direct sonic equivalent of the light cathedral, a similarly politicized space.[29] A propaganda poster, "Land of Music," shown in figure 6.2, combined the idea of the light cathedral with organ pipes, evoking its majestic sounds by means of the image.[30] As the observer moves his or her gaze up along the organ pipes, they gradually turn into stylized feathers forming the mighty wings of an eagle, the symbolic animal of the Realm. Music, space, and nation are thus combined in this powerful emblem.

FIGURE 6.2
"Germany—Land of Music"
(1935). © Deutsches Historisches
Museum—Bildarchiv.

The musicologist Heinrich Besseler, known mainly for his groundbreaking research in medieval music, also voiced a number of ideas about musical space. Unlike Schering, however, he started from the concrete performance space of medieval and Renaissance music. For him, monumental music was based "not on the employment of massed forces, but on the musico-dramatic use of large spaces, the expansion of word and sound over a powerful order, transcending normal human dimensions."[31] In Besseler's thinking, the nineteenth century typically constituted a negative pole; consequently, he set up his own concept of musical space in contrast to the idealized, internalized musical space that for him characterized nineteenth-century music. In early music, he argued, it was the performance space in which a genre emerged, that determined its musical features—such as polychoral effects or distant instrumental groups. Besseler called this, tantalizingly, its "living space" or *Lebensraum*.[32]

This *Lebensraum* of early music, however, went beyond mere acoustical concerns: as the organic connotations of the term suggest, Besseler's *Lebensraum* was inextricably bound up with the communal function of the musical traditions that emerge from and "live" in these musical spaces. Thus, he explained, to "transplant a genuine cult work such as a Bach cantata to the concert hall constitutes an intrusion into its original *Lebensraum*."[33]

Besseler was too shrewd a tactician not to be aware of the very topical political overtones of the term *Lebensraum,* and its blatant resonances with the aggressive expansionist politics of the regime.[34] He continued to describe his musical ecology of *Lebensraum:*

> What matters is not the uniqueness and particularity of a single work, but the communal, lasting, connecting element of a whole group of internally related images. For the *Lebensraum* of music is not created by the individual or arbitrarily changed. It exists *before* the individual work of art and *before* the great creator, as the result of a growing process whose roots reach deeply into race, *Volk,* landscape, history, and communal forms of living.[35]

Following Besseler's arguments, Schering's concept of the imaginary musical space would be exposed to the criticism that it is being essentially borne of the interiority of nineteenth-century symphonic aesthetics, which he imposed on the Baroque period of Bach and Handel. In his own conception, Besseler distinguished between the symphony as a "sounding cathedral" of interior space, and the church as the "space of cultish celebrations (irrespective of denominational differences)."[36] This addition, which accurately reflects National Socialist disdain for religious practice and ethics, but great interest in the ceremonial—"cultish"[37]—aspect of it, seems to suggest that Besseler was himself not free from such anachronisms.

And in fact, Besseler's underlying interest in "music and space" was guided by a very contemporary concern for "the *Fest-* und *Feiergestaltung* brought about by National Socialism"—and the "essential lived experience in contemporary life" (*das Grunderlebnis der Gegenwart*):

> The popular and state festivals of the Third Reich, the 1st of May, the Harvest festival, the events of the Nuremberg Rallies, as well as the style of festivities in the formations, orders and communities of city and countryside—not to mention the lived experience itself, the design of a great open-air space, the new use of artistic and musical forces —create a new *Lebensraum* for music today.[38]

In other words, Besseler's brand of monumental musical space was connected with the same social functions of music, in the service of festive, ceremonial, or modern cult rituals, that we already encountered in other aspects of National Socialist musical life.[39] Besseler knew, just as well as Schering and others, that art could be used to turn the masses into a nation.[40]

Nowhere do Schering's explanations of musical monumentality assume the same explicitly political tone as Besseler's do, but similarly tendentious undertones are clearly discernible. For Schering concluded that this imagined musical space of Baroque monumentality combines into an overall impression of "masculinity" that, in Schering's view, characterized the Baroque period. Glorifying "that which is the best and noblest in man: virtue, spiritual greatness, strength, valor, courage, love, faithfulness," he explained that the essential ethos of Baroque music was "severe and sturdy" [*herb und hart*].[41] In this context, Bach and Handel are more difficult to place—especially given that Schering himself declared that the music of Bach and Handel was inclined to the "gentle, soft, submissively pliable" element.[42]

Schering went on to explain that this "masculine" element of the Baroque goes hand in hand with the political system of absolutism: "This predominance of the masculine element—which, to the people, appeared to embody its highest perfection in the absolutist ruler—is connected with the fact that to the musician it did not matter whether he monumentalized divine or worldly majesty."[43] Given that Schering had also dismissed Baroque pomp and powdered wigs as "false, overblown, and unnatural," it seems that for a better understanding of Schering's position here we should not so much look back to Louis XIV's seventeenth century as to the absolutist rulers of Schering's own age and their own masculine self-image. His reference to the people [*Volk*], especially, who are handled as the ultimate arbiters over both masculinity and the degree of perfection of their absolutist ruler, would rather seem to betray a very astute contemporary political sensitivity.

In many ways, Schering's reinterpretation of Bach and Handel as masculine may seem more startling now than it would have been at the time. To a certain extent, Schering's interpretation was simply following the signs of the time. Consider, for instance, the bust of Bach (1916), depicted in figure 6.3, that had been placed in the Walhalla at Regensburg, the German Hall of Fame, as an early example of a style that was to gain prominence in the later 1920s.[44] It is easy to detect in this bust a similar kind of "severe and stark"[45] masculine traits carved into Bach's rather massive countenance that Schering associated with Baroque music. The bust exhibits simplified and cleanly articulated facial features: lips, nose, and forehead appear exaggerated. Bach's characteristic wig is so stylized as almost to resemble a helmet. This austere image is rounded off by an imposing set of arched eyebrows. And, like Schering's ideas, the bust bears a mere passing resemblance to pictorial representations dating from Bach's time. Instead, the style of the bust foreshadows that strange mixture of archaisms and disdain for ornaments or detail that has come to characterize the fascist styles of the 1930s, and that aim, as has been argued at length, to invoke images of longevity and transcendence.[46] Indeed, the masculinist ideology behind Schering's concept of Bachian monumentality here

FIGURE 6.3
Fritz Behn's bust of Johann Sebastian
Bach (1916) at the Walhalla near
Regensburg. Reproduced by permission
of Walhalla-Verwaltung, Regensburg.

resonates well, as a musicological equivalent, with the sculptures of an Arno
Breker or even the architecture of an Albert Speer.[47]

Not surprisingly, then, Schering's model placed great emphasis on the approval of the masses, while mass appeal is in turn associated with the Baroque
period:

> Music enters more powerfully than ever before into the strata of the
> leading spirits of the nations; it conquers spheres [of listeners] of an ed-
> ucational standard that it would previously have only captured in ex-
> ceptional cases. As its task consisted not only in satisfying connoisseurs
> but also amateurs of little education, even wholly unmusical ones, the
> average style had to be enhanced all the way to its greatest possible
> magnitude and force—that is: all the way to monumentality.[48]

The social task of monumentality, of uniting and shaping the masses, is clearly
articulated in Schering's model. Composers, by contrast, did not create monumental works in response to a social demand, he argued, but to follow an
innate urge to monumentalize: Bach "shared an urge with Handel to monumentalize *compulsively*."[49] In other words, Schering salvaged the Romantic idea
of the inspired genius composer, who served an essentially classical view of
the ethical purpose and function of art, dressed up in a distinctly modern and
political guise.

This insistence on an indistinct urge to monumentalize then allowed Schering to declare the object of monumentalization as being of secondary importance: Schering explained that the standard Baroque practices of recycling —such as Bach's self-borrowed cantatas, which habitually re-use profane ceremonial music in praise of divine authority—should by no means be taken as belittling of the heavenly majesty. Rather, he argued, monumentality in music is a more general phenomenon that does not simply apply to an individual person—human or divine—but rather to the "sum of the highest, super-individual characteristics, whose ethical significance remains the same, no matter on whom among mortals and immortals it is conferred."[50] In line with the National Socialists' rejection of religion while hanging on to the cult, rituals, and splendor thus decontextualized, this separation of monumental music from a specific honoree liberates transcendence as a purpose in its own right, which can then be transferred to fulfill other purposes.[51] It is hard to see how exactly Schering's argument could counter the charge of equivocating between heavenly and worldly rulers, but it could seem convincing in an intellectual context in which there is an even greater power than individuals divine or mortal.

Ultimately, in Schering's model, as well as in Besseler's musical *Lebensraum,* the spiritual substance of monumentality is provided by the nation. While Schering argued that the features of monumental music often build on religiously inspired materials—"Gregorian chant and protestant hymns, peculiar instrumental and thematic symbolisms, special contrapuntal-architectonic layout of the sound sources, room-acoustic effects etc."[52]—the communities that are shaped by and around monumental music follow strictly national lines. It is up to the composer, then, to capture the specificity of the national spirit and to monumentalize in a way befitting to the nation: "The only difference is that transcendence is found on a different level in each country."[53] It remains unclear in Schering's explanations how cosmopolitan composers fared abroad (Handel, for one, seems to be fully assimilated to the eudemonistic English spirit, while Gluck injected French music with a healthy dose of his German spirit).[54] But one thing is certain: Schering's monumentality transcends almost everything—even God—but not nationhood.

It is obvious that in developing a model of monumentality around (ostensibly) Bach's and Handel's music, Schering was looking to include other kinds of music as well. In fact, he explained that "all monumental music that has been created up to now has to measure to the standards set by Baroque models."[55] In other words, the "yearning for transcendence"[56] with which he summarized all monumental tendencies, also characterized his scholarly approach: it is less a stylistic analysis based on historical evidence than a set of guidelines; the values that Schering's Baroque period promoted transcend all subsequent stylistic periods and set binding standards for all eternity. Here again, any objections to the conflations and internal contradictions of the argument are brushed aside with reference to that deep, intuitive sense that cannot be approached with cold rationality: Schering concluded his argument by appealing to the "magical"[57] force of monumentality, contending that the mystery of monumentality "reveals itself solely to a feeling, discerning complete equilibrium of the parts, indubitable harmony of forces."[58] Meanwhile, propagandists knew that the situation was not quite as simple as Schering suggested: one could not simply rely on this indistinct "feeling," but, as we shall see, it had to be manipulated in the right way.

In this way, Besseler's and Schering's experiential conceptions of musical monumentality take us down the path into the non-rational world of the *Mütter* and play with the possibilities opened up in their alternative dimension: like the *Mütter,* the notions of musical space are "perceived wraiths"—the historical specificity of the material at hand is transformed into more general, transcendent programs, with particular relevance to their present time. We can speculate about the reasons that Schering and Besseler chose to clothe their ultimately systematic concerns in the language of historicism. One important factor is surely, first, that as music historians—and as sometime directors of the *Denkmäler deutscher Tonkunst* project (and its renamed National Socialist successor, *Das Erbe deutscher Musik,* which foregrounded the hereditary aspect of the project)—both Besseler and Schering had impeccable academic credentials.[59] Second, the cultural capital associated with the likes of Bach and Handel was such that they should serve as exemplary models, despite the obvious distortions that they had to suffer in the process. Third, while the musical traditions of the nineteenth century were undeniably central, the idealized relationship between music and society was thought to precede the bourgeois era. The sixteenth century, especially, served as the touchstone. Thus, Richard Strauss explained in his inaugural speech as director of the *Reichsmusikkammer* (Reich Music Chamber) that that age constituted the ideal synthesis, and a model, between artist and society.[60] (The sixteenth century, as Strauss imagined it, conspicuously resembled the utopian Nuremberg of Wagner's *Meistersinger.*) And fourth, considering the irrelevance of historical specificity, it appears that what matters is age per se: following Friedrich Blume's earlier argument and his insistence on unbroken national traditions, the rule of thumb seems to apply that the earlier a historical period, the more powerful the implications that the traditions are strong and worthy of preservation.[61]

Needless to say, Besseler and Schering diverge in many important respects. Besseler stressed the communal function of music, while Schering was more interested in the musical textures that can produce monumental effects. Nor need we worry whether the core of this form of monumentality, the functional musical space, should be understood in the sense of Heideggerian *Dasein* ("being-in-the-world"), in keeping with Besseler's intellectual lineage, or the Diltheyan *Erlebnis* ("lived experience"), which was more congenial to Schering's hermeneutical leanings.[62] What matters, rather, is to understand how both these attempts serve to use the unsayability topos of absolute music and refunctionalize it. While the appearance of historical research is maintained, what matters is not the accuracy of historical detail but rather the effect, the immediate experience, of the music. Schering summed it up: "So powerfully do the extraordinary, the super-normal features of its contents and the form of its representation seize us, that a long time after both have receded from our sight, not only does the elation continue in our soul but also our intellect is forced to continue pondering this experience [*das Erlebte*]."[63]

The central concern of musical space is not with meaning but with presence. We do not find out anything about the subsequent intellectual reflection of this experience: it remains a void to be filled with political content. What both scholars propose is a fantastical, immaterial building of sound that allows us temporary access into an alternative, unthinkable dimension.

The Problem of Time

Such concepts of "musical space" could be applied no better to a later composer than to Anton Bruckner. As Bruckner scholar Mathias Hansen has pointed out, "no other musician, not even Wagner or Richard Strauss, indeed no other great artist of the past was occupied so unconditionally and completely by fascist ideology as Bruckner."[64] What is more, Bruckner's music was habitually attributed to the mentality of earlier periods. Thus, in 1934 the Bruckner specialist Robert Haas declared him effectively the heir of an earlier musical sense: "The medieval feeling for spaciousness [*Weiträumigkeit*], which was retained throughout the Baroque way of life and the Enlightenment . . . could fully vibrate in ecstatic hymns praising the glory of God and the world."[65] Others, similarly, considered him the product of a "subterranean transmission of the South German-Austrian Baroque," a "continuer, indeed the consummator of an age-old world of expression, that flourished in the seventeenth and eighteenth centuries but was later swamped by other artistic currents, filled with powerful sensuality, love of brilliance, and a mighty richness of form drawn from 'preclassical,' appealingly 'objective' sense of form."[66] The attempt to classify Bruckner as a Romantic composer—that is to say a figure of his age—was resoundingly rejected, as his gigantic forms were felt to bear no relation to the formal miniatures of his Romantic contemporaries.[67]

A favorite for triumphal occasions in this respect was Bruckner's Fifth symphony, whose fugal finale—with the famous final chorale apotheosis—constituted a compendium of monumental effects just as Schering described them for Bach and Handel. What is more, the practice of performing this finale with an additional brass ensemble, positioned at the back of the concert hall, to reinforce the final chorale would seem to be the epitome of a palpable musical space. It is no surprise that in the process of replacing these versions with the *Originalfassungen* or *Urfassungen*[68] during the 1930s, this performance tradition was only given up with considerable reluctance.[69] In Bruckner's symphonies, after all, the "sounding cathedral" of absolute music and the "space of cultish celebrations" of earlier musical practices finally came together.

Thus it was only a matter of time before Bruckner was going to be associated with the *Mütter*. Richard Strauss's successor in the *Reichsmusikkammer*, Peter Raabe, made this clear in his speech for the Regensburg Bruckner festival of 1937: "For those to whom the works reveal themselves, listening [to Bruckner] is not merely an artistic enjoyment: it is a descent to the mothers, to the sources of feeling, to which leads no thinking, no knowledge or searching, but only the will to be small before the infinitude of creation, and to be great in striving for the good."[70] It is difficult in this context not to think of the popular *Dunkelkonzerte,* in which Bruckner's music was played in fully darkened concert halls, enveloping the audiences in a cathedral of sound, as a musical return into the womb.[71] Raabe's reading of the key scene describing Faust's encounter with the *Mütter,* with his strange emphasis on humility and goodness, may be a little eccentric among interpretations of *Faust,* but it shows the basic principle of individual insignificance in the presence of such overwhelming sounding bodies all the more clearly. He continued:

> What he saw in those blissful hours of creation could not be conveyed by words. For it is precisely the tremendous part of absolute music, which places it above all the other arts—including dramatic music, including song, mass, oratorio—that it is their task to pronounce that which can be said neither in words nor in gestures. And if we were to try to pin down this mysterious power of symphonic art, it could only be in the words of Goethe's *chorus mysticus* [from the end of *Faust II*]: 'the indescribable, here it is done.'[72]

Bruckner's own lack of written commentary on his work was a rarity among composers in the later nineteenth century. Here the absence of words is turned into the unsayability topos of absolute music. Like Faust, who could not express what he saw in the realm of the *Mütter,* Bruckner apparently kept silent about his music because wordlessness was the only adequate description for the ambition of his work. Bruckner's silence and his music, we are told, said more than words could say.

Werner Danckert, in picking up the same metaphor two years later, homed in particularly on the pre-Christian part of this image: "The Christian-Catholic element formed, so to speak, merely a transition to a life based on supreme antiquity, toward that primeval pagan emotional circle that venerates the eternal-feminine, the motherly, as the life-giving, the cosmic power itself."[73] In his attempt to push back the spiritual affinity of Bruckner's music to a pagan age before Christianity, he had to argue away the biographical and musical impact of Catholicism on Bruckner as a mere superficiality. He did so to endow Bruckner's music with an *ur-* quality, a raw primordial and sempiternal power, that was particularly associated with the philosophy of origins, and hence the *Mütter.* It might seem as if Dankert came unwittingly close to feminizing Bruckner. The gender discourses of National Socialism, however, predominantly excluded mothers from sexuality: their role was at once heroic and desexualized.[74]

The philological activities that surrounded Bruckner and his *Urfassungen* during those years were fed from similar sources—a belief in the superiority of the originary utterance, which was seen as a guarantee for the primeval force of Bruckner's composition.[75] Thus Wilhelm Furtwängler argued:

> For our knowledge of Bruckner's tonal language, Brucknerian will-to-style and feeling, the *Urfassungen* are exceptionally significant and instructive: the differences lie both in its instrumentation and in its tempo changes; with both it is the greater simplicity, unity, straightforwardness that characterizes the *Urfassung* and corresponds more closely to the spacious musical sensitivities of the Master.[76]

Here the connections between the crucial simplicity of the *Urfassung* (which in Schering's sense would also mean that they possess greater monumentality) and the sense of spaciousness are forged most clearly. For the genuine *Lebensraum* of Bruckner's "symphonic cathedral," in other words, the *Urfassung* is indispensable. The Eighth Symphony is a case in point: Bruckner authorized Felix Weingartner in a famous letter to cut the finale of the Eighth: "It would be much too long and is valid only for a later age, and indeed only for a circle of friends and connoisseurs."[77] For the *Urfassungen* movement, this admission was crucial: this later age, the Golden Age for Bruckner, had finally begun.[78]

Some authors, like Otto Schumann, brought a racial explanation for *Urfassungen* into play: the "Nordic" race (located in areas of Germany that conveniently coincided with the Protestant regions), austere and beholden to the whole, would consider the work with the view to preserving its integrity as a whole. By contrast, the South German and Austrian "Dinaric" race (who also were predominantly Catholic) was particularly in thrall to the splendor of the individual moment. The sensuous experience from moment to moment mattered most to them, just like Catholic mass—there could not be enough of those magical moments, their basic penchant was instinctually for long versions.[79] Not coincidentally, Schumann's explanation of the sense-driven "Dinaric" outlook matches closely Schering's concept of monumentality.

As philological exactitude was enlisted to bring about the authentic *Erlebnis,* other commentators were more emphatic in their demand for unadulterated—and uncut—versions of Bruckner's works:

> More drastic still than retouchings are cuts, for they tear up the formal
> unity and often render the developmental processes incomprehensible.
> . . . It is obvious how such interventions could disfigure the construc-
> tion of whole movements, could render it unrecognizable. . . . We have
> been deprived of the originals; not only do we have the right, we have a
> veritable duty to demand them.[80]

Indeed, the very lengths of Bruckner's music seemed to be a feature that was particularly associated with its essentially German nature. Ernst Bücken, for one, argued that the miniature "temporality of Romanticism"[81] could not be applied to Bruckner. Instead, he saw a direct correlation between the magnitude Bruckner's monumental forms and the ascent of the German nation to greatness.[82] And Karl Grunsky would go even further in a nationalistic diatribe: "For foreign audiences the length of Bruckner's symphonies is hard to bear," only to continue in an almost charming aside, which should strictly speaking cause his entire racist framework to collapse: "One can hardly claim, however, that every German could follow them without problems."[83]

This was precisely the crux with Bruckner. For all the emphatic nationalist rhetoric with which Bruckner and his spacious and expansive forms are appraised, and for all its propensity for "musical space," the music really did not enjoy as much popular support as his proponents would have wished. In this, the lengths—and especially the greater lengths of the restored *Urfassungen*— proved the biggest stumbling block. Critics could well argue that the magnitude of Bruckner's symphonies corresponded to the ascent of the German nation, but this did not mean much if the people who were to identify with them were bored or put off by the sheer lengths of the symphonies. What had to happen was to find a way to make the nation *experience* the greatness of Bruckner. In this, philology could only go so far.

Bruckner's Popularity

It is here, at last, that the wordlessness of the *Mütter* has doubled up on the National Socialist appropriation of Bruckner and led into an impasse. On the one hand, the ideology of origins valued primordial truths—or, to use the pseudo-scientific parlance of the time, it recognized Bruckner's "chthonic-telluric"[84] elements (which can best be translated as "earthy-earthy"). On this basis, the *Urfassungen* were considered to provide a more authentic, and therefore more immediate, access to his musical creation. This, in turn, added to the valorization of the lengths of the symphonies, which were already considerable. More broadly, the imperative to honor his artistic integrity meant that only the totality of his symphonic creations—without cuts or alterations —could provide access to the spiritual depths his music conveyed wordlessly. In other words, the very dimensions of Bruckner's symphonies became an expression of their quintessential Germanness. On the other hand, however, the very same ideology of the *Mütter* also built on the immediacy of a "lived experience" that preceded—or defied—rational reflection and verbal description. The more *völkisch* interpretation of this ideology, therefore, demanded a uniform and unmediated, felt understanding of Bruckner's music, irrespective of prior education. And that was evidently not forthcoming.

When put in these more general terms, in fact, the problem of Bruckner falls squarely into wider debates about popularity and high culture that occupied National Socialist policy makers at all levels.[85] More than for other political movements, the task of bringing the values of high art in line with the appeal of popular art was imperative to the cultural politics of the National Socialist regime. On the one hand, the regime was eager to cultivate an image as defenders of culture in its battle to shake off its own image as philistines.[86] (A quick glance at newspaper reports of cultural events organized for the SS, in fact, should instantly remove any doubt: these events were, more often than not, crash courses in cultural literacy.[87]) On the other hand, the populist anti-modernist polemics against elite and avant-garde art, which was typically denounced as "degenerate,"[88] insisted on the immediate communal relevance of art and advocated for a return to traditional values in art.[89] As Hitler himself explained in his speech opening the 1937 Great German Art Exhibition: "The artist not only creates for the artist. May he create, like everybody else, for the people! And we will ensure that the people [*Volk*] will from now on be called upon to be the judge of his art."[90]

How exactly the two poles of high art and popular culture should be brought together was anyone's guess.[91] This question in fact became the topic of a long debate that was mainly carried out on the pages of *Die Musik,* the official musicological organ of the National Socialist regime.[92] The bottom line, as was clear to everybody but was rarely explicitly acknowledged, was that "the cultural value of a kind of music does not always correspond to its utility value."[93] Even the National Socialist mantra that the *Volk* was the ultimate arbiter in such matters did not help, as the crucial facet whether what mattered was what the *Volk* wanted, or what it *ought* to want, remained tantalizingly vague.

It was easy to mock this problem, as did the composer and music journalist Walter Abendroth in 1934:

> Beethoven, Schubert, Schumann, Brahms, Wagner, Bruckner are supposed to have created their works only for a small stratum of educated people? They are supposed to have expressed nothing but their individual emotions, which were of no consequence to the nation [*Volk*] among which they lived? . . . Even today—after 50, 60, 70, 100, and more years—a symphony by Bruckner or Brahms, a *Tristan,* a chamber music work by Beethoven, can only be truly enjoyed by "educated" people. Millions of others are left cold, they do not get anything out of it, do not even *want* to know about it. . . . At least, that's what people say.[94]

Against this mixture of idealism and faith in the artistic instincts of the people, other commentators put a more pessimistic (but still very ambitious) outlook:

> As modernity progresses, it is advisable to pick up where the nation [*Volk*] really stands today. And if we are honest for once, this is at most at Wagner's *Meistersinger,* not yet *Tristan* or Bruckner's last symphonies, or Reger's final works. Here it is necessary to prepare an inner comprehension of these latter works by means of good performances of simpler modern works, which can be conceived as preliminary steps to the greater ones.[95]

It goes without saying that both commentators only consider works of the tonal tradition, which in most cases ends with Wagner and Bruckner, or exceptionally with Reger, Pfitzner, and Strauss. Some suggested, similarly, that composers orient themselves by the greatest composers of popular music, Schubert and Johann Strauss—the highest of the low, so to speak—to write music in a happy medium.[96]

The idea of any form of lowering standards, however, whether it be as a preliminary step for the full enjoyment of more demanding works or as a way of marking up popular music, met with vigorous rejection in some quarters. The idea, for instance, of profaning Wagner by popularizing his works, was anathema to many.[97] And speaking for German radio programming, Kurt Herbst argued vigorously against any conflation of high and low. Using Beethoven as an example, he contends: "This is not about 'Beethoven' as a concept describing a person, but about Beethoven's art and the Beethovenian capacity to capture a spiritual expressive potential in an immediate, i.e. stylish tonal context."[98] In this view, the German musical tradition is first and foremost cultural capital whose value must not be inflated with popular music. In other words, Beethoven should not so much be listened to as rather be appreciated reverently.

The values of popularity and those of culture are far from being identical. For Herbst, "popular" and "serious" music are both different forms of organizing time, both of which form necessary demands of the "natural feeling of the people" [*natürliches Volksempfinden*]: popular music is "lighthearted relief" [*heitere Auslösung*] and serious music "inner absorption" [*innere Sammlung*].[99] The attempt to conflate the two, Herbst argued, would be misguided, as the communal tasks of either genre is distinct.

The crucial category is that of entertainment. While it would be wrong to argue that one type of music was entertaining and the other was not, the different purposes of both kinds of art meant that both represent different types of entertainment:

> In popular music the entertaining element is a necessary and purposeful component or, in other words, an essential stylistic feature of the musical object itself, while the entertaining element in art music or so-called serious music is merely incidental. Put differently: in serious music the entertaining element forms the experiential state of that listener who listens to this music appropriately and correctly, while in actual popular music the entertaining element belongs to the experience or (put more simply) to the musical object.[100]

Herbst was at pains to avoid the word, or even the un-*völkisch* connotations, of elitist "intellectualism," but that is precisely what he was talking about. The purpose of popular music was an experiential kind of entertainment, while the entertainment value of art music was more intellectual. This latter kind of entertainment was not so much located in its nature or structure as rather in the intellectual capacity and educational standard of its listeners. The specific difference, Herbst continued, is that popular music tends to be well adapted to a specific non-musical purpose—it is functional, in short: *Gebrauchsmusik.*[101] The implied opposite, the essence of serious art music, was the absolute nature and the emphatic work concept of Romantic music aesthetics.

Herbst, a cultural mandarin, fell short of offering any solutions: he advocated for the strict separation of popular and serious music, each with its own specific form of entertainment. However, Schering's model suggests that even monumentality was not fully without any function, since "it implies a form of purpose, namely that of the will-to-eternalize [*Verewigenwollen*]."[102] One important facet of Schering's model, therefore, is the double-edged relation to the tradition of absolute music: while it plays with the idea of the transcendence of canonical works, he also admits that this feature is itself a function. In fact, this connection offers a way to link both aspects of entertainment—the immediate, experiential form of popular music and the more rarefied cultural appeal of great art should come together in a celebration of transcendence.

The "Regensburg Bruckner Erlebnis"

Salvation came from the modern media, which over the previous decade had been able to gather experience with the very emotional force that National Socialist policy makers were at pains to channel and manipulate. The visual media, especially, had been able to hone music as a pure emotional tool:

> Experience has taught us that only music is capable of both preparing a mood slowly and gradually, and of turning a mood into its opposite in the shortest time. Music may lose its acoustical value—as can already be gleaned from the fact that a large part [of the audiences] does not even notice the music, or at least the beginning of its acoustic effects. Their attention is drawn so strongly to the action, the moving image, that those people do not even manage also to pay attention to the—apparently incidental—music. But it is precisely this observation that shows most clearly the progress made in employing music for films: no longer does it work with the acoustic impression, but with the deeper spiritual impression.[103]

The main Bruckner celebrations could not take place in 1936, the fortieth anniversary of his death, owing to the Olympic Games. But in the following year he was honored with a bust unveiled at Walhalla—the first and only such bust to be added to the German Hall of Fame in the twelve years of the "Thousand Year Realm."

This important event, a paragon of how the National Socialist organizers availed themselves of this monumental power of music and image, has been studied carefully by scholars such as Albrecht Dümling, Bryan Gilliam, Christa Brüstle, and others.[104] In building on and adding to the work of these scholars, we will revisit the 1937 Bruckner festival, to examine how exactly the *Erlebnis* of the monument, in which so much cultural capital had been invested, was choreographed.

The celebration was billed as a veritable *"Regensburger Bruckner-Erlebnis,"* as the title of the glowing report in *Zeitschrift für Musik* had it. (In 1933, in the spirit of the times, Schumann's august journal had its epithet *"Neue"* removed.) In organizing this four-day festival of concerts and events relating to Bruckner, Joseph Goebbels had thought of everything—including hiring the entire Danube fleet, which were seen gliding up and down the river, to add to the overall impression.[105] Just how much these impressions were an integral part of the celebrations becomes clear in a passage in the official report, much-derided by subsequent commentators, where "even the decorated ships on the Danube stopped to listen to Goebbels' speech."[106] While it is unlikely that these remarkable details bear any relation to the actual events, it strongly suggests that the reporter was briefed about this feature, which otherwise might easily have gone unnoticed.

A similar facet in another news report corroborates that the press must have been supplied with highly detailed information about the event: the festivities ended with instrumental renditions of the *Deutschlandlied,* the *Horst-Wessel-Lied,* and the Austrian national anthem, as politically aligned Austrian papers were eager to report.[107] Since both anthems had identical melodies—a feature that was much discussed in the preparation for this event—it would have been impossible to tell them apart, had the reporter not been briefed accordingly.[108]

The masses, carefully arranged outside the Walhalla, became an important ornament of the festivities. In Goebbels's estimation, well over 3,000 participants and guests were expected (including 400 choral singers and 500 members of the Hitler Youth, 400 politicians, 700 guests of honor, 700 Austrian visitors).[109] On the whole, the plan for the festivities followed the tried-and-tested liturgy of National Socialist festivities.[110] The most remarkable feature, however, is the meticulous timing of the event.[111] Beginning with military music in the open (11:00 A.M.), the *Führer* arrived and watched a military tattoo. The *Führer* would enter the colonnade of the Walhalla temple (11:02 A.M.), accompanied by fanfares of themes by Richard Wagner. The *Führer* having arrived at the speaker's podium (11:04 A.M.), a massed chorus of local ensembles sang Bruckner's patriotic *Germanenzug* for seven minutes.[112] The Bavarian

Ministerpräsident would make a short speech conferring the Walhalla to the care of the *Reich*. (11:11 A.M.). Starting at 11:19 A.M., Goebbels's own speech would go on for approximately fifteen minutes. Then the president of the *Brucknergesellschaft,* Max Auer, would award the *Führer* the Bruckner medal— an award introduced especially for this purpose—and was allotted a speaking time of one minute. (Goebbels' timing is less precise from here on, as he had made use of his organizer's privilege and not timed his own speech.)

The *Führer* would then enter Walhalla. Only few members of the government and the party, as well as the Austrian guests were admitted into the inner sanctuary for the actual consecration of the bust. As for the masses outside, only the musical program would tell of the act of consecration and the emotion inside. No sooner had the *Führer* entered the inside of Walhalla, than the Munich Philharmonic, directed by Siegmund von Hausegger, began to play what Goebbels called "the festive music" from the slow movement of Bruckner's Eighth symphony for a rather un-monumental two minutes. (The curious story, whereby this movement is supposed to represent the awakening of the "German Michel," may well have been an insider joke for the occasion, but it was not thematized during the festivities.[113]) The famous cathedral choir, the *Regensburger Domspatzen,* would then sing a three-minute a capella anthem, Bruckner's *Locus iste.*[114] The *Führer* would proclaim: "I ask that the bust of the great German master Anton Bruckner be unveiled." ("Ich bitte, die Büste des großen deutschen Meisters Anton Bruckners zu enthüllen")— "or something to that effect," as Goebbels casually added in his notes. As the bust was unveiled, so-called "victory sounds" from Bruckner's Eighth Symphony were played for four minutes, while wreaths were laid down by the *Führer,* the Austrian government, the Bavarian state government, and the Bruckner Society. This moment is captured in figure 6.4. As the *Führer* left the hall, the obligatory *Deutschlandlied* and *Horst-Wessel-Lied* would be played, followed, as mentioned, by the Austrian anthem. While the *Führer* went to his car, fanfares from Bruckner's Fifth symphony were played.

The festivities follow a clear tripartite scheme. The two outer parts in front of the Walhalla temple both have a public, official character, dedicated as they are to speeches, exchanges of medals, and official emblems. They are musically framed by marches, fanfares, and a somewhat martial choral work by Bruckner. (The early and relatively little-known *Germanenzug* may have been chosen because of its patriotic—and non-Austrian—allusions, and also because it was Bruckner's first mature work, his "opus 1," as it were.) The cherished musical connection to Wagner is alluded to in the choice of fanfares at the beginning; Bruckner's music serves in the same function at the end of the ceremony, after his bust has been installed in Walhalla.

FIGURE 6.4 Adolf Hitler placing a wreath underneath Bruckner's bust in 1937.
© Ullstein Bilderdienst/Granger Collection.

The central part, inside Walhalla, is the sacred part of the ceremonial liturgy: the public is excluded here, and the spoken word is left behind—except for one moment: the unveiling of the bust. This is the first time that Hitler himself speaks. The filmed news clip of this inauguration ceremony makes this contrast even more explicit than the choreography of the event could have been: the eye of the camera enhances this transition by zooming in on the *Führer* as soon as he enters the inside of Walhalla, leaving not only the general public behind but also, visually, the chosen dignitaries who are in reality following him into the hall.

It is appropriate that this is the space for instrumental music—not only that, the selected pieces are taken from the grandest and most expansive of Bruckner's symphonic works. Unfortunately, Goebbels's notes do not indicate beyond the very general labels what passages they were, and the performance material is nonextant, but Siegmund von Hausegger's correspondence gives some indications. He wrote in a letter to the President of the International Bruckner Society, Max Auer:

> When the veil falls off Bruckner's bust, triumphal Bruckner sounds must be played. The 'non confundar' from the Seventh would be appropriate, but it would not work musically. What would also work is the grandiose entry of the final theme of the Eighth in the recapitula-

tion, up to the C major chord with the cymbal crash, and from there jumping to the C major intensification near the end with the climax unifying all the themes, as a true Walhalla sound.[115]

Most interesting about this intriguing note is the reference to the cymbal crash that Hausegger makes: the single cymbal crash (2 measures before rehearsal figure Hh), which was included in all current editions at the time, is now considered inauthentic and has been removed from the critical edition of the score.[116] Fidelity to Bruckner's music had to take a back seat behind the concision and emotional directness of Hausegger's arrangement.

Even though the score material of Hausegger's arrangement has been lost, we can catch a glimpse of it in the film material produced, in great haste, for the weekly news program.[117] The short snippet of the music played in the inner sanctum of Walhalla is indeed taken from the slow movement, what we hear is taken from the repeat of the chorale-like part of the opening material (starting at measure 39).[118] Unlike Bruckner's own version, however, with its calculated climactic use of three harps, Hausegger's arrangement adds ethereal harp sounds throughout the passage.[119] In this sense, the reference to the cymbal crash in Hausegger's letter was programmatic: he was certainly aware of the affective power of instrumental timbres.

We can therefore reconstruct the soundtrack for this ceremonial act of inaugurating Bruckner into the German Hall of Fame. The labels "victory sounds" and "festive sounds" that are used in Goebbels's memo may suggest Wagnerian leitmotivic labels, but in this case the assigning of meaning to musical phrases is based on a semantics of emotion. The mysterious, otherworldly Adagio with its slow meandering, sonorous harmonies, provides a rich carpet of sound, and within it, it is particularly the incessant harp arpeggios that guide the listener into celestial spheres. The "festive sounds" lead the masses into the realm of the *Mütter,* even where they had to wait outside the Walhalla temple. This is music, as Nietzsche once wrote, to float in—music, as Besseler knew, that invited passive listening.[120]

The finale, meanwhile, presents rousing fanfares with martial sequences, rising from the heavy low brass up to the piercing brass register. The sheer volume and brilliance of the brass sounds would surely be evocative all by itself, in the sense of wordlessly conveying victory, as Goebbels' informal label for this passage suggests, but Hausegger's note suggests an added, symbolic level of meaning for this musical choice, shown in example 6.1: the reference to the Wagnerian model—the texture of the Walhalla music at the end of *Rheingold*—is wittily related to the place in which the inauguration takes place. In the filmed version of the events, the eye of the camera anticipates and

EXAMPLE 6.1 The "Siegesklänge" (victory sounds) inside Walhalla sound the "Walhalla Motif" from the conclusion of Bruckner's Eighth Symphony.

EXAMPLE 6.1 (*continued*)

EXAMPLE 6.1 (*continued*)

reduplicates this musical association by panning over a group of indistinct busts, then cutting to Wagner, and from there to Bruckner.[121]

It is in three ways, then, Bruckner's bust is grounded musically in Walhalla: emotionally with the "victorious" sounds of his arranged symphony, historically with the firm symbolic link to the Wagnerian model, and metaphorically by articulating the space of the Hall of Fame in music. For the participants in this quasi-religious act, as well as for the viewers of the filmed version in the cinemas, the musical and emotional tissues of the Regensburg Bruckner *Erlebnis* made for an inescapably awe-inspiring moment, one that cannot but reduce the individual to silence.

Bruckner Medial

Alongside Bruckner's festive entry into Walhalla, the few selected guests inside Walhalla and the countless viewers in the cinemas also witnessed his transformation into his own soundtrack. The choreography of the whole event is marked by a cinematographic aesthetic: the music is chosen to enhance and emotionally underscore the visual aspects of this state act. What is more, cuts and links are made not in line with musical concerns but in subservience to the visual choreography of the event. Goebbels had been able to learn much from important film events, above all *Triumph des Willens* (1934) and *Olympia* (filmed in 1936), and their masterful audio-visual interaction.[122] All in all, the Bruckner experience was a meeting of modern administration with its immaculate timing and of the timeless mysticism of the *Mütter*. Even Schering knew that "the duration of a piece of music may well, but need not, be relevant for its monumental impression."[123]

In his initial speech, Goebbels had just promised to subsidize the editions of *Urfassungen* handsomely.[124] His commitment to the unadulterated, purified, and lengthy versions of Bruckner's music, however, ended at the threshold of the hall. What mattered here was the immediacy of the enhanced and concentrated "lived experience," at a speed that was commensurate with the pace of modern life, as set by the modern media, and the ever-reducing attention spans of audiences.[125] Effectively, Bruckner was just a bystander at his own party. As Bryan Gilliam and others have persuasively argued, the political overtones of the "cultish" symbolism of the Bruckner festival can be read as preparation for the annexation of Austria that was to follow on the political level only a few months later.[126] That his biography was carefully stripped of references to Austria or to Catholicism in the process was clearly picked up by those parts of the Austrian press that were still politically independent.[127]

The Catholic background of Bruckner's music—most clearly, perhaps, the "non confundar" motif from the *Te Deum* that became such an important part of his symphonies—was erased in favor of a wordless semantic void, an inarticulate sense of awe and wallowing in sounds.[128] Once replaced with the non-denominational cultish cathedral built of sounds, it could then quickly be refilled with a new significance to serve new ends. Is that the message of the *Mütter?* Is this what Faust's line of "the eternal entertainment of the eternal sense"[129] means?

To a certain extent we have to assume so. It is part and parcel of the wordlessness and absence of reason that is associated with their realm. Being lulled to silence also smothers any forms of protest. Sidestepping intellectual powers thus comes at a price: like Faust, we do not know whether the voyage to the *Mütter* will lead us upwards or downwards. Schering might well be correct that "there is an urge to serve the advanced education of mankind through art and with it to make it, if at all possible, more virtuous."[130] But in the dimensionless and unfathomable realm of the mothers any standard of virtue is possible. The mothers, after all, can only see indistinctly and schematically, they only "perceive wraiths." This is part of their strength and their weakness.

Let us not forget the underlying Freudian aspect of the descent to the *Mütter*—and one need not even be a Freudian to appreciate the sexual implications of this scene. As Faust knows well, the realm of the mothers is the most fundamental taboo of society, which he is prepared to breach.[131] Nor are Faust's aims particularly laudable: he only descends to their realm to steal the source of their power—the glowing tripod, the tool that lends them the power to create images. In fact, the sexual symbolism of the scene is not subtle: Faust is given a small golden key by Mephistopheles, which grows and sparkles as soon as Faust seizes it. He is instructed to touch the tripod with his key; then it will be his.

No concern is more central to monumentality than the power of representation, the power to manipulate emotions. In this sense, scholars such as Schering and Besseler, Moser and Blume, who tried to get beyond conventional musicological wisdom by embracing unorthodox methodologies and unorthodox political opportunities, may have done so in order to gain clearer access to pure, unadulterated insights previously hidden by the limited dimensions of our (scholarly) perception. They aimed to get beyond the textual sources to the mystical—national and racial—sources of the lived experience of music itself. "Perceiving wraiths" may give rise to the hope that we can be in more immediate contact with the Platonic idea, but it also only allows for much less clear a view.

Epilogue
The Ninth at the Wall

Ode to Freedom

The Cold War ended on November 9, 1989, with the fall of the Berlin Wall.[1] What better opportunity to celebrate this historical event, and to capture the solemn joy of the moment, than with a performance of the most sublime of musical works—Beethoven's Ninth Symphony. What better work of art to celebrate the Peaceful Revolution of East Germany, which over the previous six months had effected change without bloodshed, for instance, in the weekly Monday demonstrations in Leipzig, which reminded the autocratic Socialist Party of the simple and powerful message, *Wir sind das Volk*—"We are the people." The world press agreed that the Germans were the happiest nation in the world. And the central statement of the Ninth Symphony, "Alle Menschen werden Brüder," reflected precisely the sentiment of those days. Over the Christmas holidays of the same year, the symphony was performed in both parts of the formerly divided city of Berlin under the baton of the media star Leonard Bernstein.[2]

Bernstein felt that the unique momentous event demanded that the symphony be changed. He explained "this is a heaven-sent moment to sing '*Freiheit*' wherever the score indicates the word '*Freude*,'"[3] replacing joy with freedom. The change was academically unsound, he warned, because there is no documentary evidence of Beethoven's intentions. Instead, Bernstein referred to the unproven theory, apparently going back to Friedrich Ludwig Jahn, that Schiller originally wrote a version of the poem entitled "An die Freiheit." Jahn published an article in 1849 in which he claimed, allegedly on the basis of an account of Schiller's secretary, that a planned paean to freedom by Schiller fell prey to the censor and had to be turned into "An die Freude" to avoid recriminations.[4] This historical reference, now considered spurious, makes Bernstein's decision curiously pertinent because Jahn—whose name is commonly prefaced with the epithet *Turnvater* (the father figure of the gymnasts' movement)—was an early nineteenth-century advocate for German unification.

Jahn's 1849 article was only one instance in a historical trajectory of foregrounding the political content of Beethoven's Ninth that spanned most of the nineteenth century, and in which Bernstein's statement forms the most recent installment. The association of Beethoven's Ninth Symphony with freedom has been traced back to Wolfgang Griepenkerl's 1838 novella, *Das Musikfest oder die Beethovener.*[5] By mid-century, this association had become accepted as self-evident fact, so much so that the correspondent of the *London Illustrated News* could report from the Bonn Beethoven Festival of 1845 that "Schiller's 'Song to Joy' [was] originally intended, by the way, to 'liberty,' but German despotism was in the way."[6] Around the time of the first German unification of 1871, this association had become so entrenched as to be a founding component of national consciousness.[7] In 1927, on the occasion of the Beethoven centenary, the composer Hanns Eisler finally dismissed the association as a "legend."[8] Unsurprisingly, given the political implications, Bernstein did not cite the socialist Eisler as an authoritative source here and rather referred to unspecified musicological sources that had invalidated Jahn's claims.

In the context of this historical trajectory, Bernstein's performance amounts to a restaging of a nineteenth-century myth that had passed gradually from the realm of fiction to that of rumor and finally to culturally sanctioned truth. Accordingly, Bernstein proposed his theory in a curiously contorted argument, basing it on a historical precedent in nineteenth-century thought, which, however, he knew to be a sham.

We can perhaps make better sense of Bernstein's problem if we remember what the father of modern memory studies, Pierre Nora, has to say about the state of contemporary memory culture. Nora decried the decline of memory as it turns more and more into "sifted and sorted historical traces." This modern, archival form of memory has all but replaced the "integrated, dictatorial memory," which Nora relishes in describing as "unself-conscious, commanding, all-powerful, spontaneously, actualizing, a memory without a past that ceaselessly reinvents tradition, linking the history of its ancestors to the undifferentiated time of heroes, origins, and myth."[9] In our modern age, Nora adds wistfully, memory is separated by an unbridgeable gulf from history: "What we call memory today is therefore not memory but already history."[10] The contortions Bernstein has to go through are nothing but a demonstration of this gulf: trying to dress up memory in the guise of documented, archival history to make it presentable, Bernstein needs to perform mental gymnastics in this attempt to revive the story of *Turnvater* Jahn.

In the end, Bernstein dismissed any potential criticism of this change by asserting that any such quibbles were merely of theoretical interest and lacked the spirit of human joy that the situation demanded. He concluded: "I am sure we have Beethoven's blessing."[11]

In other words, by foregrounding the concept of "freedom" in his 1989 rendition of the symphony, Bernstein put forward a strong claim for a well-defined meaning of Beethoven's music in a specific historical situation—a meaning that bridges the gap between Beethoven's response to the 1789 revolution and the events of the very recent political history two hundred years later. Bernstein's "Ode to Freedom" is not merely a musical work that provides an aural backdrop for the historical event, but one that itself has an important political message to tell and that seeks to convey values integral to the historical events.

The monumentality of Beethoven's Ninth symphony has never been under any doubt. In many ways, this work constitutes the epitome of a musical monument—in the complex blend of sound world and cultural memory, in its perpetual presence at key moments in German history over the last two hundred years. In this sense, Bernstein's Ninth is but one chapter in the long and detailed reception history of the Ninth. But this chapter comes with a twist: how exactly does Bernstein's arrangement, his effort to upgrade its cultural relevance to the specific events of 1989, affect the monumental message of Beethoven's Ninth Symphony?

The Trouble with Freedom

Given that musical monumentality tends to encourage us to regard music as an inextricable extension of the composer, it is understandable that Bernstein would ultimately have sought legitimation from Beethoven. He may have been more successful, however, had he also asked for Schiller's blessing: Schiller's original poem "An die Freude" of 1785 shows his close allegiance to pre-revolutionary French ideas, particularly in the verses "beggars become the brothers of princes" (*Bettler werden Fürstenbrüder*) in the first stanza, and the demand for "rescue from tyrants' chains" (*Rettung von Tyrannenketten*) in the final stanza.[12] The triad of the French Revolution, *liberté–égalité–fraternité*, is clearly discernible in these lines. In this sense, it is very well possible to talk of the expression of a political concept of freedom in Schiller's poem, which is closely wedded to the central theme of joy.

Although the poem became one of Schiller's most popular creations and was set to music well over forty times,[13] Schiller was evidently unhappy with it: when editing an anthology of his poetry in 1803, he was reluctant to include "An die Freude," and eventually decided to revise it.[14] In this new version, perplexingly, Schiller removed all obvious references to the ideals of the French Revolution. It was precisely the lines cited above that fell prey to his revision: "beggars become the brothers of princes" became the much less radical—though more universal—"all humans become brothers," while the last stanza promoting freedom from tyranny was simply deleted altogether. In his correspondence Schiller expressed unhappiness with the sentiments of the poem because he had become disillusioned with the consequences of the French Revolution.[15]

In Schiller's view, the Revolution had produced, on the one hand, lawless savages, driven by external forces and internal urges alone while lacking any reason, and, on the other, merciless barbarians whose actions were solely dictated by a radical rationality devoid of any humane emotions. What the Revolution had comprehensively failed to produce were real humans in the sense of *Aufklärung,* with reason and emotions in balance.[16] Like history and memory, modernity itself was fractured, and modern humans had to suffer for it. Although we know that Beethoven was familiar with both versions of Schiller's poem, it is this revised version of the poem that he used for his "Ode an die Freude."[17] But what do Schiller's changes imply? Can we still imagine *Freude* as a code word for *Freiheit,* even though all references to it had been carefully removed in the 1803 version?[18]

Bernstein's proposal holds that we can. Between the 1785 and the 1803 versions of "An die Freude," Schiller's understanding of freedom itself had undergone some significant revisions. These are nowhere made clearer than in his epistolary treatise *On the Aesthetic Education of Man* (*Über die ästhetische Erziehung des Menschen*), published in 1795, where he sought to explain how the balance between reason and senses, such as he had found wanting in the French Revolution, could be achieved.[19] Schiller found the answer in the contemplation of beautiful forms. At the outset of his letters, he explains that it might seem inappropriate to talk about art and beauty in times of social turmoil, but this turn toward aesthetics was motivated precisely by political reasons. Accordingly, the central thesis of the treatise is: "If man is ever to solve that problem of politics in practice he will have to approach it through the problem of the aesthetic, because it is only through Beauty that man makes his way to Freedom."[20] Put differently, the central question Schiller sought to answer in his *Aesthetic Education* is this: how is it possible for imperfect humans to become free citizens? In his answer beautiful art is invested with the capacity of performing this educational task.

Schiller's leap from the political to the aesthetic was achieved through his definition of beauty as "freedom in appearance."[21] At first, this might sound circuitous: beauty will lead to freedom because beauty is itself already a kind of freedom. In this sense, one could be tempted to read Schiller's above statement as a tautology, "it is only through freedom that man makes his way to freedom." The crux is in the word *appearance:* Schiller's education is based on the idea that the appearance of freedom, in beauty, can teach us something about *actual* freedom.[22] By defining beauty in this way, he implied two things: first, freedom means autonomy, independence from external forces, and the self-imposition of laws.[23] The autonomous status of the artwork is complicated by the circumstance that, strictly speaking, it is subject to rules imposed on it by the artist, but it possesses the appearance of autonomy. And second, whereas for Schiller's teacher Kant freedom was a purely rational affair, the freedom displayed in the beauty of a work of art appeals to the senses.[24] Consequently, beauty is the analogue of freedom in the world of appearances. This second point is of crucial importance. The idea behind the aesthetic education is that mankind must be, as Schiller puts it in a rather Kantian vein, awakened from its pre-enlightened slumber and taught to use its faculty of reason through the contemplation of beautiful works of art, and in this way awaken a sense of the possibility of actualizing freedom in the human.[25] Or, in Schiller's more poetic terms: "The way to the head," he explains, "must be opened through the heart."[26]

To explain the work of art, Schiller draws on the well-known idealist categories of form and content or matter (*Stoff*). Like reason and the senses in the enlightened human, form and matter must be kept in balance in the artwork, and each aspect of the artwork is supposed to engage its correlate in the human. We can best approach these categories of form and content from the vantage point of the universal and particular. In the case of music, Schiller not only refers to the sonic material as its content, but also to the emotive response that this material evokes in the listener. That is to say, the perception of a work of art with reference to its content, by means of our senses, means that we tarry over the particular; we focus on moments and details. In extreme cases—of which the 1937 "Regensburg Bruckner Experience" surely constituted a prime example—we "live" in the piece of music, we submit to it and are enveloped by it. Schiller maintains, rightly or not, that music contains a surplus of content; it stimulates us emotionally, but it does not tend to encourage us to engage in abstract and rational thought.[27]

If we attend to form, on the other hand, we try to take in the work of art as a totality. This is done on the level of the rational reconstruction of the whole in our mind—a mode of reception requiring that we get as little involved with the sensuous stimuli of the work of art as possible. We need to hold the material at bay, because, insofar as content represents the particular, any attention to detail would necessarily interfere with our impression of the whole. In other words, the aspect of form necessitates that we distance ourselves from the work of art, that we subjugate it by means of our rational faculty and thus objectify it.[28]

In many ways, this aesthetic contemplation is best understood as a power struggle: either we submit to the work of art, or we force it to submit to us. The power within the human that comes about when he manages to objectify a work of art through its form is a manifestation of his rational autonomy, that is to say his freedom. In practice, Schiller reminds us, it is never possible to separate form from matter completely, but it is obvious that the formal part of a work of art is of greater significance in his conception of aesthetic freedom, because as the rational and non-sensuous element it is ultimately form that makes freedom possible:

> In a truly successful work of art the contents should effect nothing, the form everything; for only through the form is the whole man affected, through the subject-matter only one or other of his functions. Subject-matter, then, however sublime and all-embracing it may be, always has a limiting effect on the spirit, and it is only from form that true aesthetic freedom can be looked for. Herein, then, lies the real secret of the master in any art: that he can make his form consume his material.[29]

This final point is crucial: some critics of Schiller's aesthetics have detected a tension between his position, on the one hand, that form and content must be in balance, and, on the other hand, the postulate that freedom emerges from form—and that form is, by implication, more relevant than content. But in fact, there is no contradiction here: the aesthetic freedom that form suggests can only be *experienced* through the content. The contemplating subject cannot simply skip that part—after all, all that the subject has at the beginning of the aesthetic education are sensations and experiences. These must therefore form the starting point for an appreciation of form, and hence freedom. In this sense, Schiller calls for music to shed its abundant materiality: "music must become form," he urges, for it is only form that affects the universal.[30]

Form and Formlessness

With all this in mind, we can return to Bernstein's Ninth. Even without a thorough investigation of Schiller's own views of musical form (which in any case are few in number),[31] the problem is obvious: on the one hand, it is apparently the last movement that articulates the freedom of man, but, on the other, the single most protracted problem of this movement has been its form. From the very first review onward, which was otherwise positively brimming with praise, the inscrutable form of the last movement has been a point of criticism:

> Even the most ardent worshippers and most fervent admirers of the composer are convinced that this truly unique finale would become even more incomparably imposing in a more concentrated shape, and the composer himself would agree, had cruel fate not robbed him of the ability to hear his creation.[32]

This level of doubt, which was also manifest in Spohr's rejection of the symphony, as we saw in chapter 2, formed a constant theme of the reception of the Ninth. It was, however, two Idealist philosophers in the 1850s, Friedrich Theodor Vischer and David Friedrich Strauss, who went furthest in this argument, claiming that Beethoven's Ninth "exploded its form"[33] and possessed a certain "monstrous"[34] quality.

To be sure, they arrived at this verdict in the spirit of supreme admiration for Beethoven, and within the context of an involved philosophical argument, but it provided fodder to the notion that the last movement was in fact "formless." The suspicion of formlessness was widespread enough in the nineteenth century to warrant explicit refutations, which was the stated goal of a number of early analytical commentaries on the work.[35]

Since those days a rich analytical literature on this movement has emerged, and there is no shortage of proposals as to the form of the movement. Numerous conceptualizations of Beethoven's movement aim to capture it in simple conventional forms, which include most of the standard textbook forms— sonata form, concerto form, variation form, bar form, or a Lisztian four-movements-in-one form.[36] Beginning in the nineteenth century, meanwhile, a number of very sophisticated hybrid or multi-level models have also been proposed that blend the features of various standard forms.[37]

It seems, however, that hidden beneath these riches that formal analysis has unquestionably produced, the undercurrent of doubt as to the question of form has not gone away. This is perhaps most clearly reflected by Donald Francis Tovey, who showed himself suspicious of complicated formal solutions:

"there is no part of Beethoven's Choral Symphony which does not become clearer to us when we assume that the choral finale is right; and there is hardly a point that does not become more difficult and obscure as soon as we fall into the habit which assumes that the choral finale is wrong."[38] Tovey here effectively turned the question of analysis into a question of the analyst's underlying disposition.

One way out of this dilemma, however, would be to reconnect Tovey's associations between clarity and rightness (and obscurity with wrongness) in considering the final movement. In fact, particularly in recent years, the attempts to attain formal clarity have been counterpoised by critical voices that have instead begun to use the very ineffability of the form of the final movement as a starting point for their interpretations. Leo Treitler, for one, has called the last movement "paradoxical,"[39] in that it "blatantly confounds efforts to account for its events on strictly formalist terms"[40] While one might argue that this seems like a capitulation before a daunting challenge, it can in fact be turned into a productive vantage point. As Daniel Chua has argued, Beethoven's "'chaos' is always created."[41]—And as we shall see, the ineffable, seemingly chaotic form of the movement that seems to eschew straightforward formal understanding is in fact carefully controlled.

We could thus turn the argument around and claim, in line with Burkean–Kantian aesthetics, that the formal complexity of the movement, and our difficulty to pin down its form as a whole, is actually a sign of the sublime at work.[42] (Indeed, one defining criterion of the sublime for Vischer is that it is "at once formed and formless."[43]) This is, of course, another trope that pervades the entire reception of Beethoven Nine.[44] But from the perspective of Schiller's aesthetic education, the sublime is significantly different from the beautiful.[45] In the realm of music, Schiller found this ideal of classical, balanced beauty embodied to the highest degree in none other than Gluck's *Iphigenie in Tauris*—a far cry from Beethoven's Ninth.[46] In fact, it is noticeable how much reluctance Schiller shows in *On the Aesthetic Education of Man,* in contrast to his other aesthetic writings, to engage the sublime.[47] While for Schiller the essence of beauty resides in harmony, in the equilibrium between form and content, the sublime is quite a different aesthetic experience, namely one that "exceeds our empirical concept of the subject."[48] That is to say, the human recognizes that he cannot win the power struggle against the art object, as his sensuous capacity is overwhelmed. Consequently, as Schiller explains later, the sublime effect resides in our marveling "at the victory which the object achieves over man."[49]

To illustrate this point, consider the *poco adagio* passage near the end, shown here in example E.1 in Liszt's piano transcription, where the vocal solo

EXAMPLE E.I The quartet steps out of the tonal frame. From Franz Liszt's piano arrangement of Beethoven's Symphony no. 9, last movement.

quartet suddenly interrupts the chorus in the middle of their final stretti. The soloists seem to step out of time and lead the "Alle Menschen werden Brüder" theme into new and undreamed-of regions, winding their way somewhat self-indulgently toward B major, before the final march returns them to the universal brotherhood in the final prestissimo. Such moments of B major form a fixed reference point that spans the whole symphony and can, in fact, be found in each movement.[50] In all occurrences, these B major moments open up an immeasurable tonal space. From the home key of D minor—seven accidentals and a change of mode away—this would present an impossibly remote tonal relation. The only way to make sense of it is if we follow its path step by step. What Leo Treitler says about the last movement on the whole, rings particularly true in these passages: "We can glimpse through that the Romantic idea of music as an expression of the infinite."[51]

The fugal passage, shown in the latter half of example E.2 following the *Alla marcia* section starting at measure 424, makes this particularly evident. The fugue takes us in a variety of confounding harmonic maneuvers gradually from B flat major to the inconceivably remote regions of G flat major, across the page, and finally to our B major for a brief touchdown.—The fugue is really a centrifug(u)e, and it appears to catapult us into the outer orbits of the tonal universe.

In my descriptions of these musical passages, I have been consciously using the communal form "us," perhaps provocatively so, and thereby implying an agency of the matter of the music, as is fundamental to the workings of the musical monument: "we" are irresistibly drawn into the music; "it" draws us in. In its ineffable—though not arbitrary—form, the movement eschews definitive conceptualization, its form resists being fully captured intellectually. Following Schiller, it remains impossible for us to distance ourselves from the

EXAMPLE E.2 After the Turkish march, the fugue catapults us into the outer orbits of the tonal universe. From Liszt's piano arrangement of Beethoven's Symphony
no. 9, last movement.

content of the music and to pin down its form; we cannot objectify it and remain in turn arrested by it and in it.

Or is the issue rather that the bar is raised too high? After all, there is always form, even in the infinite. And, as example E.3 indicates, in both passages the return to the more familiar D major is achieved by the same baffling, almost mockingly simple strategy.[52] This correlation reconfirms that any apparent chaos in the form of the movement is in fact carefully controlled. Either

EXAMPLE E.3 Harmonic reductions of end of the final solo insertion and of the end of the fugue. Despite their differences, both return from "impossibly" remote B major regions by means of simple harmonic progressions.

way, however, the problem remains the same from the perspective of the aesthetic education: what matters to Schiller is the relation between the work of art and the contemplating subject.[53] Whether the problem lies with the art object or with human recognition, in the human who is not yet fully enlightened, the aesthetic experience will not be a manifestation of his or her freedom and an affirmation of the autonomy of his or her rational faculty, but is rather doomed to failure. In other words, the formal obscurity of the movement that all but the most polemical analysts have acknowledged and wrestled with does become a problem.

The consequences that Schiller envisages could be dire. He presents this case as a kind of short-circuited enlightenment: whereas the form of an artwork is supposed to stimulate our rational capacity so that we might appreciate universality and acquire an awareness of the world around us, here, without a firm handle on form, only contingent matter can be engaged.[54] In other words, where the aesthetic experience should have led to freedom, it now only leads to an awareness of the contingency of human existence, set as an absolute—in other words, a case of "bad infinity." As Schiller predicts, man will find himself alone in the world, without so much as a concept of humanity: "The first fruits which he reaps in the realm of spirit are, therefore, Sorrow and Fear; both of them products of reason, not of sense, but a reason which mistakes its object and applies its imperative directly to matter."[55] What the human is faced with in this short-circuited enlightenment, which reflects the particular and temporal rather than the universal and transcendent, then, is the overpowering force of nature, the terror of the empirical world.

This is particularly problematic with regard to the sublime: like Kant before him, Schiller considers the effect of the sublime to be a triumphant affirmation of the ability of reason to withstand the overwhelming force of nature. However, this only works if reason is fully functional, in humans that have already attained fully aesthetic maturity, which is evidently not the case here.[56] (In his study of the musical sublime, the Wagnerian Arthur Seidl pointed out, in the same vein, that "the judgment and recognition of the sublime we can only demand of those who have already developed their moral sense."[57]) Where reason has just awoken the human from his pre-enlightened slumber, and the human is, in Kant's famous dictum, freshly emerging from his self-imposed immaturity, it would seem difficult to take this last crucial step and turn the overwhelming power of nature into an affirmation of reason. Instead, the human simply stands frightened in the face of the terrifying forces of the material world. Bad news indeed for the concept of monumentality, which after all thrives on the notion of the sublime. As an educational device, at least if we follow Kant and Schiller, the monument seems to have serious inherent problems. While Sulzer, the Enlightenment encyclopedist we encountered in chapter 1, praised the monument as a tool for the education and moral betterment of the public, it now seems that the public first ought to take remedial lessons before it can appreciate the monument and derive any moral education from it.

In other words, we are worlds apart from the joyous brotherhood of humanity of which Schiller's Ode sings. Almost inevitably, the inscrutable form of the last movement of Beethoven's Ninth brings about "sorrow or fear" in the human, who was supposed to be educated toward freedom. Is this all a mistake?

Reading Monuments

The social dangers of freedom that Schiller envisaged can be found to be played out in Beethoven's symphony. Freedom is for Schiller not limited to the individual; rather, it is inseparable from the idea of a society embracing all of humanity—and Beethoven gives expression to this conceit in his unending repetitions of "Alle Menschen, alle Menschen," which saturate the entire last movement. In this context, one could even go further and suggest that these exclamations be heard as an imperative, as something not yet achieved or at stake. If we read Schiller's poem closely, we find that this "Alle Menschen" is not something we can take for granted. Particularly the second stanza, which supposedly sings the praise of the community of humanity, ends on a rather chilling note: *Und wer's nie gekonnt, der stehle weinend sich aus diesem Bund*— "And he who could never achieve this, in tears let him steal away from this community."

One critic who was troubled by these verses was Theodor W. Adorno, who was on the whole suspicious of Schiller's aesthetic-political project.[58] For him, the whole coercive gregariousness of the Enlightenment was summarized in these verses. He observed:

> The passage from Schiller's 'Ode to Joy,' in which those who are not accorded all-embracing love are banished from it, involuntarily betrays the truth about the idea of humanity, which is at once totalitarian and particular. What happens to the unloved or those incapable of love in the name of the idea in these lines unmasks that idea, as does the affirmative force with which Beethoven's music hammers it home.[59]

If we follow Adorno's line of this critique of Schiller, then man, captivated by fear and sorrow after mistakenly contemplating the matter of the work of art, is an essential part of the joyous community of brothers, precisely in his rejection from society.

Beethoven, too, took note of this particular verse. As Nottebohm reports, he scribbled in one of his sketches, slightly misquoting Schiller: "Turkish Music in 'Wer das nie gekonnt stehle.'"[60] In the final version, of course, this verse is not set to Turkish music. Instead, it makes its first appearance a little later, in the *Alla Marcia* passage in B flat major, which forms the beginning of example E.2 above. However, it is in turn possible to interpret this "Turkish March" topic in light of the verse in question and the sentiment of exclusion it may express. For Adorno, a march represents the collective figure of walking, which suggests "an idiosyncratic irreversible movement toward a goal. Withdrawal, return and repetition are unknown to it."[61]

In this situation, then, the march becomes the exact opposite, an inseparable counterpart, of the fugue discussed above, which immediately supersedes the march. Where the march stands for order and collectivity, and goal-directed motion, the fugue negates every single point: there is disorder and individuality in the polyphonic texture, and as we saw earlier on, there is no sense of any clear tonal direction. The fugue disperses the community; the music simply spirals out of control and into the sublime chaos of the B-major moment we encountered above.[62] And, in light of this interpretation, it is hardly surprising that over the course of the fugue the theme derived from the preceding "Turkish music" passage is gradually submerged by the "Freude" theme and all but disappears.[63]

From this angle, then, we can begin to reconstruct the insoluble "problem of the Ninth" of which Adorno spoke in the Beethoven fragment and bring it to bear on Bernstein's idea of freedom in Beethoven's Ninth. This problem of the Ninth looks something like this: for Schiller, freedom is grounded in the aesthetic experience of beauty, but he has some reservations about the sublime, which harbors certain dangers, since it is based on the opposition, not the harmony, of reason and the senses. The danger Schiller envisages in the sublime, in the context of an aesthetic education, is the misshapen relation between the individual and society. Rather than producing individuals who are conscious of their membership in the human species, it produces fearful individuals who cannot conceive of anything outside their individuality. Beethoven's formed-and-formless last movement, which apparently holds the key to freedom, will almost certainly result in this failed relation. At the same time, Adorno observes that Schiller's joyous utopian community thrives precisely on the exclusion of the individual who does not fit in. When Bernstein changed "joy" into "freedom," he effectively turned the conundrum into a vicious circle, which had lain dormant as long as Beethoven's Ninth did not make any overt claims to freedom: inevitability and necessity for the aesthetic education to fail now coincide. And both sides of the coin—the necessity and the inevitability of failure—can be traced back to the ineffability of Beethoven's composition.

With this sobering thought, we can finally return from the French Revolution to the bloodless German Revolution, from the aftermath of 1789 to that of 1989. It would surely be churlish to doubt the sincere spirit in which Bernstein made the change to the symphony, as a symbolic token, a musical fanfare to herald the new age of freedom and democracy, as indeed many of the press reviews at the time acknowledged. And yet, it was much more than simply a euphoric response to the historical moment. It was precisely what Pierre Nora describes as the functioning of the *lieu de mémoire:* "a site of excess closed upon itself, concentrated in its own name, but also forever open to the full range of its possible significations."[64] And as always, the Ninth resists all attempts to pin down its meaning and refuses to spell out a definitive message by itself.

Bernstein's change from "joy" to "freedom" was more prescient perhaps than he would have himself imagined at the time. For, from one angle, the years following the reunification could be described as being marked, on the one hand, by a sense of "sorrow and fear," and, on the other, by the social exclusion of the individuals who would not fit. This can emblematically be seen, as Jürgen Habermas and others have pointed out, in the transformation that the popular movement underwent shortly after the Wall came down: their slogan changed subtly but unmistakably from "We are the people" to "We are *one* nation" (*Wir sind ein Volk*), shown in figure E.1.[65] At that stage the new slogan was merely a plea for a spiritual unification alongside the economic and political unification, not dissimilar from the reading I suggested of Beethoven's incessant plea "Alle Menschen" in the Ninth Symphony. But even this innocuous slogan already resonates with the policy of exclusion that nationalism tends to be based upon, as Adorno saw in Beethoven's Ninth on the artistic level, and as was borne out politically in the 1990s, most dramatically in the rise of neo-Nazism in certain quarters.

A decade later, a number of historians came to consider the German reunification soberly as a "business transaction turned sour," resulting in little more than increases in both tax bills and unemployment figures.[66] Others, such as Wolf Lepenies, saw the initial cultural-political efforts in similarly pessimistic terms, as an "intellectual tragicomedy."[67] From the viewpoint of the aesthetic education, it might seem as if the peaceful revolution of 1989, like its predecessor two hundred years earlier, produced once again some groups

FIGURE E.1
A placard from the 1989 demonstrations in East Germany.
© Deutsches Historisches Museum–Bildarchiv.

of lawless savages and heartless barbarians. Was *that* the monumental message conveyed in Bernstein's Ninth?

We end up with three conflicting interpretations: for Bernstein, the Ninth is the fanfare heralding freedom, joy, and unification. For Schiller, meanwhile, this fanfare is dissonant, a *Schreckensfanfare,* as the people in 1989, just as in 1789, were rushed into "freedom" without first being educated toward it through the contemplation of beautiful works of art. And what rings out most strongly for Adorno is the seductive sound of our eagerness to exchange utopian "joy" for economic "freedom."

It is probably worth remembering Chou En-Lai in this context, who was asked whether he considered the French Revolution a success and allegedly replied: "it is too early to say."[68] The message for us is not so much that we need to decide in favor of one or the other, as rather to juxtapose the conflicting images that the three readings of Bernstein's Ninth have produced. Monuments, we remember, present themselves with the air of inevitable solidity, which tends to crystallize into the authoritative metaphor of the majestic mountain that we encountered so frequently in our exploration of musical monumentality. Yet no such monolith is discernible here. The monument only petrifies into a static and mountainous object once the memories that surround it solidify into a single coherent, ineluctable narrative—and "our sublime Ninth,"[69] as Scott Burnham once called it, has a habit of resisting our attempts to fix it definitively. The issue here is not that the Ninth is somehow too malleable to speak up distinctly, but rather that it has splintered: it speaks up in too many voices at the same time—or, to be precise, we have made it speak up in too many voices at once. What we end up with, then, are three monoliths, three narratives, that all vie for pre-eminence.

Is this monumental polyphony amidst a sublime chaos, a self-conscious, inconclusive anti-monumental scenario in Huyssen's sense, an appropriate note on which to end?

Before we close, let us take our story of Bernstein's Ninth one step further and turn to Richard Taruskin, whose views on Bernstein's Ninth appear to tap into some of Adorno's socio-aesthetic concerns. He drew attention to the unarticulated chasm between high and low in this event, contrasting the officially sanctioned, commercialized "packaged greatness" against the celebratory grassroots music-making on the day the Wall came down: "The true musical emblems of that glorious moment were the guitar-strumming kids in jeans atop the wall playing a music that would have landed them in jail the day before. They were the ones who symbolized *Freiheit.*"[70] In what may be seen as both historical irony and final musical triumph, it turns out that one of the joyous songs that were prominently strummed atop the wall was none other than Beethoven's *Freude* melody.[71]

The music of Beethoven's Ninth tells us of invariably monumental things, but it always tells us the story we want to hear. As with all musical monuments, and with none more so than with Beethoven's Ninth, if we listen too closely its healing magic may disappear. Ultimately, it is up to us to decide whether this is what we want.

NOTES

Introduction

1. Alfred Einstein, *Music in the Romantic Era: Musical Thought in the Nineteenth Century* (New York: Norton, 1947), 65.

2. Theodor W. Adorno, *Mahler: A Musical Physiognomy,* trans. Edmund Jephcott (Chicago: University of Chicago Press, 1996)

3. Carl Dahlhaus, *Nineteenth-Century Music,* trans. J. Bradford Robinson (Berkeley and Los Angeles: University of California Press, 1989), 266. Monumentality—variously associated with Beethoven, Berlioz, Brahms, Mendelssohn, Saint-Saens, and Schumann—is also invoked elsewhere in the book.

4. Siegfried Kross notes that Dahlhaus's notion of monumentality remains ill-defined, see Kross, ed., *Probleme der symphonischen Tradition im 19. Jahrhundert* (Tutzing: Hans Schneider, 1990), 34. The contributions to this volume can, to a certain extent, be seen as an attempt at exegesis of this and other concepts invoked by Dahlhaus.

5. Hans Ulrich Gumbrecht, "Mozarts Präsenzen oder: Wie genau kann man ein 'Musik-Erlebnis' beschreiben," presentation given as part of the lecture series, *Ästhetische Erfahrung im Zeichen der Entgrenzung der Künste,* Freie Universität Berlin, December 7, 2005. See also his *The Powers of Philology* (Champaign and Chicago: University of Illinois Press/University of Chicago, 2003).

6. Dahlhaus, *Nineteenth-Century Music,* 266 and similarly, 290.

7. Thomas Mann, "The Sorrows and Grandeur of Richard Wagner," in *Pro and Contra Wagner,* trans. Allan Blunden (Chicago: University of Chicago Press, 1985), 134.

8. A modern classic for German music in this period is Pamela Potter, *Most German of the Arts: Musicology and Society from the Weimar Republic to the End of Hitler's Reich* (New Haven: Yale University Press, 1998). For important studies of music under Italian fascismo and the Soviet regime, see Harvey Sachs, *Music in Fascist Italy* (New York: Norton, 1987); and Boris Schwarz, *Music and Musical Life in Soviet Russia 1917–1970* (New York: Norton, 1972).

9. See Fred K. Prieberg, *Musik im NS-Staat* (Frankfurt am Main: Fischer, 1983), 339–340.

10. Hanns-Werner Heister and Jochem Wolff, "Macht und Schicksal: Klassik, Fanfaren, höhere Durchhaltemusik," in Hanns-Werner Heister and Hans-Günter Klein, eds., *Musik und Musikpolitik im faschistischen Deutschland* (Frankfurt am Main: Fischer, 1984), 123. "Der Satz erscheint vereinfacht, die Streicherpassagen wie auch das Polyphonieren sind praktisch unhörbar. Um so stärker tritt das Schlagwerk hervor: Die Solostellen der Pauken, die die Streicher ersetzen, hören sich beinahe an wie Granateneinschläge." All translations are mine, unless stated otherwise. For longer quotations, the original text is provided in the footnote.

11. Adolf Weißmann, *Die Musik in der Weltkrise* (Stuttgart and Berlin: Deutsche Verlags-Anstalt, 1922), 20. "Musik sucht den Willen zu brechen."

12. On conceptions of theatricality, see the fascinating collection of essays in Erika Fischer-Lichte, ed., *Theatralität und die Krisen der Repräsentation* (Stuttgart and Weimar: Metzler, 2001).

13. Thomas Mann, *Reflections of a Nonpolitical Man,* trans. Walter D. Morris (New York: Frederic Ungar, 1983), 17; and more broadly, see also Mann, "Sorrows and Grandeur," 135.

14. Andreas Huyssen, "Monumental Seduction," *New German Critique* 69 Special Issue: Richard Wagner (1996): 181–200.

15. For a thoroughgoing investigation of the history of the term, see Reinhard Alings, *Monument und Nation: Das Bild vom Nationalstaat im Medium Denkmal—zum Verhältnis von Nation und Staat im deutschen Kaiserreich 1871–1918* (Berlin and New York: Walter de Gruyter, 1996), 3–15.

16. Huyssen, "Monumental Seduction," 198.

17. Much else has been written on commemoration and the monuments of post-unification Berlin, see, for instance, James Young, *At Memory's Edge: After-Images of the Holocaust in Contemporary Art and Architecture* (New Haven and London: Yale University Press, 2000).

18. Pierre Nora, *Les Lieux de mémoire,* 3 vols. (Paris: Gallimard, 1984–1992), ed. by Lawrence D. Kritzman and trans. by Arthur Goldhammer as *Realms of Memory: Rethinking the French Past* (New York: Columbia University Press, 1996), p. xvii. *Les Lieux de mémoire* has also been translated by David P. Jordan as *Rethinking France: Les Lieux de mémoire* (Chicago: University of Chicago Press, 2006).

19. Maurice Halbwachs developed this concept in his *The Social Frameworks of Memory,* included in *On Collective Memory,* trans. Lewis A. Coser (Chicago and London: University of Chicago Press, 1992). His essay collection, *The Collective Memory,* trans. Francis J. Ditter, Jr. and Vida Yazdi Ditter (New York: Harper and Row, 1980) is a posthumously published response to his critics.

20. Halbwachs's work, which had been almost forgotten, in turn enjoyed tremendous renaissance in the wake of memory studies. Nora's indebtedness to Halbwachs has been explored most impressively perhaps in Paul Ricoeur, *Memory, History, Forgetting,* trans. by Kathleen Blamey and David Pellauer (Chicago and London: University of Chicago Press, 2004), esp. 393–411.

21. Nora, *Realms of Memory,* vol. 1, 1. This introduction had also been published separately as "Between Memory and History: *Les Lieux de Mémoire,*" in *Representations* 26 (1989): 7–25.

22. Nora, *Realms of Memory,* vol. 1, 2. Nora's English-language editor, Lawrence Kritzman, interpolates that the word "memory" should not be taken in its literal sense: "it is to be understood in its 'sacred contexts' as the variety of forms through which cultural communities imagine themselves in diverse representational modes," in Nora, *Realms of Memory,* p. ix.

23. Wulf Kansteiner, "Finding Meaning in Memory: A Methodological Critique of Collective Memory Studies," *History and Theory* 41 (2002): 183.

24. Critics from post-colonial studies especially, who have expressed concern about some of Nora's sweeping claims, have pointed out that his diagnosis cannot be generalized. See Hue-Tam Ho Tai, "Remembered Realms: Pierre Nora and French National Memory," *American Historical Review* 106 (2001): 915; and Kerwin Lee Klein, "On the Emergence of *Memory* in Historical Discourse," *Representations* 69 Special Issue: Grounds for Remembering (2000): 137.

25. See Nancy Wood, "Memory's Remains: *Les Lieux de mémoire,*" *History and Memory* 6 (1994), 129; and Henry W. Pickford, "Conflict and Commemoration: Two Berlin Memorials," *Modernism/Modernity* 12 (2005): 134.

26. See Peter Carrier, "Pierre Noras *Les Lieux de mémoire* als Diagnose und Symptom des zeitgenössischen Erinnerungskultes," in Gerald Echterhoff and Martin Saar, eds., *Kontexte und Kulturen des Erinnerns: Maurice Halbwachs und das Paradigma des kollektiven Gedächtnisses* (Konstanz: UVK Verlagsgesellschaft, 2002), 141–162.

27. Wood draws particular attention to the overwhelming popular response to the *lieux de mémoire* project, noting that the term was quickly taken up as an entry in the *Robert* dictionary in 1993, see her "Memory's Remains," 123.

28. The literature on the monument and memory culture is too vast to be done justice in this context. Texts that have left traces on my thinking include: James E. Young, *Textures of Memory: Holocaust Memorials and Meaning* (New Haven: Yale University Press, 1993); Saul Friedlander, *Memory, History and the Extermination of the Jews of Europe* (Bloomington: University of Indiana Press, 1993); Jay M. Winter, *Sites of Memory, Sites of Mourning: The Great War in European Culture* (Cambridge: Cambridge University Press, 1995); Simon Schama, *Landscape and Memory* (London: Fontana Press, 1995); Geoffrey Hartman, *The Longest Shadow: In the Aftermath of the Holocaust* (Bloomington: University of Indiana Press, 1996); Berel Lang, *The Future of the Holocaust: Between Memory and History* (Ithaca, NY: Cornell University Press, 1999); and Rudy Koshar, *From Monuments to Traces: Artifacts of German Memory 1870–1990* (Berkeley and Los Angeles: University of California Press, 2000).

29. Francis Claudon, "Hausmusik," 138–153; Rainer Moritz, "Der Schlager," 201–220; Patrice Veit, "Bach," 239–257; Dietmar Klenke, "Der Gesangverein," 392–407; Herfried Münkler, "Richard Wagner," 549–568; Michael Jeismann, "Die Nationalhymne," 660–664; and Esteban Buch, "Beethovens Neunte," 665–680. All articles are in Etienne François and Hagen Schulze, eds., *Deutsche Erinnerungsorte,* 3 vols. (Munich: C. H. Beck, 2001), vol. 3.

30. The relation between history and memory is still a matter of considerable contention. It has become commonplace to argue that the difference is smaller than Nora pretends. Some have gone so far as to argue that history should be regarded as a subset of memory, see Kansteiner, "Finding Meaning in Memory," 184. Klein, meanwhile, adds a provocative neo-conservative twist to the argument by confirming that Nora was in fact

correct and that history and memory are irreconcilable, see his "On the Emergence of Memory in Historical Discourse," 128.

31. Nora, *Lieux de mémoire,* vol. 1,3.

32. See, for instance, Hubert Thüring, *Geschichte des Gedächtnisses: Friedrich Nietzsche und das 19. Jahrhundert* (Munich: Wilhelm Fink, 2001). Michel Foucault's influential essay "Nietzsche, Genealogy, History," in Paul Rabinow, ed., *The Foucault Reader* (London: Penguin, 1991), 76–100, was instrumental in rekindling the wide interest in Nietzsche and questions of historiography.

33. See, for instance, David Brodbeck, *Johannes Brahms: Symphony no. 1* (Cambridge: Cambridge University Press, 1997); Styra Avins, ed., *Johannes Brahms: Life and Letters* (Oxford: Oxford University Press, 1997); and Daniel Beller-McKenna, "Distance and Disembodiment: Harps, Horns, and the Requiem Idea in Brahms and Schumann," *Journal of Musicology* 2005 (22): 69–71. For a wider discussion of the exchange of memorabilia between Clara Schumann and Brahms, see also Paul Berry, "Old Love: Johannes Brahms, Clara Schumann, and the Poetics of Musical Memory," *Journal of Musicology* 24 (2007): 72–111.

Chapter One

1. On Christmann, see Mary Sue Morrow, *German Music Criticism in the Late Eighteenth Century: Aesthetic Issues in Instrumental Music* (Cambridge: Cambridge University Press, 1997); and Hans Schneider, *Der Musikverleger Heinrich Philipp Bossler 1744–1822* (Tutzing: Hans Schneider, 1985). On the *Allgemeine musikalische Zeitung,* see also Reinhold Schmitt-Thomas, *Die Entwicklung der deutschen Konzertkritik im Spiegel der Leipziger 'Allgemeinen musikalischen Zeitung' (1798–1848)* (Frankfurt: Kettenhof, 1969).

2. Christmann, "An das scheidende Jahrhundert," *Allgemeine musikalische Zeitung* 3 (1800/1801): col. 208. "Du gabst uns einen Händel und einen Gluck, einen Graun und Hasse, und gründetest durch sie die Achtung vor dem Genius der Deutschen an den Ufern der Themse, der Tiber und der Seine."

3. Friedrich Rochlitz, "Monumente deutscher Tonkünstler," *Allgemeine musikalische Zeitung* 2 (1799/1800): col. 417. "Die Werke keines Künstlers haben wohl so viel Verwesliches bey dem Unverweslichen, so viel Sterbliches bey dem Unsterblichen, als die Werke des Musikers."

4. See also John Deathridge, "The Invention of German Music c. 1800," in Tim Blanning and Hagen Schulze, eds., *Unity and Diversity in European Culture c. 1800* (Oxford: Oxford University Press, 2006), 35–60; and Matthew Head, "Music with 'No Past'? Archeologies of Joseph Haydn and *The Creation,*" *Nineteenth Century Music* 23 (2000): 191–217.

5. Johann Nikolaus Forkel, *Über Johann Sebastian Bach's Leben, Kunst und Kunstwerke für patriotische Verehrer echter musikalischer Kunst* (Leipzig: Hoffmeister und Kühnel, 1802).

6. Johann Nikolaus Forkel, *Allgemeine Literatur der Musik* (Leipzig, 1792; reprint Hildesheim: Georg Olms 2001), pp. viii–ix. Joseph Sonnleithner, "Ankündigung: Geschichte der Musik in Denkmählern von der ältesten bis auf die neueste Zeit," Sept 1799, *Intelligenzblatt der Allgemeinen musikalischen Zeitung* 1 (1798/1799): col. 91. See also Max Schneider, "'Denkmäler der Tonkunst' vor hundert Jahren," in *Festschrift Max von Liliencron* (Leipzig: Breitkopf und Härtel, 1910), 278–289.

7. Schneider "'Denkmäler der Tonkunst' vor hundert Jahren," 284.

8. Rochlitz, "Monumente deutscher Tonkünstler," col. 418. "Frankreich hat sein Paris, und Paris ein Pantheon, wo die Nation aus ihrem Schatz auch des großen Tonkünstlers Andenken würdig erhellt; England hat ein London, und London eine Westmisterabtey, wo die Nation dem Schatz der Verehrer eines solchen Verstorbenen diese Äußerung der Humanität verstattet und erleichtert. Deutschland hat keinen so ungeheuren Sammelplatz seiner Gebildeten, Reichen und Großen, hat in diesem Sinne keine Hauptstadt (nur Hauptstädte), kann bekanntlich, seiner statistischen Verhältnisse wegen, keine—und folglich auch kein Pantheon und keine Westminsterabtey haben."

9. Christmann, "An das scheidende Jahrhundert," col. 208. "Albions Mausoleum mußte den Aschenkrug eines Händels aufnehmen."

10. On the significance of Walhalla in a musical context, see particularly Albrecht Riethmüller, *Die Walhalla und ihre Musiker* (Laaber: Laaber-Verlag, 1983).

11. Johann Karl Friedrich Triest, "Bemerkungen über die Ausbildung der Tonkunst in Deutschland im achtzehnten Jahrhundert," *Allgemeine musikalische Zeitung* 3 (1800/1801): col. 241.

12. For a thorough examination of this monument and its significance in British culture, see Suzanne Aspden, "'Fam'd Handel breathing, tho' transformed to stone': The Composer as Monument," *Journal of the American Musicological Society* 55 (2002): 39–90.

13. Johann Georg Sulzer, *Allgemeine Theorie der schönen Künste* (Leipzig: Weidemann & Reich, 1771), 1: 596. "Denkmal": "Ein an öffentlichen Plätzen stehendes Werk der Kunst, das als ein Zeichen das Andenken merkwürdiger Personen oder Sachen, beständig unterhalten und auf die Nachwelt fortpflanzen soll."

14. Ibid. Sulzer's artistic concept of monument remained influential for the whole nineteenth century. See Thomas Nipperdey, "Nationalidee und Nationaldenkmal in Deutschland im 19. Jahrhundert," *Historische Zeitschrift* 206 (1968): 529–585.

15. Christmann, "An das scheidende Jahrhundert," col. 209. This praise for Breitkopf might not have been quite selfless, given that the *Allgemeine musikalische Zeitung* was published under the auspices of Breitkopf und Härtel. On the importance of music journalism in the establishment of a national musical discourse in early nineteenth-century Germany, particularly on the *Allgemeine musikalische Zeitung,* see Celia Applegate, *Bach in Berlin: Nation and Culture in Mendelssohn's Revival of the* St. Matthew Passion (Ithaca, NY: Cornell University Press, 2005), 86–101.

16. Christmann, "An das scheidende Jahrhundert," col. 209. "Vielleicht ahndetest du den Werth dieses seltenen Mannes, noch ehe er um den Lorbeerkranz wetteifern konnte, der nun seine Silberlocken schmückt: denn gleich einer zärtlichen Mutter, die für eine sichere Dauer des Glücks ihrer Kinder schon im Voraus zu sorgen pflegt, warst auch du darauf bedacht, die geistvollen Früchte der Muse dieser großen Zöglinge der Kunst und der Natur und mit ihm die Werte anderer braven Tonsetzer vor dem Untergange künftiger Zeitalter zu schützen und sie der Nachwelt zu überliefern."

17. Immanuel Kant, *Kritik der Urteilskraft,* ed. Wilhelm Weischedel (Frankfurt: Suhrkamp, 1977), para. 53. See also Hermann Parret, "Kant on Music and the Hierarchy of the Arts," *Journal of Aesthetics and Art Criticism* 56 (1998): 251–261.

18. Triest, "Bemerkungen," col. 444. "Was das neue Jahrhundert uns liefern wird, wissen wir nicht, aber, ich wiederhole es, im Einzelnen, wo die Kunst von dem Genie, dem Studium und dem Geschmack abhängt, ist sie das Werk der Menschen, die man über

ihre Fort- und Rückschritte loben oder tadeln mag, im *Ganzen* dürfen wir sie uns nur als das Werk einer höheren Kraft denken, die nie, *nie*—oder auch das Edelste in der Welt ist eine Seifenblase—wirkliche Rückschritte thun kann." For more information on Triest, see Bernd Sponheuer, "Reconstructing the Ideal Types of the 'German' in Music," in Celia Applegate and Pamela Potter, eds., *Music and German National Identity* (Chicago: University of Chicago Press, 2002), 36–58.

19. Triest, "Bemerkungen," col. 444n.

20. *Allgemeine musikalische Zeitung* 1 (1798/1799): 570–571. See Morrow, *German Music Criticism,* 154–155. This would change considerably a few years later when the *Allgemeine musikalische Zeitung,* and particularly its editor Friedrich Rochlitz, became a champion of Beethoven.

21. See, for instance, Carl Dahlhaus, *Klassische und romantische Musikästhetik* (Laaber: Laaber-Verlag, 1988), and *The Idea of Absolute Music,* trans. Roger Lustig (Chicago: University of Chicago Press, 1989); and Mark Evan Bonds, "Idealism and the Aesthetics of Instrumental Music at the Turn of the Nineteenth Century," *Journal of the American Musicological Society* 50 (1997): 387–420.

22. Sponheuer, "Reconstructing the Ideal Types," 51–52.

23. To list but the most important titles from the vast literature on this topic, see Leo Treitler, *Music and the Historical Imagination* (Cambridge, MA: Harvard University Press, 1989); Rose Rosengard Subotnik, *Developing Variations: Style and Ideology in Western Music* (Minneapolis: University of Minnesota Press, 1991); Susan McClary, *Feminine Endings* (Minneapolis: University of Minnesota Press, 1991); Lydia Goehr, *The Imaginary Museum of Musical Works: An Essay in the Philosophy of Music* (Oxford: Clarendon Press, 1992); Scott Burnham, *Beethoven Hero* (Princeton: Princeton University Press, 1995); Daniel Chua, *Absolute Music and the Construction of Meaning* (Cambridge: Cambridge University Press, 1999); and Berthold Hoeckner, *Programming the Absolute: Nineteenth-Century German Music and the Hermeneutics of the Moment* (Princeton: Princeton University Press, 2002).

24. Kant, *Kritik der Urteilskraft,* para. 42.

25. See, for instance, the related concerns raised in Erika Fischer-Lichte, ed., *Theatralität und die Krisen der Repräsentation* (Stuttgart und Weimar: Metzler, 2001).

26. Alois Riegl, "The Modern Cult of Monuments: Its Character and Its Origin," trans. Kurt W. Forster and Diane Ghirardo, *Oppositions* 25 (1982): 21.

27. Ibid.

28. Lewis Mumford, *The Culture of Cities* (New York: Harcourt, Brace and Co., 1938), 65.

29. For a thoroughgoing discussion of this notion, see Carsten Zelle, *"Angenehmes Grauen": Literaturhistorische Beiträge zur Ästhetik des Schrecklichen im 18. Jahrhundert* (Hamburg: Felix Meiner, 1987).

30. Johann Wolfgang von Goethe, "Von deutscher Baukunst," in *Werke: Schriften zur Kunst und Literatur, Maximen und Reflexionen (Hamburger Ausgabe),* ed. Erich Trunz and Herbert von Einem (Munich: C. H. Beck, 1981), 12: 7–15.

31. For a very early example, see Johann Friedrich Reichardt, "Johann Sebastian Bach," *Musikalisches Kunstmagazin* 1 (1782): 196–202.

32. Arnold Schering, "Über den Begriff des Monumentalen in der Musik," in *Von großen Meistern der Musik* (Leipzig: Koehler und Amelang, 1940), 7.

33. Franz Brendel, *Franz Liszt als Symphoniker* (Leipzig: Breitkopf und Härtel, 1857), 37. "Einer späteren Zeit wird die ganze Epoche als *ein* großer Höhenzug mit verschiedenen

Gipfeln erscheinen. Ich wiederhole: das Prinzip ist bei allen diesen größten Künstlern dasselbe; nur innerhalb desselben sind besondere Modifikationen zu unterscheiden."

34. Philipp Spitta, "Denkmäler deutscher Tonkunst," *Die Grenzboten* 52 (1893): 22–23. "Kommt auf die großen deutschen Komponisten der Vergangenheit die Rede, so denkt man zunächst immer noch an Haydn, Mozart und Beethoven. Dass Händel und Bach unter sie einzubeziehen sind, daran hat man sich wohl allmählich gewöhnt. Aber in der allgemeinen Anschauung ragen sie auf wie Berge aus der Wüste. . . . Wenn es in der Kunstgeschichte Erscheinungen giebt, denen eine überragende Größe einmütig zugestanden wird, so folgt daraus nicht, daß minder große Künstler für die Nachwelt entbehrlich wären. Mit gleichem Rechte könnte man um weniger höchsten Berge willen auf die ganze übrige Alpenwelt verzichten."

35. Ibid. 21. "Bachs und Händels Schöpfungen sind wie zwei hohe Berge, von denen das Auge gewahr werden konnte, wie weit, reich und blühend rings die Welt war."

36. It is quite possible that Brendel's conception of music history influenced the title of Richard Pohl's fascinating lecture series, *Höhenzüge der musikalischen Entwicklung* (Leipzig: B. Elischer, 1888). The appendix concretizes the "mountain ranges of musical evolution" from the title as tables covering different genres in nationally separate genealogies, showing how "instrumental music of the last 200 years" and the densely populated "nineteenth-century opera" both peak in the figure of Richard Wagner.

37. This is not to say that they cannot be thematized and scrutinized separately: the "Beethoven paradigm" has been examined from different angles in Burnham's *Beethoven Hero* and Mark Evan Bonds, *Music as Thought: Listening to the Symphony in the Age of Beethoven* (Princeton: Princeton University Press, 2006); the "Bach paradigm" has recently been examined in Celia Applegate, *Bach in Berlin: Nation and Culture in Mendelssohn's Revival of the* St. Matthew Passion (Ithaca, NY: Cornell University Press, 2005).

38. Friedrich Nietzsche, "On Uses and Disadvantages of History for Life," *Untimely Meditations,* trans. R. J. Hollingdale (Cambridge: Cambridge University Press, 1997), 68.

39. Despite its age, Donald B. Kuspit's essay "Nietzsche's Conception of Monumental History," *Archiv für Philosophie* 13 (1964): 95–115, is still an excellent introduction to and reading of Nietzsche's influential text.

40. Robert Schumann (as Florestan), "Monument für Beethoven," *Neue Zeitschrift für Musik* 4 (1836): 211. See also n. 34 in the following chapter.

41. Alfred Einstein, *Greatness in Music,* trans. César Saerchinger (New York: Oxford University Press, 1941), 3.

42. See also Chua, *Absolute Music,* 235–244.

43. See, for instance, Andreas Eichhorn, *Beethovens Neunte Symphonie: Die Geschichte ihrer Aufführung und Rezeption* (Kassel: Bärenreiter, 1993); and Albrecht Riethmüller, "Aspekte des musikalisch Erhabenen im 19. Jahrhundert," *Archiv für Musikwissenschaft* 40 (1983): 38–49.

44. Riegl, "The Modern Cult of Monuments," 22.

45. Aleida Assmann, "Kultur als Lebenswelt und Monument," in Aleida Assmann and Dietrich Harth, eds., *Kultur als Lebenswelt und Monument* (Frankfurt am Main: Fischer, 1991), 14. "Monument ist, was dazu bestimmt ist, die Gegenwart zu überdauern und in diesem Fernhorizont kultureller Kommunikation zu sprechen." See also her *Erinnerungsräume: Formen und Wandlungen des kulturellen Gedächtnisses* (Munich: C. H. Beck, 1999).

46. Schering, "Über den Begriff des Monumentalen," 8. "Denn obwohl natürlich jedes Zeitalter darin seine Großen gestellt hat und gerade auch das 19. Jahrhundert durch ein Streben nach monumentalischen Wirkungen ausgezeichnet ist, gibt es doch nur wenige Namen, mit denen wir den Begriff so schlechthin und unbedenklich verbinden können."

47. Schering, "Über den Begriff des Monumentalen," 7. "Was würdig ist, dauernd in der Erinnerung der Nachwelt festgehalten zu werden, dem setzt man ein Denkmal, ein Monument. Das kann immer nur ein Großes, Bedeutendes sein, von dem sich annehmen läßt, daß die Kraft seiner Inhalte auch in fernsten Zeiten noch lebendig zu wirken und Augenblicke der Erhebung, des Stolzes, des Selbstbewußtseins zu schaffen vermag."

48. Ibid.

49. Friedrich Nietzsche, *The Case of Wagner,* trans. Walter Kaufmann, in *The Basic Writings of Nietzsche* (New York: Modern Library, 2000), 627.

50. Jens Kulenkampff, for instance, regards "monumental" as fully synonymous with "sublime." See "Notiz über die Begriffe 'Monument' und 'Lebenswelt,'" in Assmann and Harth, eds., *Kultur als Lebenswelt und Monument,* 27–28.

51. See Adolf Zeising, *Aesthetische Forschungen* (Frankfurt am Main: Meiglinger Sohn & Co., 1855); Arthur Seidl, *Vom Musikalisch-Erhabenen: Prolegomena zur Aesthetik der Tonkunst* (Leizpig: Kahnt, 1887); Hugo Riemann, *Die Elemente der musikalischen Aesthetik* (Berlin and Stuttgart: Spemann, 1900); and Hermann Stephani, *Das Erhabene, insonderheit in der Tonkunst, und das Problem der Form im Musikalisch-Schönen und -Erhabenen* (Leipzig: Hermann Seemann, 1903).

52. Riegl, "The Modern Cult of Monuments," 21.

53. It is no coincidence that so many of these works are choral. Ryan Minor has recently examined the complex of monumentality in music specifically from the angle of the nineteenth-century choral repertory and its institutions. See his "National Memory, Public Music: Commemoration and Consecration in Nineteenth-Century German Choral Music," Ph.D. dissertation (University of Chicago, 2005). See also John Deathridge, "Germany—the Special Path," in Jim Samson, ed., *The Late Romantic Era* (Basingstoke: McMillan, 1991), 50–73.

54. See, for instance, Carl Dahlhaus, ed., *Studien zur Trivialmusik* (Regensburg: Gustav Bosse, 1967).

55. See Kuhlenkampff, "Notiz zur dem Begriffen," 27–28.

56. Idealist aesthetics specifies that the sublime is a subjective effect, not an objective property of a work of art. This caveat, however, was often ignored. See also Reinhold Brinkmann, "The Distorted Sublime: Music and National Socialist Ideology—A Sketch," in Albrecht Riethmüller and Michael Kater, eds., *Music and Nazism: Art under Tyranny 1933–1945* (Laaber: Laaber Verlag, 2003), 43–63. See also Christine Pries, ed., *Das Erhabene: Zwischen Grenzerfahrung und Größenwahn* (Weinheim: VCH Acta humaniora, 1989).

57. August Reissmann, *Allgemeine Geschichte der Musik* (Leipzig: Fries's Verlag, 1864), 3: 322. "Wirksame Akkordfolgen, wie [example 1.2] mögen wohl dem Laien gegenüber ihre Wirkung nicht verlieren, aber bei dem Musiker, der das Mechanische eines solchen Verfahrens kennt, führen sie früh Ermüdung herbei, selbst wenn er, alle andern Anforderungen beiseite setzend, sich rückhaltslos der Wirkung der Musik überläßt."

58. See note 47 above.

59. See also Riegl, "The Modern Cult of Monuments," 29.

60. Schering, "Über den Begriff des Monumentalen," 7. "Merkmal eines jeden wahrhaften Monuments wird sein, daß es über die Zeiten hinaus die Wucht des erstmaligen Eindrucks seiner Inhalte übermittelt."

61. Assmann, "Kultur als Lebenswelt und Monument," 13–14. "[D]as Monument [ist] ein aufgerichtetes, gestiftetes Zeichen, das eine Botschaft kodiert," "Monument [ist] ein Zeichen, das direkt auf einen Adressaten bezogen ist."

62. See, for instance, Andreas Huyssen, "Monumental Seduction," *New German Critique* Special Issue: Richard Wagner (1996): 198.

63. For a thoughtful discussion of related aesthetic issues, see Bernd Sponheuer, *Musik als Kunst und Nicht-Kunst* (Kassel: Bärenreiter, 1987).

64. Theodor W. Adorno, "The Fetish Character of Music and the Regression of Listening," in *Theodor W. Adorno: Essays on Music,* ed. Richard Leppert, trans. Susan Gillespie (Berkeley: University of California Press, 2001), 290.

65. For musicological treatments of this complex topic, see Peter Schleuning, *Der Bürger erhebt sich: Geschichte der deutschen Musik im achtzehnten Jahrhundert* (Stuttgart: Metzler, 2000); David Gramit, *Cultivating Music: The Aspirations, Interests and Limits of German Musical Culture 1770–1848* (Berkeley: University of California Press, 2002); Applegate, *Bach in Berlin;* and Sanna Pederson, "A. B. Marx and Berlin Concert Life, and German National Identity," *Nineteenth Century Music* 18 (1994): 87–107.

66. On historicism in general, see Annette Wittkau, *Historimus: Zur Geschichte des Begriffs und des Problems* (Göttingen: Vandenhoeck & Ruprecht, 1992). Despite its age, Walter Wiora, ed., *Die Ausbreitung des Historismus über die Musik* (Regensburg: Gustav Bosse, 1969) remains the authoritative collection on this topic in musicology.

67. On various aspects of nationalism in music, see Richard Taruskin's influential entry "Nationalism," in *New Grove,* ed. Stanley Sadie (Basingstoke: Macmillan, 2000), 17: 689–706; Jim Samson, "Nations and Nationalism," *The Cambridge History of Nineteenth Century Music* (Cambridge: Cambridge University Press, 2001), 568–600; and Philip Bohlman, *The Music of European Nationalism* (Santa Barbara, CA: ABC Clio, 2004). Celia Applegate and Pamela Potter examine forms of German nationalism in their important edited collection, *Music and German National Identity* (Chicago University of Chicago Press, 2002).

68. This idea was explored in particular by Paul Bekker. See for instance his "Deutsche Musik der Gegenwart," in Philipp Witkop, ed., *Deutsches Leben der Gegenwart* (Berlin: Volksverband der Bücherfreunde, Wegweiser Verlag, 1922), 78–126.

69. Nipperdey, "Nationalidee und Nationaldenkmal," 551–559.

70. See particularly, Georg Friedrich Wilhelm Hegel, *Vorlesungen über die Philosophie der Weltgeschichte, Bd. 1: Die Vernunft in der Geschichte,* ed. Georg Lasson (Hamburg: F. Meiner, 1988), 96–105.

71. Thomas Carlyle, *On Heroes, Hero-Worship and the Heroic in History,* reprint (New York: AMS Press, 1969), 13.

72. See Wilhelm Lange-Eichbaum, *Genie, Irrsinn und Ruhm* (Munich: E. Reinhard, 1928); and Axel Gehring, *Genie und Verehrergemeinde: Eine soziologische Analyse des Genie-Problems* (Bonn: Bouvier, 1968).

73. The canonical role of Beethoven was critically examined in Elisabeth Eleonore Bauer, *Wie Beethoven auf den Sockel kam: Die Entstehung eines musikalischen Mythos* (Stuttgart: Metzler, 1992); and Tia de Nora, *Beethoven and the Construction of Genius: Musical Politics in*

Vienna 1792–1803 (Berkeley: University of California Press, 1996). A recent reappraisal of the genius concept in music is found in Peter Kivy, *The Possessor and the Possessed: Handel, Mozart, Beethoven and the Idea of Musical Genius* (New Haven: Yale University Press, 2001).

74. Ernest Gellner, *Nations and Nationalism* (Oxford: Blackwell, 1983), 48–49.

75. Benedict Anderson, *Imagined Communities: Reflections on the Origin and Spread of Nationalism*, revised edition (London and New York: Verso, 1991). Despite (or because of) its lasting influence, Anderson's concept, which tends to stress the creative, imaginary character of the nation, has been attacked from numerous sides. An interesting critique, from the angle of German monuments, is found in Rudy Koshar, *From Monuments to Traces: Artifacts of German Memory 1870–1990* (Berkeley: University of California Press, 2000).

76. It is worth bearing in mind David Gramit's caveat that, more often than not, "*wir Deutsche* (we Germans) is a wishfully invoked metaphor for *wir Musiker* (we musicians), a claim that the prestige associated with the former category applies to the latter as well." See David Gramit, *Cultivating Music*, 32.

77. Friedrich Nietzsche, *The Gay Science*, trans. Walter Kaufmann (New York: Vintage, 1974), 158.

78. Huyssen, "Monumental Seduction," 192.

79. See Matthew Head, "Music with 'No Past'?" 426–437.

80. Triest, "Bemerkungen," col. 445. "[Lasset uns] aber auch alle ersinnliche Aufmerksamkeit denen gönnen, welche durch Genie und Fleiß ihren inneren Beruf zur Ausbildung und Erhöhung einer Kunst darthun, die auf größeren Werth als den eines flüchtenden Mittels zur sinnlichen Ergötzung Ansprüche macht, ja, die, gleich dem Geiste, der sie bearbeitet, einer Vervollkommnung ins Unendliche fähig ist."

Chapter Two

1. Hanjo Kesting, ed., *Briefwechsel Franz Liszt–Richard Wagner* (Frankfurt am Main: Insel, 1988), 425. Translated by Francis Hueffer, in *Correspondence of Wagner and Liszt*, 2 vols. (London: H. Grevel & Co., 1897), 2: 91 (translation modified).

2. Lina Ramann, *Franz Liszt als Künstler und Mensch*, 3 vols. (Leipzig: Breitkopf und Härtel, 1887), 2/ii: 46, 74, 80, 85, 101, and 110. Modern Liszt biography has tended to discredit Ramann's subjective style and tendentious conclusions. In the sense of biography as is developed here, however, Ramann's example remains the most important specimen of Liszt's hagiographic biography. For a recent reappraisal of Ramann, see Eva Rieger, "So schlecht wie ihr Ruf?: Die Liszt-Biographin Lina Ramann," *Neue Zeitschrift für Musik* 147/7–8 (1986): 16–20.

3. Ramann, *Franz Liszt*, 2/ii: 114 and 126. See also 1: 201–204: "Das Princip der Programm-Musik erscheint hiermit nicht mehr als Princip, welches an der Spitze der Instrumentalmusik steht oder dorthin gestellt werden, sondern als historisches Mittel, welches dazu berufen war, der Instrumentalmusik den Weg zu jener Idee: zu einem Weltinhalt anzubahnen. . . . Mit dieser Erkenntnis war die geistige Spirale gefunden, deren Linie die zukünftige Entwickelung der Tonkunst zum Universellen führt. Mit ihr hatte Beethoven's Prophetenwort seine volle Deutung gefunden."

4. He discusses the cycle of nine works in letters to Louis Köhler in the spring of 1854, see La Mara (pseud. Maria Lipsius), *Franz Liszts Briefe*, 8 vols. (Leipzig: Breitkopf und Härtel, 1893-1902), 1: 154 and 156; and to Wagner in a letter of January 25, 1855,

see Kesting, *Briefwechsel Liszt–Wagner,* 409. On Liszt's Beethoven reception, see particularly Axel Schröter, *"Der Name Beethoven ist heilig in der Kunst": Studien zu Liszts Beethoven-Rezeption* (Sinzig: Studio, 1999). On the number and order of the symphonic poems, see also Detlef Altenburg, "Die Schriften von Franz Liszt: Bemerkungen zu einem zentralen Problem der Liszt-Forschung," in *Festschrift Arno Forchert* (Kassel: Bärenreiter, 1986), 242–251.

5. Kesting, *Briefwechsel Liszt–Wagner,* 425; Hueffer, *Correspondence Liszt–Wagner,* 92 (translation modified).

6. Paul Bekker, *Richard Wagner: Das Leben im Werke* (Stuttgart: Deutsche Verlagsanstalt, 1924), 320–324.

7. Lina Ramann, *Lisztiana,* ed. Arthur Seidl (Mainz: Schott, 1983), 36. And even stronger in 1878: "Meine Biographie ist mehr zu erfinden denn nachzuschreiben" ("My biography should be invented rather than written down"), Ibid., 407. On Liszt's biography, see also my "Inventing Liszt's Life: Early Biography and Autobiography," in Kenneth Hamilton, ed., *The Cambridge Companion to Liszt* (Cambridge: Cambridge University Press, 2005), 14–27.

8. See, for instance, Susan Bernstein, *Virtuosity of the Nineteenth Century: Performing Music and Language in Heine, Liszt, and Baudelaire* (Stanford, CA: Stanford University Press, 1998), 109–119; and Dana Gooley, *The Virtuoso Liszt* (Cambridge: Cambridge University Press, 2004).

9. Franz Liszt, Introduction to *Tasso: Lamento e Trionfo,* trans. Humphrey Searle (London: Eulenburg, 1976), p. v. "Ce motif est en lui-même plaintif, d'une gémisante lenteur, d'un deuil monotone; mais les gondoliers lui prêtent un miroitement tout particulier en traînant certaines notes par la retenue des voix, qui à distance planent et brillent comme des traînées de gloire et de lumière. Ce chant nous avait profondément impressionnés jadis, et lorsque nous eûmes à parler du Tasse, il eût été impossible à notre sentiment ému de ne point prendre pour texte de nos pensées, cet hommage persistant rendu par sa nation à l'homme de génie dont la cour de Ferrare ne méritait ni l'attachement ni la fidélité."

10. The most explicit case of an "apotheosis" topic is found in *Die Ideale.* For a detailed discussion of this symphonic poem and its final apotheosis, see Vera Micznik, "The Absolute Limitations of Programme Music: The Case of Liszt's *Die Ideale," Music and Letters* 80 (1999): 207–240.

11. On Liszt's choice of subject matters, see Detlef Altenburg, "Franz Liszt and the Legacy of the Classical Era," *19th Century Music* 18 (1994): 46–63; and Carl Dahlhaus, "Dichtung und Symphonische Dichtung," in *Klassische und Romantische Musikästhetik* (Laaber: Laaber Verlag, 1988), 385–392.

12. Thomas Mann, "The Sorrows and Grandeur of Richard Wagner," in *Pro and Contra Wagner,* trans. Allan Blunden (Chicago: University of Chicago Press, 1985), 135. See Introduction, n. 13, above.

13. Alfred Heuß, "Eine motivisch-thematische Studie über Liszts sinfonische Dichtung 'Ce qu'on entend sur la montagne': Zur 100. Wiederkehr von Franz Liszts Geburtstag am 22. Oktober 1911," *Zeitschrift der Internationalen Musikwissenschaftlichen Gesellschaft* 13 (1911): 10–21.

14. It is noteworthy that Heuß does not mention the term "thematic transformation" in this article; yet it has been inextricably associated with it. In his *Nineteenth-Century Music* (Berkeley and Los Angeles: University of California Press, 1989), 274, Carl Dahlhaus

further suggests that Liszt might have found this technique in César Franck's Trio in F-sharp minor op. 1 no. 1 (1841). For a concise introduction to thematic transformation in the recent literature, see Keith T. Johns, *The Symphonic Poems of Franz Liszt,* ed. Michael Saffle (Stuyvesant, NY: Pendragon, 1997), 17.

15. What is remarkable about this particular apotheosis is that, contrary to mid-nineteenth-century symphonic traditions, it is based on primary material—not the more common second subject—and as such on a theme with particularly masculine associations. As James Hepokoski has shown, the archetype of the "feminine apotheosis" is found in the overture to Wagner's *Flying Dutchman* (1841), see Hepokoski, "Masculine-Feminine," *The Musical Times* 135 (1994): 494–499, and his "Beethoven Reception: The Symphonic Tradition," in *The Cambridge History of Nineteenth Century Music,* ed. Jim Samson (Cambridge: Cambridge University Press, 2001), 447–450. Michael Tusa identifies the type of apotheosis of the second, "feminine" subject in the overture of Weber's *Euryanthe,* see *Euryanthe and Carl Maria von Weber's Dramaturgy of German Opera* (Oxford: Clarendon Press, 1991), 271–274.

16. Leonard B. Meyer, *Style and Music: Theory, History, and Ideology* (Chicago: University of Chicago Press, 1989), 204.

17. Ibid. 323.

18. See also Introduction, [5–8].

19. Johns, *The Symphonic Poems of Franz Liszt,* 19. On "Liszt's Bad Style," see also Susan Bernstein, *Virtuosity of the Nineteenth Century,* 109–130.

20. Richard Wagner, *Opera and Drama,* trans. Edward Evans (London: W. Reeves, 1913), 1: 158–160. There is a certain irony in applying this term to Wagner's friend and subsequent father-in-law, given that Wagner had originally coined the term for his nemesis, the successful Jewish opera composer Giacomo Meyerbeer.

21. Charles Rosen, *The Romantic Generation* (Cambridge, MA: Harvard University Press, 1996), 492.

22. Friedrich Nietzsche, "On the Uses and Disadvantages of History for Life," in *Untimely Meditations,* ed. Daniel Breazeale, trans. R. J. Hollingdale (Cambridge: Cambridge University Press, 1997), 69.

23. Ibid. 69 and 68.

24. Ibid.

25. Ibid. 70.

26. The history of the Beethoven monument has been retold various times, most recently in Ryan Minor, "National Memory, Public Music: Commemoration and Consecration in Nineteenth-Century German Choral Music," Ph.D. dissertation (University of Chicago, 2005). The relevant chapter has been reprinted as "Prophet and Populace in Liszt's 'Beethoven' Cantatas," in Christopher Gibbs and Dana Gooley, eds., *Liszt and His World* (Princeton: Princeton University Press, 2006), 113–166. See also Theodor A. Henseler's near-exhaustive collection of materials in *Das musikalische Bonn im 19. Jahrhundert* (Bonn: [s. n.], 1959), 164–225.

27. As discussed in chapter 1, sculpted representations of German-born composers had long existed outside of Germany—notably in Britain (Handel) and France (Gluck). Also, by the time the Beethoven sculpture was finished, other kinds of memorials had been erected for some composers in other German cities. As we shall see later, however,

the special circumstances surrounding the erection of this statue sparked a controversy that none of the other examples could have caused.

28. Henseler estimates that the appeal came from Andreas Diderich, a local figure. See *Das musikalische Bonn,* 165.

29. The appeal is reproduced in full in Heinrich Karl Breidenstein, *Festgabe zur Inaugurations-Feier des Beethoven Monuments* (Bonn: T. Habicht, 1846; Reprint Bonn: Ludwig Röhrscheid Verlag, 1983), 3–4.

30. This has been described by various commentators. See above all, Alessandra Comini, *The Changing Image of Beethoven: A Study in Myth-Making* (New York: Rizzoli, 1987), 315–388; and Alan Walker, *Franz Liszt: The Virtuoso Years* (Ithaca, NY: Cornell University Press, 1987), 417–426.

31. "Jean Paul über Denkmale," *Bonner Wochenblatt* 104 (August 30, 1836): 1. See Bodsch, "Monument für Beethoven: Die Künstlerstandbilder des bürgerlichen Zeitalters als Sinnstifter nationaler Identität," in Ingrid Bodsch, *Monument für Beethoven: Zur Geschichte des Beethoven-Denkmals (1845) und der frühen Beethoven-Rezeption in Bonn* (Bonn: Bonner Stadtmuseum, 1995), 159. "Was will überhaupt ein Denkmal? Unmöglich, Unsterblichkeit zu geben—ein jedes setzt eine voraus und nicht der Thronhimmel trägt den Atlas, sondern der Riese den Himmel."

32. Ibid. "Zwei Ideale: ein geistiges durch ein plastisches."

33. Schumann's musical response to the Beethoven monument—the C-major Fantasy, op. 17, dedicated to Franz Liszt—has been discussed by John Daverio in *Nineteenth-Century Music and Romantic Ideology* (New York: Schirmer, 1995), 19–48.

34. Robert Schumann, "Monument für Beethoven: Vier kritische Stimmen hierüber," *Neue Zeitschrift für Musik* 4 (1836): 211. "Ein griechischer Bildhauer; angegangen um einen Plan zu einem Denkmal für Alexander, schlug vor, den Berg Athos zu einer Statue auszuhauen, die in der Hand eine Stadt in die Luft hinaushielte; der Mann ward für toll erklärt, wahrhaftig er ist es weniger, als diese deutschen Pfennigsubskriptionen."

35. Ibid., "ein leidlich hoher Quader, eine Lyra darauf mit Geburts- und Sterbejahr, darüber der Himmel und daneben einige Bäume."

36. Ibid.

37. Schumann-Jonathan expressed this with an aphorism: "A monument is a ruin turned forward, just as a ruin is a monument turned backward." ("Schon ein Denkmal ist eine vorwärts gedrehte Ruine, wie eine Ruine ein rückwärts gedrehtes Denkmal ist.") See ibid. 212.

38. For a modern commentary on this view, see John B. Jackson, "The Necessity for Ruins," in *The Necessity for Ruins, and Other Topics* (Amherst: University of Massachusetts Press, 1980), 91–93.

39. Schumann, "Monument für Beethoven," 212.

40. "Du Meister bist's, der Töne Hort, / Dess hohes Bild / Vor unsren Augen ward enthüllt, / An diesem Ort, / Wo Deine Wiege stand, / Denn hier bei uns am deutschen Rhein, / Ob jedes Land dich nenne sein / Gewalt'ger, ist dein Vaterland." Printed in Breidenstein, *Festgabe zur Inaugurations-Feier des Beethoven Monuments zu Bonn,* 32.

41. For some recent accounts, see the literature referenced in nn. 26 and 30 above. Accounts of Liszt's involvement can be found in Hans-Josef Irmen, "Franz Liszt in Bonn, oder: Wie die erste Beethovenhalle entstand," *Studien zur Bonner Musikgeschichte des 18. und*

19. *Jahrhunderts,* ed. Marianne Bröcker and Günther Massenkeil (Cologne: Arno Volk Verlag, 1978), 49–65; Michael Saffle, *Liszt in Germany 1840–1845: A Study of Its Sources, Documents, and the History of Reception* (Stuyvesant, NY: Pendragon Press, 1994), 174–180; Lina Ramann, *Franz Liszt als Künstler und Mensch* 2/i: 249–265; and Alan Walker, *Franz Liszt: The Virtuoso Years,* 417–426.

42. Henry F. Chorley, *Modern German Music* (London: Smith, Elder and Co., 1854), 2: 271–272.

43. See Hector Berlioz, *Evenings with the Orchestra,* trans. Jacques Barzun (New York: Alfred A. Knopf, 1956), 329.

44. See Bodsch, "Monument für Beethoven," 166.

45. Liszt tried to make up for this blunder by buying tickets for the journalists and paying for them from his own pocket. Breidenstein defends his position in *Zur Jahresfeier der Inauguration des Beethoven Monuments* (Bonn: T. Habicht, 1846; reprint Bonn: Ludwig Röhrscheid Verlag, 1983), 37–39. For modern commentaries on both conflicting positions, see Walker, *Franz Liszt: The Virtuoso Years,* 417–426; and Hans-Josef Irmen, "Franz Liszt in Bonn," 49–65.

46. A[ugust] S[chmidt], "Fliegende Blätter aus meinem Reise-Portefeuille: Nachstationen in Bonn beim Beethovenfeste, 10. bis 13. August 1845," *Wiener Allgemeine Musik-Zeitung* 5 (1845): 402. "Mag immerhin Hr. Breidenstein als Präses des Comité's, als Localdirector den billigen Wunsch gehegt haben, bei dem festlichen Acte beschäftigt zu sein, so dürfte er sich doch nimmer mit einer eigenen Composition eindrängen, wo Spohr, Lindpaintner u.v.a. beim Feste Anwesende, diese Ehre anzusprechen vermöge ihres berühmten Namens weit eher berechtigt waren; ja Hr. Breidenstein hätte, was gewiß jeder Bescheidene gethan haben würde, falls ihn das Comité zur Composition eines Festchores aufgefordert, die Ehre bestimmt ablehnen müssen, eine Ehre, der nur der älteste der ersten lebenden deutschen Tondichter theilhaftig werden sollte."

47. Goethe's original is slightly more lenient: "Wer lobt, stellt sich gleich."

48. Louis Spohr, *Lebenserinnerungen,* ed. Folker Göthel (Tutzing: Hans Schneider, 1968), 180.

49. Heinrich K. Breidenstein, *Festgabe zur Inauguration des Beethoven-Monuments zu Bonn,* 7.

50. Anton Schindler, "Ad Vocem Beethoven-Fest-Polemik," *Kölnische Zeitung,* Beilage 183 (July 2, 1845). See also Irmen "Franz Liszt in Bonn," 52. "Es sei ferne von mir, weder zum Vergnügen der Einen noch zum Mißvergnügen der Andern, . . . dem übermäßigen Geschrei über Herrn Liszt, . . . ein Sordino zu Deutsch: Dämpfer aufzusetzen. Die Wahrheit muß in jedem Falle mehr wiegen, denn zehntausend Fr., . . . vor denen aber einige Herren in Bonn auf die Knie fallen, weil ihr Klang eben derjenige ist, der ihren Gehörnerven am angenehmsten afficirt. . . . Ich war wirklich daran, dem Comite den Münchner Hofcapellmeister Lachner zum Fest-Dirigenten anzurathen, . . . weil er der einzige unter allen ist, der viele Jahre hindurch Beethoven's Musik in des Meisters Auffassungsweise in Wien kennengelernt, seit achtzehn Jahren als Musik-Director functionirt, mithin kein 'Improvisirter' ist. Lachner ist sicherlich auch von der Überzeugung durchdrungen, daß, wer die 9. Symphonie und die Missa solemnis . . . dirigiren will, sie selbsteigen mit Chor und Orchester einüben muß, um sich selbst in die Werke hineinzuarbeiten, sei er auch noch so routinirt; dabei hört es auf, wie ein hoher General vertrauend auf seinen berühmten Namen zu kommen, dem musicalischen Corps die Revue abzunehmen. . . . Wozu aber ein

Mann wie Lachner? Wozu auch Spohr, wenn Liszt da ist? Hat Lachner sich das Recht zur Direction mit einer großen Summe erkauft? Wahrscheinlich ist sein Beitrag = 0. Aber 0:10000 ist eine erschreckliche Disproportion; folglich können wir Herrn Lachner nicht einladen."

51. Walker, *Franz Liszt: The Virtuoso Years,* 421.

52. This celebrated incident has been reported repeatedly; see, for instance, Ramann, *Liszt als Künstler und Mensch,* 1: 45–47; La Mara, "Beethovens Weihekuß," *Allgemeine Musikzeitung* 40 (1913): 544–546; Allan Keiler, "Liszt and Beethoven: The Creation of a Personal Myth," *19th-Century Music* 12 (1988): 116–131; and Walker, *Franz Liszt: The Virtuoso Years,* 81–85. For a somewhat self-indulgent homosexual reading, see Kevin Kopelson, *Beethoven's Kiss: Pianism, Perversion and the Mastery of Desire* (Stanford, CA.: Stanford University Press, 1996). In connection with the Beethoven festival, see also Susanne Schaal, "Das Beethoven-Denkmal von Julius Hähnel in Bonn," in *Monument für Beethoven,* ed. Bodsch, 51; Michael Ladenburger, "Wie sich das 'neue Bonn' bewährte oder: Das Musikfest zwischen den Fronten," in Bodsch, *Monument für Beethoven,* 148–149; and Irmen, "Franz Liszt in Bonn," 57.

53. See Ladenburger, ibid.

54. Ibid. "Schreibe sogleich, ob du diesen Brief empfangen, an den Schindler—diesen verachtung[s]würdigen Gegenstand[—]werde ich dir einige Zeilen schicken, da ich unmittelbar nicht gern mit diesem elend[en] zu tun habe." The letter itself is reproduced in Bodsch, *Monument für Beethoven,* 152.

55. See Horst Hallensleben, "Das Bonner Beethoven-Denkmal als frühes 'bürgerliches Standbild'," in *Monument für Beethoven,* 35–36. On bourgeois monuments in Germany, see further Günther Hess, "Panorama und Denkmal: Erinnerung als Denkmal zwischen Vormärz und Gründerzeit," in Albert Nartino, ed., *Literatur in der sozialen Bewegung* (Tübingen: Max Niemeyer, 1977), 130–206; and Rolf Selbmann, *Dichterdenkmäler in Deutschland: Literaturgeschichte in Erz und Stein* (Stuttgart: Metzler, 1988).

56. Henseler, *Das musikalische Bonn,* 196.

57. See David Blackbourn and Richard J. Evans, eds., *The German Bourgeoisie: Essays on the Social History of the German Middle Class from the Late Eighteenth to the Early Twentieth Century* (New York: Routledge, 1991), particularly 18–20.

58. Thomas Nipperdey, "Auf der Suche nach der Identität: Romantischer Nationalismus," in *Nachdenken über die deutsche Geschichte* (Munich: C. H. Beck, 1986), 110–125.

59. The phenomenon of liberalist, democratic nationalism flipping over into aggressive chauvinism has been aptly called the "Janus face" of nationalism. See Dieter Langewiesche, "Nation, Nationalismus, Nationalstaat: Forschungsstand und Forschungsperspektive," *Neue Politische Literatur* 40 (1995): 195.

60. *Kölnische Zeitung,* November 27, 1836, Beiblatt. "Nur Eines hätte ich wenigstens anders gewünscht, nämlich die Annahme von Beiträgen des Auslandes; einem so echtdeutschen Künstler wie Beethoven, sollte die deutsche Nation auch rein aus sich, und ohne die (wenn auch noch so wohlgemeinte) Unterstützung der Fremde, die überdies noch zur Zeit den wahren und vollen Werth des großen Hingeschiedenen zu erkennen und zu fühlen nicht im Stande ist, anzunehmen, ein Monument zu errichten!" See Schaal, "Das Bonner Beethoven-Monument," 53.

61. See Ramann, *Franz Liszt als Künstler und Mensch,* 2/ii: 252. Walker follows her viewpoint in *Franz Liszt: The Virtuoso Years,* 422 n. 14. Likewise, Irmen bases his account

on K. Schorn's 1898 memoirs: writing half a century after the events, Schorn considered Liszt a non-German (see Irmen, "Franz Liszt in Bonn," 62).

62. Berlioz, *Evenings with the Orchestra*, 331. Berlioz's French perspective may have differed from German views on this matter, but to my knowledge no German newspaper ever questioned Liszt's German nationhood.

63. On this point, see Comini, *The Changing Image of Beethoven*, 328.

64. On the specific problems of German nationalism around 1848, in the absence of a unified state or a clearly defined concept of the nation, see Brian E. Vick, *Defining Germany: The 1848 Frankfurt Parliamentarians and National Identity* (Cambridge, MA: Harvard University Press, 2002).

65. Liszt had met Wolff at least once before, in Thuringia in late October 1842, when the poet offered the musician a libretto for a scene from Byron's *Manfred*. See Lothar Ehrlich, "Liszt und Goethe," in *Liszt und die Weimarer Klassik*, ed. Detlef Altenburg (Laaber: Laaber-Verlag, 1997), 37.

66. "Wenn sein Volk der Fürst vertritt / In den späteren Annalen, / Wer vertritt denn ihre Qualen, / Wer verkündet, was sie litt? / Wer steht im Buch der Weltgeschichte für sie auf? / Lässt ihren Namen strahlen durch der Zeiten Lauf? / Arme Menschheit, schweres Loos! / Wer wird von dir entsendet an der Tage Schluss? / Der Genius! / In seinem Wirken ewig gross!" Printed in Breidenstein, *Festgabe zur Inauguration des Beethoven-Monuments*, 36–37.

67. This is confirmed from all critical quarters: the gist is that Liszt possesses "enormous talent," that he shows "great promise," and possesses "princely gifts." Besides the numerous newspaper reviews on the festival, see Ignaz Moscheles, as quoted in Adrian Williams, *Portraits of Liszt: By Himself and His Contemporaries* (Oxford: Clarendon Press, 1990), 216.

68. Kesting, *Franz Liszt–Richard Wagner, Briefwechsel*, p. 52 / *Correspondence Liszt–Wagner*, 1: 2. See also Comini, *The Changing Image of Beethoven*, 321.

69. The committee knew that, too, and was obviously concerned that Liszt would carry off the trophy without leaving any of the merit to the committee, see Schaal, "Das Beethoven-Denkmal in Bonn," 51. Walker may be indulging Liszt when he disputes this point, see *Franz Liszt: The Virtuoso Years*, 420. It seems, however, that the committee's incompetence contributed to this inevitable outcome more so than Liszt's own doing.

70. See Comini, *The Changing Image of Beethoven*, 335.

71. Words and score of this unknown work had survived in separate archives and were finally put together by Günther Massenkeil in 1986. See Massenkeil, "Die Bonner Beethoven-Kantate von Franz Liszt," in *Die Sprache der Musik: Festschrift für Klaus Niemöller zum 60. Geburtstag*, ed. Jobst Peter Fricke (Regensburg: Gustav Bosse, 1989), 381–400.

72. See Henseler, *Das Musikalische Bonn*, 213–214.

73. A[ugust] S[chmidt], "Fliegende Blätter aus meinem Reise-Portefeuille," 403. "Fehlt auch dem Ganzen eben so die Einheit der Form, wie auch die Einheit der Idee, so läßt doch selbst dieses Totale der Composition etwas Außergewöhnliches erkennen. . . . Ich halte diese Composition nicht nur für eine der interessantesten Erscheinungen im Bereiche der Wirksamkeit Liszt's, sondern im Gebiete der Composition in der neuesten Zeit überhaupt, und Liszt hat dadurch das musikalische Publikum mit großen Hoffnungen für die Zukunft erfüllt."

74. Massenkeil, "Die Bonner Beethoven-Kantate," 395–397.

75. It is conspicuous that Liszt changes the key of Beethoven's Andante (from the original D major) first to C major and finally, for the apotheosis, to the home key of E major. (I thank Roger Parker for pointing this out to me.) It may be a major-third relation writ-large, which plays a big role in the harmonic language of the cantata. Alternatively, as Walker, *Franz Liszt: The Weimar Years* (Ithaca, NY: Cornell University Press, 1989), 154 n. 49, and others have noted, key symbolism is not uncommon in Liszt, and it is quite possible that these keys carry some special significance. Vladimir Jankélévitch, for instance, notes a propos of Liszt's keys that "la musique en *mi* majeur est décidément la musique des royals effusions du coeur," in *Liszt: Rhapsodie et impression* (Paris: Flammarion, 1998), 87.

76. Ramann, *Franz Liszt als Künstler und Mensch,* 2/i: 264. "Er hatte hiermit das Wesen des Beethoven'schen Genius charakterisiert und gleichsam durch sich selbst verherrlicht."

77. Julius Kapp, "Autobiographisches von Franz Liszt," *Die Musik* 11 (1911): 11.

78. See András Batta, "Die Gattung Paraphrase im Schaffen von Franz Liszt: Gattung Paraphrase—die musikalische Haßliebe Liszts," in *Liszt-Studien 4,* ed. Gottfried Scholz (Munich and Salzburg: Katzbichler, 1983), 135–142.

79. The allegorical bas-reliefs of the Beethoven statue represent Beethoven's excellence in the fields of dramatic music, sacred music, symphony, and fantasy—which, compared with our twenty-first-century perspective, presents a rather different view of Beethoven's oeuvre. For a discussion of the Beethoven statue from an art-historical viewpoint, see Schaal, "Das Beethoven-Denkmal von Ernst Julius Hähnel in Bonn," 37–116.

80. Dahlhaus points out in *Nineteenth-Century Music,* trans. J. Bradford Robinson (Berkeley and Los Angeles: University of California Press, 1989), 336, that a magnum opus must by definition be a large-scale work.

81. Nietzsche, "On the Uses and Disadvantages of History for Life," 70.

82. "Was versammelt hier die Menge? / Welch Geschäft rief Euch herbei? / Glaubt man doch an dem Gedränge, / Dass ein Festtag heute sei." Re-printed in Breidenstein, *Festgabe zur Inaugurationsfeier des Beethoven-Monuments, 33.*

83. Nietzsche, "Richard Wagner in Bayreuth," in *Untimely Meditations, 197.*

Chapter Three

1. On Liszt's Weimar activities, see Adelheid von Schorn, *Das nachklassische Weimar* (Weimar: Gustav Kiepenheuer, 1911–12); Wolfgang Marggraf, *Liszt in Weimar* (Weimar: Stadtmuseum Weimar, 1985); and Alan Walker, *Franz Liszt: The Weimar Years 1848–1861* (New York: Alfred A. Knopf, 1989). See also Ehrhard Bahr, "The Silver Age of Weimar. Franz Liszt as Goethe's Successor: A Study in Cultural Archaeology," *Yearbook of the Goethe Society* 10 (2001): 191–202; and Wolfram Huschke, "'wo Wagner und ich die Coryphäen gewesen wären, wie früher Goethe und Schiller': Franz Liszts Verhältnis zu den klassischen Traditionen Weimars," *Impulse* 5 (1982): 370–388.

2. On the Weimar Goethe jubilee, see Gerhard J. Winkler, "Liszt's 'Weimar Mythology'," in Michael Saffle, ed., *Liszt and His World* (Stuyvesant, NY: Pendragon Press, 1998), 61–73. See also Lothar Ehrlich, "Liszt und Goethe," in Detlef Altenburg, ed., *Franz Liszt und die Weimarer Klassik* (Laaber: Laaber-Verlag, 1997), 33–45.

3. Anon., "Goethes Jubelfeier in Weimar," *Leipziger Illustrirte Zeitung,* September 29, 1849, 196. "Nach Beendigung dieser Feier wurde an die Anwesenden eine elegant

ausgestattete Festgabe 'Zur Erinnerung an die Feier des 28. August 1849 auf der großher-zoglichen Bibliothek zu Weimar' vertheilt, welche interessante Facsimiles enthielt."

4. See, for instance, Burkhard Henke, Susanne Kord, and Simon Richter, eds., *Un-wrapping Goethe's Weimar: Essays in Cultural Studies and Local Knowledge* (Rochester, NY: Camden House, 2000); and Georg Bollenbeck, "Weimar," in Etienne François and Hagen Schulze, eds., *Deutsche Erinnerungsorte,* 3 vols. (Munich: C. H. Beck, 2001), 1: 207–224.

5. For a thoughtful discussion, see Matei Calinescu, *Five Faces of Modernity* (Durham, NC: Duke University Press, 1989), 223–262. German scholars have spent much time and effort in the attempt to come to terms with this phenomenon, see Ludwig Giesz, *Phänom-enologie des Kitsches: Ein Beitrag zur anthropologischen Ästhetik* (Frankfurt am Main: Fischer, 1994); Jochen Schulte-Sasse, ed., *Literarischer Kitsch* (Tübingen: Max Niemeyer, 1979); and Hans-Dieter Geuert, *Was ist Kitsch?* (Göttingen: Vandenhoeck & Ruprecht, 2000). The *locus classicus* in the English language remains Clement Greenberg's oft-reprinted "Avant-Garde and Kitsch," *Partisan Review* 6 (1939), 34–49. In the 1960s, especially, nu-merous attempts were made to isolate and define stylistic elements of *Kitsch* in music, see Carl Dahlhaus, ed., *Studien zur Trivialmusik* (Regensburg: Gustav Bosse, 1967); they have since been vigorously refuted.

6. Rena Charnin Mueller, "Sketches, Drafts and Revisions: Liszt at Work," in Detlef Altenburg and Gerhard J. Winkler, eds., *Die Projekte der Liszt-Forschung* (Eisenstadt: Bur-genländisches Landesmuseum, 1991), 26–34.

7. On this "secretive" aspect of music, see particularly Vladimir Jankélévitch, *De-bussy et le mystère* (Neuchâtel: Baconnière, 1949); and Carolyn Abbate, "Music—Drastic or Gnostic?" *Critical Inquiry* 30 (2004): 505–536.

8. Approaching the question from a compositional viewpoint, a good alternative case could be made for hearing this opening as the "cross motive" that Liszt was fond of dur-ing those years and that also features in the Bonn Beethoven Cantata. I am grateful to Ryan Minor for pointing out this relation.

9. Many of these thoughts on the souvenir could not have been formulated without Susan Stewart's groundbreaking *On Longing: Narratives of the Miniature, the Gigantic, the Souvenir, the Collection* (Durham, NC: Duke University Press, 1993).

10. Popular journals frequently took on this task of aiding and promulgating monu-ments by means of reportage. See Kirsten Belgum, "Displaying the Nation: A View of Nineteenth-Century Monuments through a Popular Magazine," *Central European History* 26 (93): 457–474.

11. Calinescu, *Five Faces of Modernity,* 234, locates the origin of *Kitsch* as an aesthetic category in Munich of the 1860s and 1870s. The very lively public and critical discourse about *Kitsch,* however, did not begin until the early twentieth century.

12. The indispensible guide to cultural life in nineteenth-century Weimar remains Adelheid von Schorn, *Das nachklassische Weimar* (Weimar: Gustav Kiepenheuer, 1911–12).

13. See Etienne François, "Die Wartburg," in François and Schulze, eds., *Deutsche Erinnerungsorte,* 2: 154–170.

14. Franz Liszt, "De la fondation-Goethe," in *Sämtliche Schriften,* 5 vols, ed. Detlev Altenburg and Britta Schilling-Wang (Wiesbaden: Breitkopf und Härtel, 1997), 3: 26. "L'Allemagne vit donc fleurir le chant et la poésie au treizième et dix-huitième siècle. Les noms les plus célèbres et les souvenirs les plus marquants de ces deux époques, se rat-tachèrent également aux beaux sites de la romanesque Thuringe. Ce furent d'abord ses

Landgraves qui immortalisèrent leurs noms par la protection qu'ils accordèrent aux poètes les plus renommés de leur temps: Wolfgang von Eschenbach, auteur du Parsifal, Walther von der Vogelweide, Heinrich d'Ofterdingen, natif d'Eisenach, Bitterolf, etc. habitèrent leur Cour, ou bien la fréquentèrent. Dans le château si pittoresque de la Wartburg, qui, pendant de longs siècles, fut la résidence des Langraves, eurent lieu ces combats des poètes (Sängerkrieg) qui restèrent à jamais fixés dans la mémoire des peuples."

15. The term "Silver Age" seems to have been established quite soon after Goethe's death, see Gitta Günther, Wolfram Huschke, and Walter Steiner, eds., *Weimar: Lexikon zur Stadtgeschichte* (Weimar: Böhlau, 1993), 401. Friederike Schmidt-Möbus and Frank Möbus, *Kleine Kulturgeschichte Weimars* (Cologne: Böhlau, 1998), 213–216, argue that the concept was in current usage by the 1850s. I am grateful to Aleksandr V. Markin for this bibliographic information. At any rate, Georg Gottfried Gervinus introduced the universal yardstick "Golden Age" in his influential literary histories of the 1830s.

16. Franz Brendel, *Die Musik der Gegenwart und die Gesammtkunst der Zukunft* (Leipzig: Bruno Hinze, 1854), 68. "Unsere Musik ist zu sehr verbreitet, um in sich abgeschlossene Kunst zu sein, um nur berufene Theilnehmer unter ihren Verehrern zu zählen, zu wenig aber, sie ist zu unpopulär in ihrem innersten Wesen, um als ächte Kunst des Volkes zu erscheinen, diesem innerlich wahrhaft eigen sein zu können. Wir haben darum in der Gegenwart die Herrschaft eines schlechten, der Kunst stets Gefahr bringenden Dilettantismus. . . . Unsere Musik ist auf dem Standpunkt, den sie insbesondere seit der zweiten Hälfte des vorigen Jahrhunderts einnimmt, einer solchen Verbreitung nicht gewachsen, sie wird dadurch innerlich vernichtet, ohne wirklich auf die Massen für die Dauer fruchtbringend wirken zu können."

17. For detailed examinations of Brendel's Hegelianism, see Johann Besser, "Die Beziehungen Franz Brendels zur Hegelschen Philosophie: Ein Beitrag zur Musikanschauung des Schumann-Kreises," in *Robert Schumann: Aus Anlaß seines 100. Todestages,* ed. Hans J. Moser and Eberhard Rebling (Leipzig: Breitkopf und Härtel, 1956), 84–91; and Bernd Sponheuer, "Zur ästhetischen Dichotomie als Denkform in der ersten Hälfte des 19. Jahrhunderts: Eine historische Skizze am Beispiel Schumanns, Brendels und Hanslicks," *Archiv für Musikwissenschaft* 37 (1980): 1–31.

18. See Franz Liszt, "Richard Wagner's Fliegender Holländer," in *Sämtliche Schriften,* ed. Dorothea Redepenning and Britta Schilling (Wiesbaden: Breitkopf und Härtel, 1989), 5: 71. "Die Gegenwart, von der Vergangenheit erzeugt, gebiert die Zukunft." In *Sämtliche Schriften,* 4: 84, Liszt originally described *Lohengrin* as a "beau monument." After Wagner's rejection of monumentality, Liszt replaced this expression with the somewhat less charged "immortal masterwork" in the version checked through by Wagner. For a detailed account of the revisions and the early reception of these essays, see Rainer Kleinertz's excellent critical commentary in *Sämtliche Schriften,* vol. 4.

19. The question of Liszt and anniversaries is an interesting one: it seems, on the one hand, that his Weimar tenure happened to coincide with an exceptionally large number of important jubilees. On the other hand, Weimar culture was such that it was more than happy to celebrate these with great pomp whenever possible.

20. Liszt, "Richard Wagner's Rheingold," 115.

21. Aleida Assmann, "Denkmäler in der Zeit: Vom Sinn und Unsinn der Gedenkjahre," *Schiller-Jahrbuch* 44 (2000): 298–302.

22. Liszt, "Richard Wagner's Rheingold," 115–116. "Seht Ihr den schimmernden

Punkt fern dort am Horizont? Es ist der gigantische Umriß eines majestätischen, großen Gebäudes wie wir im ganzen Lauf unseres Weges noch kein ähnliches erblickten. Vielleicht wird es Euch befremden, vielleicht werdet Ihr den Styl zu erhaben, den Plan zu riesig, die Ornamentik in ihrer Fülle zu reichhaltig finden—aber Ihr werdet zugestehen müssen, daß es das Großartigste unter den bestehenden Monumenten ist."

23. Letter of January 19, 1855. In Richard Wagner, *Sämtliche Briefe,* ed. Gertrud Strobel and Werner Wolf (Leipzig: Deutscher Verlag für Musik, 1969–), 6: 329. Translated in Stewart Spencer and Barry Millington, eds., *Selected Letters of Richard Wagner* (New York and London: Norton, 1987), 324–326.

24. Ibid. (translation modified). See also Liszt, *Sämtliche Schriften,* 5: 183.

25. Richard Wagner, "Eine Mitteilung an meine Freunde," *Gesammelte Schriften und Dichtungen,* 10 vols. (Leipzig: C. F. W. Siegel, 1898), 4: 237. Translation in William Ashton Ellis, *Richard Wagner's Prose Works,* Vol. 1, *The Art-Work of the Future* (Reprint; New York: Broude Brothers, 1966), 274 (translation modified, emphasis in original).

26. Ibid. 236–237 / 275–276 (translation modified). Since the published English translations of Wagner dating from the nineteenth century are notoriously unreliable, I have used them with caution. Here and in the following, the double page references refer first to the German version and then to the translation.

27. Baudelaire's understanding of modernity dwells particularly on the notion of fashion. See, for instance, Jürgen Habermas, *Der philosophische Diskurs der Moderne* (Frankfurt am Main: Suhrkamp, 1996), 17–20.

28. Wagner, "Eine Mitteilung," 238 / "A Communication," 278.

29. Where in his Zurich writings Wagner pronounced not only the death of the symphony but also that of opera, only to propose himself as the answer to both calls, Liszt countered the *creatio ex nihilo* that Wagner had invented for himself, subtly but pointedly, with a history of opera, published in twelve installments in German (not in French), that leads up to Wagner's *Fliegender Holländer* and *Rheingold* and provides his stage works with an operatic genealogy. Liszt's modern editors, Dorothea Redepenning and Britta Schilling, point out that Liszt emphasizes continuity where Wagner stresses discontinuity, particularly in his comment on Meyerbeer's (of all people) *Robert le Diable:* "In der Kunst so wenig, wie in der Natur steht je ein Genre vereinzelt da, es ist durch Kettenglieder und vermittelnde Abstufungen mit den an Form und Wesen gänzlich verschiedenen und entgegengesetzten Gattungen verbunden." See Liszt, *Sämtliche Schriften,* 5: 33.

30. While Wagner would hold that the premiere had been a disaster, it had in fact been something of a mixed bag. An extended, enthusiastic review came from none other than Eduard Hanslick, in which he praised Wagner as the "greatest dramatic talent," in *Allgemeine Wiener Musik-Zeitung* 6 (1846): 581. Wagner acknowledged Hanslick's review with a long and polite letter.

31. See Oswald Georg Bauer, *Tannhäuser zu Richard Wagners Zeit* (Munich: Bayerische Vereinsbank, 1985), 15.

32. Letter of February 26, 1849. *Richard Wagner–Franz Liszt Briefwechsel,* ed. Hanjo Kesting (Munich: Insel-Verlag, 1988), 64; trans. into English: Francis Hueffer, *Correspondence of Wagner and Liszt,* 2 vols. (New York: Scribner and Welford, 1889), 1: 16.

33. Ibid. 66 / 19.

34. The arrangement of the vocal score, including the overture alternatively set for piano duet, came out in 1846. This was the only vocal score that Wagner arranged him-

self, presumably for financial reasons. The appearance of the vocal score was advertised in the *Allgemeine Wiener Musik-Zeitung* of September 24, 1846, 464. Reprinted in Helmut Kirchmeyer, *Situationsgeschichte der Musikkritik und des musikalischen Pressewesens, IV. Teil: Das zeitgenössische Wagner-Bild, Dritter Band: Dokumente 1846–1850* (Regensburg: Gustav Bosse Verlag, 1968), col. 129.

35. Technically, Liszt's position at Weimar was no different, extraordinary court *Kapellmeister,* but due to his particular background and ambitions he tended to view the post in a very different light than Wagner.

36. Cited in Wolfgang Dömling, *Franz Liszt und seine Zeit* (Laaber: Laaber Verlag, 1985), 165. "Bescheidene Propaganda am dürftigen Klavier für den hohen Genius Wagners."

37. Liszt himself invented a variety of terms for piano arrangements—reminiscences, transcriptions, paraphrase, illustration, *partition du piano*—but did not employ them in a systematic fashion. See Dömling, *Franz Liszt,* 163. Sometimes Liszt's piano transcriptions are subdivided into faithful "partitions," and freer "paraphrases," as, for instance, in David Wilde's essay "Transcriptions for Piano," in Alan Walker, *Franz Liszt: The Man and His Music* (London: Barrie and Jenkins, 1970), 168–202; Wolfram Huschke, "Zum kulturhistorischen Stellenwert von Bearbeitungen um 1840," in Gottfried Scholz, ed., *Liszt-Studien 4: Der junge Liszt* (Munich and Salzburg: Emil Katzbichler, 1993), 95–99; and András Batta, "Die Gattung Paraphrase im Schaffen von Franz Liszt: Gattung Paraphrase —die musikalische Haßliebe Liszts," in *Liszt-Studien 4,* 135–142. For an interesting discussion of arrangements, see also Silke Leopold, ed., *Musikalische Metamorphosen: Formen und Geschichte der Bearbeitung* (Kassel: Bärenreiter, 1992); and Jonathan Kregor, "Franz Liszt and the Vocabularies of Transcription 1833–1865," Ph.D. dissertation (Harvard University, 2007).

38. See also Charles Rosen, *The Romantic Generation* (Cambridge, MA: Harvard University Press, 1996), 496–499.

39. See, for instance, Isabelle Bélance-Zank, "The Three-Hand Texture: Origins and Use," *Journal of the American Liszt Society* 38 (1995): 99–121; and Gerhard J. Winkler, "'Ein feste Burg ist unser Gott': Meyerbeers Hugenotten in der Paraphrasen Thalbergs und Liszts," in *Liszt-Studien 4,* 100–134.

40. On the recent musicological and literary interest in the concept of virtuosity, see Susan Bernstein, *Virtuosity of the Nineteenth Century: Performing Music and Language in Heine, Liszt and Baudelaire* (Stanford, CA: Stanford University Press, 1998), Paul Metzner, *Crescendo of the Virtuoso: Spectacle, Skill, and Self-Promotion in Paris during the Age of Revolution* (Berkeley: University of California Press, 1998); and Jim Samson, *Virtosity and the Musical Work: The Transcendental Studies of Liszt* (Cambridge: Cambridge University Press, 2003).

41. Franz Liszt, "Lohengrin," in *Sämtliche Schriften,* 4: 30.

42. Liszt did in fact arrange this movement, too, in an effective virtuoso setting a few years later, in 1852, and had already suggested earlier in "Tannhaüser" (*Sämtliche Schriften,* 4: 138) that it would make an attractive number when arranged for military band. The irony of this suggestion seems to have escaped Liszt.

43. In this context it is instructive to compare Carl Friedrich Weitzmann's *Geschichte des Clavierspiels und der Clavierliteratur* (Stuttgart: Cottasche Buchhandlung, 1863), which lists the arrangement of the *Tannhäuser* Overture among piano transcriptions of program

music, following Berlioz's model (p. 157) and the *Abendstern* romance among transcriptions of vocal music, for which Schubert's songs are exemplary (p. 160). While Weitzmann's categories differ from the ones employed in this essay, both arrangements clearly belonged to different sub-genres.

44. Joachim Raff, *Die Wagnerfrage* (Braunschweig: Friedrich Vieweg, 1854), 50. "Die Oper ward zum öffentlichen musikalischen Hauptgenuß Aller, und beeinflusste zugleich die Richtung dessen, was in den Salons der neuen Gesellschaft an Musik gemacht wurde. Der Kammervirtuose hatte die Wahl, in ein großes Orchester aufzugehen, oder aber sich zu isoliren. Wenn er dies Letztere that, so musste er vor allem seine Fertigkeit zum Selbstzweck nehmen. Der symphonische Concertstyl erlaubte ihm dies nicht, er ließ ihn daher bei Seite und bediente sich zur Darlegung seiner Virtuosität einer Unterlage, die, weil sie Jedermann bekannt war, Niemandes Aufmerksamkeit herausforderte, sondern derselben gefällig entgegenkam und sie einlud, sich bloß mit der Fertigkeit des Künstlers zu beschäftigen; es waren dies die 'motifs de l'opéra.' So bildete sich ein Virtuosenstyl, in welchem die Musik ein Vorwand zur Darlegung ungewöhnlicher Finger-, Lippen-, und Kehlenausbildung ist.—Im Gefolge der Oper konnte sich der Virtuosenstyl auch in dem Salon des Edelmannes und der reichen Bourgeois, sowie in das Gesellschaftszimmer des mittleren bürgerlichen Musikliebhabers einschleichen."

45. Other pedagogues went to even more drastic measures: a surgical operation recommended to aspiring pianists in the 1880s was to cut the tendon between ring and little fingers to increase the flexibility of the hand. See James Parakilas, ed., *Piano Roles: Three Hundred Years of Life with the Piano* (New Haven: Yale University Press, 1999), 152. I am grateful to Giulio Boccaletti for this reference.

46. Raff, *Wagnerfrage*, 50. "Aber hier stieß er auf zwei sehr hinderliche Elemente. Das eine davon war die Gesangslyrik, welche sich am Liede selbständig entwickelt hatte, dessen Privileg sich keine 'Tochter des Hauses' gerne nehmen lässt,—das andere der Gesellschaftstanz, durch die Mode beeinflusst und mit nationalen Elementen zersetzt, dessen Cult einen gern gesehenen Appendix zu jedem 'Gesellschaftsabend' bildetet. Hier stieß er auf das für Lied und Tanz unentbehrlich gewordene Klavier, und daneben auf einen Jüngling, der dieses Allerweltsinstrument in salonfähige Weise zu handhaben wusste. Selbiger Jüngling brauchte nur vom Lied die Worte, und vom Tanze die Beine wegzulassen, und fertig war der—Salonstyl."

47. See Andreas Balstaedt and Tobias Widmaier's groundbreaking study, *Salonmusik: Zur Geschichte und Funktion einer bürgerlichen Musikpraxis* (Stuttgart: Franz Steiner Verlag Wiesbaden, 1989). On the gendering of pianists, see also Richard Leppert, *Music and Image: Domesticity, Ideology and Socio-Cultural Formation in Eighteenth-Century England* (Cambridge: Cambridge University Press, 1988); Arthur Loesser, *Men, Women and Pianos: A Social History* (New York: Simon and Schuster, 1954); and Parakilas, *Piano Roles.*

48. See Balstaedt and Widmaier, *Salonmusik,* 200–235.

49. See Daniel Pick, *Faces of Degeneration* (Cambridge: Cambridge University Press, 1989).

50. Raff, *Wagnerfrage,* 184. "Wagner thut zwar in seiner Weise nur, was die Klaviervirtuosen [tun], welche sich seit zwanzig Jahren abmühen, auf ihren Instrumenten die Vocalmelodie zu verarbeiten (in Wahrheit ähnelt seine Art, die Geigen über dem tenorisirenden Gesang weg zu figuriren, sehr der Manier moderner Klaviercomponisten); aber diese Sünde am Style entschuldigt die seine nicht. Die Unkeuschheit im künstlerischen

Schaffen rächt sich stets durch Krankheiten der Kunst, welche gefährlich auf den Künstler zurückwirken."

51. See Paul Marsop, "Joachim Raff und 'Die Wagnerfrage,'" *Neue Musik-Zeitung* 43 (1922): 252–254.

52. This did not actually stop Raff from producing a plethora of virtuosic arrangements himself. However, Liszt got his own back when he wrote about Raff: "Ohne der Salonliteratur für Klavier weiter gedenken zu wollen, die er in Form von Transkriptionen, Arrangements, Phantasien, Klavierauszügen, leichten Stücken über beliebte Melodien und über einige Themen größtenteils kommerziellen Verlegerinteressen und dem Geschmack des Publikums nachkommend bereicherte, haben wir Werke von ihm zu nennen, die eine erhöhte Aufmerksamkeit beanspruchen." Cited in Dömling, *Franz Liszt,* 160.

53. See, among myriad other sources, *Allgemeine Musikalische Zeitung* (1842): 605. "In den vollgriffigen neumodischen Pianofortekompilationen findet man selten noch Musik, die edle Kunst ist zur Künstelei herabgesunken, von werthvoller Musik ist wenig Spur vorhanden, von einer schönen, regelrechten, gesangreichen Stimmenführung, von kunstreicher Verwebung der Themen, u.s.w., lauter Necessariis, die man durch Studium der Theorie erlangt, ist keine Rede mehr; und so dürften wohl die unbefangenen älteren Zuhörer nicht Unrecht haben, wenn sie, wie ich es neuerdings erlebt, beim Anhören solcher Neumodischen Klaviermusik ausrufen: 'es ist keine Musik darinne.'"

54. Thomas Christensen, "Four-Hand Piano Transcription and Geographies of Nineteenth-Century Musical Reception," *Journal of the American Musicological Society* 52 (1999): 275–280. Liszt, too, drew on this popular comparison in his essay, "Wagner's Fliegender Holländer," in *Sämtliche Werke,* 5: 108. For a recent reassessment of the copper engraving trope in its larger context, see Kregor, "Franz Liszt and the Vocabularies of Transcription 1833–1865," 16–75.

55. See *Allgemeine Musikalische Zeitung* (1842): 1047. "Wenn bei größern und bedeutendern Orchesterwerken nur eine öftere Aufführung ein vollständiges Verständnis bringen kann, so sind Klavierauszüge um so erwünschter, je seltener solche Werke in ihrer Originalgestalt zu Gehör gebracht werden, weil sie Gelegenheit bieten, mit Form und Inhalt vertrauter zu werden, die Intention des Komponisten besser zu verfolgen, und sich mit dem Fremden, Ungewohnten vertrauer zu machen. Kommen zu solchen Privatstudien öffentliche Aufführungen, so wird sich bald die frische Färbung der Instrumentation dem Ohre dergestalt einprägen, dass bei Wiederholung des Werkes am Piano dasselbe immer mehr in seiner Urgestalt in das Licht treten wird. Ein Vortheil, der nicht gering anzuschlagen ist, weshalb uns Klavierauszüge immer von bedeutendem Nutzen erschienen sind. Ihnen hat ja meistens das Publikum das Verständnis unsrer größten Meisterwerke zu verdanken, und wo z. B. in einem Concertsaale dasselbe aufmerksam den Klängen einer Symphonie Beethoven's lauscht, da lässt sich immer schließen, dass das häusliche Musikleben diesen Kunstgenüssen zugewandt ist."

56. Ibid. 46. "Es wird sowohl den zahlreichen Freunden und Verehrern wie den Gegnern des berühmten, um das Beethoven-Denkmal unstreitig hochverdienten Componisten lieb sein, seine vielfach besprochene, gerühmte Cantata nunmehr wenigstens in einem reich ausgestatteten Clavierauszuge . . . erlangen zu können und somit Gelegenheit zu gewinnen, sich, so weit es in solcher Gestalt möglich ist, eine genauere Kenntniss des Werkes zu verschaffen, das jedenfalls zu den besten und interessantesten des Verfassers gehört."

57. Ibid. 337. "Halten wir aber die Bestimmung eines Arrangements im Auge, sich nämlich durch Vergegenwärtigung des Stoffes des Eindrucks zu erinnern, den das Werk in seiner Urgestalt gemacht, und dasselbe wieder zu geniessen, so findet nicht nur bei Instrumentalwerken, sondern auch bei Gesangswerken, die viele und größere Mittel erfordern, eine gewisse Nothwendigkeit und, wenn wir so sagen dürfen, Entschuldigung eines Arrangements statt."

58. He spelled this out in *Neue Zeitschrift für Musik* 49 (1858): 75. "Was bei uns populär werden, wirklich in die Menge eindringen soll, muß in vierhändiger Gestalt für ein Instrument allein arrangiert vorliegen." See also Christensen, "Four-Hand Piano Transcriptions," 267.

59. Johann Christian Lobe, *Fliegende Blätter: Wahrheit über Tonkunst und Tonkünstler* (Leipzig: Baumgärtner's Buchhandlung, 1855–1857), 155. "Statt also die Salonmusik unbedingt und in Bausch und Bogen zu verwerfen und zu verdammen, könnte man vielleicht wohl gar sagen, in diese Musik—natürlich ist von der schlechten nicht die Rede— habe sich in neuerer Zeit der gute Geist der Tonkunst geflüchtet."

60. von Schorn, *Das nachklassische Weimar*, 257, writes about the Weimar premiere of *Tannhäuser* on February 16, 1849: "Das Publikum war so enthusiasmiert, daß sogar eine alte Sitte umgeworfen wurde: An Geburtstagen wird—beim Eintritt der Fürstlichkeiten in die Hofloge—von dem Publikum zum Empfang applaudiert, für die Künstler rühren sich aber die Hände an diesem Abend nicht. Die Begeisterung durchbrach die Etikette, Liszt und die Mitwirkenden, unter diesen besonders Tichatschek, ernteten stürmischen Applaus."

61. See, for instance, the anonymous review in the *Gemeinde-Verhandlungsblatt und Volksorgan für das Großherzogtum Sachsen-Weimar-Eisenach* 8 (1849): 74–76.

62. See Ernest Newman, *The Life of Richard Wagner* (London: Cassell, 1937), 2: 102–104; and Alan Walker, *Franz Liszt: The Weimar Years* (Ithaca, NY: Cornell University Press, 1993), 112–119.

63. For the Parisian version of *Tannhäuser*, see, for instance, Carolyn Abbate, "The Parisian *Vénus* and the 'Paris' *Tannhäuser*," *Journal of the American Musicological Society* 36 (1983): 73–122.

64. August Wilhelm Ambros, "Die neu-deutsche Schule," in *Culturhistorische Bilder aus dem Musikleben der Gegenwart* (Leipzig: Breitkopf und Härtel, 1860), 139. "Jedenfalls hat Liszt das Verdienst, durch sein brilliantes Buch und durch sein Auftreten in Weimar den Werken Wagners wie mit einem Zauberschlage die Bahn gebrochen zu haben." It is difficult to overestimate the importance of these essays. Christian Thorau has drawn attention to the impact of Liszt's essay on *Lohengrin* in providing a language to the experience of listening to Wagner, which is partly analytical and partly descriptive. See his *Semantisierte Sinnlichkeit: Studien zu Rezeption und Zeichenstruktur der Leitmotivtechnik Richard Wagners* (Stuttgart: Franz Steiner Verlag, 2003), 38–58.

65. The difference between both is in the key—the overture is in E major, the Act III chorus in Eb major. Given the frequent key changes and transposition, however, it is impossible to identify the source for sure, except in Alfred Jaëll's arrangement in E major.

66. Most of these arrangements now survive only in individual (or very few) copies. I have used the copies from Bayerische Staatsbibliothek Munich 2 Mus.pr 2943 (Raff Sextett) and 4 Mus.pr 46956 (Raff Fantasie), and Landesbibliothek Coburg Mus 2243:8 (Voss).

67. Bayerische Staatsbibliothek Munich, 4 Mus.pr 912318.

68. Otto Jahn, "Tannhäuser, Oper von Richard Wagner," *Gesammelte Aufsätze über Musik* (Leipzig: Breitkopf und Härtel, 1866), 82–83.

69. Bayerische Landesbibliothek Munich, 2 Mus.pr. 1710–2.

70. Bayerische Landesbibliothek Munich, 4 Mus.pr 19079.

71. Due to the long-lasting neglect of the genre of piano arrangements, the source situation in libraries and publishing catalogues is very difficult to assess. As many of these arrangements have been lost, it is not possible to make any real comparisons. Publication catalogues, above all the Hofmeister-Whistling catalogue, offer a glimpse into what was once available, but they are often unreliable sources because of the complex questions of authorship in arrangements. A reasonably good sense can also be gained from newspaper reviews at the time.

72. Wagner himself attributed this term to his critic, the editor of the *Niederrheinische Musikzeitung,* Ludwig Bischoff. More recent scholarship suggests that Wagner's source was misattributed. While a number critics certainly engaged in similar polemics, the first mention has recently been attributed to Clara Schumann's father, the conservative Leipzig music teacher, Friedrich Wieck, as early as 1852 (to be precise, it appears in a review by August Ferdinand Riccius, of the as-yet unpublished book by Wieck). See Christa Jost and Peter Jost, "'Zukunftsmusik': Zur Geschichte eines Begriffs," *Musiktheorie* 10 (1995): 119–135.

73. See especially Brendel, "Zur Anbahnung einer Verständigung," *Neue Zeitschrift für Musik* 50 (1859): 265–273.

74. See Klaus Kropfinger, *Wagner and Beethoven: Richard Wagner's Reception of Beethoven,* trans. Peter Palmer. (Cambridge: Cambridge University Press, 1991).

75. See Christensen, "Four-Hand Piano Arrangements," 290. On the practice of analysis in Schumann, see Ian Biddle, "Policing Masculinity: Schumann, Berlioz and the Gendering of the Music-critical Idiom," *Journal of the Royal Musical Association* 124 (1999): 196–220.

76. Liszt, "Tannhaüser," 138. "Lorsqu'elle sera plus connue[,] on disséquera le squelette de cette belle oeuvre, et on ne manquera point d'en compter toutes les articulations."

77. Lobe, "Briefe an einen jungen Komponisten über Wagner," in *Fliegende Blätter,* 418.

78. Hanslick, review of *Tannhäuser,* 609. "Das große Publikum . . . mag keine Musik, aus der man sich nicht aus der ersten Aufführung gleich einige achttaktige Marschmelodien summend nach Hause tragen kann, um sie daselbst unverzüglich dem Fortepiano beizubringen." See also Thorau, *Semantisierte Sinnlichkeit,* 44.

79. Lobe writes about the first bars of the Venusberg music in "Briefe an einen jungen Komponisten," 455: "In den ersten drei Takten werden schon fünf verschiedene Tonarten durchlaufen. Welche Menge dissonirender Akkorde hierauf ! In einundsechzig Takten zweiundvierzig ! . . . Die Mannigfaltigkeit ist in überschwenglichem Maße vorhanden, die Einheit fehlt ganz und gar."

80. T[heodor] U[hlig], "Die Ouvertüre zu Wagner's Tannhäuser," *Neue Zeitschrift für Musik* 34 (1851): 166.

81. Liszt, "Tannhaüser," 146. "Dans le *Tannhaüser,* il a inauguré pour l'opéra une innovation frappante, par laquelle la mélodie, non seulement exprime, mais représente certaines émotions, en revenant au moment où elles réapparaissent, en se reproduisant dans l'orchestre indépendement du chant de la scène, souvent avec des modulations qui caractérisent les modifications des passions auxquelles elle correspond."

82. Liszt, too, singles out the Rome narration as one of the "most astonishing creations of Wagner's genius," see "Tannhaüser," 133.

83. As before, the uncertain situation of the sources makes it difficult to make any statistically verifiable claims. Few of the arrangements consulted survive in more than a single copy, and it is likely that many have been lost, largely due to lack of interest in the genre of piano arrangements. Liszt's own output of Wagner arrangements, which steadily declines after *Tannhäuser* and *Lohengrin,* however, should give us a good indication. As the importance of piano arrangements gradually declines, a more analytical discourse takes its place, which culminates in the *Leitmotivtabellen* that become the inevitable guide to understanding Wagner's later works. There is hardly a vocal score, libretto, or introductory text in the later nineteenth century that dispenses with such *Leitmotivtabellen.* See Thorau, *Semantisierte Sinnlichkeit,* 157–254.

84. Raff, *Wagnerfrage,* 93. "Im 'Holländer' had man noch accidentale Scenen, wie den lyrischen Matrosen, die Spinnstube, den Auftritt zwischen den beiden Schiffen im letzten Acte; im 'Tannhäuser' giebt's eine Landschaft . . . und einen 'Abendstern.' Im 'Lohengrin' findet sich nichts dergleichen: Alles ist unmittelbar und nothwendig an und aus dem Stoffe entstanden."

85. Brendel, "Die bisherige Sonderkunst und das Kunstwerk der Zukunft," *Neue Zeitschrift für Musik* 38 (1853): 90. "Tannhäuser ist das Werk des Überganges, er ist Oper, nach der einen Seite von dem Unsinn der Neuzeit befreite, auf höherem Standpunkte und mit reicheren Mitteln wiedergeborene Gluck'sche Oper, nach der anderen Seite allerdings schon in sehr Vielem die Elemente des weiteren Fortschritts enthaltend."

86. Brendel, *Die Musik der Gegenwart,* 118. "In Leipzig machte die Ouvertüre zum 'Tannhäuser' bei einer Aufführung in Concert Fiasco. Man muß dies natürlich finden, wenn man bedenkt, dass das Publicum von der ganzen Oper nicht das Geringste kannte, dass man sogar dem Componisten mit dem ungünstigsten, durch jene Gerüchte genährten Vorurtheilen entgegentrat."

87. Theodor Uhlig, "Zeitgemäße Betrachtungen," *Neue Zeitschrift für Musik* 42 (May 28, 1850): 218. Reprinted in Kirchmeyer, *Situationsgeschichte der Musikkritik,* 4/iii: col. 633. "Wie Wenige wird es geben, die da im Herzen nicht ausgerufen hätten: Ach, wie ist das schön! Wie so Manchem traten nicht schon Thränen der Rührung in die Augen, wenn er sich diese Scene am Clavier in Erinnerung zurückrief."

88. *Signale für die musikalische Welt,* 8/22 (May 29, 1850): 213. Reprinted in Kirchmeyer, *Situationsgeschichte der Musikkritik,* 4/iii: col. 635. "Besonderes Verdienst hat sich Liszt durch Bearbeitung der reizenden Romanze aus Richard Wagner's Tannhäuser gemacht, indem er derselben dadurch hoffentlich *die* Verbreitung verschafft, welche ihr aber ohne die Transcription schwerlich zu Theil geworden, da der Tannhäuser bisher nur auf so wenigen Bühnen heimisch geworden."

Chapter Four

1. Richard Wagner, *My Life,* trans. Andrew Gray (New York: Da Capo Press, 1992), 62.
2. Ibid. 37.
3. E. T. A. Hoffmann, *Selected Writings,* trans. and ed. Elizabeth Knight and Leonard Kent (Chicago and London: University of Chicago Press, 1969), 59.

4. According to Hans Mayer, the answer to this question is decisive for one's entire approach to Hoffmann's romanticism. See Hans Mayer, "Die Wirklichkeit E. T. A. Hoffmanns," in *Das unglückliche Bewußtsein: Zur deutschen Literaturgeschichte von Lessing bis Heine* (Frankfurt am Main: Suhrkamp, 1986), 469–511.

5. For a recent survey of different views, see Ricarda Schmitt, "Klassische, romantische und postmoderne musikästhetische Paradigmen in E. T. A. Hoffmanns *Ritter Gluck*," in Werner Keil and Charis Goer, eds., *"Seelenaccente"—"Ohrenphysiognomik": Zur Musikanschuung E. T. A. Hoffmanns, Heinses und Wackenroders* (Hildesheim: Georg Olms, 2000), 11–61.

6. Wagner, *My Life*, 190–191.

7. James Webster discusses the ramifications of different concepts of "Classicism" in his *Haydn's 'Farewell' Symphony and the Idea of Classical Style* (Cambridge: Cambridge University Press, 1991), 353–373.

8. This marble bust, based on an earlier bronze by Jean-Antoine Houdon, was installed in the Opéra in 1778. It was destroyed by fire in 1873. See Patricia Howard, *Gluck: An Eighteenth-Century Portrait in Letters and Documents* (Oxford: Clarendon Press, 1995), 164. Edgar Istel, *Das große Buch der Oper* (Berlin: Max Hesse, 1919), 39, asserts that the motto goes back to Christoph Martin Wieland.

9. Thomas Grey, "Wagner, the Overture, and the Aesthetics of Musical Form," *Nineteenth Century Music* 12 (1988): 3–4.

10. Richard Wagner, "Über die Ouvertüre," *Gesammelte Schriften und Dichtungen*, 10 vols., 3d ed. (Leipzig: C. F. W. Siegel, 1898), 1: 194. Translation William Ashton Ellis, *Wagner's Prose Works*, Vol. 7, *In Paris and Dresden* (Reprint New York: Broude Brothers, 1966), 153.

11. Ibid.

12. There are small but interesting differences between the French and German versions. See Thomas Grey, "Wagner, the Overture, and the Aesthetics of Musical Form," *Nineteenth-Century Music* 12 (1988): 3–22.

13. Wagner, "Über die Ouvertüre," 196 / "On the Overture," 155.

14. Ibid. 197 / 157. (As before, in light of the slippery state of Wagner translations, I first reference the German version, followed by the published English translation.)

15. Wagner, "Beethoven," *Gesammelte Schriften und Dichtungen*, 10: 105. Translation in Ellis, *Richard Wagner's Prose Works*, Vol. 5, *Actors and Singers*, 106.

16. Wagner, "Über die Ouvertüre," 199–200 / "On the Overture," 158–159.

17. For a discussion of these types, see also José Antonio Bowen, "The Conductor and the Score: The Relationship between Interpreter and Text in the Generation of Mendelssohn, Berlioz and Wagner," Ph.D. dissertation (Stanford University, 1994), 350–351.

18. Wagner, "Über die Ouvertüre," 204 / "On the Overture," 163.

19. Ibid. 203 / 161 (translation modified).

20. For an excellent discussion of different approaches to sonata form, chiefly from the nineteenth century, see Scott Burnham, "Form," in Thomas Christensen, ed., *The Cambridge History of Western Music Theory* (Cambridge: Cambridge University Press, 2001), 880–906.

21. See Ian Bent, ed., *Music Analysis in the Nineteenth Century*, 2 vols. (Cambridge: Cambridge University Press, 1993); Adolf B. Marx, *Musical Form in the Age of Beethoven:*

Selected Writings on Theory and Method, trans. and ed. Scott Burnham (Cambridge University Press, 1997); and Torsten Brandt, *Johann Christian Lobe (1797–1881): Studien zu Biographie und musikschriftstellerischem Werk* (Göttingen: Vandenhoeck & Ruprecht, 2002).

22. Hegel's views on tragedy are explored particularly in Georg W. F. Hegel, *Ästhetik,* vol. 2. See also Helmut Pillau, *Die fortgedachte Dissonanz: Hegels Tragödientheorie und Schillers Tragödie* (Munich: Wilhelm Fink Verlag, 1981).

23. Wagner, "Über die Ouvertüre," 203 / "On the Overture," 162 (translation modified).

24. Ibid. 202 / 161.

25. See Johann Jakob Winckelmann, *Gedanken über die Nachahmung der griechischen Werke in der Malerei und Bildhauerkunst* (1755). Typically, though, Wagner cautioned against the imitation of Greek art as advocated by Winckelmann.

26. Wagner, "Über die Ouvertüre," 206 / "On the Overture," 165 (translation modified.)

27. Ibid. 198 / 157.

28. Eduard Hanslick had drawn up a similar typology of overtures in his exhaustive—and predominantly positive—review of *Tannhäuser,* going back to Gluck and Mozart. It must have been disheartening for Wagner to read that his overture types were grouped together with the potpourri type. See Eduard Hanslick, "Richard Wagner, und seine neueste Oper, 'Tannhäuser,'" *Allgemeine Wiener Musik-Zeitung,* 6 (1846): 589–590.

29. See also Grey, "Wagner and the Aesthetics of the Overture," 7.

30. Johann Christian Lobe, "Die Opernouvertüre von einer anderen Seite betrachtet," in *Fliegende Blätter: Wahrheit über Tonkunst und Tonkünstler,* 3 vols. (Leipzig: Baumgärtner, 1855–1857), 1: 362.

31. Ibid. 366. There are, incidentally, a number of *Wallenstein* programmatic works, including an overture by the Swiss composer Otto Oberholzer, the *Wallenstein* symphonic trilogy by Vincent d'Indy, and *Wallenstein's Camp* by Bedřich Smetana.

32. Franz Brendel, *Geschichte der Musik in Frankreich, Deutschland und Italien* (Leipzig: Breitkopf und Härtel, 1852), 286. "Gluck ist die noch unaufgeschlossene Knospe, Mozart die in reichster Fülle entfaltete Blume. Die damalige Oper culminiert in zwei Gipfeln, Gluck und Mozart; beide haben in gewisser Hinsicht das Höchste geleistet, je nachdem man den Gesichtspunct feststellt."

33. Ibid. 284.

34. See chapter 3, 82–84.

35. Eduard Schelle [Wilhelm Fröhner?], *Der Tannhäuser in Paris und der dritte musikalische Krieg* (Leipzig: Breitkopf und Härtel, 1861). "Gleich Wagner hat Gluck diejenige seiner Opern zum Debut seiner Pariser Laufbahn gewählt, welche in ihrer Diktion das neue Prinzip vollständig darlegte." The copy in the Herzogin Anna Amalia Library in Weimar (M 9 : 158 [a] [1]) has a damning inscription on the front page: "Diese Broschüre, mit Ausnahme der Vorrede, ist von mir. Schelle lieferte mir nur einige Notizen über Gluck. Fröhner."

36. Karl Maria Klob, *Die Oper von Gluck bis Wagner* (Ulm: Heinrich Kerler, 1913), 55. "Gluck und Wagner, sie verfolgten beide das gleiche Prinzip; sie zertrümmerten die Form der alten Oper, sie verhalfen auch der Dichtung im gesungenen Drama wieder zu ihrem

Rechte und führten so eine Verschwisterung von Ton und Wort herbei, von der bereits unsere deutschen Klassiker Lessing, Herder, Klopstock geträumt hatten."

37. Ludwig Nohl, *Gluck und Wagner: Ueber die Entwicklung des Musikdramas* (Munich: Louis Finsterlin, 1870), 136. "Wie kam es nun aber, daß trotz all dieser Anzeichen einer innigen Sehnsucht nach dem Ziele, zu dem am erfolgreichsten Gluck die Bahn gebrochen hatte, fast ein Jahrhundert hingehen konnte, ehe das Ziel selbst erreicht ward, ja daß Gluck die Erfüllung seiner Bestrebungen völlig nur im Auslande und obendrein bei den unmusikalischesten dieser Fremden, bei den Franzosen hatte erreichen können?"

38. See Istel, *Das große Buch der Oper,* 70.

39. For an exploration of the trope of the *creatio ex nihilo,* see Jean-Jacques Nattiez, *Wagner Androgyne,* trans. Stewart Spencer (Princeton: Princeton University Press, 1993); and Liszt's dramaturgical essays in *Sämtliche Schriften,* ed. Detlef Altenburg (Wiesbaden: Breitkopf und Härtel, 1989), vol. 5, which consciously create a non-Wagnerian pre-history of the Wagnerian music drama.

40. Klob, *Die Oper von Gluck bis Wagner,* 297. "Spontini war das letzte Glied einer Reihe von Komponisten, deren erstes Glied in Gluck zu finden ist."

41. Wagner, *My Life,* 336.

42. See, for instance, Carl Dahlhaus, *Klassische und romantische Musikästhetik* (Laaber: Laaber-Verlag, 1988).

43. See, among many others, Ludwig Uhlig, ed., *Griechenland als Ideal: Winckelmann und seine Rezeption in Deutschland* (Tübingen: Günter Narr Verlag, 1988); and Philip J. Kain, *Schiller, Hegel and Marx: State, Society, and the Aesthetic Ideal of Ancient Greece* (Kingston and Montreal: McGill-Queen's University Press, 1982). For Wagner's views of ancient Greece, see Wolfgang Schadewaldt, "Richard Wagner and the Greeks," trans. David C. Durst, *Hellenic Studies Review: Dialogos* 6 (1999): 108–133. John Deathridge, "Wagner, the Greeks and Wolfgang Schadewaldt," *Hellenic Studies Review: Dialogos* 6 (1999): 133–140, rightly cautions that Wagner's approach to ancient Greece is mediated by neo-Hellenism. See also Arno Forchert, "Droysen und Wagner," in Josef Kuckertz, Helga de la Motte-Haber, Christian Martin Schmidt, and Wilhelm Seidel, eds., *Neue Musik und Tradition: Festschrift Rudolf Stephan* (Laaber: Laaber-Verlag, 1990), 251–257.

44. Lauriana Sapienza, "Euripides: Eine disziplinierte Polemik?" in Glenn W. Most, ed., *Disciplining Classics / Diszplinierte Klassik* (Göttingen: Vandenhoeck & Rupprecht, 2002), 55–71. For Wagner's views of Euripides, see M. Owen Lee, *Athena Sings: Wagner and the Ancient Greeks* (Toronto: University of Toronto Press, 2003), 27.

45. See Wagner, *Gesammelte Schriften,* 12: 280. Fragment "Das Künstlertum der Zukunft."

46. This translation, taken from Ellis, *Richard Wagner's Prose Works,* Vol. 7, *In Paris and Dresden,* 95, is based on the German version, "Über deutsches Musikwesen," *Gesammelte Schriften und Dichtungen,* 1: 160, while Pohl cites his own German translation from the French version of Wagner's text.

47. Reinhard Strohm notes this in "Gedanken zu Wagners Opernouvertüren," in Carl Dahlhaus and Egon Voss, eds., *Wagnerliteratur—Wagnerforschung* (Mainz: Schott, 1985), 69–84.

48. In the early essay, "Die deutscher Oper" (1834), even Wagner declares Gluck a French composer.

49. Richard Wagner, *Oper und Drama,* 3: 293–294, trans. in Ellis, *Richard Wagner's Prose Works,* Vol. 2, *Opera and Drama,* 87–88 (translation modified.)

50. Ibid. 245 / 35–36.

51. Wagner, "Gluck's Ouvertüre zu 'Iphigenia in Aulis,'" *Gesammelte Schriften und Dichtungen,* 5: 114, trans. William Ashton Ellis, *Richard Wagner's Prose Works,* Vol. 3, *The Theatre,* 158 (translation modified). See also Wilhelm Kleefeld, "Richard Wagner als Bearbeiter fremder Werke," *Die Musik* 4 (1904): 231–249.

52. Wagner was correct that the Paris score that he perused did not contain the Allegro marking. What he did not know, however, was that Gluck himself had later added *Animé* at exactly the same point (which is now added in the critical edition).

53. It would be pedantic to hold it against Wagner, but is not without a certain irony, that E. T. A. Hoffmann's Ritter Gluck comments on precisely this Allegro and deems it vital to his overture.

54. Wagner, "Gluck's Ouvertüre," 113–114 / 157–158.

55. Wagner declares textual fidelity to be the prerequisite of any valid performance as early as his essay, "Der Virtuos und der Künstler": "Was ihr von Tönen euch da aufzeichnet, soll nun laut erklingen: ihr wollt es hören und von Anderen hören lassen. Nun ist euch das Wichtigste, ja das Unerläßlichste, da euer Tonstück genau so zu Gehör gelange, wie ihr es bei seiner Aufzeichnung in euch vernahmt, das heißt, mit gewissenhafter Treue sollen die Intentionen des Komponisten wiedergegeben werden, damit die geistigen Gedanken unentstellt und unverkümmert den Wahrnehmungsorganen übermittelt werden," in *Gesammelte Schriften und Dichtungen,* 1: 169 (*Richard Wagner's Prose Works,* 7: 111).

56. Wagner, "Gluck's Ouverture," 114 / 158 (translation modified). The attribute "deformed" [*entstellt*] is used repeatedly in the context of Gluck's *Iphigenie,* see also "Über das Dirigieren," 7: 309.

57. Ibid. 115 / 159 (translation modified).

58. Ibid. 118–119 / 162.

59. Richard Wagner, "Über Franz Liszt's symphonische Dichtungen," *Gesammelte Schriften und Dichtungen,* 5: 189. Trans. in *Richard Wagner's Prose Works,* 3: 245.

60. Ibid. 190 / 245.

61. Wagner, "On Franz Liszt's Symphonic Poems," 190 / 245–246 (translation modified).

62. On the concept of the "outmoded" position in music history, see also my "Wagner, Liszt, Berlioz and the New German School," in Mary Ann Perkins and Martin Liebscher, eds., *Nationalism versus Cosmopolitanism in German Thought and Culture 1789–1914: Essays on the Emergence of Europe* (Lewiston, NY: Edwin Mellen Press, 2006), 159–187.

63. Wagner, "Gluck's Ouverture," 117 / 161.

64. Bowen, "Conductor and Score," 378.

65. See ibid. 397.

66. See particularly Wagner, "Über das Dirigiren," *Gesammelte Schriften und Dichtungen,* 8: 275. Translated as "On Conducting," in *Richard Wagner's Prose Works,* Vol. 4, *Art and Politics,* 304. "To sum up in one word the question of a tone-work's right performance, so far as depends on the conductor, it is this: Has he given throughout the proper *tempo?*" Crucial to the correct understanding of a piece of music is what Wagner calls the *melos*: "But a correct conception of the *melos* alone can give the proper tempo: the two are indivisible" (275 / 303). The notion of the *melos* Wagner attributes to his experience of Wilhelmine

Schröder-Devrient, and it might best be understood as a combination of dramatic spirit, expression, and poetic content. See also Bowen, "Conductor and Score."

67. Wagner, "Über das Dirigiren," 318 / "On Conducting," 344.

68. See ibid. 318 / 345.

69. Wagner, "On Franz Liszt's Symphonic Poems," 185 / 240.

70. Ibid.

71. Letter to Theodor Uhlig, February 13, 1852, trans. in Stewart Spencer and Barry Millington, eds., *Selected Letters of Richard Wagner* (New York and London: Norton, 1987), 251 (translation modified).

72. José Bowen draws particular attention to the importance of this parenthetical qualification. See his "Conductor and Score," 397–398.

73. For a collection of contemporary reviews, see Helmut Kirchmeyer, *Situations-geschichte der Musikkritik und des musikalischen Pressewesens in Deutschland,* Vol. 4/iii, *Das zeitgenössische Wagner-Bild* 1846–1850 (Regensburg: Gustav Bosse, 1968). The complex relationship between Wagner and his former friend Carl Banck is explored in Kirchmeyer, *Situationsgeschichte der Musikkritik,* Vol. 4/i, *Wagner in Dresden* (Regensburg: Gustav Bosse Verlag, 1972), 657–672, the significance of *Iphigenie* for Dresden on 717–730.

74. Wagner, "Gluck's Ouverture," 116 / 160.

75. Wagner, "Über das Dirigieren," 287–295 / "On the Art of Conducting," 317–324.

76. Wagner, "Gluck's Ouverture," 115 / 159.

77. Wagner, "Zum Vortrag der neunten Symphonie Beethoven's," 9: 233. Translated by William Ashton Ellis as "The Rendering of Beethoven's Ninth Symphony," in *Richard Wagner's Prose Works,* 5: 232.

78. Wagner, "Gluck's Ouverture," 116 / 159.

79. Ibid. 122 / 165–166.

80. This has been noted by different writers across the ages, going back to Nietzsche. See Theodor W. Adorno, *In Search of Wagner,* trans. Rodney Livingstone (London: Verso, 1991); Peter Gay, *Freud, Jews and Other Germans: Masters and Victims in Modernist Culture* (London and New York: Oxford University Press, 1978); to Susan Bernstein, *Virtuosity of the Nineteenth Century: Performing Music and Language in Heine, Liszt, and Baudelaire* (Stanford, CA: Stanford University Press, 1998).

Chapter Five

1. Letter by Johannes Brahms to Eusebius Mandyczewski: "Haben Sie den ersten Bd. Denkmäler? (Schöne Orgelsachen) u. schwelgen Sie in Betrachtung u. Bewunderung ihn u.—Bach angehend? Eine wie große und tiefe Natur er selbst u. von wie hohem Interesse—Bach vor Augen—alles was Contrapunkt, Fuge, Choral u. Variation angeht! Das ist ein üppiger Sommer! Ein neuer Band Schütz liegt da, ein Bach ist zu erwarten." Reproduced in Karl Geiringer, "Johannes Brahms im Briefwechsel mit Eusebius Mandyczewski," *Zeitschrift für Musikwissenschaft* 15 (1933): 352. See also Imogen Fellinger, "Brahms und die Musik vergangener Epochen," in Walter Wiora, ed., *Die Ausbreitung des Historismus in der Musik* (Regensburg: Gustav Bosse, 1969), 147.

2. Michael Musgrave reports that the appearance of the *Bach Gesellschaft* complete edition in 1851 "was the main musicological event of Brahms's youth and clearly ranked with Bismarck's creation of the German Empire in 1871 as a major national event of his

life." See *A Brahms Reader* (New Haven: Yale University Press, 2000), 161. This comparison seems particularly a propos in this context.

3. Historicism is, like many such –isms, notoriously difficult to define and has been subject to much discussion. See for instance Friedrich Meinecke, *Historicism: The Rise of a New Historical Outlook,* trans. J. E. Anderson (London: Routledge and K. Paul, 1972); and Friedrich Jaeger and Jörn Rüsen, *Geschichte des Historismus: Eine Einführung* (Munich: C. H. Beck, 1992).

4. Philipp Spitta, preface in Samuel Scheidt, *Tabulatura nova,* ed. Max Seiffert (Leipzig: Breitkopf und Härtel, 1892).

5. On the problems of a specific Austrian music history, see Carl Dahlhaus, "Die Musikgeschichte Österreichs und die Idee der deutschen Musik," in Richard A. Kann and Friedrich E. Prinz, eds., *Deutschland und Österreich* (Vienna and Munich: Jugend und Volk, 1980), 322–349.

6. Friedrich Chrysander, "'Des einigen deutschen Reiches Musikzustände,'" *Leipziger allgemeine musikalische Zeitung,* 11 (1874): col. 4. "Sodann ist das *musikalische* deutsche Reich größer als das politische, weil Oesterreich dazu gehört. Diese nackte Tatsache sollte allein schon genügen, uns von dem patriotischen Bombast zu befreien."

7. In addition, Brahms was also a member of the editorial board of the German *Denkmäler,* though most probably in a largely ceremonial function. See Elisabeth Th. Hilscher, *Denkmalpflege und Musikwissenschaft: Einhundert Jahre Gesellschaft zur Herausgabe der Tonkunst in Österreich (1893–1993)* (Tutzing: Hans Schneider, 1995), 59.

8. The Austrian *Denkmäler* were also fostered by two important musical events at the time: the finding of the important Trent Codices and the successful International Exhibition for Music and Theater in Vienna. See Elsa Bienenfeld, "Köpfe im Profil: Guido Adler," *Die Musik* 28 (1925): 113–124.

9. The Austrian project is generally better documented than its German counterpart, Important insights on the German project, however, can be found in the archive of the publisher of *Denkmäler der deutschen Tonkunst,* Breitkopf und Härtel. See Oskar von Hase, *Breitkopf und Härtel: Gedenkschrift und Arbeitsbericht* (Wiesbaden: Breitkopf und Härtel, 1968), 3 vols.

10. The specific problem of an Austrian (Viennese) and a German (Mannheim) classicism arising from this division has been discussed in my *Hugo Riemann and the Birth of Modern Musical Thought* (Cambridge: Cambridge University Press, 2003), 138–149.

11. Federico Celestini points out that the German emperor was invoked as the spirit of a *captatio benevolentiae Imperatoris,* whereas the problematic approach to Austrian nationhood meant that the focus on the Austrian emperor was far more central to the whole enterprise. See his "'Denkmäler italienischer Tonkunst': D'Annunzios Roman *Il fuoco* und die Mythologisierung alter Musik in Italien um 1900," in Rudolf Jaworski and Peter Stachel, eds., *Die Besetzung des öffentlichen Raumes: Politische Plätze, Denkmäler und Straßennamen im europäischen Vergleich* (Berlin: Timme & Frank, 2007), 277–292.

12. See Hans Joachim Moser, *Das musikalische Denkmälerwesen in Deutschland* (Kassel: Bärenreiter, 1952), 20. Bismarck's characteristic attitude that "the Reich did not know art or science" was evidently still in place, even after the Iron Chancellor had retired to the outskirts of Hamburg where he lived close to Friedrich Chrysander, who supplied the Bismarcks with fruit and vegetables from his garden. This intransigence from the political platform set the German project back by a few years after the initial volume.

13. Of course, this was not restricted to Germany. See for instance Katherine Bergeron, *Decadent Enchantments: The Revival of Gregorian Chant at Solesmes* (Berkeley: University of California Press, 1998).

14. It becomes apparent from Spitta's proclamation of 1892 that the tensions with some regions—presumably Bavaria—go back to the earlier stages of the project. Spitta feels it necessary to remind the regional governments that in funding the project, Prussia has put its trust in their support of all national institutions and hopes "not to be left stranded." See Spitta, "Denkmäler deutscher Tonkunst," *Die Grenzboten* 52/2 (1893): 22. This concern becomes even more urgent in light of the state's initial reluctance to finance the publication of non-Prussian music.

15. A number of studies have examined the history of musical *Denkmäler*. See Max Schneider, "'Denkmäler der Tonkunst' vor hundert Jahren," in *Festschrift Rochus von Liliencron* (Leipzig: Breitkopf und Härtel, 1910), 278–289; Hans Joachim Moser, *Das musikalische Denkmälerwesen in Deutschland* (Kassel: Bärenreiter, 1952); Ludwig Finscher, "Musikalische Denkmäler und Gesamtausgaben," in Hanspeter Bennwitz, Georg Feder, Ludwig Finscher, and Wolfgang Rehm, eds., *Musikalisches Erbe und Gegenwart: Musikgesamtausgaben in der Bundesrepublik Deutschland* (Kassel: Bärenreiter, 1975), 1–13; Ottmar Wessely, *Zur Vorgeschichte des musikalischen Denkmalschutzes* (Vienna: Verlag der österreichischen Akademie der Wissenschaften, 1976); Hilscher, *Denkmalpflege und Musikwissenschaft;* Anselm Gerhard, "Für den 'Butterladen,' die Gelehrten oder 'das practische Leben'? Denkmalsidee und Gesamtausgaben in der Musikgeschichte vor 1850," *Die Musikforschung* 57 (2004): 363–382.

16. Spitta, "Händel, Bach und Schütz," *Zur Geschichte der Musik: Musikwissenschaftliche Aufsätze* (Berlin: Gebrüder Paetel, 1894), 72. This dictum is also discussed in Rudolf Heinz, *Geschichtsbegriff und Wissenschaftscharakter in der Musikwissenschaft in der zweiten Hälfte des neunzehnten Jahrhunderts* (Regensburg: Gustav Bosse, 1969), 31, and his "Geschichte als angewandte Ästhetik: Zum Verhältnis zwischen Musikästhetik und Musikhistorie bei Friedrich Chrysander und Hermann Kretzschmar," in Walter Wiora, ed., *Die Ausbreitung des Historismus über die Musikwissenschaft* (Regensburg: Gustav Bosse, 1969), 257–258; as well as in Wolfgang Sandberger, "Philipp Spitta und die Geburt der Musikwissenschaft aus dem Geiste der Philologie," in Anselm Gerhard, ed., *Musikwissenschaft—eine verspätete Disziplin? Die akademische Musikforschung zwischen Fortschrittsglauben und Modernitätsverweigerung* (Stuttgart: Metzler, 2001), 59.

17. Spitta, "Denkmäler deutscher Tonkunst," 19: "nur wenige Schlußsteine fehlen heute zur Vollendung dieses ältesten und vielleicht folgenreichsten 'Denkmals deutscher Tonkunst.'" The chauvinistic nationalist overtones of this article are striking, but they reflect, at least partly, the overall patriotic style of journal in which they appear. Thus, French claims over Gluck and English claims over Handel are seen as signs of impertinence, while the German edition of Palestrina's works is a sign of German superiority over Italian editorship. Patriotic sentiments are still occasionally found in modern comments, see Christian Martin Schmidt, "Zwischen Quellentreue und Werkrezeption, oder: Dem Wandel des historischen Bewußtseins ist nicht zu entkommen," in Helga Lühning, ed., *Musikedition: Mittler zwischen Wissenschaft und musikalischer Praxis* (Tübingen: Max Niemeyer, 2002), 3–17.

18. Practically the entire literature on the topic treats *Denkmäler* and complete editions together. Spitta and Chrysander make this link explicit in Spitta, "Denkmäler

deutscher Tonkunst," 16–27, and Chrysander, "Denkmäler der Tonkunst: Eine Ankündigung," *Leipziger allgemeine musikalische Zeitung* 4 (1869): col. 1. Moser reports that when writing a history of monumental editions he found it impossible to "separate [it] from that of musical complete editions" (in *Das musikalische Denkmälerwesen*, 5). Gerhard, "Für den 'Butterladen,'" traces this confluence in the first half of the nineteenth century.

19. Susan Stewart, *On Longing: Narratives of the Miniature, the Gigantic, the Souvenir, the Collection* (Durham, NC: Duke University Press, 1993), 151–169. For other important insights in the collection, see also Aleida Assmann, Monika Gomille, and Gabriele Rippl, eds., *Sammler—Bibliophile—Exzentriker* (Tübingen: Gunter Narr Verlag, 1998); John Elsner and Roger Cardinal, eds., *The Cultures of Collecting* (London: Reaktion Books, 1994); and Susan Crane, *Collecting & Historical Consciousness in Early Nineteenth-Century Germany* (Ithaca, NY: Cornell University Press, 2000).

20. See Werner Breig, "Probleme in der Edition älterer deutscher Orgelmusik," in Helga Lühning, ed., *Musikedition: Mittler zwischen Wissenschaft und musikalischer Praxis* (Tübingen: Max Niemeyer, 2002), 51. See also preface of Max Seiffert's edition of Scheidt's *Tabulatura nova, Denkmäler deutscher Tonkunst* 1 (1892).

21. Heinrich Reimann, "Philipp Spitta und seine Bach-Biographie," in *Musikalische Rückblicke* (Berlin: Harmonie Verlagsgesellschaft für Literatur und Kunst, 1900), 60.

22. Spitta, "Denkmäler deutscher Tonkunst," 23.

23. Ibid. 22–23. "Der Griff um ein Jahrhundert weiter zurück zu Heinrich Schütz erschien der Mehrzahl unsrer Musiker als eine antiquarische Thorheit, die sie nichts angehe, und wurde von vorsichtiger Urteilenden wenigstens mit zweifelnder Verwunderung angesehen."

24. The compositional impact of Schütz's style, and ultimately the publication of the Schütz complete edition, is perhaps most manifest in Brahms's opus 109 and 110. See Ryan Minor, "National Memory, Public Music: Commemoration and Consecration in Nineteenth-Century German Choral Music," Ph.D. dissertation (University of Chicago, 2005), 382–446.

25. Spitta, "Denkmäler deutscher Tonkunst," 23. "Diesen wiederherzustellen ist nichts förderlicher, als wenn gezeigt wird, wie ein ganzes Jahrhundert in solchen und ähnlichen Formen musikalisch dachte, wie Schütz zwar unter den Zeitgenossen der größte war, aber doch mit ihnen an demselben Strange zog. Dann sondert sich von selbst das Typische vom Individuellen, jenes wird am leichtesten begriffen und auf der so gewonnenen Grundlage allmählich auf dieses verständlich und endlich vertraut. So setzt Schütz die Bekanntschaft mit Andreas Hammerschmidt, mit Johann Hermann Schein und Samuel Scheidt voraus, von denen wenigstens die beiden letzten der Stolz ihrer Zeit waren und nach einigen Geschlechtern auf wieder unser Stolz sein können."

26. Ibid. 22. See also note 97 below.

27. Moser, *Das musikalische Denkmälerwesen*, 17.

28. See Spitta, "Kunst und Kunstwissenschaft," *Zur Geschichte der Musik*, 6.

29. Spitta, "Denkmäler deutscher Tonkunst," 27. "Es gab eine Zeit, da fühlten sich die deutschen Musiker reich genug, von dem zu leben, was sie selbst aufbrachten. Dies Selbstgefühl fängt an, wankend zu werden. Aber sie brauchen nicht zu verzagen; im Rücken liegt ihnen ein kostbares Erbe, an das sie sich lehnen können. Noch ahnen sie kaum, wie umfangreich es ist. Die 'Denkmäler deutscher Tonkunst' werden helfen, seine Größe offenbar zu machen."

30. Spitta, "Vom Mittleramte der Poesie," *Zur Geschichte der Musik,* 24.

31. Cited in Friedrich Chrysander, "Was Herr Prof. Hanslick sich unter 'Kunst-zeloten' vorstellt," *Leipziger allgemeine musikalische Zeitung* 3 (1869): 387. "Sie scheint uns redlicher für das Interesse des Kunstwerkes thätig, als jene Puristen, welche dessen lebendige Wirkung gerne der philologischen Buchstabentreue opfern. Sie möchten ein für uns unzureichend instrumentirtes Tonwerk lieber in der Originalgestalt durchfallen sehen, als durch bescheidene Nachhilfe zu neuer lebendiger Wirksamkeit erweckt."

32. Chrysander calls Hanslick "the official representative of musicology in Austria." See "Was Herr Prof. Hanslick," 388. Heinrich Bellermann makes the same point more strongly in "Robert Franz' Bearbeitungen älterer Tonwerke," *Leipziger allgemeine musika-lische Zeitung* 7 (1872): col. 489.

33. Chrysander's biography is treated in detail in Waltraut Schardig, *Friedrich Chry-sander: Leben und Werk* (Hamburg: K. D. Wagner, 1986).

34. On Robert Franz, see Konrad Sasse, *Beiträge zur Forschung über Leben und Werk von Robert Franz 1815–1892,* ed. Edwin Werner (Halle an der Saale: Händel-Haus, 1986); and Konstanze Musketa, ed., *Robert Franz (1815–1892)* (Halle an der Saale: Händel-Haus, 1993).

35. A good part of the protracted debate was spent on the question of whether organ or harpsichord, or both, had been used in Bach's time. The harpsichord being obsolete in the nineteenth century, most of Chrysander's supporters argued that the modern piano was an adequate replacement. See Dieter Gutknecht, "Robert Franz als Bearbeiter der Werke von Bach und Händel und die Praxis seiner Zeit," in Konstanze Musketa, ed., *Robert Franz (1815–1892)* (Halle an der Saale: Händel-Haus, 1993), 219–247; Hans-Joachim Hinrichsen, "Die Bach-Gesamtausgabe und die Kontroversen um die Aufführungspraxis der Vokalwerke," in Michael Heinemann and Hans-Joachim Hinrichsen, eds., *Bach und die Nachwelt* (Laaber: Laaber-Verlag, 1997), 2: 227–297; and Elaine Kelly, "Evolution versus Authenticity: Johannes Brahms, Robert Franz, and Continuo Practice in the Late Nineteenth Century," *Nineteenth Century Music* 30 (2006): 182–204.

36. Robert Franz, *Offener Brief an Eduard Hanslick über die Bearbeitung älterer Tonwerke* (Leipzig: F. E. C. Leuckart, 1871), 8.

37. Ibid., 7.

38. Robert Franz, *Mittheilungen über J. S. Bach's 'Magnificat'* (Halle: Heinrich Karm-rodt, 1863), 1.

39. See Johann S. Bach, *36 Arien aus verschiedenen Kantaten mit Begleitung des Pianoforte,* ed. Robert Franz (Leipzig: Whistling, 1859/60), preface. See also Gutknecht, "Robert Franz als Bearbeiter," 219–220.

40. The *St Matthew Passion* is, of course, the *locus classicus* of historical performance practice. See Martin Geck, *Die Geburtsstunde des Mythos "Bach": Mendelssohns Wiederent-deckung der Matthäuspassion* (Stuttgart: Carus, 1998); and Celia Applegate, *Bach in Berlin: Nation and Culture in Mendelssohn's Revival of the St Matthew Passion* (Ithaca, NY: Cornell University Press, 2005).

41. The *Bach Gesellschaft* version is confused by the indication "Chor II," as the only viola da gamba is found in Chor I. Their editorial decision is to rescore the aria for obbligato cello.

42. Franz, *Offener Brief,* 2–3.

43. Anon., "Bearbeitungen älterer Vocalwerke von Robert Franz," *Leipziger allgemeine musikalische Zeitung* 3 (1865): col. 435. See also Gutknecht, "Robert Franz als Bearbeiter," 225.

44. Franz, *Offener Brief,* 2–3 and 13.

45. Ibid. 5. "Das Accompagnement hatte fast überall mitzuwirken, und zwar lag in ihm recht eigentlich der Schwerpunkt derartiger Musik."

46. Bellermann, "Robert Franz' Bearbeitungen älterer Tonwerke," col. 495. "denn auch diese, obgleich sie fast stets eine Instrumentalbegleitung anwandten und keine eigentliche Acapella-Musik mehr schrieben, räumten dennoch dem Gesange den *ersten Platz* in der Musik ein, indem sie sich noch wohl bewusst waren, dass der Ursprung aller Musik der Gesang ist." It seems Chrysander and Spitta were not in agreement with Bellermann, but kept silent in this highly partisan situation, not least since Bellermann was Spitta's colleague in Berlin. See Ulrike Schilling, *Philipp Spitta: Leben und Wirken im Spiegel seiner Briefwechsel mit einem Inventar des Nachlasses und einer Bibliographie der gedruckten Werke* (Kassel: Bärenreiter, 1994), 67 and 132–133.

47. Spitta, *Johann Sebastian Bach* (Leipzig: Breitkopf und Härtel, 1873), 1: 713. "Solchen Thatsachen gegenüber kann man sich des niederschlagenden Gefühles nicht erwehren, daß eine gänzlich dem Sinne Bachs genügende Ausführung seiner Instrumentalsoli mit beziffertem Basse für uns jetzt unmöglich geworden ist. Hätte jedoch der Meister seine Art der Begleitung für die Gesammtwirkung als wesentlich erachtet, so würde er auch hier eine obligate Clavierstimme hingeschrieben haben."

48. He justifies this preference with reference to a chordal accompaniment to the trio from the Musical Offering, realized by Bach's student Kirnberger. See Spitta, "Der Bach-Verein zu Leipzig," *Leipziger allgemeine musikalische Zeitung* 10 (1875): col. 309.

49. The relevant correspondence between Brahms and Chrysander is found in Gustav Fock, "Brahms und die Musikforschung," in Heinrich Husmann, ed., *Beiträge zur Hamburger Musikgeschichte* (Hamburg: Selbstverlag des musikwissenschaftlichen Instituts der Universität Hamburg, 1956), 62–67. Brahms made the same point to Spitta, see Carl Krebs, ed., *Johannes Brahms im Briefwechsel mit Philipp Spitta* (Reprint Tutzing: Hans Schneider, 1974), 72. See also Karl Geiringer, "Brahms als Musikhistoriker," *Die Musik* 25 (1933): 571–578; "Brahms and Chrysander," *Monthly Musical Record* 67 (1937): 97–99, 131–132, 178–180, 463–464; and "Brahms as Reader and Collector," *Musical Quarterly* 19 (1933): 158–168. For a recent reassessment of Brahms and philology, see Roger Moseley, "Brief Immortality: Recasting History in the Music of Brahms," Ph.D. dissertation (University of California at Berkeley, 2004).

50. Letter Julius Schaeffer to Robert Franz, January 2, 1881, in Wolfgang Golther, ed., *Robert Franz und Arnold Freiherr Senfft von Pilsach: Ein Briefwechsel 1861–1888* (Berlin: Alexander Duncker, 1907), 310. "er meinte, er habe den Baß freigelassen, damit man auf Grund desselben spielen könne, 'was man wolle,' er selber würde ganz etwas anderes spielen, als er geschrieben habe; dies letztere sei vielleicht anzugreifen, und er würde es vielleicht 8 Tage später wieder anders gemacht haben." It is quite likely that Brahms knew he was being provocative, see fn. 53 below.

51. Franz, *Offener Brief,* 4.

52. See Spitta, *Johann Sebastian Bach,* 1: 716–717.

53. See Fock, "Brahms und die Musikforschung," 64. "Glauben Sie, fragte ich ihn, daß Bach, wenn er an der Orgel saß und Arien begleitete, sich mit der einfachen harmonischen Auflösung der bezifferten Basses begnügt haben würde? 'Quod licet Bacho, not licet Francisco,' replizierte er schlagfertig." (This citation is from Max Kalbeck, *Johannes Brahms* [Vienna and Leipzig: Wiener Verlag, 1904], 1: 281.)

54. Franz, *Offener Brief,* 3–4. "Und siehe da: zu meiner freudigen Ueberraschung wurde plötzlich Alles lebendig, die Stimmen schienen nur darauf gewartet zu haben, dass man sie niederschriebe und waren offenbar prämeditirt worden."

55. The mystical marriage from artist to artist, which is reminiscent of Wagner's musical encounters with Gluck, is clearest in Franz's final peroration, in *Offener Brief,* 36: "Ihren Werken wird nur gerecht werden, wer ihnen mit der bestimmten Voraussetzung nahet, dass sie in allen Theilen von der geheimnissvollen Macht eines poetischen Tonlebens durchdrungen sind. Beide Meister [Bach und Handel] unter anderen Gesichtspunkten begreifen zu wollen, würde sicher zu der Gefahr führen, sich mehr und mehr von ihren wirklichen Absichten zu entfernen."

56. On this particularly contentious point, see Julius Schaeffer, *Friedrich Chrysander in seinen Klavierauszügen zur deutschen Händel-Ausgabe* (Leipzig: F. E. C. Leuckart, 1876), 13.

57. See Franz, *Offener Brief,* 11–24; Schaeffer, *Friedrich Chrysander in seinen Klavierauszügen,* and *Seb. Bachs Cantate "Sie werden alle kommen aus Saba." in den Ausgaben von Robert Franz und dem Leipziger Bachverein* (Leipzig: F. E. C. Leuckart, 1877).

58. Kelly, "Brahms, Franz and *Continuo* Practice," 187–189.

59. See, for instance, Schaeffer, *Friedrich Chrysander,* 41; and Franz, *Offener Brief,* 35.

60. *Leipziger allgemeine musikalische Zeitung* 6 (1871): 299: "Hoffentlich wird die Akademie, nach diesem ihr abermals gelungenen Versuche, eine vollständige Aufführung des 'Allegro' zu wege bringen, wobei wir uns dem Wunsche des obigen Referenten um Benutzung der 'ursprünglichen' Orchester-Begleitung (mit Ausschluss der leidigen modernen 'Bearbeitungen') anschliessen, weil nur dadurch die volle Wirkung verbürgt ist. Was wäre es anders als eine barbarische Geschmacklosigkeit, wollte man alte Gemälde neu überpinseln? Ist es aber in der Musik nicht genau dasselbe?" Schaeffer comments on this passage in his *Friedrich Chrysander,* 9.

61. Alois Riegl, "The Modern Cult of Monuments: Its Character and Its Origin," trans. Kurt W. Forster and Diae Ghirardo, *Oppositions* 25 (1982): 21.

62. Ibid. 44.

63. Ibid. 34.

64. Ibid. 35.

65. Spitta, "Kunst und Kunstwissenschaft," 13. "Die Arbeitswege der Kunstwissenschaft und der Kunst dürfen niemals ineinander laufen." Rudolf Heinz conjectures that this strict separation was mainly to protect Johannes Brahms from criticism, see *Geschichtsbegriff und Wissenschaftscharakter,* 35 and 55–56. It is worth noting, however, that Spitta was at times rather critical of Brahms's music, as he expresses freely in his letters to von Herzogenberg. For Spitta's views on Brahms's music, see Schilling, *Spitta,* 176–179.

66. Spitta, "Kunst und Kunstwissenschaft," 4–6. This separation became an important guideline for editing practice. As Max Friedlander, *Ueber musikalische Herausgeberarbeit* (Weimar: Gesellschaft der Bibliophilen, 1922), 5, underlines in almost comical terms, it is "a fateful error of publishers to commission creative masters with the edition of works of art . . . although experience has shown for centuries that geniuses, of all people, are not suited to purely philological tasks."

67. Spitta, "Kunst und Kunstwissenschaft," 12. "Er kann nicht beanspruchen, in sich vereinigen zu wollen, was sich von Natur ausschließt."

68. Ibid. 11. "Wird also einmal die Nothwendigkeit einer literarischen Vermittelung anerkannt, so muß es der Künstler selber sein, der sie besorgt. Das Unbehagen, welches

ihm daraus erwachsen dürfte, wird er ertragen, wenn er überzeugt ist, daß es sich um eine Lebensfrage handelt."

69. Ibid. "Kein Kunstwerk wirkt voraussetzungslos. Immer ist es auf den Hintergrund bezogen, welchen mit ihren Sitten, Anschauungen und Stimmungen diejenige Zeit bildet, in der es entstanden ist. Im Laufe der Jahrhunderte verschiebt sich allmählich dieser Hintergrund, oder sinkt auch ganz zusammen. Die Kunstwerke erscheinen alsdann in schiefen Verhältnissen, oder stehen gar einsam und fremd im öden Raum. Diese ihre nothwendige Zubehör ihnen zurückzugeben, dazu muß zunächst der Gelehrte die Hand anlegen."

70. Anton Friedrich Justus Thibaut, *Über Reinheit der Tonkunst* (Heidelberg: J. C. B. Mohr, 1825), 38.

71. Spitta, "Kunst und Kunstwissenschaft," 11–12. "Es gibt einige wenige alte Kunstwerke, die auch auf die Gegenwart, mochte sie zeitlich noch so weit von ihnen getrennt sein, immer mit überzeugender Kraft gewirkt haben. Auf sie pflegt man sich zu stützen, wenn man behauptet, das wahrhaft Schöne bleibe zu allen Zeiten dasselbe. Zutreffender aber wäre es wohl zu sagen: es wird in ihnen die Fülle des Kunstgehalts sowohl der schaffenden Persönlichkeit als ihrer ganzen Zeit mit einer solchen Energie zur Erscheinung gebracht, daß diese den Beschauer oder Hörer unwiderstehlich in die Vergangenheit zurückzieht, aber in der Weise, daß ihm das Fremde sofort vertraut, das zeitlich Zufällige als künstlerisch nothwendig erscheint."

72. Schaeffer, *Seb. Bach's Cantate:"Sie werden aus Saba alle kommen,"* 6.

73. Just how common this notion of classicism has become shows Riemann's popular *Musiklexikon,* which changes its entry on "klassisch" in the fourth edition, to mean "a work of art resistant to the destructive power of time. Since this trait can only become evident over the course of time, there are no living composers who are 'classical.'" *Musiklexikon* (Leipzig: Max Hesse, 1894), 540. For a recent reconsideration of Riemann's classicism, see Rudolf Stefan, "'Klassizismus' bei Hugo Riemann," in Tatjana Böhme-Mehner und Klaus Mehner, eds., *Hugo Riemann (1849–1919): Musikwissenschaftler mit Universalanspruch* (Cologne: Böhlau, 2001), 131–137.

74. Chrysander, "Instrumentalmusik," *Leipziger allgemeine musikalische Zeitung* 7 (1872): col. 106. "Nichts Höheres existirt in der Kunst, als das einzelne vollendete Werk, und keine größere Erscheinung bietet die Kunstgeschichte dar, als den Künstler, der solches zu erzeugen vermochte. Die Verehrung, welche den wenigen sogenannten Classikern gezollt wird, ist daher eine berechtigte; ihre Werke zeigen uns die ganze Kunst, zwar nicht in ihrer ganzen Länge und Breite, aber im Durchschnitt und in der höchsten Höhe. Der Besitz der Classiker in Drucken und Aufführungen wird also immer der kürzeste und gemeinsamste Weg bleiben, um zum Vollgenuss der Kunst zu gelangen."

75. Ibid., col. 105. "Das so Entstandene hatte in seiner Zeit zunächst nur eine relative Bedeutung als das Beste unter vielen ähnlichen Versuchen Mitlebender. Bald aber zeigte es sich—zunächst in der Erlahmung der Production der Mitbewerber—, dass die Bedeutung eine *absolute* war und dass das Werk im letzten Grunde weder durch einen glücklichen Griff entstand, noch durch ein günstiges Zusammenwirken äusserer Umstände zur Anerkennung gelangte, sondern dass bei seinem Entstehen neue geistige Kräfte wirksam waren, Ideen eigenthümlicher Art, wodurch es wie eine völlig neue Schöpfung ins Dasein trat."

76. Ibid. "Es ist gegen den Lauf der Natur, dass diese Kräfte, diese Ideen je zum zweiten Male unter gleichen und gleich günstigen Bedingungen sollten zur Wirksamkeit gelan-

gen können. Alle Gestaltung ist individuell, und wie in Sachen der Erkenntniss nicht einmal von Zweien ein Gedanke von irgendwelcher Originalität zu gleicher Zeit und bei Betrachtung desselben Gegenstandes genommen werden kann, so ist die Wiederholung und Ueberholung einer künstlerischen Schöpfung in späterer Zeit noch viel unmöglicher."

77. Friedrich Nietzsche, "On the Uses and Disadvantages of History for Life," *Untimely Meditations*, trans. R. J. Hollingdale (Cambridge: Cambridge University Press, 1997), 72. Note that the question of whether antiquarian history is in fact identical with academic history has been questioned, see Kurt Hübner, "Vom theoretischen Nachteil und praktischen Nutzen der Historie: Unzeitgemäßes über Nietzsches unzeitgemäße Betrachtungen," in Dieter Borchmeyer, ed., *"Vom Nutzen und Nachteil der Historie für das Leben": Nietzsche und die Erinnerung in der Moderne* (Frankfurt am Main: Suhrkamp, 1996), 43. For thought-provoking interpretations of Nietzsche's text as a critique of academic history, see Dieter Jähnig, "Nietzsches Kritik der historischen Wissenschaften," *Praxis* 6 (1970): 223–236; Katrin Meyer, *Ästhetik der Historie: Friedrich Nietzsches "Vom Nutzen und Nachteil der Historie für das Leben"* (Würzburg: Königshausen & Neumann, 1998), 69–70; and Glenn W. Most, "Vom Nutzen und Nachteil der Antike für das Leben: zur modernen deutschen Selbstfindung anhand der alten Griechen," *Humanistische Bildung* 19 (1996): 35–52. I take it that Nietzsche refers to particular antiquarian and monumental tendencies within academic history, which would seem to apply here.

78. Recent scholarship has suggested that Spitta in fact responded directly to Nietzsche's *Untimely Meditations*. See Laurenz Lütteken, "Vom Umgang mit Quellen," *Die Musikforschung* 57 (2004): 329. The question of the precise relation between monumental and antiquarian history is unsettled. Heidegger, for one, fits Nietzsche into a scheme where monumental history is forward-looking and antiquarian is backward-looking, whereas it would be misguided—as we see here—to construct them as completely opposed. See Achim Geisenhanslüke, "Der Mensch als Eintagswesen: Nietzsches Kritische Anthropologie in der Zweiten Unzeitgemäßen Betrachtung," *Nietzsche-Studien* 28 (1999): 132–135.

79. Chrysander's colleague on the Handel edition, Gervinus, would argue in a similar vein from the perspective of the literary scholar. See his *Händel und Shakespeare: Zur Ästhetik der Instrumentalkunst* (Leipzig: Wilhelm Engelmann, 1868). Chrysander's article, "Instrumentalmusik," was written in response to Gervinus's somewhat conflicting aesthetic views of instrumental music.

80. For an insightful reflection on the nature of musical editions, see Carl Dahlhaus, "Philologie und Rezeptionsgeschichte: Bemerkungen zur Theorie der Edition," in Thomas Kohlhase und Volker Scherliess, eds., *Festschrift Georg von Dadelsen zum 60. Geburtstag* (Neuhausen-Stuttgart: Hänssler, 1978), 45–58, and "Ideengeschichte musikalischer Editionsprinzipien," *Fontes Artes Musicae* 25 (1978): 19–27.

81. To be sure, *"oeuvres complettes,"* already existed in the first half of the nineteenth century, but these editions usually did not aspire to anything approaching completion, nor did their editorial policy have much to do with the philological ideals of the latter half of the century. See Annette Oppermann, *Musikalische Klassikerausgaben des 19. Jahrhunderts* (Göttingen: Vandenhoeck & Oppermann, 2001).

82. Moritz Hauptmann in a letter to Franz Hauser of 1860. Cited in Moser, *Das musikalische Denkmälerwesen,* 14.

83. Chrysander, "Instrumentalmusik," col. 108. "Die Fülle der Anschauung ist und bleibt der allererste Grund wahrer umfassender Kunsterkenntniss. Nur wenn diese zu

Grunde liegt, dann ist Gefahr zu vermeiden, welche bei ästhetischen Untersuchungen so nahe liegt, die Gefahr nämlich, einzelne Beobachtungen vorschnell zu allgemeinen Gesetzen zu erheben."

84. Spitta, "Denkmäler deutscher Tonkunst," 21. "Andererseits konnte nun bei Bach, Händel und Schütz der Welt zum erstenmale ganz augenscheinlich gemacht werden, wie unerläßlich für das geschichtliche Verständnis einer zurückliegenden künstlerischen Persönlichkeit die genaue und vollständige Kenntnis aller ihrer Werke ist. Das klingt so selbstverständlich, daß man Anstand nehmen möchte, es auszusprechen."

85. Ibid. "daß eine allgemeine Musikgeschichte so lange nicht geschrieben werden kann, als man die Thaten der Männer nicht kennt, die die Geschichte gemacht haben."

86. This was in marked contrast to the low regard in which Guido Adler held biography: for him, it was an object of "enthusiasm" that declared a "hobby," but excluded from his musicological style history. See Heinz, *Geschichtsbegriff und Wissenschaftscharakter,* 37–38.

87. Spitta, "Denkmäler deutscher Tonkunst," 21."die Darstellung der einzelnen Persönlichkeit wächst sich aus in die ihrer Umgebung, Zeit und Vorzeit: das Licht, an einem Punkte hell entzündet, wirft seinen Schein in das ringsum lagernde Dunkel."

88. Nietzsche, "On the Uses and Disadvantages of History for Life," 75.

89. Ibid.

90. Ibid. 73.

91. Spitta, "Musikalische Seelenmessen," *Zur Geschichte der Musik,* 434. "Aber es ist nur nöthig, die Phantasie der Menschheit von Neuem mit den Anschauungen zu erfüllen, die einstmals die Voraussetzung der Kunstwerke bildeten, und sie zur lebendigen Verknüpfung derselben zu erziehen, dann fangen auch die Kunstwerke selbst, wie Dornröschen im Märchen, wieder an zu athmen und schlagen die hellen Augen auf."

92. Samuel Scheidt, *Tabulatura nova,* ed. Max Seiffert, preface. "Nicht alles, was uns Scheidt in seiner 'Tabulatura nova' darbietet, hat bis heute seine erfrischende Kraft bewahrt, aber die wenigen noch grünenden Zweige sind aufmerksamer Betrachtung in vollem Maße würdig. Man pflanze sie nur wieder auf den Boden, der ihnen taugt, und unter den Händen eines wackeren Organisten werden sie wieder zu den lebensvollen Gestalten erblühen, wie sie ehedem die Herzen frommer Kirchgänger erbauten."

93. In fact, Seiffert's presentation of the *Tabulatura nova* poses an interesting problem: despite the importance of the score layout of the original, which necessarily required further editing by the performer before the works could be played, Seiffert summarizes the parts into a modern two-system score notation. Subsequent editors have not followed him in this practice; either reverting to open score or to a two-manual-plus-pedal organ layout. See Breig, "Probleme in der Edition älterer deutscher Orgelmusik," 49–62.

94. Reimann, "Philipp Spitta und seine Bach-Biographie," 61.

95. Spitta, "Denkmäler deutscher Tonkunst," 25–26. "daß man die Kunstwerke als Urkunden auffaßt und mit allen Mitteln bestrebt sein will, sie ohne Rücksicht auf ästhetischen Genuß vor allem richtig zu lesen und zu deuten, darin sehe ich einen der wichtigsten Fortschritte der jüngsten Zeit."

96. Spitta's comrade-in-philology, Otto Jahn, was clear about the consequences and difficulties: "Ein Eingehen auf historische Auffassung setzt freilich nicht nur ein gewisses Maß an Kenntnissen voraus, sondern auch die bewußte Absicht, dem Kunstwerk gegenüber einen anderen Standpunkt einzunehmen als den eines einfachen Genießers, ferner die

Fähigkeit, von den gewohnten Formen teilweise wenigstens abzusehen, ohne durch das eine wie das andere die Empfänglichkeit für das eigentlich Musikalische und Künstlerische zu schwächen—Anforderungen, welche besonders auf diesem Gebiet nicht leicht zu befriedigen sind." See his "Beethoven und die Ausgabe seiner Werke" in *Gesammelte Aufsätze über Musik,* 2d ed. (Leipzig: Breitkopf und Härtel, 1867), 277–278.

97. Spitta, "Denkmäler deutscher Tonkunst," 22. "Nur ganz wenige haben Kenntnis von dem, was um sie her besteht, obschon die gewöhnlichste geschichtliche Erfahrung sagen müßte, daß diese Männer zu ihrer riesigen Größe nicht haben aufwachsen können, ohne daß mächtige Kräfte vor und neben ihnen thätig gewesen sind, die ihnen zu dieser Größe verhalfen." By contrast, in Spitta's *Antrittsrede 1876,* "Bildende Kunst und Musik in ihrem gegenseitigen geschichtlichen Verhältnisse," *Leipziger allgemeine musikalische Zeitung* 11 (1876): col. 305–313, he argued in favor of a begotten-not-made genius, though this might have been a concession to the ceremonial occasion.

98. Chrysander, "Denkmäler der Tonkunst: Eine Ankündigung," *Leipziger allgemeine musikalische Zeitung* 4 (1869): col. 1.

99. See also Chrysander, "Die Verwendung der Schlüssel bei der Herausgabe älterer Meisterwerke, mit besonderer Beziehung auf die 'Denkmäler der Tonkunst,'" *Leipziger allgemeine musikalische Zeitung* 5 (1870): 356–359. Chrysander's example is briefly discussed in Gerhard, "Für den 'Butterladen,'" 364 and 380.

100. See Chrysander, "Instrumentalmusik," and "Die Oratorien von Carissimi," in *Leipziger allgemeine musikalische Zeitung* 11 (1876): cols. 67–69, 81–83, 113–115, 129–132, 145–147.

101. Moser, *Das musikalische Denkmälerwesen,* 17.

102. Stewart, *On Longing,* 155.

103. See note 74 above.

104. Cited in Minor, "National Memory, Public Music," 248.

105. Franz Gehring, "Triumphlied (auf den Sieg der deutschen Waffen) von Johannes Brahms," *Leipziger allgemeine musikalische Zeitung* 7 (1872): col. 414.

106. Spitta, "Johannes Brahms," *Zur Geschichte der Musik,* 427. "Er gehört auch so, wie er jetzt dasteht, zu den mächtigsten Schützern und Mehrern des vielhundertjährigen Reiches deutscher Tonkunst. An diesem Urtheil wird die Nachwelt nichts zu berichtigen finden."

Chapter Six

1. Johann Wolfgang von Goethe, *Faust: Der Tragödie zweiter Teil,* in *Goethe: Werke (Hamburger Ausgabe)* (Frankfurt am Main: Deutscher Taschenbuch Verlag, 1998), Act I, vv. 6222–6224. "Ins Unbetrene / Nicht zu Betretende; ein Weg ans Unerbetene / Nicht zu Erbittende." Trans. Stuart Atkins, *Goethe: The Collected Works,* Vol. 2, *Faust I & II* (Princeton: Princeton University Press, 1984), translation modified. This scene caused considerable interpretive difficulties throughout the nineteenth century. One enlightening interpretation is found in the parody by Friedrich Theodor Vischer, *Faust: Der Tragödie dritter Teil* (1886).

2. Goethe, *Faust II,* vv. 6246–6248. "Nichts wirst du sehn in ewig leerer Ferne, / Den Schritt nicht hören, den du tust, / Nichts Festes finden, wo du ruhst."

3. Ibid., vv. 6275–6276. "Versinke denn! Ich könnt' auch sagen: steige! / 's ist einerlei."

4. Ibid., vv. 6303–6304. "Dein Wesen strebe nieder; / Versinke stampfend, stampfend steigst du wieder."

5. M. Nadeem Niazi, "Violating the *Mütter*: Staging the Semiotics of Desire, or, Aspects of the Eternal-Feminine in 'Faust,'" *Orbis Litterarum* 55 (2000): 103–117. A Lacanian would effortlessly recognize the realm of the *Mütter* as a site of the "real."

6. See, for instance, Michael Neumann, *Das Ewig-Weibliche in Goethes "Faust"* (Heidelberg: C. Winter, 1985).

7. Goethe, *Faust II,* vv. 6216 and 6272–6274. "*Faust:* Mütter! *Mephistopheles:* Schaudert's dich? . . . *Faust:* Das Schaudern ist der Menschheit bestes Teil; / Wie auch die Welt ihm das Gefühl verteure, / Ergriffen, fühlt er tief das Ungeheure."

8. Ibid., v. 6306. "Neugierig bin ich, ob er wiederkommt."

9. Ibid., vv. 6213 and 6218. On the mythological facets of the *Mütter,* see Gottfried Diener, *Fausts Weg zu Helena: Urphänomen und Archetypus* (Stuttgart: Ernst Klett Verlag, 1961), 56–62.

10. Goethe, *Faust II,* vv. 6286–6287. "Die einen sitzen, andre stehn und gehn, / Wie's eben kommt."

11. Ibid., vv. 6427–6432. "In eurem Namen, Mütter, die ihr thront / Im Grenzenlosen, ewig einsam wohnt, / Und doch gesellig. Euer Haupt umschweben / Des Lebens Bilder, regsam, ohne Leben. / Was einmal war, in allem Glanz und Schein, / Es regt sich dort; denn es will ewig sein."

12. Ibid., vv. 6290. "Sie sehn dich nicht, denn Schemen sehn sie nur" (translation modified).

13. Oswald Spengler, *The Decline of the West,* trans. Charles Atkinson (New York: Knopf, 1950).

14. Interesting though it may be, I refrain from drawing on Germanists' interpretations of this scene from the era of National Socialism here, since the music scholars who make reference to the *Mütter* often seem to have a personal, and sometimes idiosyncratic, understanding of the text.

15. Friedrich Blume, *Wesen und Werden der deutschen Musik* (Kassel: Bärenreiter, 1944), 6. "Das Reich der Mütter enträtselt kein Faustischer Wissensdrang."

16. See Pamela Potter, *Most German of the Arts: Musicology and Society from the Weimar Republic to the End of Hitler's Reich* (New Haven: Yale University Press, 1998); and Bernd Sponheuer, "Musik, Faschismus, Ideologie: Heuristische Überlegungen," *Die Musikforschung* 46 (1993): 241–253.

17. On Blume, see also Bernd Sponheuer, "The National Socialist Discussion on the 'German Quality' in Music," in Michael Kater and Albrecht Riethmüller, eds., *Music and Nazism: Art und Tyranny 1933–1944* (Laaber: Laaber-Verlag, 2003), 32–42. Sponheuer here refers to Herder's and Dahlhaus's explanation of the "Volksseele," which often took on a racial basis during the 1930s and 1940s, as we shall see below.

18. Lydia Goehr, *The Quest for Voice: On Music, Politics, and the Limits of Philosophy* (Berkeley: University of California Press, 1998) has captured the irrational "Wahn" as the basis of her philosophical reflections.

19. Hans Joachim Moser, *Kleine deutsche Musikgeschichte* (Stuttgart: Cotta'sche Buchhandlung, 1938), 323. "Wir wollen in der Kunst nicht das Physische, sondern das Metaphyische, nicht das bequem Nahe, sondern die ferne Idee, nicht das schlaue Wachsein,

sondern den kindhaften Traum, nicht die taschenspielerische Geschicklichkeit des glaube-losen Blenders, sondern noch im Schein des künstlerischen Spiels den bitteren Ernst um den letzten Sinn. . . . wir wollen (und nicht erst in der Romantik!) Musik als Ausdruck von menschlich Wesentlichem, als Darstellung von Dingen, die im Mittelpunkt des Gefühls stehen, als feiertägliche Bindung eines auf anderen Wegen so nicht ausdrück-baren Geheimnisses; es darf sehr wohl auch ein heiteres, lächelndes, frohes Geheimnis sein, aber ein Stück Seelisches muss damit übermittelt werden. Und der Drang, noch das im Wort Nicht-Sagbare zu sagen, drängt den Deutschen immer wieder zur Instrumen-talmusik als zu einer Verständigungssprache des Geistes und der Geister jenseits des platterdings Mitteilbaren, als zu einer Einsiegelung von Symbolen."

20. On *Feiern* and *Feste* of the National Socialists, see for instance Klaus Vondung, *Magie und Manipulation: Ideologischer Kult und politische Religion des Nationalsozialismus* (Göttingen: Vandenhoeck & Ruprecht, 1971); and George L. Mosse, *The Nationalization of the Masses: Political Symbolism and Mass Movements in Germany from the Napoleonic Wars through the Third Reich* (Ithaca, NY: Cornell University Press, 1991).

21. The point that the autonomy of absolute music is only relative, or imaginary, has been made by many commentators. Dahlhaus particularly explores the "relative auton-omy" of absolute music in his *The Idea of Absolute Music,* trans. Roger Lustig (Chicago: University of Chicago Press, 1989).

22. Besseler explains *Gebrauchsmusik* and its sphere of influence in Besseler, "Grund-fragen des musikalischen Hörens," in Peter Gülke, ed., *Aufsätze zur Musikgeschichte und Musikästhetik* (Leipzig: Reclam Leipzig, 1978), 29–53. As the Second World War turned increasingly desperate, this music became "höhere Durchhaltemusik," as Heister quips. See Hanns-Werner Heister, "Klassik, Fanfaren, höhere Durchhaltemusik," in Hanns-Werner Heister and Hans-Günter Klein, eds., *Musik und Musikpolitik im faschistischen Deutschland* (Frankfurt am Main: Fischer, 1984), 115–125.

23. Adolf Hitler, "Rede auf der Kulturtagung des Reichsparteitages 1935," in *Die Malerei im deutschen Faschismus: Kunst und Konterrevolution,* ed. Berthold Hinz (Munich: Hanser, 1974), 151. "Nichts ist mehr geeignet, den kleinen Nörgler zum Schweigen zu bringen als die ewige Sprache der großen Kunst." See also Robert Eikmeyer, ed., *Adolf Hitler: Reden zur Kunst- und Kulturpolitik 1933–1939,* with introd. by Boris Groys (Frank-furt am Main: Revolver, 1999).

24. On Schering's political engagement during the 1930s, see Potter, *Most German of the Arts.*

25. Arnold Schering, "Über den Begriff des Monumentalen in der Musik," *Von großen Meistern in der Musik* (Leipzig: Breitkopf und Härtel, 1935), 10. "Ein monumentales Ton-stück kann niemals in einem beschränkten Tonraume gedacht werden. Dessen Weite aber wird erreicht durch das Erklingen einer breiten tonalen Basis, durch das Vorwiegen ein-facher, aber voller Harmonien und eine gewisse Pracht und Stärke des Klangs. Weit ent-fernt nämlich, diese Dinge als bloße Steigerung des Normalen aufzufassen, ergänzt das Gemüt hier den sinnlichen Eindruck nach der Seite der Vorstellung, indem es unbewußt die solchen außergewöhnlichen Klangerzeugnissen entsprechenden akustischen Räum-lichkeiten mit reproduziert."

26. Ibid. 10–11.

27. Ibid. 14–15. On the musical sublime and National Socialist ideology, see Reinhold

Brinkmann, "The Distorted Sublime: Music and National Socialist Ideology—A Sketch," in Michael Kater and Albrecht Riethmüller, eds., *Music and Nazism: Art under Tyranny 1933–1945* (Laaber: Laaber-Verlag, 2003), 43–63.

28. See Siegfried Kracauer, *The Mass Ornament: Weimar Essays,* trans. Thomas Y. Levin (Cambridge, MA: Harvard University Press, 1995), 75–86.

29. Vondung, *Magie und Manipulation,* 150.

30. On the political and ethical significance attributed to the organ, see Albrecht Riethmüller, "Zur Politik der unpolitischen Musik," in *Funkkolleg Musikgeschichte* (Tübingen, Weinheim, Basel, and Mainz: Deutsches Institut für Fernstudien, 1988), 111–125.

31. Heinrich Besseler, "Musik und Raum," in Heinrich Besseler, ed., *Musik und Bild: Festschrift Max Seiffert* (Kassel: Bärenreiter, 1938), 156. "Monumentalwirkung beruht hier nicht auf dem Einsatz großer Massen, sondern auf der musikalisch-dramatischen Auswertung des Großraumes, dem Ausgreifen von Wort und Klang über eine mächtige, das gewohnte Menschenmaß überschreitende Ordnung."

32. Ibid. 152. "Bezeichnet man diese Welt, in der die Musik gewachsen ist, als Lebensraum, so ist damit schon angedeutet, dass es hier nicht allein um akustische und klangräumliche Fragen geht. Ein echtes Kultwerk wie eine Bachsche Kantate in den Konzertsaal verpflanzen, bedeutet gewiss einen Eingriff in seinen ursprünglichen 'Lebensraum.'"

33. Ibid.

34. See Besseler's final paragraph, which makes explicit the political import of his ideas, 160: "Es ist hier nicht der Ort, ausführlich den Umbruch darzulegen, den die Fest- und Feiergestaltung des Nationalsozialismus heraufgeführt hat. Aber eine Betrachtung des Verhältnisses von Musik und Raum würde den entscheidenden Gesichtspunkt beiseite lassen, wenn sie nicht wenigstens mit einem Hinweis auf das Grunderlebnis der Gegenwart schlösse, das unserem Blick in die Vergangenheit und Zukunft Richtung gibt."

35. Ibid. 153. "Dabei geht es nicht um das Einmalige und Besondere eines bestimmten Werkes, sondern um das Gemeinsame, Bleibende, Verbindende einer ganzen Gruppe innerlich verwandter Bilder. Denn der Lebensraum einer Musik wird nicht vom Einzelnen geschaffen oder willkürlich geändert. Er ist *vor* dem Einzelkunstwerk und *vor* dem großen Schöpfer da, als Ergebnis eines Wachstums, dessen Wurzeln tief hinabreichen in Rasse, Volk, Landschaft, Geschichte und gemeinsame Lebensform."

36. Ibid. 156. "Hier alles übergreifend die Sinfonie als 'tönende Kathedrale,' dort der Kirchenraum als Ort der kultischen Feier (ungeachtet konfessioneller Unterschiede)." (Additionally, in conjunction with the church space, Besseler lists the "höfische Festraum mit Ritterspiel, Ballett und Oper.")

37. For a discussion of the double-edged significance of "cult" in National Socialism, see Vondung, *Magie und Manipulation,* 42–47.

38. Besseler, "Musik und Raum," 160. "Die Volks- und Staatsfeiern des Dritten Reiches, der 1. Mai, das Erntedankfest, die Veranstaltungen auf dem Nürnberger Parteitag ebenso wie der Feierstil in den Formationen, Gliederungen und Gemeinschaften von Stadt und Land schaffen heute—ganz abgesehen von dem Erlebnis selbst, von der Gestaltung des Groß- und Freiluftraumes, vom neuen Einsatz künstlerischer und musischer Kräfte—der Musik einen echten neuen *Lebensraum.*"

39. For a recent reflection on the role of music in festive culture, see Hermann Danuser and Herfried Münkler, ed., *Kunst—Fest—Kanon: Inklusion und Exklusion in Gesellschaft und Kultur* (Berlin: Staatsoper Unter den Linden, 2004).

40. See, for instance, Wolfgang von Bartels, "Unterhaltung und Kultur im Rundfunk," *Zeitschrift für Musik* 101 (1934): 412, who startlingly claims: "Der Führer formt die Masse zum Volke; formt das Volk zur Nation." See also Karl Gustav Fellerer, "Musik und Feier," *Die Musik* 31 (1939): 433–437; and Robert Unger, *Die mehrchörige Aufführungspraxis bei Michael Praetorius und die Feiergestaltung der Gegenwart* (Wolfenbüttel and Berlin: Georg Kallmeyer, 1941).

41. Schering, "Über den Begriff des Monumentalen," 18.

42. Ibid.

43. Ibid. 19. "Mit dem Hang zum Männlichen, wie es dem Volke in höchster Vollkommenheit im absolutistischen Herrscher verkörpert erschien, hängt auch zusammen, daß es dem Musiker nichts ausmachte, ob er die göttliche oder die weltliche Majestät monumentalisierte."

44. See Albrecht Riethmüller, *Die Walhalla und ihre Musiker* (Laaber: Laaber-Verlag, 1993).

45. Schering, "Über den Begriff des Monumentalen," 18.

46. See, for instance, Peter Adam, *Art of the Third Reich* (New York: Harry N. Abrams, 1992).

47. The controversial classic of gender politics in the National Socialist regime remains Klaus Theweleit, *Male Fantasies,* trans. Stephen Conway (Cambridge: Polity Press, 1987–1989). Needless to say, all these trends could look back on powerful precursors preceding the Third Reich. As Jost Hermand has argued, National Socialist cultural politics preceded the political "seizure of power" in 1933, as one of its crucial organs, Rosenberg's *Kampfbund für deutsche Kultur* was active as early as 1928. See his "Bewährte Tümlichkeiten: Der Völkisch-Nazistische Traum einer ewig-deutschen Kunst," *Stile, Ismen, Etiketten: Zur Periodisierung der modernen Kunst* (Wiesbaden: Wissenschaftliche Verlagsgesellschaft Athenaion, 1978), 94–110.

48. Schering, "Über den Begriff des Monumentalen," 23. "Die Musik dringt damit machtvoller denn je in die Schichten der führenden Geister der Nationen ein; sie erobert sich Bildungssphären, die sie früher nur ausnahmsweise erfasst hatte. Da es dabei nicht nur Kenner, sondern auch musikalisch wenig vorgebildete Liebhaber, ja Unmusikalische zu befriedigen galt, musste der Durchschnittsstil zur höchsten möglichen Größe und Schlagkraft, d.h. eben zum Monumentalen gesteigert werden."

49. Ibid. 36. "Den Drang, monumentalisieren zu *müssen,* teilte er [Bach] mit Händel."

50. Ibid. 20. "Was hier in Tönen monumentalisiert wird, ist nicht die Person, die menschliche oder göttliche vorgestellte Erscheinung, sondern eine gewisse Summe höchster, überindividueller Eigenschaften, deren ethische Bedeutung immer dieselbe bleibt, wem unter Sterblichen oder Unsterblichen wir sie auch zuweisen."

51. Among the many publications on this complex topic, see Klaus Vondung, "National Socialism as Political Religion," *Totalitarian Movements and Political Religion* 6 (2005): 87–95; and Robert A. Pois, *National Socialism and the Religion of Nature* (New York: St Martin's Press, 1986).

52. Ibid., 17. "gregorianischer oder evangelischer Choral, eigenthümliche Instrumenten- und Themensymbolik, besondere Maßnahmen kontrapunktisch-architektonischer Anordnung der Klanggruppen, raumakustische Effekte und anderes."

53. Ibid. 24. "Nur daß das Transzendente in den einzelnen Ländern auf verschiedenen Ebenen gefunden wird, macht den Unterschied aus."

54. Ibid. 26 and 32.

55. Ibid. 16. "Was bis zur Stunde an monumentaler Musik geschaffen wird, muß dulden, daß es mit dem Maßstab barocker Vorbilder gemessen wird."

56. Ibid. 22. "Sehnsucht nach dem Transzendenten."

57. Ibid. 42.

58. Ibid. 43. "In der Regel läßt sich das weder aus- noch nachrechnen, sondern enthüllt sich schon dem reinen Gefühl, wenn es feststellt: hier herrscht vollkommene Ausgewogenheit der Teile, unbezweifelbare Harmonie der Kräfte."

59. Their story is detailed in Hans Joachim Moser, *Das musikalische Denkmälerwesen in Deutschland* (Kassel: Bärenreiter, 1952). See also Albrecht Riethmüller, "Deutsche Musik aus Sicht der deutschen Musikwissenschaft nach 1933," in Marion Demuth, ed., *Das Deutsche in der Musik* (Dresden: UniMedia, 1997), 68–80.

60. The speech is reprinted in Gerhard Splitt, *Richard Strauss 1933–1935* (Pfaffenweiler: Centaurus, 1987), 93–96.

61. See Blume, *Wesen und Werden der deutschen Musik.*

62. See Laurenz Lütteken, "Das Musikwerk im Spannungsfeld von 'Ausdruck' und 'Erleben': Heinrich Besselers musikhistoriographischer Ansatz," in Anselm Gerhard, ed., *Musikwissenschaft—eine verspätete Disziplin?: Die akademische Musikforschung zwischen Fortschrittsglauben und Modernitätsverweigerung* (Stuttgart, Weimar: J. B. Metzler, 2000), 213–232; and Pamela Potter, *Most German of the Arts* (New Haven: Yale University Press, 1998). See also Anselm Gerhard, "Musicology in the 'Third Reich': A Preliminary Report," *Journal of Musicology* 18 (2001): 517–543.

63. Schering, "Über den Begriff des Monumentalen," 21. "So mächtig packt uns das Außergewöhnliche, Übernormale seines Inhalts und seiner Darstellungsform, daß noch lange, nachdem beides außer Sicht getreten, nicht nur in unserer Seele ein Hochgefühl weiterschwingt, sondern auch der Verstand zu sinnendem Weiterdenken des Erlebten gezwungen wird."

64. Mathias Hansen, "Die faschistische Bruckner-Rezeption und ihre Quellen," *Beiträge zur Musikwissenschaft* 28 (1986): 53. "Kein anderer Musiker, nicht einmal Wagner oder Richard Strauss, . . . ist so vorbehaltlos und vollständig von der faschistischen Ideologie okkupiert worden wie Bruckner." Since his pioneering studies, a considerable number of other important articles and books have been written on the subject. Bryan Gilliam, "The Annexation of Anton Bruckner: Nazi Revisionism and the Politics of Appropriation," *Musical Quarterly* 78 (1994): 584–604; Benjamin Korstvedt, "Anton Bruckner in the Third Reich and After: An Essay on Ideology and Bruckner Reception," *Musical Quarterly* 80 (1996): 132–160; Steven McClatchie, "Bruckner and the Bayreuthians: Or, *Das Geheimnis der Form bei Anton Bruckner*," in Paul Hawkshaw and Timothy L. Jackson, eds., *Bruckner Studies* (Cambridge: Cambridge University Press, 1997), 110–121; Christa Brüstle, *Anton Bruckner und die Nachwelt: Zur Rezeptionsgeschichte des Komponisten in der ersten Hälfte des 20. Jahrhunderts* (Stuttgart: Metzler, 1998); Julian Horton, *Bruckner's Symphonies: Analysis, Reception and Cultural Politics* (Cambridge: Cambridge University Press, 2004).

65. Robert Haas, *Anton Bruckner* (Potsdam: Akademische Verlagsanstalt Athenaion, 1934), 3. "Das mittelalterliche Gefühl für Weiträumigkeit, das durch den barocken Lebensinhalt hindurch und über die Aufklärung hinweg gewahrt geblieben war . . . konnte da voll ausschwingen zu ekstatischen Hymnen von der Größe Gottes und der Welt."

66. Werner Danckert, "Bruckner und das Natursymbol," *Die Musik* 30 (1938): 306. "Fortsetzer, ja Vollender einer älteren, im 17. und 18. Jahrhundert lebendigen, späterhin aber von anderen künstlerischen Strömungen überfluten Ausdruckswelt, erfüllt von kräftiger Sinnlichkeit, Freude an Glanz und wuchernder Gestaltenfülle, getragen von einem 'vorklassisch' anmutenden 'objektiven' Formensinn." Trans. from Korstvedt, "Ideology and Bruckner Reception," 140.

67. See, for instance, Ernst Bücken, *Die Musik der Nationen* (Leipzig: Alfred Kröner, 1937), 383.

68. While the correct term, employed by the Bruckner *Gesamtausgabe,* was *Originalfassungen,* the term that gained popular currency, especially during the 1930s, was *Urfassungen*—the organic and primordial connotation of this term were, of course, part and parcel of the ideology of the *Mütter.*

69. For a history of versions and editions of Bruckner's symphonies, see Wolfgang Doebel, *Bruckners Symphonien in Bearbeitungen: Die Konzepte der Bruckner-Schüler und ihre Rezeption bis zu Robert Haas* (Tutzing: Hans Schneider, 2001); and Manfred Wagner, *Wandel des Konzepts: Zu verschiedenen Fassungen von Bruckners 3., 4. und 8. Symphonie* (Vienna: Musikwissenschaftlicher Verlag, 1980). On the contemporary discussion in the 1930s, see Max Auer, "Der Streit um den 'echten' Bruckner im Licht biographischer Tatsachen," *Zeitschrift für Musik* 103 (1935): 538–545; and Victor Junk, "Zur Urfassung von Bruckners Fünfter Symphonie," *Zeitschrift für Musik* 103 (1936): 545–546.

70. Peter Raabe, "Anton Bruckner: Rede gehalten 7. Juni 1937," *Zeitschrift für Musik* 104 (1937): 744. "Darum ist das Anhören dieser Werke für den, dem sie sich erschließen, etwas anderes als nur ein Kunstgenuß: es ist ein Gang zu den 'Müttern,' zu den Quellen der Empfindung, zu denen kein Denken führt, kein Wissen und Forschen, sondern nur der Wille, klein zu sein vor der Unendlichkeit der Schöpfung, aber groß in dem Streben nach dem Guten."

71. See Gilliam, "The Annexation of Anton Bruckner," 597.

72. Raabe, "Anton Bruckner," 743. "Was er in seligen Schaffensstunden erblickte, war durch Worte nicht wiederzugeben. Das ist ja das Gewaltige der Absoluten Musik, was sie über alle anderen Künste stellt, auch über die dramatische Musik, auch über das Lied, die Messe, das Oratorium, dass es ihre Aufgabe ist, das auszusprechen, was sich weder durch das Wort noch Geberde sagen läßt, und wenn man in einen Ausspruch die geheimnisvolle Macht der symphonischen Kunst dahin bannen wollte, so kann es nur das Wort aus Goethes Chorus mysticus sein: 'Das Unbeschreibliche, hier ist's getan.'"

73. Danckert, "Bruckner und das Natursymbol," 308. "Das Christlich-Katholische bildete gewissermaßen nur einen Durchgangsweg zu einem Lebensgrunde von höchster Altertümlichkeit, zu jenem urheidnischen Gefühlskreise, der das Ewigweibliche, das Mütterliche als die lebenspendende, die kosmische Macht schlechthin verehrt."

74. See Theweleit, *Male Fantasies;* and Ilse Erika Korotin, *"Am Muttergeist soll die Welt genesen": Philosophische Dispositionen zum Frauenbild im Nationalsozialismus* (Vienna, Cologne, Weimar: Böhlau, 1992).

75. When the concept of *Urfassung* was first formulated, in 1895, the express goal was to "prevent the danger of a swamping of sources" ("der Gefahr der Quellenversumpfung vorzubeugen"). See Ludwig Finscher, "Gesamtausgabe—Urtext—Musikalische Praxis: Zum Verhältnis von Musikwissenschaft und Musikleben," in Martin Bente, ed., *Musik, Edition, Interpretation: Gedenkschrift Günter Henle* (Munich: Henle, 1980), 194.

76. Wilhelm Furtwängler, "Rede zum 1. Großdeutschen Brucknerfest (1939)," in *Bruckner Blätter* (1939): 10–16. Cited in Hanns Kreczi, *Das Bruckner Stift St. Florian und das Linzer Reichs-Bruckner-Orchester (1942–1945): Anton Bruckner: Dokumente und Studien* (Graz: Akademische Druck und Verlagsanstalt, 1986), 5: 28. "Für unsere Kenntnis Brucknerscher Tonsprache, Brucknerschen Stilwillens und Fühlens sind die Urfassungen außerordentlich bedeutsam und aufschlußreich: die Unterschiede liegen sowohl in der Instrumentation als auch in der Tempoführung; beidemale ist es die größere Einfachheit, Einheitlichkeit, Geradlinigkeit, die die Urfassung kennzeichnet und dem weiträumigen Musikempfinden des Meisters mehr zu entsprechen scheint."

77. Letter January 27, 1891, in Max Auer, ed., *Anton Bruckner: Gesammelte Briefe, Neue Folge* (Regensburg: Gustav Bosse, 1924), 237. "es wäre viel zu lang und gilt nur späteren Zeiten und zwar für einen Kreis von Freunden und Kennern."

78. On *Urfassungen*, see Benjamin M. Korstvedt, "'Return to the Pure Sources': The First Bruckner Gesamtausgabe," in Timothy L. Jackson and Paul Hawkshaw, eds., *Bruckner Studies* (Cambridge: Cambridge University Press, 1997), 91–109; and his *Bruckner: Symphony no. 8* (Cambridge: Cambridge University Press, 2000). See also Morten Solvik, "The International Bruckner Society and the NSDAP: A Case Study of Robert Haas and the Critical Edition," *Musical Quarterly* 83 (1998): 362–382. On the ideology of *ur-,* see also Norbert Nagler, "Bruckners gründerzeitliche Monumentalsymphonie: Reflektionen zur Heteronomie kompositorischer Praxis," in *Musik-Konzepte: Anton Bruckner* 23/24 (1982): 86–118.

79. Otto Schumann, *Geschichte der deutschen Musik* (Leipzig: Bibliographisches Institut, 1940), 341–343.

80. Oskar Lang, "Der Ur-Bruckner," *Die Musik* 28 (1935): 260. "Einschneidender noch als die Retuschen sind die Kürzungen, denn sie zerreissen das Formgefüge und machen dadurch zu öfteren Malen den Entwicklungsablauf unverständlich. . . . Wie durch solche Ausmerzungen der Bau des ganzen Satzes entstellt, ja geradezu unkenntlich gemacht wurde, ist einleuchtend. . . . Die Originale sind uns bisher vorhenthalten worden; wir haben nicht nur ein Recht, sondern die Pflicht, sie zu verlangen."

81. Bücken, *Musik der Nationen,* 382.

82. Ibid. 383.

83. Karl Grunsky, *Kampf um die deutsche Musik* (Stuttgart: Erhard Walther, Verlag für Nationalsozialistisches Schrifttum, 1933), 10. "Die Länge der Brucknerschen Symphonie ist im Ausland schwer erträglich. Allerdings kann man nicht behaupten, daß ohne weiteres jeder Deutsche folgen könne."

84. Danckert, "Bruckner und das Natursymbol," 307.

85. Most of the research on this complex topic has been carried out with specific reference to the medium of film. See Linda Schulte-Sasse, *Entertaining the Third Reich* (Durham, NC: Duke University Press, 1996); Eric Rentschler, *The Ministry of Illusion: Nazi Cinema and its Afterlife* (Cambridge, MA: Harvard University Press, 1996); and especially Brian Currid, *A National Acoustics: Music and Mass Publicity in Weimar and Nazi Germany* (Minneapolis: University of Minnesota Press, 2006).

86. See Adelheid von Saldern, "'Kunst für's Volk': Vom Kulturkonservatismus zur nationalsozialistischen Kulturpolitik," in Harald Wetzer, ed., *Das Gedächtnis der Bilder: Ästhetik und Nationalsozialismus* (Tübingen: Edition Diskord, 1995), 45–104.

87. The first glowing inauguration of concerts for the SS, Oscar von Pander, "SS-Konzerte," *Die Musik* 27 (1934): 205–206, is followed by a much more down-to-earth series of concerts and opera introductions.

88. See Albrecht Dümling and Peter Girth, eds., *Entartete Musik: Eine kommentierte Rekonstruktion* (Düsseldorf: Service-Druck Kleinherne, 1988); Hanns Werner Heister, ed.,"*Entartete Musik*" *1938: Weimar und die Ambivalenz*, 2 vols. (Saarbrücken: Pfau, 2001); Eckhardt John, *Musikbolschewismus: Die Politisierung der Musik 1918–1938* (Stuttgart: Metzler, 1994).

89. See Jost Hermand, "Die Kulturszene im Dritten Reich," in Brunhilde Sonntag, Hans-Werner Boresch, and Detlev Gojowy, eds., *Die dunkle Last: Musik und National-sozialismus* (Cologne: Bela Verlag, 1999), 9–22.

90. Adolf Hitler, "Rede bei der Eröffnung der Ersten Grossen Deutschen Kunstausstellung 1937," in Berthold Hinz, *Die Malerei im deutschen Faschismus, 167.* "Denn der Künstler schafft nicht nur für den Künstler. Sondern er schaffe genau so wie alle anderen für das Volk! Und wir werden dafür Sorge tragen, dass gerade das Volk von jetzt ab wieder zum Richter über seine Kunst aufgerufen wird."

91. This matter was not helped by the fact that there were two rivaling institutions that were in charge of cultural matters, Goebbels's ministry for *Volksaufklärung und Propaganda* as well as Rosenberg's *Kampfbund für deutsche Kultur,* both of which had different ideas about the future of German culture.

92. The main topics of discussion concerned folk music, the maintenance and restoration of traditions, the ennobling of mass culture, and the search for a moderate modernism. See von Saldern, "'Kunst für's Volk,'" 45–66. See also Riethmüller, "Komposition im Deutschen Reich um 1936," 255.

93. Friedrich W. Herzog: "Warum Unterhaltungsmusik?," *Die Musik* 28 (1935): 321. "Der Kulturwert einer Musik deckt sich nicht immer mit dem Gebrauchswert."

94. Walter Abendroth, "Kunstmusik und Volkstümlichkeit," *Die Musik* 26 (1934): 414–415. "Beethoven, Schubert, Schumann, Brahms, Wagner, Bruckner sollen nur für eine kleine Bildungsschicht geschaffen haben? Sie sollen in ihrer Kunst nichts als ihre individuellen Regungen ausgesprochen haben, die das Volk, in dem sie lebten, nichts angehen? . . . Auch heute noch, nach 50, 60, 70, 100 und mehr Jahren ist es so, dass eine Sinfonie Bruckners oder Brahms's, ein 'Tristan' ein Beethovensches Kammermusikwerk nur von gewissen, 'gebildeten' Leuten wirklich genossen werden kann. Millionen andere bleiben dabei kalt, haben nichts davon, *wollen* auch gar nichts davon wissen. . . . So wird gesagt."

95. Ludwig Schrott, "Vom Musizieren und Musik-Erleben," *Die Musik* 28 (1935): 346. "Bei dem Fortschreiten der Moderne empfiehlt es sich, dort anzuknüpfen, wo das Volk heute wirklich steht, und das ist, wenn man endlich einmal ehrlich sein soll, höchstens der Wagner der 'Meistersinger' noch nicht der Wagner des 'Tristan' oder der Bruckner der letzten Sinfonien oder der Reger in den Spätwerken. Hier ist es notwendig, durch gute Aufführungen derjenigen leichteren modernen Werke, die als Vorstufe für die größeren und schwereren empfunden werden können, das innerliche Erfassen dieser vorzubereiten."

96. Hansheinrich Dronsmann, "Kritische Anmerkungen zur Unterhaltungsmusik," *Die Musik* 28 (1935): 335–336.

97. See Rudolf Sommer, "Unterhaltungsmusiker als Kulturträger," *Die Musik* 28 (1935): 336–341. See also the editorial "Unsere Meinung" on 846–847, supporting Richard Strauss's proposed ban of arrangements and potpourris.

98. Kurt Herbst, "Musikchronik des deutschen Rundfunks," *Die Musik* 28 (1935): 63. "Es handelt sich nämlich nicht um einen Personalbegriff 'Beethoven,' sondern um die Beethovensche Kunst und das Beethovensche Vermögen, ein seelisches Ausdrucksvermögen in einen unmittelbaren, d.h. stilvollen Tonzusammenhang gebracht zu haben. "

99. Ibid.

100. Kurt Herbst, "Leitfaden zu einer musikalischen Gesamtreform," *Die Musik* 28 (1935): 276. "Ist das unterhaltende Moment in der unterhaltungsmusikalischen Gebrauchsmusik ein notwendiger Zweckbestandteil oder, mit anderen Worten, ein notwendiges Stilmerkmal am musikalischen Gegenstand selbst, so ist das unterhaltende Moment in der Kunstmusik oder in der sogenannten ernsten Musik dem Kunstwerk nur beigegeben, mit anderen Worten: Das unterhaltende Moment wird bei der ernsten Musik zum Erlebniszustand desjenigen Hörers, der diese Musik entsprechend, d.h. richtig hört, während bei der eigentlichen Unterhaltungsmusik das unterhaltende Moment dem Erlebnis oder (einfacher gesagt) dem musikalischen Gegenstand angehört."

101. Ibid. 275.

102. Schering, "Über den Begriff des Monumentalen," 9. "denn es schließt eine sachliche Zweckhaftigkeit, eben die des Verewigenwollens ein."

103. Irmgard Otto, "Tonfilm—Ein Problem?," *Die Musik* 28 (1935): 113. "Die Erfahrung lehrte, dass nur die Musik imstande ist, auf lange Zeit eine Stimmung vorzubereiten oder in kürzester Spanne eine Stimmung in ihr Gegenteil zu verkehren. Dabei verliert die Musik an akustischem Wert, was schon daraus hervorgeht, dass ein großer Teil gar nicht eigentlich die Musik, zum mindesten den Beginn ihrer akustischen Wirksamkeit spürt. Die Aufmerksamkeit ist so stark auf die Handlung, d.h. also auf das gesprochene Wort und das bewegte Bild gerichtet, dass solche Menschen es gar nicht vermögen, ausserdem noch auf die anscheinend nebensächliche Musik zu achten. Aber gerade diese Feststellungen verdeutlichen am ehesten den Fortschritt, den die Tonfilmpraxis bei der Anwendung der Musik gemacht hat: sie arbeitet nicht mehr mit dem akustischen Eindruck, sondern mit dem tieferen seelischen Eindruck."

104. See Albrecht Dümling and Peter Girth, eds., *Entartete Musik: Eine kommentierte Rekonstruktion* (Düsseldorf: Service-Druck Kleinherne, 1988), 8–18; Gilliam, "The Annexation of Anton Bruckner," and Christa Brüstle, *Anton Bruckner und die Nachwelt,* particularly 99–122.

105. See Bundesarchiv R/55 20582 (Old: X 10019–01), 31.

106. Paul Ehlers, "Das Regensburger Bruckner-Erlebnis," *Zeitschrift für Musik* 104 (1937): 747. "wo die wimpelgeschmückten Schleppschiffe auf der Donau im Laufe innehielten und der Rede des Reichsministers Dr. Goebbels lauschten."

107. See … zel, "Bruckners Einzug in die Walhalla," {*Linzer*} *Tagespost,* June 8, 1937. Similarly, the *Linzer Volksblatt,* June 8, 1937, reports that the "*Siegesklänge*" from Bruckner's Eighth symphony were played, implying that this was a generally known term, whereas in fact it was an ad hoc label of Goebbel's planning committee, which was probably communicated to the newspaper staff along with the itinerary for the whole event.

108. Bundesarchiv R/55 20582 (Old: X 10019–01), 27. This detail may add to Gilliam's observation that the event foreshadows and prepares the Austrian annexation of the following year. See n. 126 below.

109. Ibid. 30.

110. Vondung, *Magie und Manipulation,* 113.

111. The whole schedule is reproduced in Christa Brüstle, *Anton Bruckner und die Nachwelt,* 109.

112. Brüstle notes that the text of *Germanenzug* by August Silberstein would have probably been replaced with an Aryan version, see *Anton Bruckner und die Nachwelt,* 106–107. See also Alexander L. Ringer, *"Germanenzug* bis *Helgoland:* Zu Bruckners Deutschtum," in Albrecht Riethmüller, ed., *Bruckner-Probleme* (Stuttgart: Steiner, 1999), 25–34.

113. The significance of the program is discussed in Korstvedt, *Bruckner: Symphony no.* 8, 49–53. This topic was vigorously debated by Dahlhaus and Floros, see Constantin Floros, *Brahms und Bruckner: Studien zur musikalischen Exegetik* (Wiesbaden: Breitkopf und Härtel, 1980), 182–210; and Dahlhaus, "Bruckner und die Programmusik: Zum Finale der Achten Symphonie," in Christoph-Hellmut Mahling, ed., *Anton Bruckner: Studien zu Werk und Wirkung* (Tutzing: Hans Schneider, 1985), 40–78. See also Albrecht Riethmüller, "Der deutsche Michel erwacht: Zur Bruckner-Rezeption im NS-Staat," *Bruckner-Probleme,* 202–214.

114. . . . zel, "Bruckners Einzug in die Walhalla," [*Linzer*] *Tagespost,* June 8, 1937.

115. Siegmund von Hausegger, letter to Max Auer, July 29, 1936. "Wenn die Hülle von Bruckner's Büste fällt, müssen triumphale Brucknerklänge ertönen. 'Non confundar' aus der VII. wäre sinngemäß, geht aber musikalisch nicht. Es ginge aber der grandiose Einsatz des Hauptthemas des Finales der VIII. in der Reprise bis zum C-Dur-Akkord mit dem Beckenschlag, von da gleich überspringend auf die C-Dur-Steigerung des Schlusses mit dem Climax der Themenvereinigung, als wahrhaften Walhall-Klängen." Cited in Brüstle, *Anton Bruckner und die Nachwelt,* 115. On Hausegger, see also Christa Brüstle, "Siegmund von Hausegger: A Bruckner Authority from the 1930s," in Crawford Howie, Paul Hawkshaw, and Timothy Jackson, eds., *Perspectives on Anton Bruckner* (Aldershot: Ashgate, 2001), 341–352.

116. In 1937 the Schalk edition, based on the second version of the symphony of 1890, was the only authoritative edition at the time. It was almost certainly used here, as the Haas edition was not completed until 1939. On the versions, see Korstvedt, *Bruckner: Symphony no. 8,* 68–110. I am grateful to Christa Brüstle for pointing me to the finer points of the edition history of Bruckner's score.

117. Bundesfilmarchiv Wochenschau 353/1937.

118. Why Hausegger preferred this instance, beginning on C, over the first occurrence, starting on Bb, is probably impossible to reconstruct without access to further materials.

119. On the sublime aesthetics of the slow movement, see also Margaret Notley, "Formal Process as Spiritual Progress: The Symphonic Slow Movements," in John Willliamson, ed., *The Cambridge Companion to Bruckner* (Cambridge: Cambridge University Press, 2004), 190–204; and her "Late-Nineteenth-Century Chamber Music and the Cult of the Classical Adagio," *Nineteenth-Century Music* 23 (1999): 33–61.

120. See Besseler, "Das musikalische Hören der Neuzeit," in Gülke, ed., *Aufsätze zur Musikästhetik und Musikgeschichte,* 163.

121. It is an irony of history, given the amount of preparation that went into the production of this event, that the filmed version, which had evidently been edited in great haste, cuts off just before the final chord and stops on the unresolved dominant of this grandiose musical passage.

122. See Michael Walter, "Die Musik des Olympiafilms von 1938," *Acta musicologica* 62 (1990): 82–113; Wolfgang Thiel, "Filmmusik im NS-Staat: Sechs Annäherungen und ein Nachwort," in Hanns-Werner Heister, ed., *"Entartete Musik" 1938: Weimar und die Ambivalenz* (Saarbrücken: Pfau, 2001), 599–613; and Albrecht Riethmüller, "Komposition im Deutschen Reich um 1936," *Archiv für Musikwissenschaft* 38 (1981): 241–278. See also Albrecht Riethmüller, "Das Tonsignet: Versuch einer Bestimmung seiner Eigenarten und Aufgaben," *Archiv für Musikwissenschaft* 30 (1973): 69–79.

123. Schering, "Über den Begriff des Monumentalen," 10. "Die Dauer eines Musikstücks kann wohl, aber braucht für den monumentalen Eindruck nicht ausschlaggebend zu sein."

124. The English translation of this speech by John Michael Cooper is found in *Musical Quarterly* 78 (1994): 605–609.

125. See Jeffrey Herf, *Reactionary Modernism: Technology, Culture, and Politics in Weimar and the Third Reich* (Cambridge: Cambridge University Press, 1987).

126. Gilliam, "The Annexation of Anton Bruckner," 584–604. (Note also the ensuing interchange with Manfred Wagner, "Response to Bryan Gilliam Regarding Bruckner and National Socialism" and "Bruckner's Annexation Revisited: A Response to Manfred Wagner," in *Musical Quarterly* 79 (1995): 118–131.) As Ludwig I, the founder of Walhalla, had supported the idea of a greater Germany, including Austria, the worthies honored in Walhalla had therefore been Austrian and German right from the beginning. Similarly, Jews had been excluded.—All this was very helpful, as Goebbels noted approvingly in his diaries.

127. See the anonymous reviews, "Eine Weiherede vor einer Brucknerbüste," *{Wiener}* *Reichspost,* June 8, 1937 and "Bruckner in der Walhalla," *Linzer Volksblatt,* June 8, 1937.

128. This is the principle that Sponheuer calls "disarticulation," see "Musik, Faschismus, Ideologie," 242–243. His theoretical background is from Manfred Behrens, ed., *Faschismus und Ideologie,* Vols. 1 and 2, *Das Argument Sonderband 60 and 62* (Berlin: Argument-Verlag, 1980).

129. Goethe, *Faust II,* vv. 6288. "Des ewigen Sinnes ewige Unterhaltung." (translation modified).

130. Schering, "Über den Begriff des Monumenten," 23. "Es ist ein Trieb vorhanden, mit der Kunst der Höherbildung des Menschengeschlechts zu dienen, es über das zeitlich Begrenzte hinaus auf das Ewige zu weisen und damit, wenn irgend möglich, tugendhafter zu machen."

131. See also M. Nadeem Niazi, "Violating the *Mütter:* Staging the Semiotics of Desire, or, Aspects of the Eternal-Feminine in 'Faust,'" *Orbis Litterarum* 55 (2000): 103–117.

Epilogue

1. It is an irony of history that what was perhaps the blackest day in the German past, the *Reichskristallnacht* of 1938, also occurred on November 9. It is for this reason that the

national holiday is the more neutral October 3, the day on which the constitution was ratified by the new East German states.

2. For critical engagements with this performance, see David B. Dennis, *Beethoven in German Politics 1870–1989* (New Haven: Yale University Press, 1996), 200–203; Esteban Buch, *Beethoven's Ninth: A Political History*, trans. Richard Miller (Chicago: University of Chicago Press, 2003), 260–262.

3. Leonard Bernstein, "Aesthetic News Bulletin," *Ode an die Freiheit: Bernstein in Berlin*, CD booklet (Hamburg: Deutsche Grammophon, 1990), 2.

4. See Uwe Martin, "Freude, Freiheit, Götterfunken: Über Schillers Schwierigkeiten beim Schreiben von Freiheit," *Cahiers d'études germaniques*, 8 (1990): 9–10.

5. Nicholas Cook, *Beethoven: Symphony no. 9* (Cambridge: Cambridge University Press, 1993), 94; Andreas Eichhorn, *Beethovens Neunte Symphonie: Die Geschichte ihrer Aufführung und Rezeption* (Kassel: Bärenreiter, 1993), 302–306; and David Benjamin Levy, *Beethoven: The Ninth Symphony* (New York: Schirmer, 1995), 162–164.

6. *Illustrated London News*, August 16, 1845, 102. This snippet, which has not been noted in the literature, may indeed constitute the "missing link" in the reception history of this trope, mediating as well-known rumor between fictional origin and accepted truth. For a detailed account of the reception history of the symphony, see particularly Buch, *Beethoven's Ninth*, 116–117 and 258–262.

7. Jacob Venedey, Die deutschen Republikaner unter der französischen Republik (Leipzig: Brockhaus, 1870), 1; and Ludwig Nohl, *Beethovens Leben*, 2d ed. (Berlin: Schlesische Verlagsanstalt, 1913), 3/i: 188. Though not explicitly concerned with freedom, one might further add Otto Baensch's extraordinary analytical interpretation of the symphony as a world-historical allegory, *Aufbau und Sinn des Chorfinales von Beethovens Neunter Symphonie* (Berlin and Leipzig: Walter de Gruyter, 1930).

8. Hanns Eisler, *Musik und Politik: Schriften 1924–1948*, ed. Günther Mayer, in *Hanns Eisler: Gesammelte Werke*, eds. Stephanie Eisler and Manfred Grabs (Leipzig: VEB Deutscher Verlag für Musik, 1973), 31 n. 8.

9. Pierre Nora, "Between Memory and History," *Representations* 26 (1989): 8. This text is reprinted, in a slightly different translation, in Pierre Nora, *Realms of Memory*, trans. Arthur Goldhammer, ed. Lawrence D. Kritzman (New York: Columbia University Press, 1996), 2.

10. Nora, "Between Memory and History," 13, and *Realms of Memory*, 4.

11. Bernstein, "Aesthetic News Bulletin," 2.

12. For a full comparison of both versions with an English translation, see Levy, *Beethoven: The Ninth Symphony*, 9–12; or Appendix D of Parsons, "'Deine Zauber binden wieder': Beethoven, Schiller and the Joyous Reconciliation of Opposites," *Beethoven Forum* 9 (2002): 1–54.

13. See Appendix A of Parsons, "'Deine Zauber binden wieder.'"

14. Maynard Solomon, "Beethoven and Schiller," *Beethoven-Essays* (Cambridge, MA: Harvard University Press, 1988), 209.

15. This context is explored in Rudolf Dau, "Friedrich Schillers Hymne 'An die Freude' zu einigen Problemen ihrer Interpretation und aktuellen Rezeption," *Weimarer Beiträge* 24/10 (1978): 38–40.

16. Friedrich Schiller, *On the Aesthetic Education of Man*, trans. Elizabeth M. Wilkinson and L. A. Willoughby (Oxford: Clarendon Press, 1967), 21. On Schiller's savages and

barbarians, see, for instance, Kenneth Parmelee Wilcox, *Anmut und Würde: Die Dialektik der menschlichen Vollendung bei Schiller* (Frankfurt am Main: Peter Lang, 1981), 146–170.

17. Whereas Schiller's title was simply "An die Freude," Beethoven habitually added the word "Ode," which has now become standard. Andreas Eichhorn shows in *Beethovens Neunte Symphonie*, 225–236, how Beethoven's cuts emphasize the Ode character of the poem.

18. I am grateful to Reinhold Brinkmann for pointing out to me that the alliterative similarity between *Freiheit* and *Freude* might constitute another point of connection. This point holds true particularly in the context of Schiller's tragedies: Johanna's dying words in *Die Jungfrau von Orleans,* "Kurz ist der Schmerz / und ewig ist die Freude," express a sense of freedom, besides joy, precisely in a sense that Schiller espoused in his writings on the sublime and on the pathetic—which amounts, broadly speaking, to the right to self-denial and self-sacrifice. (Beethoven, incidentally, set these verses as a canon in WoO 163 and 166.) Presumably, however, this level of meaning of *Freude/Freiheit* is not one that was on Bernstein's mind when he proposed the change to "An die Freude."

19. As a central philosophical document, the *Aesthetic Education* has been subject to countless interpretations, and its exegesis is far from self-evident. See Lesley Sharpe's detailed bibliographical essay, *Schiller's Aesthetic Essays: Two Centuries of Criticism* (Columbia, SC: Camden House, 1995) for the main lines of argument.

20. Schiller, *Aesthetic Education,* 9.

21. Ibid. 167n. He first introduced this notion in his *Kallias* letters.

22. This is not to downplay the considerable body of critical debate that has amassed around these central concepts, whose relationship is anything but settled. Schiller's position toward freedom and the significance of the aesthetic state seems to change somewhat over the course of the twenty-seven letters that make up the treatise. See Schiller, *Aesthetic Education,* pp. xlii–lx. For a thoughtful consideration of the structure of Schiller's treatise in the context of Beethoven, see also Karol Berger, "Beethoven and the Aesthetic State," *Beethoven Forum* 7 (1999): 38–44.

23. See R. D. Miller, *Schiller and the Ideal of Freedom* (Oxford: Clarendon Press, 1970), 89–91.

24. The difference between Kant and Schiller's approaches is perhaps best expressed by Kant's maxim *sapere aude,* which he translates as the encouragement "to use your own reason." Schiller, by contrast, renders this as "dare to be wise" (*Aesthetic Education,* 51). Nicholas Till draws attention to this difference in *Mozart and the Enlightenment: Truth, Virtue and Beauty in Mozart's Operas* (New York and London: W. W. Norton, 1992), 283.

25. Schiller, *Aesthetic Education,* 205.

26. Ibid. 53.

27. Ibid. 153–155.

28. Ibid. 185.

29. Ibid. 155–157.

30. Ibid. 155. Translation modified.

31. Schiller's comments explicitly on music in letters to his friend Theodor Körner. See R. M. Longyear, *Schiller and Music* (Chapel Hill, NC: University of North Carolina Press, 1966).

32. *Allgemeine musikalische Zeitung* (1824): col. 442. See Stefan Kunze, ed., *Ludwig van Beethoven: Die Werke im Spiegel der Zeit* (Laaber: Laaber-Verlag, 1989), 473. "[D]ie glühend-sten Verehrer und feurigsten Bewunderer des Tonsetzers sind fest überzeugt, dass dieses

wahrhaft einzige Finale in einer concentrirten Gestalt noch ungleich mehr imponieren müsste, und der Componist selbst diese Ansicht theilen würde, wenn das grausame Geschick ihm nicht das Vemögen, seine eigenen Schöpfungen zu hören, geraubt hätte." On the cultural importance of Beethoven's deafness, see K. M. Knittel, "Wagner, Deafness, and the Reception of Beethoven's Late Style," *Journal of the American Musicological Society*, 51 (1998): 49–82.

33. Friedrich Theodor Vischer, Ästhetik oder Wissenschaft des Schönen (Stuttgart: Carl Mäcken, 1857), 3/ii: 1146. Note that the parts on music in Vischer's treatise were actually written by Karl Köstlin. On Vischer's music aesthetics, see Barbara Titus, "Conceptualizing Music: Friedrich Theodor Vischer and Hegelian Currents in German Music Criticism 1848–1887," Ph.D. dissertation (Oxford University, 2005).

34. David Friedrich Strauss, "Beethoven's Neunte Symphonie und ihre Bewunderer" (originally published anonymously in *Augsburger Allgemeine Zeitung* 1853), reprinted in *Allgemeine musikalische Zeitung* 12 (1877): col. 129. On the negative reception of Strauss's essay, see also Ruth Solie, "Beethoven as a Secular Humanist: Ideology and the Ninth Symphony in Nineteenth-Century Criticism," in Eugene Narmour and Ruth Solie, eds., *Explorations in Music, the Arts and Ideas: Essays in Honor of Leonard B. Meyer* (Stuyvesant, NY: Pendragon, 1988), 10–11 and 32–33.

35. Selmar Bagge, "L. van Beethoven's Neunte Symphonie," *Allgemeine musikalische Zeitung* 12 (1877): 53–54; and C. R. Hennig, *Beethoven's Neunte Symphonie: Eine Analyse* (Leipzig: F. E. C. Leuckart, 1888), which includes a long polemic against Vischer's aesthetic views. The reproach of formlessness became particularly prominent in the context of aesthetic discussions surrounding the genre of the symphonic poem. These debates form the tacit background to the aesthetic-analytical controversy surrounding Beethoven's final symphonic movement.

36. Ernest Sander is a prominent proponent of sonata form, see his "Form and Content in the Finale of Beethoven's Ninth Symphony," *Musical Quarterly* 50 (1964): 59–76. Charles Rosen has proposed a reading as concerto form, see his *The Classical Style: Haydn, Mozart, Beethoven* (New York: Viking, 1971), 439–440. Vincent d'Indy proposes variation form in *Beethoven: A Critical Biography,* trans. Theodore Baker (Boston and New York: The Boston Music Company/G. Schirmer, 1912), 117. Ernest Livingstone explores the four-movement-in-one type, see "Das Formproblem des 4. Satzes in Beethovens 9. Symphonie," in Carl Dahlhaus and Hans-Heinrich Eggebrecht, eds., *Bericht über den internationalen musikwissenschaftlichen Kongress Bonn 1970* (Kassel: Bärenreiter, 1971), 494–497. Otto Baensch proposes extended bar form (in the wake of Lorenz-style Wagner analysis), see his *Aufbau und Sinn des Chorfinales von Beethovens Neunter Symphonie* (Berlin and Leipzig: Walter de Gruyter, 1930). For very useful discussions of the analytical history of this movement, see Webster, "The Finale in Beethoven's Ninth Symphony," 36–44; and Tusa, "Noch einmal: Form and Content in the Finale of Beethoven's Ninth Symphony," *Beethoven Forum* 7 (1999): 113–126.

37. The analytical exploration of such hybrid forms may indeed begin with Selmar Bagge's proposed "fantasia" form, see his "L. van Beethoven's Neunte Symphonie," col. 53. Neither Donald Francis Tovey, "Beethoven: Ninth Symphony in D Minor, p. 125. Its Place in Musical Art," in *Essays in Musical Analysis,* Vol. 2, *Symphonies* (Oxford: Oxford University Press, 1935), 1–45, nor Heinrich Schenker, *Beethoven's Ninth Symphony,* trans. John Rothgeb (New Haven: Yale University Press, 1992) follow established formal types in their thoroughgoing analyses. The four-movement-in-one type (see previous note) may

also be counted as a hybrid, as may David Levy's proposal of considering the form as a "fractal," see his *Beethoven: The Ninth Symphony*, 91. For a recent multivalent analysis, see James Webster, "The Finale in Beethoven's Ninth Symphony," *Beethoven Forum* 1 (1991): 25–62; and Michael C. Tusa, "Noch einmal," 113–137.

38. Tovey, "Beethoven: Ninth Symphony op. 125," 3.

39. Leo Treitler, *Music and the Historical Imagination* (Cambridge, MA: Harvard University Press, 1989).

40. Ibid., 55.

41. Daniel Chua, *The 'Galitzin' Quartets of Beethoven* (Princeton: Princeton University Press, 1995), 193.

42. See, for instance, Jean-François Lyotard, *Lessons on the Analytic of the Sublime: Kants Critique of Judgment 23–29,* trans. Elizabeth Rottenberg (Stanford, CA: Stanford University Press, 1994), 74–75.

43. Vischer, *Ästhetik oder Wissenschaft des Schönen,* 1: 228. Michael Tusa also points toward the link between Vischer's views of Beethoven's Ninth Symphony and his discussion of formlessness and the sublime. See Tusa, "Noch einmal," 114n.

44. In fact, this began even before the Ninth Symphony was written, when Schiller's friend Theodor Körner recommended Beethoven to the poet as a man who is "interested in the great and the sublime." See Solomon, "Beethoven and Schiller," 206. Eichhorn lists particular instances of the sublime in Beethoven's Ninth in *Beethovens Neunte Symphonie,* 191–288.

45. See Philip J. Kain, *Schiller, Hegel and Marx: State, Society, and the Aesthetic Ideal of Ancient Greece* (Kingston, Ont.: McGill-Queen's University Press, 1982), 15–19.

46. See Carl Dahlhaus, *Klassische und romantische Musikästhetik* (Laaber: Laaber-Verlag, 1988), 55. In fact, despite his self-declared ignorance in musical matters, Schiller prepared a performance of Gluck's *Iphigenie* for Weimar in 1796.

47. There is considerable debate about the philological legitimacy of interpreting Schiller's concepts of "melting" and "energizing beauty," which he introduces in letter 16, in terms equivalent to the beautiful and the sublime.

48. Schiller, *Aesthetic Education,* 166.

49. Ibid. 166.

50. These occur in the first movement at measures 108–115, in the second at measure 177, and in the third at measures 91–98. Robert Fink has shown, in "'Arrows of Desire': Long-Range Linear Structure and the Transformation of Musical Energy," Ph.D. dissertation (University of California Berkeley, 1994), 202–204, how the quartet reproduced in my example E.1 is motivically related to the B major moment in the first movement.

51. Leo Treitler, "'To Worship that Celestial Sound': Motives for Music Analysis," in *Music and the Historical Imagination* (Cambridge, MA: Harvard University Press, 1989), 61.

52. Stephen Hinton makes a related observation in "Not 'which' tones? The Crux of Beethoven's Ninth," *Nineteenth-Century Music* 22 (1998): 62–64. His analytical framework makes it clear that an alternative interpretation of the move to the "impossibly remote" region of B major might be motivically motivated. Tovey, "Beethoven: Ninth Symphony," 41–45; and James Webster, "The Form of the Finale," 54–56, also draw attention to this procedure.

53. Schiller, *Aesthetic Education,* 157.

54. Ibid. 175.

55. Ibid. 175–177. Translation modified.

56. See Schiller's very different assessment of the Sublime in his other aesthetic writings, above all *Über das Pathetische, Vom Erhabenen,* and the later *Über das Erhabene.*

57. Arthur Seidl, *Ueber das Musikalisch-Erhabene,* 37. "[Die] Beurtheilung und Anerkennung als eines Erhabenen wir schlechterdings nur von denen fordern können, welche ihr moralisches Gefühl bereits entwickelt haben."

58. See Adorno, *Negative Dialectics,* trans. E. B. Ashton (New York: Seabury Press, 1973), 296; and *Aesthetic Theory,* trans. Robert Hullot-Kentor (Minneapolis: University of Minnesota Press, 1997), 62. Several other commentators have regarded Schiller's attempt to turn Kant's aesthetics into a social program as a misreading of his teacher, see, for instance, Paul de Man, *The Rhetoric of Romanticism* (New York: Columbia University Press, 1984), 263–265.

59. Adorno, *Gesammelte Schriften,* 20 vols. (Frankfurt am Main: Suhrkamp, 1970), 10/ii: 620. Trans. from Adorno, *Beethoven: The Philosophy of Music,* ed. Rolf Tiedemann, trans. Edmund Jephcott (Stanford: Stanford University Press, 1998), 212. For related comments on this passage, see also *Beethoven,* 32–33, and "Fortschritt," in *Stichworte: Kritische Modelle 2 (Gesammelte Schriften,* 10/ii), 619–620.

60. Gustav Nottebohm, *Zweite Beethoveniana* (Leipzig: J. Rieter-Biedermann, 1887), 186.

61. Adorno, "Wiener Rede," in *Gustav Mahler* (Tübingen: Rainer Wunderlich Verlag, 1966), 218; cited in Eichhorn, *Beethovens Neunte Symphonie,* 232.

62. Bernstein's musical interpretation recognizes the close relationship between these two radically diverse topics, but clings to a sense of precise rhythmic control throughout the fugue, thus effectively carrying over the march into the next section.

63. It is difficult not to think here of August Halm's interpretation of fugue and sonata in light of the individual and the state, respectively. For discussions of this topic, see Lee Rothfarb, "Music Analysis, Cultural Ethics, and Sociology in the Writings of August Halm," *Indiana Theory Review* 16 (1995): 171–196; and my "August Halm's Two Cultures as Nature," in Suzannah Clark and Alexander Rehding, eds., *Music Theory and Natural Order from the Renaissance to the Early Twentieth Century* (Cambridge: Cambridge University Press, 2001), 142–160.

64. Nora, "Between Memory and History," 23–24; and *Realms of Memory,* 20.

65. On this much-discussed point, see, for instance, Jürgen Habermas, *Die nachholende Revolution* (Frankfurt am Main: Suhrkamp, 1990), 181. On Habermas's position, see also Jan Müller, *Another Country: German Intellectuals, Unification and National Identity* (New Haven: Yale University Press, 2000), 90–119.

66. Harold James and Maria Stone, eds., *When the Wall Came Down: Reactions to German Unification* (London and New York: Routledge, 1992), 70.

67. Wolf Lepenies, *The Seduction of Culture in German History* (Princeton: Princeton University Press, 2006), 165–175.

68. I thank Tracy Strong for the attribution of this legend.

69. Scott Burnham, "Our Sublime Ninth," *Beethoven Forum* 5 (1996): 155–163. See also Richard Taruskin, "Resisting the Ninth," in *Text and Act: Essays on Music and Performance* (New York and Oxford: Oxford University Press, 1995), 235–261.

70. Taruskin, "Another Beethoven Season," *New York Times,* September 10, 1995, H51.

71. I thank Thomas Christensen, who was an eye-witness in East Berlin during these days, for this information.

Abbate, Carolyn. *In Search of Opera.* Princeton: Princeton University Press, 2001.

———. "Music—Drastic or Gnostic?" *Critical Inquiry* 30 (2004): 505–536.

———. "The Parisian *Vénus* and the 'Paris' *Tannhäuser.*" *Journal of the American Musicological Society* 36 (1983): 73–122.

———. *Unsung Voices: Opera and Musical Narrative in the Nineteenth Century.* Princeton: Princeton University Press, 1991.

Abendroth, Walter. "Kunstmusik und Volkstümlichkeit." *Die Musik* 26 (1934): 413–417.

Adam, Peter. *Art of the Third Reich.* New York: Harry N. Abrams, 1992.

Adorno, Theodor. *Aesthetic Theory.* Translated by Robert Hullot-Kentor. Minneapolis: University of Minnesota Press, 1997.

———. *Beethoven: The Philosophy of Music.* Edited by Rolf Tiedemann. Translated by Edmund Jephcott. Stanford, CA: Stanford University Press, 1998.

———. *Essays on Music.* Edited by Richard Leppert. Translated by Susan H. Gillespie. Berkeley: University of California Press, 2001.

———. *Gesammelte Schriften.* 20 vols. Edited by Rolf Tiedemann. Frankfurt am Main: Suhrkamp, 1970–1997 .

———. *In Search of Wagner.* Translated by Rodney Livingstone. London: Verso, 1991.

———. *Mahler: A Musical Physiognomy.* Translated by Edmund Jephcott. Chicago: University of Chicago Press, 1996.

———. *Negative Dialectics.* Translated by E. B. Ashton. New York: Seabury Press, 1973.

Alings, Reinhard. *Monument und Nation: Das Bild vom Nationalstaat im Medium Denkmal—zum Verhältnis von Nation und Staat im deutschen Kaiserreich 1871–1918.* Berlin and New York: Walter de Gruyter, 1996.

Altenburg, Detlef. "Franz Liszt and the Legacy of the Classical Era." *Nineteenth-Century Music* 18 (1994): 46–63.

———. "Die Schriften von Franz Liszt: Bemerkungen zu einem zentralen Problem der Liszt-Forschung." In *Festschrift Arno Forchert,* edited by Gerhard Allroggen and Detlef Altenburg, 242–251. Kassel: Bärenreiter, 1986.

Ambros, August Wilhelm. *Culturhistorische Bilder aus dem Musikleben der Gegenwart.* Leipzig: Breitkopf und Härtel, 1860.

Anderson, Benedict R. *Imagined Communities: Reflections on the Origin and Spread of Nationalism.* Rev. ed. London and New York: Verso, 1991.

Anonymous. "Bearbeitungen älterer Vocalwerke von Robert Franz." *Leipziger allgemeine musikalische Zeitung* 3 (1865): cols. 417–422, 433–436.

Anonymous. "Bruckner in der Walhalla." *Linzer Volksblatt* (June 8, 1937), [no page]. In Bundesarchiv Berlin, Bestandssignatur: R/55, Archivsignatur: 20582 (Alt: X 10019–01).

Anonymous. "Eine Weiherede vor einer Brucknerbüste." *Wiener Reichspost* (June 8, 1937), [no page]. In Bundesarchiv Berlin, Bestandssignatur: R/55, Archivsignatur: 20582, (Alt: X 10019–01).

Anonymous. "Goethes Jubelfeier in Weimar." *Leipziger Illustrirte Zeitung* 13 (September 29, 1849): 195–197.

Anonymous. Review of Beethoven, *Tre sonate per il Clav. o Fortepiano con un Violino* op. 12. *Allgemeine musikalische Zeitung* 1 (1798/1799): cols. 570–571.

Anonymous. "The Beethoven Festival." *Illustrated London News* 7 (August 16, 1845): 101–102.

Applegate, Celia. *Bach in Berlin: Nation and Culture in Mendelssohn's Revival of the St. Matthew Passion.* Ithaca, NY: Cornell University Press, 2005.

Applegate, Celia, and Pamela Potter, eds. *Music and German National Identity.* Chicago: University of Chicago Press, 2002.

Aspden, Suzanne. "'Fam'd Handel breathing, tho' transformed to stone': The Composer as Monument." *Journal of the American Musicological Society* 55 (2002): 39–90.

Assmann, Aleida. "Denkmäler in der Zeit: Vom Sinn und Unsinn der Gedenkjahre." *Schiller-Jahrbuch* 44 (2000): 298–302.

———. *Erinnerungsräume: Formen und Wandlungen des kulturellen Gedächtnisses.* Munich: C. H. Beck, 1999.

———. "Kultur als Lebenswelt und Monument." In *Kultur als Lebenswelt und Monument,* edited by Aleida Assmann and Dietrich Harth, 11–25. Frankfurt am Main: Fischer, 1991.

Assmann, Aleida, Monika Gomille, et al., eds. *Sammler—Bibliophile—Exzentriker.* Tübingen: Gunter Narr Verlag, 1998.

Assmann, Jan. "Collective Memory and Cultural Identity." Translated by John Czaplicka. *New German Critique* 65 (1995): 125–133.

Auer, Max. "Der Streit um den 'echten' Bruckner im Licht biographischer Tatsachen." *Zeitschrift für Musik* 103 (1935): 538–545.

———, ed. *Anton Bruckner: Gesammelte Briefe, Neue Folge.* Regensburg: Gustav Bosse, 1924.

Avins, Styra, ed. *Johannes Brahms: Life and Letters.* Oxford: Oxford University Press, 1997.

Bach, Johann S. *36 Arien aus verschiedenen Kantaten mit Begleitung des Pianoforte.* Edited by Robert Franz. Leipzig: Whistling, 1859/60.

Baensch, Otto. *Aufbau und Sinn des Chorfinales von Beethovens Neunter Symphonie.* Berlin and Leipzig: Walter de Gruyter, 1930.

Bagge, Selmar. "L. van Beethoven's Neunte Symphonie," *Allgemeine musikalische Zeitung* 12 (1877): cols. 49–53, 65–71.

Bahr, Ehrhard. "The Silver Age of Weimar. Franz Liszt as Goethe's Successor: A Study in Cultural Archaeology." *Yearbook of the Goethe Society* 10 (2001): 191–202.

Balstaedt, Andreas, and Tobias Widmaier. *Salonmusik: Zur Geschichte und Funktion einer bürgerlichen Musikpraxis.* Stuttgart: Franz Steiner Verlag Wiesbaden, 1989.

Bartels, Wolfgang von. "Unterhaltung und Kultur im Rundfunk." *Zeitschrift für Musik* 101 (1934): 410–413.

Batta, András. "Die Gattung Paraphrase im Schaffen von Franz Liszt: Gattung Paraphrase—die musikalische Hassliebe Liszts." In *Liszt-Studien 4: Der junge Liszt,* edited by Gottfried Scholz, 135–142. Munich and Salzburg: Emil Katzbichler, 1993.

Bauer, Elisabeth Eleonore. *Wie Beethoven auf den Sockel kam: Die Entstehung eines musikalischen Mythos.* Stuttgart: Metzler, 1992.

Bauer, Oswald Georg. *Tannhäuser zu Richard Wagners Zeit.* Munich: Bayerische Vereinsbank, 1985.

Behrens, Manfred, ed. *Faschismus und Ideologie.* 2 vols. Berlin: Argument-Verlag, 1980.

Bekker, Paul. "Deutsche Musik der Gegenwart." In *Deutsches Leben der Gegenwart,* edited by Philipp Witkop, 77–126. Berlin: Volksverband der Bücherfreunde Wegweiser Verlag, 1922.

———. *Richard Wagner: Das Leben im Werke.* Stuttgart: Deutsche Verlagsanstalt, 1924.

Bélance-Zank, Isabelle. "The Three-Hand Texture: Origins and Use." *Journal of the American Liszt Society* 38 (1995): 99–121.

Belgum, Kirsten. "Displaying the Nation: A View of Nineteenth-Century Monuments through a Popular Magazine." *Central European History* 26 (93): 457–474.

Beller-McKenna, Daniel. "Distance and Disembodiment: Harps, Horns, and the Requiem Idea in Brahms and Schumann." *Journal of Musicology* 2005 (22): 47–89.

Bellermann, Heinrich. "Robert Franz' Bearbeitungen älterer Tonwerke." *Leipziger allgemeine musikalische Zeitung* 7 (1872): cols. 489–495, 505–510, 521–526.

Bent, Ian, ed. *Music Analysis in the Nineteenth Century.* 2 vols. Cambridge: Cambridge University Press, 1993.

Berger, Karol. "Beethoven and the Aesthetic State." *Beethoven Forum* 7 (1999): 17–44.

Berlioz, Hector. *Evenings with the Orchestra.* Translated by Jacques Barzun. New York: Alfred A. Knopf, 1956.

Bernstein, Leonard. "Aesthetic News Bulletin." Program notes to *Ode an die Freiheit: Bernstein in Berlin.* 429 861–2. Hamburg: Deutsche Grammophon, 1990.

Bernstein, Susan. *Virtuosity of the Nineteenth Century: Performing Music and Language in Heine, Liszt, and Baudelaire.* Stanford, CA: Stanford University Press, 1998.

Berry, Paul. "Old Love: Johannes Brahms, Clara Schumann, and the Poetics of Musical Memory." *Journal of Musicology* 24 (2007): 72–111.

Besseler, Heinrich. *Aufsätze zur Musikgeschichte und Musikästhetik.* Edited by Peter Gülke. Leipzig: Reclam, 1978.

———. "Musik und Raum." In *Musik und Bild: Festschrift Max Seiffert,* edited by Heinrich Besseler, 151–160. Kassel: Bärenreiter, 1938.

Besser, Johann. "Die Beziehungen Franz Brendels zur Hegelschen Philosophie: Ein Beitrag zur Musikanschauung des Schumann-Kreises." In *Robert Schumann: Aus Anlaß seines 100. Todestages,* edited by Hans J. Moser and Eberhard Rebling, 84–91. Leipzig: Breitkopf und Härtel, 1956.

Biddle, Ian. "Policing Masculinity: Schumann, Berlioz and the Gendering of the Music-critical Idiom." *Journal of the Royal Musical Association* 124 (1999): 196–220.

Bienenfeld, Elsa. "Köpfe im Profil: Guido Adler." *Die Musik* 28 (1925): 113–124.

Blackbourn, David, and Richard J. Evans, eds. *The German Bourgeoisie: Essays on the Social History of the German Middle Class from the Late Eighteenth to the Early Twentieth Century.* New York: Routledge, 1991.

Blume, Friedrich. *Wesen und Werden der deutschen Musik.* Kassel: Bärenreiter, 1944.

Bodsch, Ingrid. "Monument für Beethoven: Die Künstlerstandbilder des bürgerlichen Zeitalters als Sinnstifter nationaler Identität." In *Monument für Beethoven: Zur Geschichte des Beethoven-Denkmals (1845) und der frühen Beethoven-Rezeption in Bonn,* edited by Ingrid Bodsch, 157–177. Bonn: Bonner Stadtmuseum, 1995.

Bohlman, Philip. *The Music of European Nationalism.* Santa Barbara, CA: ABC Clio, 2004.

Böhme-Mehner, Tatjana, and Klaus Mehner, eds. *Hugo Riemann (1849–1919): Musikwissenschaftler mit Universalanspruch.* Cologne: Böhlau, 2001.

Bonds, Mark Evan. "Idealism and the Aesthetics of Instrumental Music at the Turn of the Nineteenth Century." *Journal of the American Musicological Society* 50 (1997): 387–420.

———. *Music as Thought: Listening to the Symphony in the Age of Beethoven.* Princeton: Princeton University Press, 2006.

Bowen, José Antonio. "The Conductor and the Score: The Relation between Interpreter and Text in the Generation of Mendelssohn, Berlioz and Wagner." Ph.D. diss., Stanford University, 1989.

Brandt, Torsten. *Johann Christian Lobe (1797–1881): Studien zu Biographie und musikschriftstellerischem Werk.* Göttingen: Vandenhoeck & Ruprecht, 2002.

Breidenstein, Heinrich Karl. *Festgabe zur Inaugurations-Feier des Beethoven-Monuments.* Bonn: T. Habicht, 1845; reprint Bonn: Ludwig Röhrscheid, 1983.

———. *Zur Jahresfeier der Inauguration des Beethoven Monuments.* Bonn: T. Habicht, 1846; reprint Bonn: Ludwig Röhrscheid, 1983.

Breig, Werner. "Probleme in der Edition älterer deutscher Orgelmusik." In *Musikedition: Mittler zwischen Wissenschaft und musikalischer Praxis,* edited by Helga Lühning, 49–62. Tübingen: Max Niemeyer, 2002.

Brendel, Franz. "Die bisherige Sonderkunst und das Kunstwerk der Zukunft." *Neue Zeitschrift für Musik* 38 (1853): 77–79, 89–92, 101–104, 109–113, 121–126, 133–136.

———. *Franz Liszt als Symphoniker.* Leipzig: Breitkopf und Härtel, 1857.

———. *Geschichte der Musik in Frankreich, Deutschland und Italien.* Leipzig: Breitkopf und Härtel, 1852.

———. *Die Musik der Gegenwart und die Gesammtkunst der Zukunft.* Leipzig: Bruno Hinze, 1854.

———. "Zur Anbahnung einer Verständigung." *Neue Zeitschrift für Musik* 50 (1859): 265–273.

Brinkmann, Reinhold. "The Distorted Sublime: Music and National Socialist Ideology—A Sketch." In *Music and Nazism: Art under Tyranny 1933–1945,* edited by Michael Kater and Albrecht Riethmüller, 43–63. Laaber: Laaber Verlag, 2003.

Brodbeck, David. *Johannes Brahms: Symphony no. 1* (Cambridge: Cambridge University Press, 1997).

Brüstle, Christa. *Anton Bruckner und die Nachwelt: Zur Rezeptionsgeschichte des Komponisten in der ersten Hälfte des 20. Jahrhunderts.* Stuttgart: Metzler, 1998.

————. "Siegmund von Hausegger: A Bruckner Authority from the 1930s." In *Perspectives on Anton Bruckner,* edited by Crawford Howie, Paul Hawkshaw, and Timothy L. Jackson, 341–352. Aldershot: Ashgate, 2001.

Buch, Esteban. *Beethoven's Ninth: A Political History.* Translated by Richard Miller. Chicago: University of Chicago Press, 2003.

Bücken, Ernst. *Die Musik der Nationen.* Leipzig: Alfred Kröner, 1937.

Burnham, Scott. *Beethoven Hero.* Princeton: Princeton University Press, 1995.

————. "Form." In *The Cambridge History of Western Music Theory,* edited by Thomas Christensen, 880–906. Cambridge: Cambridge University Press, 2001.

————. "Our Sublime Ninth." *Beethoven Forum* 5 (1996): 155–163.

Calinescu, Matei. *Five Faces of Modernity.* Durham, NC: Duke University Press, 1989.

Carlyle, Thomas. *On Heroes, Hero-Worship, and the Heroic in History.* Reprint ed. New York: AMS Press, 1969.

Carrier, Peter. "Pierre Noras *Les Lieux de mémoire* als Diagnose und Symptom des zeitgenössischen Erinnerungskultes." In *Kontexte und Kulturen des Erinnerns: Maurice Halbwachs und das Paradigma des kollektiven Gedächtnisses,* edited by Gerald Echterhoff and Martin Saar, 141–162. Konstanz: UVK Verlagsgesellschaft, 2002.

Celestini, Federico. "'Denkmäler italienischer Tonkunst': D'Annunzios Roman *Il fuoco* und die Mythologisierung alter Musik in Italien um 1900." In *Die Besetzung des öffentlichen Raumes: Politische Plätze, Denkmäler und Straßennamen im europäischen Vergleich,* edited by Rudolf Jaworski and Peter Stachel, 277–292. Berlin: Timme & Frank, 2007.

Choay, Françoise. *The Invention of the Historic Monument.* Trans. Lauren M. O'Connell. Cambridge: Cambridge University Press, 2001.

Chorley, Henry F. *Modern German Music: Recollections and Criticisms.* 2 vols. London: Smith, Elder and Co., 1854.

Christensen, Thomas. "Four-Hand Piano Transcription and Georgaphies of Nineteenth-Century Musical Reception." *Journal of the American Musicological Society* 52 (1999): 255–298.

Christmann, Johann Friedrich. "An das scheidende Jahrhundert." *Allgemeine musikalische Zeitung* 3 (1800/1801): cols. 201–211.

Chrysander, Friedrich. "Berichte. Nachrichten und Bemerkungen. Wien." *Leipziger allgemeine musikalische Zeitung* 6 (1871): col. 299.

————. "Denkmäler der Tonkunst: Eine Ankündigung." *Leipziger allgemeine musikalische Zeitung* 4 (1869): cols. 1–2.

————. "'Des einigen deutschen Reiches Musikzustände.'" *Leipziger allgemeine musikalische Zeitung* 11 (1874): cols. 1–5.

————. "Instrumentalmusik." *Leipziger allgemeine musikalische Zeitung* 7 (1872): cols. 105–110, 121–124, 137–141.

————. "Die Oratorien von Carissimi." *Leipziger allgemeine musikalische Zeitung* 11 (1876): cols. 67–69, 81–83, 113–115, 129–132, 145–147.

————. "Die Verwendung der Schlüssel bei der Herausgabe älterer Meisterwerke, mit besonderer Beziehung auf die 'Denkmäler der Tonkunst.'" *Leipziger allgemeine musikalische Zeitung* 5 (1870): cols. 356–359.

————. "Was Herr Prof. Hanslick sich unter 'Kunstzeloten' vorstellt." *Leipziger allgemeine musikalische Zeitung* 3 (1869): cols. 387–389.

Chua, Daniel. *Absolute Music and the Construction of Meaning.* Cambridge: Cambridge University Press, 1999.

————. *The 'Galitzin' Quartets of Beethoven.* Princeton: Princeton University Press, 1995.

Comini, Alessandra. *The Changing Image of Beethoven: A Study in Myth-Making.* New York: Rizzoli, 1987.

Cook, Nicholas. *Beethoven: Symphony no. 9.* Cambridge: Cambridge University Press, 1993.

Crane, Susan. *Collecting and Historical Consciousness in Early Nineteenth-Century Germany.* Ithaca, NY: Cornell University Press, 2000.

Currid, Brian. *A National Acoustics: Music and Mass Publicity in Weimar and Nazi Germany.* Minneapolis: University of Minnesota Press, 2006.

Dahlhaus, Carl. "Bruckner und die Programmusik: Zum Finale der Achten Symphonie." In *Anton Bruckner: Studien zu Werk und Wirkung,* edited by Christoph-Hellmut Mahling, 40–78. Tutzing: Hans Schneider, 1985.

————. *The Idea of Absolute Music.* Translated by Roger Lustig. Chicago: University of Chicago Press, 1989.

————. "Ideengeschichte musikalischer Editionsprinzipien." *Fontes Artes Musicae* 25 (1978): 19–27.

————. *Klassische und romantische Musikästhetik.* Laaber: Laaber Verlag, 1988.

————. "Die Musikgeschichte Österreichs und die Idee der deutschen Musik." In *Deutschland und Österreich,* edited by Richard A. Kann and Friedrich E. Prinz, 322–349. Vienna and Munich: Jugend und Volk, 1980.

————. *Nineteenth-Century Music.* Translated by J. Bradford Robinson. Berkeley and Los Angeles: University of California Press, 1989.

————. "Philologie und Rezeptionsgeschichte: Bemerkungen zur Theorie der Edition." In *Festschrift Georg von Dadelsen zum 60. Geburtstag,* edited by Thomas Kohlhase and Volker Scherliess, 45–58. Neuhausen-Stuttgart: Hänssler, 1978.

Dahlhaus, Carl, ed. *Studien zur Trivialmusik.* Regensburg: Gustav Bosse, 1967.

Danckert, Werner. "Bruckner und das Natursymbol." *Die Musik* 30 (1938): 306–309.

Danuser, Hermann, and Herfried Münkler, eds. *Kunst—Fest—Kanon: Inklusion und Exklusion in Gesellschaft und Kultur.* Berlin: Staatsoper unter den Linden, 2004.

Dau, Rudolf. "Friedrich Schillers Hymne 'An die Freude' zu einigen Problemen ihrer Interpretation und aktuellen Rezeption." *Weimarer Beiträge* 24 (1978): 38–60.

Daverio, John. *Nineteenth-Century Music and the German Romantic Ideology.* New York: Schirmer, 1993.

Deathridge, John. "Germany—the Special Path." In *The Late Romantic Era,* edited by Jim Samson, 50–73. Basingstoke: McMillan, 1991.

————. "The Invention of German Music c. 1800." *Unity and Diversity in European Culture c. 1800,* edited by Tim Blanning and Hagen Schulze, 35–60. Oxford: Oxford University Press 2006.

————. "Wagner, the Greeks and Wolfgang Schadewaldt." *Dialogos: Hellenic Studies Review* 6 (1999): 133–140.

De Man, Paul. *The Rhetoric of Romanticism.* New York: Columbia University Press, 1984.

Dennis, David B. *Beethoven in German Politics 1870–1989.* New Haven: Yale University Press, 1996.

DeNora, Tia. *Beethoven and the Construction of Genius: Musical Politics in Vienna 1792–1803.* Berkeley: University of California Press, 1995.

Diener, Gottfried. *Fausts Weg zu Helena: Urphänomen und Archetypus.* Stuttgart: Ernst Klett Verlag, 1961.

D'Indy, Vincent. *Beethoven: A Critical Biography.* Translated by Theodore Baker. Boston and New York: Boston Music Company/G. Schirmer, 1912.

Doebel, Wolfgang. *Bruckners Symphonien in Bearbeitungen: Die Konzepte der Bruckner-Schüler und ihre Rezeption bis zu Robert Haas.* Tutzing: Hans Schneider, 2001.

Dömling, Wolfgang. *Franz Liszt und seine Zeit.* Laaber: Laaber-Verlag, 1985.

Dronsmann, Hansheinrich. "Kritische Anmerkungen zur Unterhaltungsmusik." *Die Musik* 28 (1935): 335–336.

Dümling, Albrecht, and Peter Girth, eds. *Entartete Musik: Eine kommentierte Rekonstruktion.* Düsseldorf: Service-Druck Kleinherne, 1988.

Ehlers, Paul. "Das Regensburger Bruckner-Erlebnis." *Zeitschrift für Musik* 104 (1937): 745–748.

Ehrlich, Lothar. "Liszt und Goethe." In *Liszt und die Weimarer Klassik,* edited by Detlef Altenburg, 33–45. Laaber: Laaber-Verlag, 1997.

Eichhorn, Andreas. *Beethovens Neunte Symphonie: Die Geschichte ihrer Aufführung und Rezeption.* Kassel: Bärenreiter, 1993.

Eikmeyer, Robert. *Adolf Hitler: Reden zur Kunst- und Kulturpolitik 1933–1939.* Introduction by Boris Groys. Frankfurt am Main: Revolver, 1999.

Einstein, Alfred. *Greatness in Music.* Translated by César Saerchinger. New York: Oxford University Press, 1941.

———. *Music in the Romantic Era: Musical Thought in the Nineteenth Century.* New York: Norton, 1947.

Eisler, Hanns. *Gesammelte Werke.* Edited by Stephanie Eisler and Manfred Grabs. Leipzig: VEB Deutscher Verlag für Musik, 1968–.

Elsner, John, and Roger Cardinal, eds. *The Cultures of Collecting.* London: Reaktion Books, 1994.

Fellerer, Karl Gustav. "Musik und Feier." *Die Musik* 31 (1939): 433–437.

Fellinger, Imogen. "Brahms und die Musik vergangener Epochen." In *Die Ausbreitung des Historismus in der Musik,* edited by Walter Wiora, 147–167. Regensburg: Gustav Bosse, 1969.

Fink, Robert. "'Arrows of Desire': Long-Range Linear Structure and the Transformation of Musical Energy." Ph.D. diss., University of California Berkeley, 1994.

Finscher, Ludwig. "Gesamtausgabe—Urtext—Musikalische Praxis: Zum Verhältnis von Musikwissenschaft und Musikleben." In *Musik, Edition, Interpretation: Gedenkschrift Günter Henle,* edited by Martin Bente, 193–198. Munich: Henle, 1980.

———. "Musikalische Denkmäler und Gesamtausgaben." In *Musikalisches Erbe und Gegenwart: Musikgesamtausgaben in der Bundesrepublik Deutschland,* edited by Hanspeter Bennwitz, Georg Feder, Ludwig Finscher, and Wolfgang Rehm, 1–13. Kassel: Bärenreiter, 1975.

Fischer-Lichte, Erika, ed. *Theatralität und die Krisen der Repräsentation.* Stuttgart: Metzler, 2001.

Floros, Constantin. *Brahms und Bruckner: Studien zur musikalischen Exegetik* Wiesbaden: Breitkopf und Härtel, 1980.

Fock, Gustav. "Brahms und die Musikforschung." In *Beiträge zur Hamburgischen Musikgeschichte,* edited by Heinrich Husmann, 46–69. Hamburg: Selbstverlag des musikwissenschaftlichen Instituts der Universität Hamburg, 1956.

Forchert, Arno. "Droysen und Wagner." In *Neue Musik und Tradition: Festschrift Rudolf Stephan,* edited by Josef Kuckertz, Helga de la Motte-Haber, Christian Martin Schmidt, and Wilhelm Seidel, 251–257. Laaber: Laaber-Verlag, 1990.

Forkel, Johann Nikolaus. *Allgemeine Literatur der Musik.* Leipzig, 1792; reprint Hildesheim: Georg Olms, 2001.

———. *Über Johann Sebastian Bach's Leben, Kunst und Kunstwerke für patriotische Verehrer echter musikalischer Kunst.* Leipzig: Hoffmeister und Kühnel, 1802.

Foucault, Michel. "Nietzsche, Genealogy, History." In *The Foucault Reader,* edited by Paul Rabinow, 76–100. London: Penguin, 1991.

François, Etienne, and Hagen Schulze, eds. *Deutsche Erinnerungsorte.* 3 vols. Munich: C. H. Beck, 2001.

Franz, Robert. *Mittheilungen über J. S. Bach's 'Magnificat.'* Halle: Heinrich Karmrodt, 1863.

———. *Offener Brief an Eduard Hanslick über die Bearbeitung älterer Tonwerke.* Leipzig: F. E. C. Leuckart, 1871.

Friedlander, Max. *Ueber musikalische Herausgeberarbeit.* Weimar: Gesellschaft der Bibliophilen, 1922.

Friedlander, Saul. *Memory, History and the Extermination of the Jews of Europe.* Bloomington: University of Indiana Press, 1993.

Furtwängler, Wilhelm. "Rede zum 1. Großdeutschen Brucknerfest (1939)." In *Bruckner-Blätter (Mitteilungen der Internationalen Bruckner-Gesellschaft)* 10 (1939): 10–16.

Gay, Peter. *Freud, Jews and Other Germans: Masters and Victims in Modernist Culture.* London, New York: Oxford University Press, 1978.

Geck, Martin. *Die Geburtsstunde des Mythos "Bach": Mendelssohns Wiederentdeckung der Matthäuspassion.* Stuttgart: Carus, 1998.

Gehring, Axel. *Genie und Verehrergemeinde: Eine soziologische Analyse des Genie-Problems.* Bonn: Bouvier, 1968.

Gehring, Franz. "Triumphlied (auf den Sieg der deutschen Waffen) von Johannes Brahms." *Leipziger allgemeine musikalische Zeitung* 7 (1872): cols. 409–414.

Geiringer, Karl. "Brahms als Musikhistoriker." *Die Musik* 25 (1933): 571–578.

———. "Brahms and Chrysander." *Monthly Musical Record* 67 (1937): 97–99, 131–132, 178–180, 463–464.

———. "Brahms as Reader and Collector." *Musical Quarterly* 19 (1933): 158–168.

———. "Johannes Brahms im Briefwechsel mit Eusebius Mandyczewski. " *Zeitschrift für Musikwissenschaft* 15 (1933): 337–370.

Geisenhanslüke, Achim. "Der Mensch als Eintagswesen: Nietzsches Kritische Anthropologie in der Zweiten Unzeitgemäßen Betrachtung." *Nietzsche-Studien* (28) 1999: 125–140.

Gellner, Ernest. *Nations and Nationalism.* Oxford: Blackwell, 1983.

Gerhard, Anselm. "Für den 'Butterladen,' die Gelehrten oder 'das practische Leben'? Denkmalsidee und Gesamtausgaben in der Musikgeschichte vor 1850." *Die Musikforschung* 57 (2004): 363–382.

————. "Musicology in the 'Third Reich': A Preliminary Report." *Journal of Musicology* 18 (2001): 517–543.

Gervinus, Georg G. *Händel und Shakespeare: Zur Ästhetik der Instrumentalkunst.* Leipzig: Wilhelm Engelmann, 1868.

Geuert, Hans-Dieter. *Was ist Kitsch?* Göttingen: Vandenhoeck & Ruprecht, 2000.

Giesz, Ludwig. *Phänomenologie des Kitsches: Ein Beitrag zur anthropologischen Ästhetik.* Frankfurt am Main: Fischer, 1994.

Gilliam, Bryan. "The Annexation of Anton Bruckner: Nazi Revisionism and the Politics of Appropriation." *Musical Quarterly* 78 (1994): 584–604.

————. "Bruckner's Annexation Revisited: A Response to Manfred Wagner." *Musical Quarterly* 80 (1996): 124–131.

Goebbels, Joseph. "Bruckner Address in Regensburg (6 June 1937)." Translated by John Michael Cooper. *Musical Quarterly* 78 (1994): 605–609.

Goehr, Lydia. *The Imaginary Museum of Musical Works: An Essay in the Philosophy of Music.* Oxford: Clarendon Press, 1992.

————. *The Quest for Voice: On Music, Politics, and the Limits of Philosophy.* Berkeley: University of California Press, 1998.

Goethe, Johann Wolfgang von. *Faust: Der Tragödie zweiter Teil.* Edited by Ulrich Gaier. Stuttgart: Reclam, 2004.

————. *Faust I & II.* Vol. 2 of *Goethe: The Collected Works.* 12 vols. Edited and translated by Stuart Atkins. Princeton: Princeton University Press, 1994.

————. *Werke. (Hamburger Ausgabe).* Edited by Erich Trunz. 14 vols. Munich: C. H. Beck, 1981.

Golther, Wolfgang, ed. *Robert Franz und Arnold Freiherr Senfft von Pilsach: Ein Briefwechsel 1861–1888.* Berlin: Alexander Duncker, 1907.

Gooley, Dana. *The Virtuoso Liszt.* Cambridge: Cambridge University Press, 2004.

————. "Warhorses: Liszt, Webers *Konzertstück,* and the Cult of Napoléon." *Nineteenth-Century Music* 24 (2000): 62–88.

Gramit, David. *Cultivating Music: The Aspirations, Interests, and Limits of German Musical Culture 1770–1848.* Berkeley: University of California Press, 2002.

Greenberg, Clement. "Avant-Garde and Kitsch." *Partisan Review* 6 (1939): 34–49.

Grey, Thomas. "Wagner, the Overture, and the Aesthetics of Musical Form." *Nineteenth-Century Music* 12 (1988): 3–22.

Grunsky, Karl. *Kampf um die deutsche Musik.* Stuttgart: Erhard Walther, Verlag für Nationalsozialistisches Schrifttum, 1933.

Gumbrecht, Hans Ulrich. *The Powers of Philology.* Champaign and Chicago: University of Illinois Press and University of Chicago Press, 2003.

————. *The Production of Presence: What Meaning Cannot Convey.* Stanford, CA: Stanford University Press, 2004.

Günther, Gitta, Wolfram Huschke, et al., eds. *Weimar: Lexikon zur Stadtgeschichte.* Weimar: Böhlau, 1993.

Gutknecht, Dieter. "Robert Franz als Bearbeiter der Werke von Bach und Händel und die Praxis seiner Zeit." In *Robert Franz (1815–1892),* edited by Konstanze Musketa, 219–247. Halle an der Saale: Händel-Haus, 1993.

Haas, Robert. *Anton Bruckner.* Potsdam: Akademische Verlagsanstalt Athenaion, 1934.

Habermas, Jürgen. *Die nachholende Revolution.* Frankfurt am Main: Suhrkamp, 1990.

————. *Der philosophische Diskurs der Moderne.* Frankfurt am Main: Suhrkamp, 1996.

Halbwachs, Maurice. *On Collective Memory.* Translated by Lewis A. Coser. Chicago and London: University of Chicago Press, 1992.

————. *The Collective Memory.* Translated by Francis J. Ditter, Jr. and Vida Yazdi Ditter, with an introduction by Mary Douglas. New York: Harper and Row, 1980.

Hallensleben, Horst. "Bonner Beethoven-Denkmal als frühes 'bürgerliches Standbild.'" In *Monument für Beethoven,* edited by Ingrid Bodsch, 29–38. Bonn: Bonner Stadtmuseum, 1995.

Hansen, Mathias. "Die faschistische Bruckner-Rezeption und ihre Quellen." *Beiträge zur Musikwissenschaft* 28 (1986): 53–61.

Hanslick, Eduard. "Richard Wagner, und seine neueste Oper, 'Tannhäuser.'" *Allgemeine Wiener Musik-Zeitung* 6 (1846): 581, 585, 589–590, 601–602, 606, 613–614, 617–618, 625–627, 629–630, 637–638.

Hartman, Geoffrey. *The Longest Shadow: In the Aftermath of the Holocaust.* Bloomington: University of Indiana Press, 1996.

Hase, Oskar von. *Breitkopf und Härtel: Gedenkschrift und Arbeitsbericht.* 3 vols. Wiesbaden: Breitkopf und Härtel, 1968.

Head, Matthew. "Music with 'No Past'? Archeologies of Joseph Haydn and *The Creation.*" *Nineteenth-Century Music* 23 (2000): 191–217.

Hegel, Georg Wilhelm Friedrich. *Ästhetik.* 3 vols. Berlin: DEB Das Europäische Buch, 1985.

————. *Vorlesungen über die Philosophie der Weltgeschichte, Bd. 1: Die Vernunft in der Geschichte.* Edited by Georg Lasson. Hamburg: F. Meiner, 1988.

Heinz, Rudolf. "Geschichte als angewandte Ästhetik: Zum Verhältnis zwischen Musikästhetik und Musikhistorie bei Friedrich Chrysander und Hermann Kretzschmar." In *Die Ausbreitung des Historismus über die Musikwissenschaft,* edited by Walter Wiora, 251–259. Regensburg: Gustav Bosse, 1969.

————. *Geschichtsbegriff und Wissenschaftscharakter in der Musikwissenschaft in der zweiten Hälfte des neunzehnten Jahrhunderts.* Regensburg: Gustav Bosse, 1968.

Heister, Hanns-Werner. "Macht und Schicksal: Klassik, Fanfaren, höhere Durchhaltemusik." In *Musik und Musikpolitik im faschistischen Deutschland,* edited by Hanns-Werner Heister and Hans-Günter Klein, 115–125. Frankfurt am Main: Fischer, 1984.

————, ed. *"Entartete Musik" 1938: Weimar und die Ambivalenz.* 2 vols. Saarbrücken: Pfau, 2001.

Henke, Burkhard, Susanne Kord, et al., eds. *Unwrapping Goethe's Weimar: Essays in Cultural Studies and Local Knowledge.* Rochester, NY: Camden House, 2000.

Hennig, C. R. *Beethoven's Neunte Symphonie: Eine Analyse.* Leipzig: F. E. C. Leuckart, 1888.

Henseler, Theodor A. *Das musikalische Bonn im 19. Jahrhundert.* Bonn, 1959.

Hepokoski, James. "Beethoven Reception: The Symphonic Tradition." In *The Cambridge History of Nineteenth-Century Music,* edited by Jim Samson, 424–459. Cambridge: Cambridge University Press, 2001.

————. "Masculine-Feminine." *The Musical Times* 135 (1994): 494–499.

Herbst, Kurt. "Leitfaden zu einer musikalischen Gesamtreform." *Die Musik* 28 (1935): 268–276.

———. "Musikchronik des deutschen Rundfunks." *Die Musik* 28 (1935): 61–65.

Herf, Jeffrey. *Reactionary Modernism: Technology, Culture, and Politics in Weimar and the Third Reich.* Cambridge: Cambridge University Press, 1987.

Hermand, Jost. "Die Kulturszene im Dritten Reich." In *Die dunkle Last: Musik und Nationalsozialismus,* edited by Brunhilde Sonntag, Hans-Werner Boresch and Detlev Gojowy, 9–22. Cologne: Bela Verlag, 1999.

———. *Stile, Ismen, Etiketten: Zur Periodisierung der modernen Kunst.* Wiesbaden: Wissenschaftliche Verlagsgesellschaft Athenaion, 1978.

Herzog, Friedrich W. "Warum Unterhaltungsmusik?" *Die Musik* 28 (1935): 321.

Hess, Günther. "Panorama und Denkmal: Erinnerung als Denkmal zwischen Vormärz und Gründerzeit." In *Literatur in der sozialen Bewegung,* edited by Albert Nartino, 130–206. Tübingen: Max Niemeyer, 1977.

Heuß, Alfred. "Eine motivisch-thematische Studie über Liszts sinfonische Dichtung 'Ce qu'on entend sur la montagne': Zur 100. Wiederkehr von Franz Liszts Geburtstag am 22. Oktober 1911." *Zeitschrift der Internationalen Musikwissenschaftlichen Gesellschaft* 13 (1911): 10–21.

Hilscher, Elisabeth Th. *Denkmalpflege und Musikwissenschaft: Einhundert Jahre Gesellschaft zur Herausgabe der Tonkunst in Österreich (1893–1993).* Tutzing: Hans Schneider, 1995.

Hinrichsen, Hans-Joachim. "Die Bach-Gesamtausgabe und die Kontroversen um die Aufführungspraxis der Vokalwerke." In *Bach und die Nachwelt,* 4 vols., edited by Michael Heinemann and Hans-Joachim Hinrichsen, ii. 227–297. Laaber: Laaber-Verlag, 1997.

Hinton, Stephen. "Not 'Which' Tones? The Crux of Beethoven's Ninth." *Nineteenth-Century Music* 22 (1998): 61–77.

Hinz, Berthold, ed. *Die Malerei im deutschen Faschismus: Kunst und Konterrevolution.* Munich: Hanser, 1974.

Hobsbawm, Eric, and Terence Ranger, eds. *The Invention of Tradition.* Cambridge: Canto, 1984.

Hoeckner, Berthold. *Programming the Absolute: Nineteenth-Century German Music and the Hermeneutics of the Moment.* Princeton: Princeton University Press, 2002.

Hoffmann, E. T. A. *Selected Writings.* Edited by Elizabeth Knight and Leonard Kent. Chicago and London: University of Chicago Press, 1969.

Horton, Julian. *Bruckner's Symphonies: Analysis, Reception, and Cultural Politics.* Cambridge: Cambridge University Press, 2004.

Howard, Patricia. *Gluck: An Eighteenth-Century Portrait in Letters and Documents.* Oxford: Clarendon Press, 1995.

Hübner, Kurt. "Vom theoretischen Nachteil und praktischen Nutzen der Historie: Unzeitgemäßes über Nietzsches unzeitgemäße Betrachtungen." In *"Vom Nutzen und Nachteil der Historie für das Leben": Nietzsche und die Erinnerung in der Moderne,* edited by Dieter Borchmeyer, 28–47. Frankfurt am Main: Suhrkamp, 1996.

Huschke, Wolfram. "'. . . wo Wagner und ich die Coryphäen gewesen wären, wie früher Goethe und Schiller': Franz Liszts Verhältnis zu den klassischen Traditionen Weimars." *Impulse* 5 (1982): 370–388.

———. "Zum kulturhistorischen Stellenwert von Bearbeitungen um 1840." In *Liszt-Studien 4: Der junge Liszt,* edited by Gottfried Scholz, 95–99. Munich and Salzburg: Emil Katzbichler, 1993.

Huyssen, Andreas. "Monumental Seduction." *New German Critique* 69 (1996): 181–200.

———. *Twilight Memories: Marking Time in a Culture of Amnesia.* Routledge: New York: 1995.

Irmen, Hans-Josef. "Franz Liszt in Bonn, oder: Wie die erste Beethovenhalle entstand." In *Studien zur Bonner Musikgeschichte des 18. und 19. Jahrhunderts,* edited by Marianne Bröcker and Günther Massenkeil, 49–65. Cologne: Arno Volk Verlag, 1978.

Istel, Edgar. *Das große Buch der Oper.* Berlin: Max Hesse, 1919.

Jackson, John. *The Necessity for Ruins, and Other Topics.* Amherst: University of Massachusetts Press, 1980.

Jaeger, Friedrich, and Jörn Rüsen. *Geschichte des Historismus: Eine Einführung.* Munich: C. H. Beck, 1992.

Jahn, Otto. *Gesammelte Aufsätze über Musik.* Leipzig: Breitkopf und Härtel, 1866.

———. *Gesammelte Aufsätze über Musik.* 2d ed. Leipzig: Breitkopf und Härtel, 1867.

Jähnig, Dieter. "Nietzsches Kritik der historischen Wissenschaften." *Praxis* 6 (1970): 223–236.

James, Harold, and Maria Stone, eds. *When the Wall Came Down: Reactions to German Unification.* London and New York: Routledge, 1992.

Jankélévitch, Vladimir. *Debussy et le mystère.* Neuchâtel: Baconnière, 1949.

———. *Liszt: Rhapsodie et impression* Paris: Flammarion, 1998.

John, Eckhardt. *Musikbolschewismus: Die Politisierung der Musik 1918–1938.* Stuttgart: Metzler, 1994.

Johns, Keith T. *The Symphonic Poems of Franz Liszt.* Edited by Michael Saffle. Stuyvesant, NY: Pendragon, 1997.

Jost, Christa, and Peter Jost. "'Zukunftsmusik': Zur Geschichte eines Begriffs." *Musiktheorie* 10 (1995): 119–135.

Junk, Victor. "Zur Urfassung von Bruckners Fünfter Symphonie." *Zeitschrift für Musik* *103* (1936): 545–546.

Kain, Philip J. *Schiller, Hegel, and Marx: State, Society, and the Aesthetic Ideal of Ancient Greece.* Kingston and Montreal: McGill-Queen's University Press, 1982.

Kalbeck, Max. *Johannes Brahms.* 2 vols. Vienna and Leipzig: Wiener Verlag, 1904.

Kansteiner, Wulf. "Finding Meaning in Memory: A Methodological Critique of Collective Memory Studies." *History and Theory* 41 (2002): 179–197.

Kant, Immanuel. *Kritik der Urteilskraft.* Edited by Wilhelm Weischedel. Frankfurt: Suhrkamp, 1977.

Kapp, Julius. "Autobiographisches von Franz Liszt," *Die Musik* 11 (1911): 10–21.

Keiler, Allan. "Liszt and Beethoven: The Creation of a Personal Myth." *Nineteenth-Century Music* 12 (1988): 116–131.

Kelly, Elaine. "Evolution versus Authenticity: Johannes Brahms, Robert Franz, and Continuo Practice in the Late Nineteenth Century." *Nineteenth Century Music* 30 (2006): 182–204.

Kesting, Hanjo, ed. *Briefwechsel Franz Liszt-Richard Wagner.* Frankfurt am Main: Insel, 1988.

Kirchmeyer, Helmut. *Situationsgeschichte der Musikkritik und des musikalischen Pressewesens.* Regensburg: Gustav Bosse Verlag, 1967–.

Kivy, Peter. *The Possessor and the Possessed: Handel, Mozart, Beethoven, and the Idea of Musical Genius.* New Haven: Yale University Press, 2001.

Kleefeld, Wilhelm. "Richard Wagner als Bearbeiter fremder Werke." *Die Musik* 4 (1904): 231–249.

Klein, Kerwin Lee. "On the Emergence of Memory in Historical Discourse." *Representations* 69 (2000): 127–150.

Klob, Karl Maria. *Die Oper von Gluck bis Wagner.* Ulm: Heinrich Kerler, 1913.

Knittel, K. M. "Wagner, Deafness, and the Reception of Beethoven's Late Style," *Journal of the American Musicological Society,* 51/1 (Spring 1998): 49–82.

Kopelson, Kevin. *Beethoven's Kiss: Pianism, Perversion, and the Mastery of Desire.* Stanford, CA: Stanford University Press, 1996.

Korotin, Ilse Erika. *"Am Muttergeist soll die Welt genesen": Philosophische Dispositionen zum Frauenbild im Nationalsozialismus.* Vienna, Cologne, Weimar: Böhlau, 1992.

Korstvedt, Benjamin. "Anton Bruckner in the Third Reich and After: An Essay on Ideology and Bruckner Reception." *Musical Quarterly* 80 (1996): 132–160.

———. "'Return to the Pure Sources': The Ideology and Text-Critical Legacy of the First Bruckner *Gesamtausgabe.*" In *Bruckner Studies,* edited by Timothy L. Jackson and Paul Hawkshaw, 91–109. Cambridge: Cambridge University Press, 1997.

———. *Symphony no. 8.* Cambridge: Cambridge University Press, 2000.

Koshar, Rudy. *From Monuments to Traces: Artifacts of German Memory, 1870–1990.* Berkeley: University of California Press, 2000.

Kracauer, Siegfried. *The Mass Ornament: Weimar Essays.* Translated by Thomas Y. Levin. Cambridge, MA: Harvard University Press, 1995.

Kreczi, Hanns. *Das Bruckner Stift St. Florian und das Linzer Reichs-Bruckner-Orchester (1942–1945).* Graz: Akademische Druck und Verlagsanstalt, 1986.

Kregor, Jonathan. "Franz Liszt and the Vocabularies of Transcription 1833–1865," PhD diss. Harvard University, 2007.

Kropfinger, Klaus. *Wagner and Beethoven: Richard Wagner's Reception of Beethoven.* Translated by Peter Palmer. Cambridge: Cambridge University Press, 1991.

Kross, Siegfried, ed. *Probleme der symphonischen Tradition im 19. Jahrhundert.* Tutzing: Hans Schneider, 1990.

Kulenkampff, Jens. "Notiz über die Begriffe 'Monument' und 'Lebenswelt.'" In *Kultur als Lebenswelt und Monument,* edited by Aleida Assmann and Dietrich Harth, 26–33. Frankfurt am Main: Fischer, 1991.

Kunze, Stefan, ed. *Ludwig van Beethoven: Die Werke im Spiegel der Zeit.* Laaber: Laaber-Verlag, 1989.

Kuspit, Donald B. "Nietzsche's Conception of Monumental History," *Archiv für Philosophie* 13 (1964): 95–115.

Ladenburger, Michael. "Wie sich das 'neue Bonn' bewährte oder: Das Musikfest zwischen den Fronten." In *Monument für Beethoven,* edited by Ingrid Bodsch, 135–155. Bonn: Bonner Stadtmuseum, 1995.

Lang, Berel. *The Future of the Holocaust: Between Memory and History.* Ithaca, NY: Cornell University Press, 1999.

Lang, Oskar. "Der Ur-Bruckner." *Die Musik* 28 (1935): 256–260.

Lange-Eichbaum, Wilhelm. *Genie, Irrsinn und Ruhm.* Munich: E. Reinhard, 1928.

Langewiesche, Dieter. "Nation, Nationalismus, Nationalstaat: Forschungsstand und Forschungsperspektive." *Neue Politische Literatur* 40 (1995): 195–236.

Lee, M. Owen. *Athena Sings: Wagner and the Ancient Greeks.* Toronto: University of Toronto Press, 2003.

Leopold, Silke, ed. *Musikalische Metamorphosen: Formen und Geschichte der Bearbeitung.* Kassel: Bärenreiter, 1992.

Lepenies, Wolf. *The Seduction of Culture in German History.* Princeton: Princeton University Press, 2006.

Leppert, Richard. *Music and Image: Domesticity, Ideology and Socio-Cultural Formation in Eighteenth-Century England.* Cambridge: Cambridge University Press, 1988.

Levy, David Benjamin. *Beethoven: The Ninth Symphony.* New York: Schirmer, 1995.

Lipsius, Maria [= La Mara]. "Beethovens Weihekuß." *Allgemeine Musikzeitung* 40 (1913): 544–546.

Liszt, Franz. *Briefe.* Edited by Maria Lipsius [=La Mara]. 8 vols. Leipzig: Breitkopf und Härtel, 1893–1902.

———. "Introduction to *Tasso: Lamento e Trionfo.*" Translated by Humphrey Searle. London: Eulenburg, 1976.

———. *Sämtliche Schriften.* Edited by Detlef Altenburg. Wiesbaden: Breitkopf und Härtel, 1989–.

Liszt, Franz, and Richard Wagner. *Correspondence of Wagner and Liszt.* Translated by Francis Hueffer. 2 vols. New York: Scribner and Welford, 1889.

Livingstone, Ernest. "Das Formproblem des 4. Satzes in Beethovens 9. Symphonie." In *Bericht über den internationalen musikwissenschaftlichen Kongress Bonn 1970.* Edited by Carl Dahlhaus, Hans Joachim Marx, Magda Marx-Weber, and Günther Massenkeil, 494–497. Kassel: Bärenreiter, 1971.

Lobe, Johann Christian. *Fliegende Blätter: Wahrheit über Tonkunst und Tonkünstler.* 3 vols. Leipzig: Baumgärtner's Buchhandlung, 1855–1857.

Loesser, Arthur. *Men, Women, and Pianos: A Social History.* New York: Simon and Schuster, 1954.

Longyear, R. M. *Schiller and Music.* Chapel Hill: University of North Carolina Press, 1966.

Lütteken, Laurenz. "Das Musikwerk im Spannungsfeld von 'Ausdruck' und 'Erleben': Heinrich Besselers musikhistoriographischer Ansatz." In *Musikwissenschaft—eine verspätete Disziplin?: Die akademische Musikforschung zwischen Fortschrittsglauben und Modernitätsverweigerung,* edited by Anselm Gerhard, 213–232. Stuttgart and Weimar: J. B. Metzler, 2000.

———. "Vom Umgang mit Quellen." *Die Musikforschung* 57 (2004): 329–332.

Lyotard, Jean-François. *Lessons on the Analytic of the Sublime: Kants Critique of Judgment 23–29.* Translated by Elizabeth Rottenberg. Stanford, CA: Stanford University Press, 1994.

Mann, Thomas. *Pro and Contra Wagner.* Translated by Allan Blunden. Chicago: University of Chicago Press, 1985.

———. *Reflections of a Nonpolitical Man.* Translated by Walter D. Morris. New York: Frederic Ungar, 1983.

Marggraf, Wolfgang. *Liszt in Weimar.* Weimar: Stadtmuseum Weimar, 1985.

Marsop, Paul. "Joachim Raff und 'Die Wagnerfrage.'" *Neue Musik-Zeitung* 43 (1922): 252–254.

Martin, Uwe. "Freude, Freiheit, Götterfunken: Über Schillers Schwierigkeiten beim Schreiben von Freiheit." *Cahiers d'études germaniques* 18 (1990): 9–18.

Marx, A. B. *Musical Form in the Age of Beethoven: Selected Writings on Theory and Method.* Edited and translated by Scott Burnham. Cambridge: Cambridge University Press, 1997.

Massenkeil, Günther. "Die Bonner Beethoven-Kantate von Franz Liszt." In *Die Sprache der Musik: Festschrift für Klaus Niemöller zum 60. Geburtstag,* edited by Jobst Peter Fricke, 381–400. Regensburg: G. Bosse, 1989.

Mayer, Hans. *Das unglückliche Bewußtsein: Zur deutschen Literaturgeschichte von Lessing bis Heine.* Frankfurt am Main: Suhrkamp, 1986.

McClatchie, Steven. "Bruckner and the Bayreuthians: Or, *Das Geheimnis der Form bei Anton Bruckner.*" In *Bruckner Studies,* edited by Paul Hawkshaw and Timothy L. Jackson, 110–121. Cambridge: Cambridge University Press, 1997.

Meinecke, Friedrich. *Historicism: The Rise of a New Historical Outlook.* Translated by J. E. Anderson. London: Routledge and K. Paul, 1972.

Metzner, Paul. *Crescendo of the Virtuoso: Spectacle, Skill, and Self-Promotion in Paris during the Age of Revolution.* Berkeley: University of California Press, 1998.

Meyer, Katrin. *Ästhetik der Historie: Friedrich Nietzsches "Vom Nutzen und Nachteil der Historie für das Leben."* Würzburg: Königshausen & Neumann, 1998.

Meyer, Leonard B. *Style and Music: Theory, History, and Ideology.* Chicago: University of Chicago Press, 1989.

Micznik, Vera. "The Absolute Limitations of Programme Music: The Case of Liszt's *Die Ideale.*" *Music and Letters* 80 (1999): 207–240.

Miller, R. D. *Schiller and the Ideal of Freedom.* Oxford: Clarendon Press, 1970.

Minor, Ryan. "National Memory, Public Music: Commemoration and Consecration in Nineteenth-Century German Choral Music." Ph.D. diss., University of Chicago, 2005.

———. "Prophet and Populace in Liszt's 'Beethoven' Cantatas." In *Franz Liszt and His World,* edited by Christopher Gibbs and Dana Gooley, 113–166. Princeton: Princeton University Press, 2006.

Möbus, Frank, and Frederike Schmidt-Möbus. *Kleine Kulturgeschichte Weimars.* Cologne: Böhlau, 1998.

Morrow, Mary Sue. *German Music Criticism in the Late Eighteenth Century: Aesthetic Issues in Instrumental Music.* Cambridge: Cambridge University Press, 1997.

Moseley, Roger. "Brief Immortality: Recasting History in the Music of Brahms." Ph.D. diss., University of California at Berkeley, 2004.

Moser, Hans Joachim. *Kleine deutsche Musikgeschichte.* Stuttgart: Cotta'sche Buchhandlung, 1938.

———. *Das musikalische Denkmälerwesen in Deutschland.* Kassel: Bärenreiter, 1952.

Mosse, George L. *The Nationalization of the Masses: Political Symbolism and Mass Movements in Germany from the Napoleonic Wars through the Third Reich.* Ithaca, NY: Cornell University Press, 1991.

Most, Glenn W. "Vom Nutzen und Nachteil der Antike für das Leben: Zur modernen deutschen Selbstfindung anhand der alten Griechen." *Humanistische Bildung* 19 (1996): 35–52.

Mueller, Rena Charnin. "Sketches, Drafts and Revisions: Liszt at Work." In *Die Projekte der Liszt-Forschung,* edited by Detlef Altenburg and Gerhard J. Winkler, 26–34. Eisenstadt: Burgenländisches Landesmuseum, 1991.

Müller, Jan. *Another Country: German Intellectuals, Unification, and National Identity.* New Haven: Yale University Press, 2000.

Mumford, Lewis. *The Culture of Cities.* New York: Harcourt, Brace and Co., 1938.

Musgrave, Michael. *A Brahms Reader.* New Haven: Yale University Press, 2000.

Musketa, Konstanze, ed. *Robert Franz (1815–1892)* Halle an der Saale: Händel-Haus, 1993.

Nagler, Norbert. "Bruckners gründerzeitliche Monumentalsymphonie: Reflektionen zur Heteronomie kompositorischer Praxis." In *Musik-Konzepte: Anton Bruckner,* edited by Heinz-Klaus Metzger and Rainer Riehn, 86–118. Munich: Text + Kritik, 1982.

Nattiez, Jean-Jacques. *Wagner Androgyne.* Translated by Stewart Spencer. Princeton: Princeton University Press, 1993.

Neumann, Michael. *Das Ewig-Weibliche in Goethes "Faust."* Heidelberg: C. Winter, 1985.

Newman, Ernest. *The Life of Richard Wagner.* 4 vols. London: Cassell, 1933–1947.

Niazi, M. Nadeem. "Violating the *Mütter:* Staging the Semiotics of Desire, or, Aspects of the Eternal-Feminine in 'Faust.'" *Orbis Litterarum* 55 (2000): 103–117.

Nietzsche, Friedrich. *Basic Writings of Nietzsche.* Translated and edited by Walter Kaufmann, with an introduction by Peter Gay. New York: The Modern Library, 2000.

———. *The Gay Science.* Translated by Walter Kaufmann. New York: Vintage, 1974.

———. *Untimely Mediations.* Edited by Daniel Breazeale. Translated by R. J. Hollingdale. Cambridge: Cambridge University Press, 1997.

Nipperdey, Thomas. "Nationalidee und Nationaldenkmal in Deutschland im 19. Jahrhundert." *Historische Zeitschrift* 206 (1968): 529–585.

———. *Nachdenken über die deutsche Geschichte.* Munich: C. H. Beck, 1986.

Nohl, Ludwig. *Beethovens Leben.* 2d ed. 3 vols. Berlin: Schlesische Verlagsanstalt, 1913.

———. *Gluck und Wagner: Ueber die Entwicklung des Musikdramas.* Munich: Louis Finsterlin, 1870.

Nora, Pierre. "Between Memory and History: *Les Lieux de Mémoire.*" *Representations* 26 (1989): 7–25.

———. *Les Lieux de mémoire,* 3 vols. Paris : Gallimard, 1984–1992. Edited by Lawrence D. Kritzman and translated by Arthur Goldhammer as *Realms of Memory: Rethinking the French Past.* New York: Columbia University Press, 1996, and by David P. Jordan as *Rethinking France: Les Lieux de mémoire.* Chicago: University of Chicago Press, 2006.

Notley, Margaret. "Formal Process as Spiritual Progress: The Symphonic Slow Movements." In *The Cambridge Companion to Bruckner,* edited by John Willliamson, 190–204. Cambridge: Cambridge University Press, 2004.

———. "Late-Nineteenth-Century Chamber Music and the Cult of the Classical Adagio." *Nineteenth-Century Music* 23 (1999): 33–61.

Nottebohm, Gustav. *Zweite Beethoveniana.* Leipzig: J. Rieter-Biedermann, 1887.

Oppermann, Annette. *Musikalische Klassikerausgaben des 19. Jahrhunderts.* Göttingen: Vandenhoeck & Oppermann, 2001.

Otto, Irmgard. "Tonfilm—Ein Problem?" *Die Musik* 28 (1935): 111–117.

Pander, Oscar von. "SS-Konzerte." *Die Musik* 27 (1934): 205–206.

Parakilas, James, ed. *Piano Roles: Three Hundred Years of Life with the Piano.* New Haven: Yale University Press, 1999.

Parret, Hermann. "Kant on Music and the Hierarchy of the Arts." *Journal of Aesthetics and Art Criticism* 56 (1998): 251–261.

Parsons, James. "'*Deine Zauber binden wieder*': Beethoven, Schiller, and the Joyous Reconciliation of Opposites." *Beethoven Forum* 9 (2002): 1–54.

Pederson, Sanna. "A. B. Marx and Berlin Concert Life, and German National Identity." *Nineteenth-Century Music* 18 (1994): 87–107.

Pick, Daniel. *Faces of Degeneration.* Cambridge: Cambridge University Press, 1989.

Pickford, Henry W. "Conflict and Commemoration: Two Berlin Memorials." *Modernism/Modernity* 12 (2005): 133–172.

Pillau, Helmut. *Die fortgedachte Dissonanz: Hegels Tragödioentheorie und Schillers Tragödie.* Munich: Wilhelm Fink Verlag, 1981.

Pohl, Richard. *Höhenzüge der musikalischen Entwicklung.* Leipzig: B. Elischer, 1888.

Pois, Robert A. *National Socialism and the Religion of Nature.* New York: St Martin's Press, 1986.

Potter, Pamela. *Most German of the Arts: Musicology and Society from the Weimar Republic to the End of Hitler's Reich.* New Haven: Yale University Press, 1998.

Prieberg Fred K. *Musik im NS-Staat.* Frankfurt am Main: Fischer, 1982.

Pries, Christine, ed. *Das Erhabene: Zwischen Grenzerfahrung und Größenwahn.* Weinheim: VCH Acta humaniora, 1989.

Raabe, Peter. "Anton Bruckner: Rede gehalten 7. Juni 1937." *Zeitschrift für Musik* 104 (1937): 741–744.

Raff, Joachim. *Die Wagnerfrage.* Braunschweig: Friedrich Vieweg, 1854.

Ramann, Lina. *Franz Liszt als Künstler und Mensch.* 3 vols. Leipzig: Breitkopf und Härtel, 1880–1894.

———. *Lisztiana.* Edited by Arthur Seidl. Mainz: Schott, 1983.

Rehding, Alexander. "August Halm's Two Cultures as Nature." In *Music Theory and Natural Order from the Renaissance to the Early Twentieth Century,* edited by Suzannah Clark and Alexander Rehding, 142–160. Cambridge: Cambridge University Press, 2001.

———. *Hugo Riemann and the Birth of Modern Musical Thought.* Cambridge: Cambridge University Press, 2003.

———. "Inventing Liszt's Life: Early Biography and Autobiography." In *The Cambridge Companion to Liszt,* edited by Kenneth Hamilton, 14–27. Cambridge: Cambridge University Press, 2005.

———. "Wagner, Liszt, Berlioz and the New German School." In *Nationalism* versus *Cosmopolitanism in German Thought and Culture 1789–1914: Essays on the Emergence of Europe,* edited by Mary Ann Perkins and Martin Liebscher, 159–187. Lewiston, NY: Edwin Mellen Press, 2006.

Reichardt, Johann Friedrich. "Johann Sebastian Bach." *Musikalisches Kunstmagazin* 1 (1782): 196–202.

Reimann, Heinrich. *Musikalische Rückblicke.* 2 vols. Berlin: Harmonie Verlagsgesellschaft für Literatur und Kunst, 1900.

Reissmann, August. *Allgemeine Geschichte der Musik.* Leipzig: Fries's Verlag, 1864.

Rentschler, Eric. *The Ministry of Illusion: Nazi Cinema and its Afterlife.* Cambridge, MA: Harvard University Press, 1996.

[Richter], Jean Paul. "Jean Paul über Denkmale." *Bonner Wochenblatt* 104 (30 August 1836): 1.

Rieger, Eva. "So schlecht wie ihr Ruf?: Die Liszt-Biographin Lina Ramann." *Neue Zeitschrift für Musik* 147/7–8 (1986): 16–20.

Riegl, Alois. "The Modern Cult of Monuments: Its Character and Its Origin." Translated by Kurt W. Forster and Diane Ghirardo. *Oppositions* 25 (1982): 21–51.

Riemann, Hugo. *Die Elemente der musikalischen Aesthetik.* Berlin and Stuttgart: Spemann, 1900.

———. *Musiklexikon.* 4th ed. Leipzig: Max Hesse, 1894.

Riethmüller, Albrecht. "Aspekte des musikalisch Erhabenen im 19. Jahrhundert." *Archiv für Musikwissenschaft* 40 (1983): 38–49.

———. "Der deutsche Michel erwacht: Zur Bruckner-Rezeption im NS-Staat." In *Bruckner-Probleme,* edited by Albrecht Riethmüller, 202–214. Stuttgart: Steiner, 1999.

———. "Deutsche Musik aus Sicht der deutschen Musikwissenschaft nach 1933." In *Das Deutsche in der Musik,* edited by Marion Demuth, 68–80. Dresden: UniMedia, 1997.

———. "Komposition im Deutschen Reich um 1936." *Archiv für Musikwissenschaft* 38 (1981): 241–278.

———. "Das Tonsignet: Versuch einer Bestimmung seiner Eigenarten und Aufgaben." *Archiv für Musikwissenschaft* 30 (1973): 69–79.

———. *Die Walhalla und ihre Musiker.* Laaber: Laaber-Verlag, 1983.

———. "Zur Politik der unpolitischen Musik." In *Funkkolleg Musikgeschichte,* 111–125. Tübingen, Weinheim, Basel, and Mainz: Deutsches Institut für Fernstudien, 1988.

Ringer, Alexander L. "*Germanenzug* bis *Helgoland:* Zu Bruckners Deutschtum." In *Bruckner-Probleme,* edited by Albrecht Riethmüller, 25–34. Stuttgart: Steiner, 1999.

Rochlitz, Friedrich. "Monumente deutscher Tonkünstler." *Allgemeine musikalische Zeitung* 2 (1799/1800): cols. 417–423.

Rosen, Charles. *The Romantic Generation.* Cambridge, MA: Harvard University Press, 1996.

Rothfarb, Lee. "Music Analysis, Cultural Ethics, and Sociology in the Writings of August Halm." *Indiana Theory Review* 16 (1995): 171–196.

Sachs, Harvey. *Music in Fascist Italy.* New York: Norton, 1987.

Saffle, Michael. *Liszt in Germany 1840–1845: A Study in Sources, Documents, and the History of Reception.* Stuyvesant, NY: Pendragon Press, 1994.

Saldern, Adelheid von. "'Kunst für's Volk': Vom Kulturkonservatismus zur national-sozialistischen Kulturpolitik." In *Das Gedächtnis der Bilder: Ästhetik und National-sozialismus,* edited by Harald Wetzer, 45–104. Tübingen: Edition Diskord, 1995.

Samson, Jim. *Virtuosity and the Musical Work: The* Transcendental Studies *of Liszt.* Cambridge: Cambridge University Press, 2003.

———, ed. *The Cambridge History of Nineteenth-Century Music.* Cambridge: Cambridge University Press, 2001.

Sandberger, Wolfgang. "Philipp Spitta und die Geburt der Musikwissenschaft aus dem Geiste der Philologie." In *Musikwissenschaft—eine verspätete Disziplin? Die akademische Musikforschung zwischen Fortschrittsglauben und Modernitätsverweigerung,* edited by Anselm Gerhard, 55–68. Stuttgart: Metzler, 2001.

Sanders, Ernest. "Form and Content in the Finale of Beethoven's Ninth Symphony." *Musical Quarterly* 50 (1964): 59–76.

Sapienza, Lauriana. "Euripides: Eine disziplinierte Polemik?" In *Disciplining Classics/Diszplinierte Klassik* edited by Glenn W. Most, 55–71. Göttingen: Vandenhoeck & Rupprecht, 2002.

Sasse, Konrad. *Beiträge zur Forschung über Leben und Werk von Robert Franz 1815–1892.* Edited by Edwin Werner. Halle an der Saale: Händel-Haus, 1986.

Schaal, Susanne. "Das Beethoven-Denkmal von Julius Hähnel in Bonn." In *Monument für Beethoven,* edited by Ingrid Bodsch, 39–134. Bonn: Bonner Stadtmuseum, 1995.

Schadewaldt, Wolfgang. "Richard Wagner and the Greeks." Translated by David C. Durst. *Dialogos: Hellenic Studies Review* 6 (1999): 108–133.

Schaeffer, Julius. *Friedrich Chrysander in seinen Klavierauszügen zur deutschen Händel-Ausgabe.* Leipzig: F. E. C. Leuckart, 1876.

———. *Seb. Bachs Cantate "Sie werden alle kommen aus Saba." in den Ausgaben von Robert Franz und dem Leipziger Bachverein.* Leipzig: F. E. C. Leuckart, 1877.

Scharding, Waltraut. *Friedrich Chrysander: Leben und Werk.* Hamburg: K. D. Wagner, 1986.

Scheidt, Samuel. *Tabulatura nova.* Edited by Max Seiffert. Preface by Philipp Spitta. Leipzig: Breitkopf und Härtel, 1892.

Schelle, Eduard. *Der Tannhäuser in Paris und der dritte musikalische Krieg.* Leipzig: Breitkopf und Härtel, 1861.

Schenker, Heinrich. *Beethoven's Ninth Symphony: A Portrayal of Its Musical Content, with Running Commentary on Performance and Literature As Well.* Translated by John Rothgeb. New Haven: Yale University Press, 1992.

Schering, Arnold. *Von großen Meistern der Musik.* Leipzig: Breitkopf und Härtel, 1935.

Schiller, Frierich. *On the Aesthetic Education of Man.* Translated by Elizabeth M. Wilkinson and L. A. Willoughby. Oxford: Clarendon Press, 1967.

Schilling, Ulrike. *Philipp Spitta: Leben und Wirken im Spiegel seiner Briefwechsel mit einem Inventar des Nachlasses und einer Bibliographie der gedruckten Werke.* Kassel: Bärenreiter, 1994.

Schindler, Anton. "Ad Vocem Beethoven-Fest-Polemik." *Kölnische Zeitung* 183 (2 July 1845): unnumbered *Beilage.*

Schleuning, Peter. *Der Bürger erhebt sich: Geschichte der deutschen Musik im achtzehnten Jahrhundert.* Stuttgart: Metzler, 2000.

Schmidt, August. "Fliegende Blätter aus meinem Reise-Portefeuille: Nachstationen in Bonn beim Beethovenfeste, 10. bis 13. August 1845." *Allgemeine Wiener Musik-Zeitung* 5 (1845): 393–394, 397–398, 401–406.

Schmidt, Christian Martin. "Zwischen Quellentreue und Werkrezeption, oder: Dem Wandel des historischen Bewußtseins ist nicht zu entkommen." In *Musikedition: Mittler zwischen Wissenschaft und musikalischer Praxis,* edited by Helga Lühning, 3–17. Tübingen: Max Niemeyer, 2002.

Schmitt, Ricarda. "Klassische, romantische und postmoderne musikästhetische Paradigmen in E. T. A. Hoffmanns *Ritter Gluck.*" In *"Seelenaccente"—"Ohrenphysiognomik": Zur Musikanschuung E. T. A. Hoffmanns, Heinses und Wackenroders,* edited by Werner Keil and Charis Goer, 11–61. Hildesheim: Georg Olms, 2000.

Schmitt-Thomas, Reinhold. *Die Entwicklung der deutschen Konzertkritik im Spiegel der Leipziger 'Allgemeinen musikalischen Zeitung' (1798–1848).* Frankfurt: Kettenhof, 1969.

Schneider, Hans. *Der Musikverleger Heinrich Philipp Bossler 1744–1822.* Tutzing: Hans Schneider, 1985.

Schneider, Max. "'Denkmäler der Tonkunst' vor hundert Jahren." In *Festschrift Max von Liliencron,* edited by Hermann Kretzschmar, 278–289. Leipzig: Breitkopf und Härtel, 1910.

Schorn, Adelheid von. *Das nachklassische Weimar.* Weimar: G. Kiepenheuer, 1911–12.

Schröter, Axel. *"Der Name Beethoven ist heilig in der Kunst": Studien zu Liszts Beethoven-Rezeption.* Sinzig: Studio, 1999.

Schrott, Ludwig. "Vom Musizieren und Musik-Erleben." *Die Musik* 28 (1935): 341–347.

Schulte-Sasse, Jochen, ed. *Literarischer Kitsch: Texte zu seiner Theorie, Geschichte und Einzelinterpretation.* Tübingen: Max Niemeyer, 1979.

Schulte-Sasse, Linda. *Entertaining the Third Reich: Illusions of Wholeness in Nazi Cinema.* Durham, NC: Duke University Press, 1996.

Schumann, Otto. *Geschichte der deutschen Musik.* Leipzig: Bibliographisches Institut, 1940.

Schumann, Robert. "Monument für Beethoven: Vier kritische Stimmen hierüber." *Neue Zeitschrift für Musik* 4 (1836): 211–213.

Schwarz, Boris. *Music and Musical Life in Soviet Russia 1917–1970.* New York: Norton, 1972.

Seidl, Arthur. *Vom Musikalisch-Erhabenen: Prolegomena zur Aesthetik der Tonkunst.* Leipzig: Kahnt, 1887.

Selbmann, Rolf. *Dichterdenkmäler in Deutschland: Literaturgeschichte in Erz und Stein.* Stuttgart: Metzler, 1988.

Sharpe, Lesley. *Schiller's Aesthetic Essays: Two Centuries of Criticism.* Columbia, SC: Camden House, 1995.

Sisman, Elaine. *Mozart: The 'Jupiter' Symphony.* Cambridge: Cambridge University Press, 1997.

Solie, Ruth. "Beethoven as a Secular Humanist: Ideology and the Ninth Symphony in Nineteenth-Century Criticism." In *Explorations in Music, the Arts and Ideas: Essays in Honor of Leonard B. Meyer,* edited by Eugene Narmour and Ruth Solie, 1–42. Stuyvesant, NY: Pendragon, 1988.

Solomon, Maynard. *Beethoven Essays.* Cambridge, MA: Harvard University Press, 1988.

Solvik, Morten. "The International Bruckner Society and the NSDAP: A Case Study of Robert Haas and the Critical Edition." *Musical Quarterly* 83 (1998): 362–382.

Sommer, Rudolf. "Unterhaltungsmusiker als Kulturträger." *Die Musik* 28 (1935): 336–341.

Sonnleithner, Joseph. "Ankündigung: Geschichte der Musik in Denkmählern von der ältesten bis auf die neueste Zeit." *Intelligenzblatt der Allgemeinen musikalischen Zeitung* 1 (1798/1799): cols. 91–92.

Spengler, Oswald. *The Decline of the West.* Translated by C. F. Atkinson. 2 vols. New York: Knopf, 1950.

Spitta, Philipp. "Der Bach-Verein zu Leipzig." *Leipziger allgemeine musikalische Zeitung* 10 (1875): cols. 305–312.

———. "Bildende Kunst und Musik in ihrem gegenseitigen geschichtlichen Verhält-nisse." *Leipziger allgemeine musikalische Zeitung* 11 (1876): cols. 305–313.

———. "Denkmäler deutscher Tonkunst." *Die Grenzboten* 52/2 (1893): 16–27.

———. *Johann Sebastian Bach.* 2 vols. Leipzig: Breitkopf und Härtel, 1873–80.

———. *Zur Geschichte der Musik. Musikgeschichtliche Aufsätze.* Berlin: Gebrüder Paetel, 1894.

Splitt, Gerhard. *Richard Strauss 1933–1935.* Pfaffenweiler: Centaurus, 1987.

Spohr, Louis. *Lebenserinnerungen.* Edited by Folker Göthel. Tutzing: Hans Schneider, 1968.

Sponheuer, Bernd. *Musik als Kunst und Nicht-Kunst.* Kassel: Bärenreiter, 1987.

———. "Musik, Faschismus, Ideologie: Heuristische Überlegungen." *Die Musik-forschung* 46 (1993): 241–253.

———. "The National Socialist Discussion on the 'German Quality' in Music." In *Music and Nazism: Art und Tyranny 1933–1944,* edited by Michael Kater and Albrecht Riethmüller, 32–42. Laaber: Laaber-Verlag, 2003.

———. "Reconstructing the Ideal Types of the 'German' in Music." In *Music and German National Identity,* edited by Celia Applegate and Pamela Potter, 36–58. Chicago: University of Chicago Press, 2002.

———. "Zur ästhetischen Dichotomie als Denkform in der ersten Hälfte des 19. Jahrhunderts: Eine historische Skizze am Beispiel Schumanns, Brendels und Hanslicks." *Archiv für Musikwissenschaft* 37 (1980): 1–31.

Stephani, Hermann. *Das Erhabene insonderheit in der Tonkunst und das Problem der Form im Musikalisch-Schönen und Erhabenen.* Leipzig: Hermann Seemann, 1903.

Stewart, Susan. *On Longing: Narratives of the Miniature, the Gigantic, the Souvenir, the Collection.* Durham, NC: Duke University Press, 1993.

Strauss, David Friedrich. "Beethoven's Neunte Symphonie und ihre Bewunderer." In *Allgemeine musikalische Zeitung* 12 (1877): cols. 129–133.

Strohm, Reinhard. "Gedanken zu Wagners Opernouvertüren." In *Wagnerliteratur—Wagnerforschung,* edited by Carl Dahlhaus and Egon Voss, 69–84. Mainz: Schott, 1985.

Sulzer, Johann Georg. *Allgemeine Theorie der schönen Künste.* 2 vols. Leipzig: Weidemann & Reich, 1771.

Tai, Hue-Tam Ho, "Remembered Realms: Pierre Nora and French National Memory," *American Historical Review* 106 (2001): 906–922.

Taruskin, Richard. "A Beethoven Season? Like Last Season, the One Before . . . " *The New York Times,* Arts and Leisure section (September 10, 1995).

———. "Nationalism." In *The New Grove Dictionary of Music and Musicians.* 29 vols. Edited by Stanley Sadie. Rev. ed. xvii: 689–706. Basingstoke: Macmillan, 2000.

———. "Resisting the Ninth." In *Text and Act: Essays on Music and Performance,* 235–261. New York and Oxford: Oxford University Press, 1995.

———. "Speed Bumps." *Nineteenth-Century Music* 29 (2005): 185–207.

Theweleit, Klaus. *Male Fantasies.* 2 vols. Translated by Stephen Conway. Cambridge: Polity Press, 1987–1989.

Thibaut, Friedrich Justus. *Über Reinheit der Tonkunst.* Heidelberg: J. C. B. Mohr, 1825.

Thiel, Wolfgang. "Filmmusik im NS-Staat: Sechs Annäherungen und ein Nachwort." In *"Entartete Musik" 1938: Weimar und die Ambivalenz,* edited by Hanns-Werner Heister, 599–613. Saarbrücken: Pfau, 2001.

Thorau, Christian. *Semantisierte Sinnlichkeit: Studien zu Rezeption und Zeichenstruktur der Leitmotivtechnik Richard Wagners.* Stuttgart: Franz Steiner Verlag, 2003.

Thüring, Hubert. *Geschichte des Gedächtnisses: Friedrich Nietzsche und das 19. Jahrhundert* Munich: Wilhelm Fink, 2001.

Till, Nicholas. *Mozart and the Enlightenment: Truth, Virtue, and Beauty in Mozart's Operas.* New York and London: W. W. Norton, 1992.

Titus, Barbara. "Conceptualizing Music: Friedrich Theodor Vischer and Hegelian Currents in German Music Criticism 1848–1887," Ph.D. diss. Oxford University, 2005.

Tovey, Donald Francis. "Beethoven: Ninth Symphony in D Minor, p. 125. Its Place in Musical Art," In *Essays in Musical Analysis.* Vol. 2, *Symphonies,* 1–45. Oxford: Oxford University Press, 1935.

Treitler, Leo. *Music and the Historical Imagination.* Cambridge, MA: Harvard University Press, 1989.

Triest, Johann Karl Friedrich. "Bemerkungen über die Ausbildung der Tonkunst in Deutschland im achtzehnten Jahrhundert." *Allgemeine musikalische Zeitung* 3 (1800/1801): cols. 225–235, 241–249, 257–264, 273–286, 297–308, 321–331, 369–379, 389–401, 405–410, 421–432, 437–445.

Tusa, Michael C. *Euryanthe and Carl Maria von Weber's Dramaturgy of German Opera.* Oxford: Clarendon Press, 1991.

———. "Noch einmal: Form and Content in the Finale of Beethoven's Ninth Symphony." *Beethoven Forum* 7 (1999): 113–137.

Uhlig, Ludwig, ed. *Griechenland als Ideal: Winckelmann und seine Rezeption in Deutschland.* Tübingen: Günter Narr Verlag, 1988.

Uhlig, Theodor. "Die Ouvertüre zu Wagner's Tannhäuser." *Neue Zeitschrift für Musik* 34 (1851): 153–156, 165–168.

Unger, Robert. *Die mehrchörige Aufführungspraxis bei Michael Praetorius und die Feiergestaltung der Gegenwart.* Wolfenbüttel and Berlin: Georg Kallmeyer, 1941.

Venedey, Jacob. *Die deutschen Republikaner unter der französischen Republik.* Leipzig: Brockhaus, 1870.

Vick, Brian E. *Defining Germany: The 1848 Frankfurt Parliamentarians and National Identity.* Cambridge, MA: Harvard University Press, 2002.

Vischer, Friedrich Theodor. *Aesthetik oder Wissenschaft des Schönen.* 5 vols. in 10. Reutlingen, Leipzig, and Stuttgart: Carl Mäcken, 1846–1858.

———. *Faust: Der Tragödie dritter Teil.* Tübingen: H. Laupp, 1886.

Vondung, Klaus. *Magie und Manipulation: Ideologischer Kult und politische Religion des Nationalsozialismus.* Göttingen: Vandenhoeck & Ruprecht, 1971.

———. "National Socialism as Political Religion." *Totalitarian Movements and Political Religion* 6 (2005): 87–95.

Wagner, Manfred. "Response to Bryan Gilliam Regarding Bruckner and National Socialism." *Musical Quarterly* 80 (1996): 118–123.

———. *Wandel des Konzepts: Zu verschiedenen Fassungen von Bruckners 3., 4. und 8. Symphonie.* Vienna: Musikwissenschaftlicher Verlag, 1980.

Wagner, Richard. *Gesammelte Schriften und Dichtungen,* 3d ed. 10 vols. Leipzig: C. F. W. Siegel, 1898.

———. *My Life.* Translated by Andrew Gray. New York: Da Capo Press, 1992.

————. *Opera and Drama.* Translated by Edward Evans. 2 vols. London: W. Reeves, 1913.

————. *Richard Wagner's Prose Works.* 10 vols. Translated by William Ashton Ellis. Reprint New York: Broude Brothers, 1966.

————. *Sämtliche Briefe.* Edited by Gertrud Strobel and Werner Wolf. Leipzig: Deutscher Verlag für Musik, 1967–.

————. *Selected Letters of Richard Wagner.* Translated and edited by Stewart Spencer and Barry Millington. New York and London: Norton, 1987.

Walker, Alan. *Franz Liszt: The Virtuoso Years.* Ithaca, NY: Cornell University Press, 1987.

————. *Franz Liszt: The Weimar Years.* Ithaca, NY: Cornell University Press, 1989.

Walter, Michael. "Die Musik des Olympiafilms von 1938." *Acta musicologica* 62 (1990): 82–113.

Webster, James. "The *Creation,* Haydn's Late Vocal Music, and the Musical Sublime." In Elaine Sisman, ed., *Haydn and his World,* 57–102. Princeton: Princeton University Press, 1997.

————. "The Finale in Beethoven's Ninth Symphony." *Beethoven Forum* 1 (1991): 25–62.

————. *Haydn's "Farewell" Symphony and the Idea of Classical Style.* Cambridge: Cambridge University Press, 1991.

Weißmann, Adolf. *Die Musik in der Weltkrise.* Stuttgart and Berlin: Deutsche Verlags-Anstalt, 1922.

Weitzmann, Carl Friedrich. *Geschichte des Clavierspiels und der Clavierliteratur.* Stuttgart: Cottasche Buchhandlung, 1863.

Wessely, Ottmar. *Zur Vorgeschichte des musikalischen Denkmalschutzes.* Vienna: Verlag der österreichischen Akademie der Wissenschaften, 1976.

Wilcox, Kenneth Parmelee. *Anmut und Würde: Die Dialektik der menschlichen Vollendung bei Schiller.* Frankfurt am Main: Peter Lang, 1981.

Wilde, David. "Transcriptions for Piano." In *Franz Liszt: The Man and His Music,* edited by Alan Walker, 168–202. London: Barrie and Jenkins, 1970.

Williams, Adrian. *Portraits of Liszt: By Himself and His Contemporaries.* Oxford: Clarendon Press, 1990.

Winckelmann, Johann Jakob. *Gedanken über die Nachahmung der griechischen Werke in der Malerei und Bildhauerkunst.* Dresden and Leipzig: Verlag der Waltherischen Handlung, 1755.

Winkler, Gerhard J. "'Ein feste Burg ist unser Gott': Meyerbeers Hugenotten in der Paraphrasen Thalbergs und Liszts." In *Liszt-Studien 4: Der junge Liszt,* edited by Gottfried Scholz, 100–134. Munich and Salzburg: Emil Katzbichler, 1993.

————. "Liszt's 'Weimar Mythology.'" In *Liszt and His World,* edited by Michael Saffle, 61–73. Stuyvesant, NY: Pendragon Press, 1998.

Winter, Jay M. *Sites of Memory, Sites of Mourning: The Great War in European Culture.* Cambridge: Cambridge University Press, 1995.

Wiora, Walter, ed. *Die Ausbreitung des Historismus über die Musik.* Regensburg: Gustav Bosse, 1969.

Wittkau, Annette. *Historimus: Zur Geschichte des Begriffs und des Problems.* Göttingen: Vandenhoeck & Ruprecht, 1992.

Wood, Nancy. "Memory's Remains: *Les lieux de mémoire.*" *History and Memory* 6 (1994), 123–149.

Young, James E. *At Memory's Edge: After-Images of the Holocaust in Contemporary Art and Architecture.* New Haven and London: Yale University Press, 2000.

———. *Textures of Memory: Holocaust Memorials and Meaning.* New Haven: Yale University Press, 1993.

Zeising, Adolf. *Aesthetische Forschungen.* Frankfurt am Main: Meidlinger Sohn & Co., 1855.

. . . zel. "Bruckners Einzug in die Walhalla." [*Linzer*] *Tagespost,* June 8, 1937, [no page]. In Bundesarchiv Berlin, Bestandssignatur: R/55, Archivsignatur: 20582 (Alt: X 10019–01).

Zelle, Carsten. *"Angenehmes Grauen": Literaturhistorische Beiträge zur Ästhetik des Schrecklichen im 18. Jahrhundert.* Hamburg: Felix Meiner, 1987.

intelligibility, 4, 9, 24, 28, 34, 39–40, 76, 105, 118, 140

Italy, Italian music, 3, 5, 24, 43, 121–123

Jahn, Friedrich Ludwig "Turnvater," 197–200

Jahn, Otto, 99, 143, 170

Jaëll, Alfred, 99–101

  Aus Richard Wagner's Lohengrin und Tannhäuser, 99

Jean Paul. *See* Richter

jingle, 5–8, 190–195

Joachim, Joseph, 166

Kallbeck, Max ,153

Kansteiner, Wulf, 12

Kant, Immanuel, 24, 26, 172, 201, 204, 211

Kelly, Elaine, 154

kings. *See* royalty *and individual monarchs*

kitsch, 35, 76, 78, 105

Kleinmeister, 144–145

Klopstock, Friedrich Gottlieb, 120

Lachner, Franz, 61

Lepenies, Wolf, 214

Lessing, Gotthold Ephraim, 120

Lieu de mémoire. *See* memory

Lindpaintner, Peter Joseph von, 59

listeners. *See* audience

Liszt, Franz, 3, 5, 8, 29–30, 32, 47–49, 54, 56, 59–62, 64–71, 73–74, 77–79, 81–85, 87–90, 93, 95–96, 99, 101–103, 107–108, 119, 134–135, 203–204

  Cantata for the Inauguration of the Bonn Beethoven Monument, 59–60, 65–67, 69–70, 93–94, 106

  Chor der Engel (Faust II), 73

  Goethe-Festmarsch, 73

  "Mehr Licht," 73–75, 78

  Les Préludes, 5–8, 77

  O du mein holder Abendstern, 85, 88, 90–91, 95, 106, 108

  Overture to *Tannhäuser* 85, 87, 91, 95

  Pilgrims' Chorus, 88–89, 99

  Réminiscences de Lucia di Lammermoor, 69

  Réminiscences de Norma, 69

  Tasso, Lamento e Trionfo, 48–49, 73

  "Wanderers Nachtgesang," 73

  "Weimars Toten," 73

Lobe, Johann Christian, 95, 102–104, 116, 118

Louis XIV, King of France, 176

Ludwig I, King of Bavaria, 20

Lukács, Georg, 43

Lully, Jean-Baptiste, 24, 112, 122

Luther, Martin, 78

Mahler, Gustav, 3–5, 15

  Symphony no. 8, 35

Mandyczewski, Eusebius, 141–142

Mann, Thomas, 5, 8, 9, 49

Maria Pavlovna, Grand-Duchess of Weimar, 78

Marx, Adolf Bernhard, 116

Marx, G. W., 99

masses, 4, 11–14, 38–40, 42–43, 56, 70, 76, 78, 80–82, 116, 136, 156, 173–175, 177, 188–189, 191, 195

material, 11, 16, 94, 162–163, 201–202, 211–212

  musical material, 15, 87, 94, 128–129, 139

medium, media, 10, 13, 15, 34, 46, 136, 159, 195

  cinema, 5, 15, 187, 195

  mass media, 13, 91, 187, 195

  radio, 186

memory

  aide-mémoire, 94

  collective memory, 12–13, 26, 28, 30, 35, 39–40, 42, 215–216

  cultural memory, 14, 21, 28, 33, 74, 198–199

  lieu de mémoire (memory site), 12–13, 78, 198, 214

  memorial, 10, 20, 21, 27, 60

  memory studies, 11–13, 33, 198

Mendelssohn-Bartholdy, Felix, 32, 167

  Symphony no. 2 *"Lobgesang,"* 69

Meyer, Leonard B., 52

Meyerbeer, Giacomo, 37, 59, 122–123

  Le Prophète 101

Midas touch, 8, 14, 32, 40, 45

miniature, 28, 69, 77–78, 106–107, 110, 181, 183

modernism, 10, 12, 184

modernity, 40–41, 43, 46, 77, 80–81, 84, 105–106, 134, 139–140, 148, 150, 155, 158, 177, 185, 198, 200

monarchy, 41, 46, 63, 143. *See also* royalty
Monteverdi, Claudio, 147, 166
Monumenta Germaniae Historica, 143
monumentality, 3–5, 7–9, 14–15, 19–25,
    27–28, 33–35, 37–40, 42, 45–46,
    53–54, 57–58, 71, 82–84, 172,
    212–216
  cultural-political use of 5, 8–9, 17, 21,
    24–25, 27–28, 30, 32, 35, 37–39,
    43, 78, 142–143, 171–180, 183–187,
    195–196, 197–199
  See also aesthetics; agency; ahistoricity;
    ambivalence; anti-monumentality;
    architecture; authority; awe; classicism;
    commemoration; communication;
    complexity; effect; elite; enjoyment;
    excess; experience; form; greatness;
    ideology; immediacy; immortality; in-
    telligibility; morality; mountain range;
    philology; popularity; power; presence;
    progress; reflection; representation; se-
    duction; self-evidence; simplicity; size;
    solidity; sound; style; subtlety; super-
    ficiality; transcendence; will
morality, 5, 8–9, 21, 25, 30–32, 39, 42, 93,
    177–178, 196, 211–212
Moser, Hans-Joachim, 170–171, 196
mountain range, 29–32, 34, 37, 45, 53,
    119, 145, 215–216
Mount Rushmore. *See* Hall of Fame
Mozart, Wolfgang Amadeus, 20, 29–30, 80,
    112–119, 122–123, 128, 134, 137,
    140
  Don Giovanni, 114–117
  Entführung aus dem Serail, 114, 117
  Jupiter Symphony, 129
  "Mozart" ending of overture to Gluck's
    Iphigenie in Aulis (see Schmidt, Johann
    Philipp)
  Zauberflöte, 40
Mueller, Rena, 76
Müller, Joseph, 167
Mumford, Lewis, 28
museum, 27, 144, 156
music
  chamber 69
  choral 69, 189
  instrumental 25, 73, 94, 103, 113–114,
    116–117, 119, 123, 130–131, 171,
    182, 190

musical object 15, 26, 40
  orchestral 3, 15, 34, 49, 61, 67, 69, 73.
    87, 91, 93–94, 118, 129, 136, 138,
    148–150
  piano (keyboard), 69, 93, 85–88, 95–99,
    102, 135, 145, 149, 153
  vocal 25, 34, 92–93, 103, 152
  See also absolute music; analysis; compo-
    sition; criticism; dance; institution;
    material; music pedagogy; opera, per-
    formance; soundtrack; space; work
music history, 3, 15, 19, 24–25, 29, 32, 37,
    45, 47, 54, 69, 84, 96, 110, 112–113,
    118–121, 123, 125, 129, 134, 139,
    141, 143–144, 146–147, 156, 160,
    162–163, 179
musicology, 4, 9, 37, 141, 143–144,
    147–149, 157–158, 161, 164, 166,
    170, 174, 176, 185, 196
music pedagogy, 20, 24, 45, 47, 145
music theory, 5, 24, 47, 102, 112, 137
Musik, Die, 185

nation, 13, 20, 24–25, 41–43, 53, 63–64,
    69, 78, 122–123, 141, 143–144,
    147–148, 164–165, 173, 175,
    177–179, 183, 197–198, 214
national anthem, 13, 188–189
nationalism, 13, 41–42, 63–65, 122, 141,
    143–144, 147–148, 165, 183, 196
National Socialism, 5, 8, 16, 28, 35,
    175–191, 194–195, 214
  Deutsche Wochenschau 5–8, 191
Neudeutsche Schule, 4, 29
Neue Zeitschrift für Musik, 29, 57, 80,
    105–106, 188
newness, 40, 81, 102–103, 106, 155–156
Nietzsche, Friedrich, 13–14, 16, 31–32, 34,
    38, 41–43, 53, 56, 69–71, 155, 161,
    163–164, 191
  antiquarian history *and* monumental
    history (*see under* history)
nineteenth century, 3, 5, 9, 11, 13–14, 16,
    24–26, 28, 30–34, 36, 42–43, 45–46,
    48–49, 52, 54, 69, 76, 80–81, 91, 93,
    104, 111, 116, 126, 129, 138, 141,
    147, 153, 155–156, 165, 171,
    174–175, 179, 181, 198, 203
Nipperdey, Thomas, 13, 41, 63
Nohl, Ludwig, 120–122

Nora, Pierre, 12–13, 198, 214
nostalgia, 12–13, 79
notation, 21, 74, 110, 125–127, 129,
     134–137, 145
Nottebohm, Gustav, 213
Novalis, 43

Ockeghem, Johannes, 24
oldness, 40, 81, 119, 127, 154–156, 163,
     167, 179
opera, 80, 87, 91, 93, 105–106, 109, 118,
     120, 123
origin, 34, 38, 43, 46, 121, 145, 148,
     152–158, 163, 166, 169, 181–184,
     198
Originalfassung. See Bruckner
overture, 15, 113, 116–119, 122–123, 129,
     131–133, 135–136

Palestrina, Giovanni Pierluigi da, 165
pantheon. *See* Hall of Fame
past. *See* time; history
performance, 21, 45, 74, 78, 85, 88, 91,
     93–95, 106, 112, 123, 125, 135–140,
     152, 156–158, 164–166, 172, 174,
     185
performer. *See also* virtuoso
Pfitzner, Hans, 185
philology, 15, 16, 19, 29–30, 134,
     141–144, 146–149, 152, 154–158,
     162–165, 167, 170, 182–184
pleasure, 10–11, 41, 48, 91. *See also*
     enjoyment; entertainment
Poland, 8
polyphony, 8, 52, 118, 141, 145, 149, 150,
     152–154, 178, 213, 216
popularity, 4–5, 11, 13–17, 24–25, 37–41,
     80–81, 84–85, 91, 94–95, 108, 138,
     157–159, 183–187, 214, 216
populism, 5
possession. *See* comsumption
postmodernism, 10, 13
power, 8–10, 28, 34, 38–39, 41, 52, 69–70,
     81, 114, 118, 123, 125, 134, 147,
     158, 164, 172–180, 182, 188, 196,
     202
presence, 14, 28, 32, 34, 42, 53, 108,
     159–160, 180–181, 199
present. *See* time
private, 15, 77–78, 91, 106
progress. *See* history

Proust, Marcel, 12
public, 10–12, 15, 24, 29, 37–38, 45, 56,
     69, 82, 91, 93, 149, 158, 189–190,
     212. *See also* bourgeoisie; masses
publishing, 20, 24, 45

Quantz, Johann Joachim, 121

Raabe, Peter, 88, 181
Raff, Joachim, 91–93, 99, 105
     *Fantasie über Motive aus Richard Wagners
        Tannhäuser*, 98–99
     Sextett aus Richard Wagners Tannhäuser, 96
     Weltende—Gericht—Neue Welt, 35
Ramann, Lina, 47, 64, 67
Rameau, Jean Philippe, 112, 122
Ranger, Terence, 13
Ranke, Leopold von, 144
reflection, 3, 8–10, 16–17, 21, 45, 82,
     147–148, 158, 180, 184, 202
regeneration, 147, 157, 160, 164
Reger, Max, 185
Reissmann, August, 37–38
religion, religiosity, 13, 42, 66–67, 74, 175,
     178, 180–182, 190, 195–196
representation, 28, 31–33, 41, 43, 49,
     56–57, 65, 67, 69, 79, 93–95, 103,
     118, 133, 163, 170–173, 176, 180,
     188, 196
revolution. *See* France; Germany
Richter, Jean Paul, 25, 56–57, 67, 69
Riefenstahl, Leni
     Olympia, 195
     Triumph des Willens, 195
Riegl, Alois, 13, 27, 32, 35, 38, 155–156
     historical monument, 27–28, 38, 40,
        155–156, 164
Riemann, Hugo, 34, 147
ritual. *See* tradition
Rochlitz, Friedrich, 19–20
Romanticism, 25–26, 52, 56, 64, 78, 139,
     156, 171, 177, 180–181, 183, 206
Rosen, Charles, 52
Rossini, Giacomo, 118
Roullet, François Gand-Leblanc du, 110
Royalty, 62–63, 65, 143
Russia, Russian Music, 3, 5
Rußlandfanfaren. See Liszt, Franz, *Les Préludes*

Saint-Saëns, Camille, 3
salon music, 85, 88, 91–93, 95, 105–106